KYOTO AREA STUDIES ON ASIA

CENTER FOR SOUTHEAST ASIAN STUDIES, KYOTO UNIVERSITY

VOLUME 3

Commodifying Marxism

KYOTO AREA STUDIES ON ASIA

CENTER FOR SOUTHEAST ASIAN STUDIES, KYOTO UNIVERSITY

The Nation and Economic Growth: Korea and Thailand
YOSHIHARA Kunio

One Malay Village: A Thirty-Year Community Study
TSUBOUCHI Yoshihiro

Commodifying Marxism: The Formation of Modern Thai Radical Culture,
1927–1958
Kasian TEJAPIRA

KYOTO AREA STUDIES ON ASIA

CENTER FOR SOUTHEAST ASIAN STUDIES, KYOTO UNIVERSITY

VOLUME 3

Commodifying Marxism:

The Formation of Modern Thai Radical Culture, 1927–1958

Kasian TEJAPIRA

Kyoto University Press

First published in 2001 jointly by:

Kyoto University Press
Kyodai Kaikan
15-9 Yoshida Kawara-cho
Sakyo-ku, Kyoto 606-8305, Japan
Telephone: +81-75-761-6182
Fax: +81-75-761-6190
Email: sales@kyoto-up.gr.jp
Web: http://www.kyoto-up.gr.jp

Trans Pacific Press
PO Box 120, Rosanna, Melbourne
Victoria 3084, Australia
Telephone: +61 3 9459 3021
Fax: +61 3 9457 5923
E-mail: enquiries@transpacificpress.com
Website: http://www.transpacificpress.com

Copyright © Kyoto University Press and Trans Pacific Press 2001

Set by digital environs Melbourne: enquiries@digitalenvirons.com

Printed in Melbourne by Brown Prior Anderson

Distributors

Australia
Bushbooks
PO Box 1958, Gosford, NSW 2250
Telephone: (02) 4323-3274
Fax: (02) 9212-2468
Email: bushbook@ozemail.com.au

USA and Canada
International Specialized Book
Services (ISBS)
5824 N. E. Hassalo Street
Portland, Oregon 97213-3644
USA
Telephone: (800) 944-6190
Fax: (503) 280-8832
Email: orders@isbs.com
Web: http://www.isbs.com

ISSN 1445–9663 (Kyoto Area Studies on Asia)
ISBN 4–876–984–52–2 (hardcover)
ISBN 1–876–843–98–5 (softcover)

National Library of Australia Cataloging in Publication Data

Tejapira, Kasian.
Commodifying Marxism.

Bibliography.
Includes index.

ISBN 4 87698452 2 (Kyoto).
ISBN 1 876843 98 5 (pbk. : Trans Pacific).

1. Communism – Thailand – History. 2. Thailand – Politics
and government – 20th century. 3. Thailand – Social life
and customs – 20th century. I. Title. (Series : Kyoto
area studies on Asia ; v. 3).

335.4309593

Contents

Tables

Plates

To Ah Tia, Ah Yi, Jeed, and Kloy
whose "pid thong lang phra" love and support
saw me through many storms in my life as well as this book

Biographical Sketch

Born into a Teochiu Chinese family in Bangkok, Thailand, in 1957, the author spent the first sixteen years of his life being Thaified by the state and Sinofied by his father under absolutist military dictatorship. The student-led popular rising of 1973 and the mass movement afterwards turned him into a radical democrat and populist nationalist student activist at Thammasat University. The right-wing reactionary massacre and military coup in 1976 drove him to join the communist-led guerrilla movement in Cambodia and the jungle in northeastern Thailand until 1981 when the guerrilla movement collapsed and he left the jungle to resume his undergraduate studies. After graduating with a B.A. in International Affairs (first class honors) in 1983, he joined the Faculty of Political Science at Thammasat as a lecturer and went to Cornell University for further studies, earning a Ph.D. in Government in 1992. Since then, he has been teaching at Thammasat, publishing academic papers in English, and contributing articles on Thai cultural politics and political economy to Thai-language newspapers and magazines as a regular columnist.

Cover Photographs

A rally of 3,000 students at Sanam Luang in the middle of Bangkok, protesting insufficient schooling capacity and demanding the Thai government s withdrawal from the American-led, anti-communist Southeast Asian Treaty Organization. *Photo taken on 19 May 1957; photo credit: Nitisat Rab Satawas Mai [Journal of Law: The New Century Issue] VII:4 (1957).*

Students confronted army soldiers in a protest march against dirty election. *Photo taken on 2 March 1957; photo credit: Nitisat Rab Satawas Mai [Journal of Law: The New Century Issue] VII:4 (1957).*

Preface

This book is long in the making. It originated as a doctoral dissertation submitted to the Department of Government at Cornell University in early 1992, the research for which was carried out in Thailand from mid-1988 to mid-1989 and the writing in Ithaca, New York, during the following two and a half years. Despite the enthusiastic urging of the narrow circle of the dissertation's readers, I could not afford the time to revise and publish it due to ceaseless pressure and obligations, some of which were imposed on me, others I took on willingly as a Third World university lecturer-cum-practicing public intellectual, in the course of which I published a score of academic papers in English and Thai, ten books, and up to a thousand articles in various Thai newspapers and magazines. Yet though the manuscript was lying idle in a filing cabinet, I never felt distant from it, for I have been trying to practice, test, and live its findings and message in a present-day Thailand whose intervening years have seen another popular uprising and political reform, economic boom and bust, cultural commodification and resistance.

So, it was to my great delight and gratitude that the Faculty of Political Science, Thammasat University, granted me a full-year leave of absence to take a visiting research fellowship at the Center for Southeast Asian Studies, Kyoto University, Japan. Leaving behind my usual hectic Thai cultural political self, I calmly and continuously focused on revising my dusty dissertation in the paradisiacal serenity of Kyoto in 1999. Cuts in the length, a number of factual corrections, and extensive grammatical and stylistic improvements have been made to the text, especially as kindly and meticulously suggested by its anonymous readers.

In addition, a number of significant new studies that touch on or partly cover the subject have appeared since the dissertation's initial completion, in particular, Somsak Jeamteerasakul's unpublished doctoral dissertation on the communist movement in Thailand (1993), Scot Barmé's study of Kulap Saipradit's post-war sojourn in Australia (1995), Eiji Murashima's research on early modern Sino-Siamese political movements (1996) and on wartime relationships between the Thai government, the Japanese imperial power, and the Chinese community in Thailand (1998), and Chirstopher E. Goscha's book on Vietnamese revolutionary activities and networks in Thailand and Southeast Asia (1999). Where relevant and appropriate, I have taken cognizance of their new empirical findings and modified or revised my manuscript accordingly, but I have not found any cause in them for a serious reconsideration and overhaul of its theoretical conception, architectonic structure, or essential arguments. As a matter of fact, quite the contrary. I have tried to do justice to them all, but rather than integrate them wholly with my manuscript into a single fat, ugly text, I think it is better to let interested readers go to these important studies themselves.

The considerable time that has passed since I first crafted the dissertation and the further experience I have gained from putting its lessons into real-life practice have also furnished me with a broader and clearer perspective on, and deeper understanding of, Thai cultural politics and the profound influence it has had on the collective intellectual and identity formation of people of my generation. These insights I have incorporated into a newly-written conclusion.

This book owes its existence to too many teachers, colleagues, friends, and informants to list all their names in a brief preface, but it would be an act of ingratitude on my part not to mention a few indispensable ones among them: Benedict Anderson, Craig J. Reynolds, Susan Buck-Morss, Takashi Shiraishi, and Chaiwat Satha-Anand. Many participants in the Thai radical cultural movements of the 1950s and 1970s also kindly shared with me their precious personal memories and experience as well as rare documents and publications, especially the late Supha Sirimanond, his surviving widow Chinda Sirimanond, Thaweep Voradilok, Khamsing Srinawk, Phichit Dijai, Swai Malayavej, Sujin Akharasamit, Suchart Sawatsri, the late Yutthaphong Phurisamban alias "Rawi Domephrajan," and Kanya Lilalai.

At various stages in the lengthy research for, as well as the write-up and revision of this book, I received timely and generous financial support from the following institutions: the Social Science Research Council (U.S.A.), the Southeast Asia Program at Cornell University, Thammasat University's Faculty of Political Science, Foundation for Promoting Education in Political Science, and Foundation for Development and Democracy, and last but not least, the Center for Southeast Asian Studies at Kyoto University. I am very grateful to all of them.

In the course of writing this book, it has struck me many times as a tragic irony that the few people who matter most to me personally are unable to read this most time-consuming and painstaking of my works. Ah Yi passed away in Bangkok while I was writing at Cornell. Ah Tia can read only Chinese. Jeed is too preoccupied with keeping house and raising Kloy, who, in turn, can't understand what this mysterious "work" is, which has taken "Papa" away from her almost every day. And yet, it is clear to me that their fates and mine are no less affected by the Thai cultural political regime than those of the Chinese,

Vietnamese, *lookjin* (people of Chinese descent born in Thailand), and Thai radical intellectuals of yesteryear. My only consolation and hope is that this "work" will contribute in some modest way to the re-imagination and remaking of Thai culture and politics into an Uttarakuru Thaweep that is freely and equally open and belonging to all of them.

Note on Transliteration and Translation

As will quickly be noticed, the transliteration of Thai proper names into the Roman alphabet in this book seems inconsistent. It indeed is, for several good reasons. To begin with, there is as yet no universally accepted system of romanization of Thai words. The current official version of the Thai Royal Institute is constrictive, rigid, and hence highly disputed. Other attempts to find a consensus on this controversial and slippery issue have so far ended in vain. Without a pre-existing satisfactory alternative, one has no choice but to invent one's own system.

Mine is primarily sound-based and aims to help speakers of English pronounce these names in a manner as close as possible to their original Thai pronunciations without making the resultant transliterations look too grotesque. Hence "traiphoom" instead of "traiphum" and "lookjin" instead of "lukjin" or "lookjiin." I have tried to maintain this principle and apply its derivative system of transliteration consistently throughout the book. However, two types of exception are made. Firstly, I follow some widely-used and well-known transliterations, even though I may disagree with their sounds, simply to avoid unnecessary confusion, for example, "Kuomintang" instead of "Guomaindang," and "Phibun" instead of "Phiboon." Secondly, I accord Thai persons and organizations the final say on how to transliterate their own names, hence, "Pridi Banomyong," "Thaweep Voradilok," and "Karnmuang Weekly." One should not presume, I think, to know better than these people how to fix such a personal mark of identity as their name.

All translations are mine unless otherwise stated.

1

Introduction: Manifesto for a Post-Communist Ghost Story

To English-reading audiences at the post-communist beginning of the third millennium A.D., reading a book on the now defunct doctrine of Marxism-communism in its reincarnation half a century ago in a remote and reposeful Third World capitalist country must seem superfluous; even the book's "right to exist" appears dubious. After all, during the last two decades, the theory, practice, and organization of Marxism-communism has proven bankrupt and utterly collapsed in Thailand, as in most countries around the world. Why bother to read, let alone write, such a lengthy and tedious obituary to this political corpse?

My answer is that, though dead, the Specter of Communism is still haunting us; that having had such a long and stormy engagement with the living, the dead did not depart without leaving deep imprints on the cultural soul of its intimate interlocutors; and that only through the writing, reading, and understanding of a post-communist ghost story can the living become fully aware of their own subconscious cultural selves.

What is attempted here, therefore, is a paradigmatic blasting away and overhaul of the pre-existing approaches to the study of the naturalization of Marxism-communism, both anti-communist and Marxist alike, and, by implication, of the relationship and interaction between national culture and foreign-derived discourse. Its point of departure is the rejection of the complacent, anti-communist, essentialist view that uses the political defeat of Marxism-communism to claim the incompatibility between what is presumed to be the "national cultural essence" and Marxist-communist ideology. At the same time, it also refuses the theoreticist, Marxist-communist view that is fixated on the "right" or "wrong" application of the "universal" truth of Marxism-communism to the concrete analysis of the social formation of a particular nation as the measure of its success. Instead, it rethinks the problematic from a decidedly non-essentialist and culturalist point of view which holds that political defeat or theoretical invalidity need not accurately reflect the cultural influence of Marxism-communism; that although beaten politically and disproved theoretically, Marxism-communism can still have a strong impact on national culture and vice versa; and that the only way to see this impact is to capture Marxism-communism and national culture in their actual moments of articulation—that is, when they are mutually interacting, interpenetrating, and transforming each other in the specific social, political, and economic conditions of a country.

The new problematic demands new objects of analysis. The investigation can proceed only by breaking up the phantasmagoric wholes into their real component parts and then scrutinizing the transformations they have brought about in one another. Consequently, the study emphatically regards national culture not as an immutable essence but as a repertoire of changeable and dynamic material practices and institutions, and Marxism-communism not as a universal theory but as a distinct set of always particularized cultural artifacts and discourses. Hence I deliberately abstain from any analysis of wholes (e.g., the overall contents of Thai culture or of Marxist-communist theory), but concentrate on apparently insignificant or marginal cultural bits and pieces (e.g., accented speech, books, bookshops, words, neologisms, advertisements, and prisons). This is where the generally overlooked or denied profound influence and complicity between the two is best revealed.

This new problematic also dictates the style of presentation which, in view of the objects of analysis, proceeds from a rather thick description of the particular context of the articulation between national culture and Marxist-communist discourse to an analysis of that articulation itself. And by force of repeated illustrations of this articulation, it seeks to illuminate the pattern of transformative effects each has had upon the other. Hence, the choice of a satirical novelistic narrative strategy in which historical facts, events, characters, and objects are first paraded to reconstruct in minute detail the setting and the scene, and then built up to the act of articulation itself.

There is also a non-academic reason for the choice of a satirical novelistic presentation, for in retelling the ghost story of Thai Marxism-communism, one simultaneously and inevitably has to recount the story of its alter-egos, namely the ethno-ideology of Thainess and the politics of anti-communism. Thus a post-communist attempt at cultural self-analysis is inseparably tied to the demystification of the "Thainess" ideology and anti-communist politics. Self-consciously informed by this double purpose, the book itself becomes an exercise in cultural politics, with a premeditatedly irreverent attitude, mocking tone, and ironic plot. Therefore, for all the many weaknesses it may contain, political innocence is assuredly not one of them.

For readers who may feel daunted and perplexed by the thick maze of narrative that will ensue, the following is offered as a synoptic guide to the whole book.

Chapter 2 begins with the characterization of the specific conditions of Siam in the early twentieth century as a singularly uncolonized absolute monarchy in Southeast Asia, strategically situated next to Indochina and near China, having substantial communities of Chinese and Vietnamese immigrants. These characteristics determined the overwhelmingly Chinese and Vietnamese origins and ethnic composition of the early communist movement and the relative absence of western-educated Marxist-communist native intellectuals in Siam. Rather, what dominated the cultural political life of the country was the Anglophile conservative royalism of the Chakri dynasty that put up a double-layered cultural resistance to foreign radical ideas through the conservative ethno-ideology of Thainess and the anti-socialist hegemony of the ancient Thai utopias of Uttarakuru-Phra Sri Arya.

Chapter 3 explores how the emerging *lookjin* (Thai-born Chinese) communists and Thai socialists tried to overcome these layers of cultural resistance in the aftermath of the fall of the absolute monarchy in 1932. It traces the varied attempts of lookjin communists to Thaify themselves both in and outside prison, as well as the effort of the constitutionalist, nationalist, and socialist Pridi Banomyong and the left-wing of the anti-monarchical People's Party under his leadership to de-utopianize Phra Sri Arya and acclimatize socialistic ideas to Thai Buddhism and culture in his Economic Plan of 1933. The opportunity for political breakthrough for both groups came with the invasion of Thailand by Japanese troops and the subsequent alliance between Japan and the Phibun government during the Second World War. Both the communist movement and the Pridi group organized underground resistance to the Japanese and the Phibun government, thus emerging after the war more powerful politically and more acceptable ethno-ideologically as Thai patriots and legitimate participants in national politics.

Chapters 4 and 5 present the particular circumstances of the post-war commodification of Marxism-communism in the Thai capitalist market economy under anti-communist authoritarian rule. Chapter 4 analyses in detail the demographic, international, and socio-economic conditions underlying the demand for Marxist-communist printed commodities in post-war Thailand. Chapter 5 discusses the immediate political and intellectual currents precipitating an upsurge in this demand. The chapter ends with a discussion of two contemporary pieces of writing that serve as an illustration of the change in the attitude of Thai intellectuals towards Uttarakuru, whose actuality had then become imaginable and mappable.

Chapter 6 continues the story of the post-war commodification of Marxism-communism on two separate tracks. On the surface, it surveys the cultural infrastructure of the supply of foreign Marxism-communism in Thailand, focusing on such cultural institutions as bookshops, libraries, private collections, and foreign embassies and their political connections and activities. On a deeper level, it deals with the interaction between communism and anti-communism, or between the leftist-communist opposition movement and the anti-communist authoritarian Phibun government, and with how the anti-communist authoritarianism of the latter affected and intertwined with the communism of the former. Included in the discussion are the following aspects of the Phibun government: the wax and wane of its political-intelligence Santibal Police, its mutual double dealing with the United States, its spurious and opportunistic anti-communist policy, and conflicts within its ruling elite.

The next two chapters follow the same narrative strategy. Chapter 7 deals ostensibly with different groups of Thai reproducers of Marxism-communism and their inter- and intra-group relationships and conflicts, Chapter 8 with their respective press organs. But together these chapters pursue a second and more important theme: the interaction between the commodification of Marxism-communism and print capitalism. Various aspects of the topic that are discussed include financing, advertising, patronage, and protection, concluding with the coercive character of bourgeois civil society, as against those liberal aspects covered earlier.

The concluding chapter brings together key analytical and conceptual findings from the text concerning the ethno-ideology of Thai official nationalism and its relationship with Thai cultural politics, the commodification of Marxism-communism in a capitalist cultural market, the politics and semiotics of translating foreign-derived radical discourse into Thai, the rhyming of Marxist-communist discourse in Thai poetry, and parting thoughts on what, if any, is still left of Marxism-communism-constituted Thai radical culture.

2

Lookjin Communists: The Bridgehead of Siamese Communism

[People who believe in communism like Mr. Piatoe]...are likely to cause a lot of troubles. It should not be taken simply for granted that he is a Thai by birth since his disposition is by no means Thai...[He] should not be allowed to depend on His Majesty's merciful protection any further.

Prince Boriphat, Minister of Interior[1]

Immigrant Communism from the East

With the coming of the modern European colonial powers to Southeast Asia in the nineteenth century, all of Siam's formerly belligerent neighboring states were colonized and pacified one by one until Siam stood alone as the only non-colonized country in the region. But her non-colonized status by no means implied a completely independent and sovereign nation-state. Rather, with the traditional ruling monarchy still in power and actually gaining strength from the newly available technology of colonial state-building, and with the overwhelming military superiority, political influence, and economic domination of the colonial powers codified in a series of unequal treaties, Siam arguably was transformed into an indirectly colonized dynastic state in a reluctant transition to modern nation-statehood under the leadership of a modernizing and conservative socio-political elite.[2]

The key to early modern Siam's real situation lies not in her absolute monarchs' official nationalist rhetoric nor in the formal-legal and diplomatic regalia frequently and grandly exhibited to an audience of visiting dignitaries and foreign residents, but in their actual relationship with their subjects and with the country's natural resources. Economically, the Chakri rulers linked resource-rich Siam to the burgeoning global chain of colonial commodity production as the British Empire's most important rice depot; as Siam's biggest landlords and real-estate developers, they enriched themselves enormously in the process. Politically, they visited and learned from the British and Dutch colonial authorities' methods of governing India, Singapore, and Java and applied that knowledge to the administrative reform of their relatively weak and decentralized traditional patrimonial kingdom into an authoritarian and centralized modernizing auto-colonial state. And culturally, they inhabited a mental, intellectual, and discursive "civilized" world wishfully close to their sovereign counterparts in the European metropolises and far from their compatriots in the villages. Regarding themselves subjectively as almost a supra-ethnic or supranational cosmopolitan ruling caste, they lorded it over the Siamese nation-people as colonial masters with a royal Thai face.

This particular situation of Siam at the turning point in her history brought mixed blessings to the country, with far-reaching consequences for the future. One of those mixed blessings was communism.

As a result of Siam's indirect colonization, the origins and early development of communism in Siam assumed specific characteristics. The first was that communism was introduced into the country from the Asiatic East rather than the European West. Since non-colonial Siam retained sovereign authority over her domestic affairs, including education, her population did not undergo a European-language, colonial system of education, but neither did it receive a system of mass education. Instead, the dynastic state gave it belated, half-hearted, and underfunded measures which resulted in an underdeveloped, narrowly-based, Thai-language, elitist education, the upper echelons of which were specifically intended to train loyal bureaucrats or *kharajkan* (royal servants).

The contrast between Siam and Japan, another non-colonized Asian country, is instructive. Although they opened to the West and began modernizing reform in about the same period (1855 and 1885 in Siam, 1858 and 1868 in Japan), the disparities between them in educational progress were immense. By 1914, 98.5 percent of Japanese children of school age were in school, whereas the corresponding figure in Siam in 1918 was only 10 percent. Allowing for the seventeen-year gap between the beginnings of reform in the two countries does not help; the Siamese figure was still a dismal 52.73 percent in 1932, the year the absolute monarchy was overthrown. While the Japanese imperial government enacted a compulsory primary education law as early as 1872, the equivalent decree was only passed in Siam some forty-nine years later, due to the persistent efforts of two consecutive reform-minded ministers of public instruction to create "national education" against the strong resistance of their conservative cabinet colleagues. As to higher education, while Japan opened the Imperial University in Tokyo in 1869, it was not until 1917, almost half a century later, that the first full-fledged university (Chulalongkorn University) was inaugurated in Siam. And during the forty-year period from 1892 to 1932, at no point was more than 7.05 percent of the state budget allocated to the

Ministry of Public Instruction; the average was less than 4 percent. Thus, the Ministry usually found its place near the bottom of the list of budget priorities, slightly above the Ministry of Foreign Affairs and well below His Majesty's Civil List and Other Royal Expenses. When compulsory primary education was finally enacted, a special educational surcharge tax (*ngoen seuksa phli*) was needed to finance it.[3]

Despite the slow development of educational policy, the material preconditions for the rise of a European-languages-translating class had begun to emerge in the reign of King Rama III (1824–1851)—the printing press and Thai type characters were introduced into Siam in 1835 and the first Thai biweekly newspaper was published in 1844, both by Dan Beach Bradley, an American missionary. A few far-sighted members of the royalty and nobility, on their own initiative, began to study English from western missionaries and to translate English technical texts into Thai. Also, the first Thai student was sent to study in Europe in this reign. The reign of King Rama IV (1851–1868) saw the publication of the first English-Thai dictionary in 1865 and the teaching of translation to some members of the royalty and nobility as part of their education. In the reign of King Rama V (1868–1910), seventeen newspapers and forty-seven magazines were published in Bangkok, mostly in Thai, usually containing Thai translations of English or French tales, short stories, novels, news, articles, plays, and academic texts. Almost without exception, the translators of these works belonged to the royalty and nobility. By the reign of King Rama VI (1910–1925), translation had become a dependable profession, generating lucrative fees from the publication in installments of popular foreign romantic, detective, and adventure novels.[4]

But it remained difficult for ordinary Thais to get much formal education, even more so to climb the educational ladder and become well-versed in a European language. For most Thais who were domestically educated under absolute monarchy, the linguistic means to communist literature in European languages were simply not there.[5] How uncommon the route to Western-language proficiency was is illustrated by the story of Supha Sirimanond (1914–1986), the first domestically educated Thai student of Marxism to undertake an extensive, conceptual, and analytical study of Marx's *Capital* (from an English translation) in his *Khaepitalist* (1951). Among the many factors that contributed to his very good knowledge of English prior to his fateful encounter with Marxism were a well-off, aristocratic family, formal primary and secondary education in several good public schools in Bangkok, special evening tutorial classes in English, subscriptions to two English-language newspapers, two years of English language study at Chulalongkorn

University, four years of correspondence courses in advertising and journalism with the International Correspondence School and the London School of Journalism, a one-year trip to China and Japan as a foreign war correspondent for a Thai newspaper, and two years of monitoring and translating English radio broadcasts for the Supreme Command Headquarters of the Armed Forces. It was within the intellectually eye-opening and stimulating environment of career journalism that he discovered Marx in a book by the Fabians Sydney and Beatrice Webb and began a painstaking nine-year study of *Capital* in 1943. Obviously, such a concurrence of factors did not happen often.

Of those who were sent to study in Europe, most were offspring of the royalty, nobility, or bourgeoisie, destined to join the bureaucratic or business elite after graduation. Hence their general aversion to radicalism of any persuasion.[6] A good example of this anti-radical, royalist political attitude among Thai students in Europe, especially in Britain, can be found in *Lakhorn haeng chiwit* (The circus of life), the first celebrated novel of Prince Akatdamkoeng Raphiphat, a pioneering modern Thai novelist-cum-princeling of the blood. In this novel as well as its sequel, the embittered member of the royal family, in socio-economic decline, aims his most virulent invective not at the undemocratic political regime in Siam nor at the wealthy white imperialists in Europe, but at the "Bolshevik Hindus" who dare try to incite him against his beloved Chakri absolute monarchs, to whom the Siamese nation owes her survival and independence.[7] This kind of political conservatism was uncannily mixed with progressive, middle-class social values, causing some later critics to mistake him for a revolutionary democrat!

Thai students abroad also had to live and study under the watchful eyes of Siamese diplomatic authorities who were ready to punish them for any suspicious political activity.[8] As a matter of fact, worry over dangerous, contracted-abroad political ideas and activism had persistently troubled the minds of successive Chakri rulers. King Chulalongkorn (Rama V) confided his concern to Prince Naresworarit, his brother and then Siamese envoy to Britain, in a letter written in 1885:

> About the *political* affairs in England, those who go near them and listen to them a lot usually take sides with the idea of one group or another. Even though they can't do anything in England, they will often use that idea in their homeland, where the official tradition of government is very different from the one in England. This will cause an even more serious trouble, leading to all kinds of whimsies. As far as I have heard, if they get the so-called *radical* thought, they will become big hindrances to Thailand. Especially in the case of royalty, it will amount to cutting off

one's own fortune [words in italics appeared as transliterations in the Thai original].[9]

His successor, King Vajiravudh (Rama VI), took the same concern to fantastic extremes. He wrote to Thai students abroad in 1925 that whenever they heard political conversations in their schools or colleges, they should ask themselves first whether those doctrines or methods were suitable for the Thais and useful to the people in general before accepting them as good and fashionable. "Don't forget," the King emphasized, "that the conditions of European countries and Thailand are different. So things that are beneficial to them may be harmful to us." In case sheer advice was not enough, he required everyone taking an examination for the King's Scholarship for study abroad to sign a written oath to all sorts of angels and ghosts that if they ever became traitorous to the King and rebelled, they would die a horrible death and be sent to hell.[10]

In any case, the number of Thai students studying abroad was very small (see Table 2-1), and most were not exposed to radical socialism. From the late nineteenth century to the 1920s, socialism in general and revolutionary Marxism in particular was far less central and influential as an intellectual and political force in Great Britain and the United States, where over 80 percent of Thai students on government scholarships studied, than in countries such as France and Germany. This might help explain the rareness of socialists and communists among them, although there were growing socialist movements of a moderate, reformist, and strongly ethical kind in both countries during that period, the British movement being the stronger and more successful of the two.[11]

The few Thai students, mainly of commoner origin and studying in France, who despite royal warnings and gruesome curses were secretly interested and

Table 2-1
Thai Students Abroad on Government Scholarship
by Country of Study, 1921–1924

YEAR	GREAT BRITAIN	UNITED STATES	FRANCE	OTHER COUNTRIES	TOTAL
1921	140	41	26	15	222
1922	182	39	23	21	265
1923	204	49	24	26	303
1924	301	47	24	-	(400)*

* An estimate. There was also a small, but undetermined number of students studying on private funds.
Sources: Laortong, "Kansong," 166; Batson, *The End*, 78.

active in anti-royalist politics, went on to form the core of the People's Party. Established in Paris in 1927 and eventually including about one hundred army and navy officers and civilian bureaucrats, the People's Party would stage the 1932 coup against the absolute monarchy, establish a constitutionalist regime, and rule Siam for the next fifteen years. But only a few of the several hundred Thai students who studied in the West before the fall of absolute monarchy considered themselves a socialist of any kind. One was Pridi Banomyong, top civilian leader and strategist of the 1932 coup, key architect and minister of the subsequent constitutional regime, leader of the Free Thai resistance underground during World War II, onetime prime minister, and first senior statesman of modern Siam. Pridi converted to socialism under the influence of the French Solidarist School of Professor Charles Gide during his doctoral study in France in the 1920s, a study which later formed the basis of his aborted National Economic Plan of 1933.[12] Another was Prince Sakol Wannakon Worawan, who claimed to have become a member of the socialist Fabian Society while studying in Britain sometime in the 1900s. During the controversy over Pridi's National Economic Plan in 1933, he was appointed to a special government committee formed to study the Plan. Not only did he staunchly support it, but considered it insufficiently thorough and radical in some respects. Widely dubbed the "Red Prince," he played a prominent advisory role in the pro-Pridi social democratic Sahachip (Unionist) Party and in the communist labor movement after the Second World War.[13]

Pridi and Prince Sakol were exceptional; until the end of World War II there was no significant overlap between the growing European-language-translating class and the Siamese communists. But if the flow of communism from the European West was dammed, communism from the Asiatic East, namely China and Indochina, flowed profusely into Siam. Since the early nineteenth century, it had been a deliberate and consistent policy of successive Chakri monarchs to encourage the immigration of Chinese coolies into the kingdom to serve as an increasingly needed and taxable pool of wage labor, while events in the Middle Kingdom itself, never lacking in natural and man-made calamities, also pushed them outward. To a lesser number and degree, Vietnamese immigrants left Indochina, mostly for Siam's Northeast, due to the internal wars and foreign invasions of their homeland from the early nineteenth century, especially after French colonization in 1883. In contrast to the foreign-invaded, war-torn, and often economically depleted lands they left behind, the non-colonized, peaceful, and resource-rich Kingdom of Siam must have appeared a blessed heaven indeed. By 1927, large communities of these immigrants were settled in Siam—about 1.3 million Chinese and twenty thousand Vietnamese.[14]

In the early twentieth century a new breed of Chinese and Vietnamese immigrant entered Siam, no longer economic and war refugees in search of work and peace, but nationalist propagandists and organizers in search of money and recruits for their revolutionary causes. Among them were such well-known nationalist leaders as Sun Yatsen and Phan Boi Chau.[15] They were joined in the 1920s by their communist fellow countrymen, who came for the same immediate political purposes but with a fundamentally different doctrine and ultimate political program. As the single non-colonial country in Southeast Asia, situated next to Indochina, enjoying regular marine transportation with southern China and Hong Kong, and having substantial immigrant communities of their compatriots, Siam offered the new immigrants an ideal sanctuary from pursuing European colonial authorities and anti-communist governments and a perfect base of training and operation to recuperate, reorganize, and relaunch anti-colonial and anti-government activities.[16] No sooner had the Chinese and Vietnamese communist movements been established than communist political immigrants began to enter Siam.[17] The most prominent was Nguyen Ai Quoc (Ho Chi Minh), who used Siam as his base for anti-French colonial and Comintern operations from 1928 to 1930. Among the Southeast Asian communist sojourners was Tan Malaka, who came after Indonesia's failed communist uprisings of 1926–1927, stayed from December 1926 until August 1927, and with his comrades established the Partai Republik Indonesia in Bangkok.[18]

Pro-communist Chinese newspapers, libraries, and book and newspaper clubs began to appear in Bangkok as early as 1922,[19] the first publicly-known Chinese communist organization emerged out of a split in the local rightist-dominated Kuomintang branch in November 1924,[20] and Chinese communist activities increased conspicuously after the breakdown of the first Kuomintang-CCP alliance in China in 1927.[21] As to their Vietnamese counterparts, a few members of the Viet Nam Thanh Nien Kach Menh Hoi (Vietnamese Revolutionary Youth League) were sent to Siam to carry out nationalist propaganda and organizational work among the Vietnamese immigrants beginning in 1925. They were able to set up friendship and cooperative societies in Vietnamese immigrant communities at various places around the country in 1926 and began to publish a Vietnamese newsmagazine called *Dong Tranh* in 1927. Following his arrival in Siam in mid-1928, Nguyen Ai Quoc, one of whose at least six *noms de guerre* in Siam was "Thau Chin" (Old Chin), reorganized the various friendship societies into the Hoi Than Ai Nguoi Annam O Xiem (Annamite Fraternity of Siam), improved the newsmagazine and changed its name to Than Ai (Friendship), and with the permission of the Siamese government opened

schools for Vietnamese and nearby Thai children.[22] The Chinese and
Vietnamese comrades, usually in close cooperation, set up front and party
organs, imported communist literature, opened bookshops and book and
newspaper clubs, published newspapers and pamphlets, established private
schools for the immigrants' children, and put up posters in public places.[23]

In early 1928, in response to communist setbacks in China and Indonesia,
the Nan Yang or South Seas Communist Party was established in Singapore by
order of the Comintern, with Chinese immigrants in Southeast Asian countries
as its customary mass base. The Party was charged with supervising the
organization of national-revolutionary movements under strict communist
leadership among the revolutionary forces of workers, peasants, and
intelligentsia in Malaya, Siam, Burma, Indochina, and Indonesia. Organizationally, it was under the joint control of the Comintern's Far Eastern Bureau
and the Central Committee of the Chinese Communist Party, both situated in
Shanghai.[24] In July 1929, a branch of the South Seas Communist Party, the
Siam Special Committee, was set up in Siam under its guidance to take charge
of the local, mainly Chinese, communist movement.[25]

Nevertheless, much to the dismay of their foreign supervisors and to the
relief of Siamese police, the early Chinese communists in Siam usually carried
out their tasks incautiously. Among the numerous ideological, political,
organizational, disciplinary, and administrative mistakes committed by them
and severely censured by the South Seas Communist Party around November
1929 were the following: arranging party meetings in tea houses and
restaurants in contempt of police capability, resulting in the arrest of many
members; being careless with organizational secrets; recruiting new members
without a probation period; setting up a store to sell cheap bread to workers
but ending up pursuing profit; and depositing funds in the bank to earn interest
instead of spending them to expand operations among workers.[26] It was
probably this type of careless activity which invited the Siamese authority's
first explicitly anti-communist measure, a secret deportation order by the
Ministry of Interior in April 1929, as well as a series of big police catches of
over one hundred communists from late 1929 through 1930.[27]

Meanwhile, the general failure of the South Seas Communist Party's
operations, especially in recruiting native peoples into the communist
movement in Siam and elsewhere, caused by its persistently narrow ethnic
Chinese emphasis and the ethnically un-diversified CCP channels, led the
Comintern to replace it with several communist parties organized more "along
racial lines," including the Communist Party of Siam (CPS), the first national
communist organization in the country, nominally at least.[28] The Comintern
agent responsible for setting up the CPS was none other than "Old Chin," alias

Nguyen Ai Quoc. During his visits from Siam to Hong Kong and Shanghai from late November or early December 1929 to February 1930, Quoc took over as chief of the Shanghai-based Far Eastern Bureau of the Comintern, formed a Hong Kong-based Southern Bureau—a sub-office of the Far Eastern Bureau directly responsible for communist operations in Southeast Asia—and helped found a unified Vietnamese Communist Party. Equipped with the addresses of Chinese communists in Siam obtained from their comrades in Hong Kong, he returned to Siam in March with the definite instruction to establish the Communist Party of Siam by combining Chinese communists affiliated with the South Seas branch in Bangkok with their Vietnamese counterparts in the Northeast. There was some argument from local Vietnamese comrades who were disinclined to reorient their anti-French patriotic activities towards the Comintern-prescribed internationalist cause of Siamese proletarian revolution, thereby risking a backlash from the Siamese authorities. But with perseverance and the help of CCP Southern Bureau member Fu Ta Chang, Quoc finally convened and chaired a meeting of Chinese and Vietnamese communists in Bangkok on April 20, 1930. Resolutions were officially adopted to unify the two groups, establish the Communist Party of Siam, and appoint a Bangkok-based Provisional Central Committee, which later became the Central Executive Committee of the Party, pending official recognition of full party status by the Comintern (granted, perhaps in 1935). From its inception until 1934, the CPS remained under the direct responsibility of the Communist Party of Malaya (CPM), which superseded the South Seas Communist Party in April 1930.[29]

Royal Anti-Communism from the West

The second characteristic of the initial development of communism in Siam resulting from her non-colonial situation was that anti-communism predated communism both in its introduction into the country and its articulation with Thai culture. Whereas communism began to emerge among the Sino-Vietnamese immigrant communities in Siam in the early 1920s, anti-communism had made its first appearance among the European-cultured ruling elite in the late nineteenth century. King Chulalongkorn reportedly sent a letter in 1881 to an American diplomat, expressing his hope that all rulers in the world would some day be saved by Providence from "...those based classes Sociallist, Nihilist, Communists etc."[30]

Much more crucial is the fact that anti-communism took a vantaged position in Thai culture long before communism did. On April 26/27, 1912, shortly after a series of political incidents at home and abroad had unexpectedly shaken the seeming stability of the Siamese throne—the Chinese Republican Revolution in October 1911, the abdication of the Manchu emperor in February 1912, and the aborted coup attempt by junior army officers at home in March of the same year—the English-educated King Vajiravudh, deeply alarmed, penned two consecutive diary entries of great length, in Thai, dealing exclusively with what he perceived as the threat of "latthi khong sochialist" (the doctrine of socialism).[31]

In them, the King tried to work out a critique of socialism, likening it to the Buddhist mythology of Sassana Phra Sri Arya (the religion of Phra Sri Arya) in their presumed common impracticality and unreality. Phra Sri Arya, more fully Phra Sri Arya Mettraya, was the name of the Future Buddha. According to the Tripitaka, he would arise after the religion of the present Buddha (Gautama Shakyamuni) came to an end, when the average age of human beings reached 80,000 years. In the popular Thai folktale version, millenarian elements joined the story, such as material abundance, common property, absolute equality, perfect human beauty, universal resemblance, universal moral behavior, the absence of crime and war, Kalpa Phruksa (magic wish-granting trees), monks no longer wearing a yellow robe but only tying a piece of yellow cloth to their ear, and the dating of Phra Sri Arya Mettraya's appearance to B.E. 5000.[32]

King Vajiravudh began by listing the coming "benefits" of an ideal socialist rule, namely, universal peace, absolute social and political equality, forced equalization of wealth, nationalization of the country's wealth and resources, abolition of religion, and community of women.[33] Having constructed a caricature of socialism, reducing it to either impossible absolute egalitarianism or anarcho-liberal individualism and making it an easy target of attack, he then proceeded to the absurd logical implications which "proved" socialism's impracticality and unreality. Throughout, his arguments relied heavily on an implicit presupposition of a reality that was partly common sense and partly an underlying philosophical-anthropological assumption of human nature as unequal, greedy, vainglorious, ambitious, envious, lazy, and foolish, all the more so among the working class. Finally, the King delivered a below-the-belt blow by arbitrarily setting up a religious-like, taxing, moral standard for socialists, using their failure to meet that standard to assassinate their characters, and thereby triumphantly proclaiming the impossibility of true socialism and the resultant danger of fake socialists. These "phasa sontaphai" (literally, leading-people-by-the-nose-language) polemical techniques, as later characterized by Supha Sirimanond, were typical of his writing on other such controversial subjects as the Chinese, parliamentary democracy, and revolution.[34]

The King's diary entries on *latthi khong sochialist* were soon followed by a satirical essay in English entitled "Uttarakuru: An Asiatic Wonderland," first published in the English magazine *Siam Observer* and translated into Thai by Prince Dhani and Phraya Burinawaras (Chuan Singhaseni) shortly thereafter.[35] In the essay, the King further developed the theme of his diary entries, proceeding to idealize or utopianize modern socialism by equating it not only with Sir Thomas More's *Utopia* and the Buddhist millenarian era of Phra Sri Arya Mettraya, but with the Brahmanic ideal land of Uttarakuru. Literally meaning "Land to the North," Uttarakuru was a Hindu utopia described in the ancient texts of the Vedas and Brahmanas. It first appeared in Thai in the fourteenth century Mahayana Buddhist treatise *Trai Bhumi Phra Ruang* (The Three Worlds of King Reuang), on which the King's essay was based. In the Thai version, Uttarakuru was situated to the north of Mount Sumeru. Its inhabitants were all virtuous people, blessed with permanent youth, good health, and physical beauty. There was no disease, conflict, or crime, no manner of work, productive or domestic, no private property, even in personal clothing, and no marriage, family, or childcare. Food and material abundance was brought by a gigantic Kalpa Phruksa and other miraculous plants, while people dwelt in trees, with no need for houses.[36]

Utopia, Sassana Phra Sri Arya, Uttarakura—they were all lumped together as so many old and new symptoms of the same recurrent "Unrest Fever," "New Mania," and "Revolution Plague," having their place only in "Dreamland or the Lunatic Asylum." The King executed this *tour de force* in the following manner. He equated More's *Utopia* with the ancient Brahmanic ideal land of Uttarakuru, "a land apparently every whit as Utopian"; he identified Brahmanic Uttarakuru with modern socialism by arbitrarily selecting such common elements as common property and material abundance, while glossing over or downplaying historical and substantial differences between them; and he highlighted the more outlandish elements in Uttarakuru as proof of its ideality, summarily projecting that ideality onto socialism.

In itself, there was nothing unique or even peculiar about this second characteristic of early Siamese communism. After all, it was only natural for the Siamese aristocracy to bring anti-radicalism back to their un-colonized home from turn-of-the-century Europe. But the crux of the matter lay in the far-reaching consequences this had for future Thai radical culture. We can begin to understand this by noticing a peculiar point in King Vajiravudh's anti-socialist diary entries and essay: no contemporary Siamese socialist was ever mentioned or identified by the King. None of the "socialists" mentioned in the texts were Thai (George Bernard Shaw, Keir Hardie)[37] and some were not really socialist (Kang Youwei and Sun Yatsen).[38] As it turned out, the only Siamese socialist therein was an anonymous Brahman of yore who allegedly sandwiched his Uttarakuru socialism within a lot of dull religious stuff to get it past the censor over 500 years ago![39] In fact, the 1912 coup plotters, whose action most likely provoked the King's writings, were merely limited monarchists or republicans, and by no means socialist.[40] Why then so much ado about no socialists?

The reason seemed to lie in the growing Chinese republican movement in Siam at the time. The first pro-revolutionary Chinese newspaper in Siam, *Meinan Ribao*, began publication in 1906. The Siamese branch of Sun Yatsen's Tongmenghui (Revolutionary Alliance) was established in 1907. And in 1908, Sun himself visited the Chinese community in Siam for ten days.[41] These developments prompted King Chulalongkorn to comment in 1909: "Our *interests* are opposed to those Chinese who have come here to instigate a *political party*. We should keep a watch on them. Whenever there is a chance to destroy the Chinese *political party*, we must do it."[42] One year later and only a few months before King Vajiravudh came to the throne, the Chinese in Bangkok flexed their political muscle by launching the first general strike in Thai history against a capitation tax increase. This strike almost completely paralyzed the capital for three to four days and sent a shock wave among the Siamese rulers.[43] All these incidents were omens of political trouble for the new King, especially if the dangerous and alien ideas of the Tongmenghui, with all its "socialist" leanings, were to spread to the Thai population.[44] It was obvious to him that something must be done to culturally immunize the Thai against this political plague. This was all the more crucial since the legal hands of his indirectly colonized dynastic state were partly tied and could not reach the many independent press owners and editors who, as extraterritorial subjects of western colonial powers, remained outside Siamese jurisdiction. This might well have been the reason behind this curious, bemoaning passage in *Uttarakuru*:

> ...the good old kings were not piffling jokers to snap your fingers at; they did do all kinds of unpleasant things to Socialists....The Sword of Justice and the Sword of Power was the same, and held by the same man. What a difference between then and now! The World had not become so frightfully civilised in the days of our author to permit a man's airing his socialistic opinions as such...[45]

Perforce, the King could do little but argue with them.[46]

The King's motive was clearly stated near the end of his diary entries on socialism. Candid in its conception and prescient in its anticipation, this remarkable statement can be read essentially as a program of anti-socialist hegemony, a declaration of war of position against socialism in the field of culture, à la Gramsci. It deserves to be quoted in full:

People with such ill will cover themselves with the title of socialism like a beautiful gown to deceive others into admiring them. So they are tough enemies who couldn't be easily suppressed. To use force or penalty against them as we do against other criminals is useless for it will make them more respectable in the eyes of the fools who will think that they are punished for speaking the truth. Therefore, the expedient method which we should use to fight these people is their very own method. We must speak up, explain, oppose what they say. But not just opposing, we must also show that while what they say is a good idea, can it really be put into practice? If we can clearly show that it is impossible, the audience will become aware and change its mind. We can't force people to change their mind. We can only explain until they see by themselves that their old idea is incorrect due to misunderstanding. Only thus can they really change their mind. The important thing is not to forbid people to express their opinion, on the contrary, we ought to open a channel for them to do so. We can then know how incorrect that opinion is, and how to correct it.[47]

In this light, *Uttarakuru* was a deliberate anticipatory move of cultural politics to discredit socialism before it took root in Siam or partook of Thai culture, an attempt to carve out a Thai utopian identity of Uttarakuru or Sri Arya Mettraya for socialism before its Siamese inception, a prenatal birth certificate, or an anti-Gramscian text before Gramsci.[48] True to King Vajiravudh's program, *Uttarakuru* was soon followed by more anti-socialist and anti-Bolshevik works like *Chuai amnaj!* (Coup d'état!), *Kanjalajol nai russia* (Chaos in Russia), and *Latthi ao yang* (The cult of imitation). By the 1930s, "Phra Sri Arya Mettraya" had become so significant a part of Thai political parlance that it found its way into newspapers, poetry, the Supreme Council of State's meetings, and the First Declaration of the People's Party, while "Uttarakuru" entered the rank of officially recognized words in the Thai dictionary of the Ministry of Public Instruction. The upshot was that, for years to come, the ideas of socialism and communism would almost automatically be associated with, or referred to in Thai as, "Uttarakuru" or "Phra Sri Arya," with all their inherent utopian connotations.

Nonetheless, what the far-sighted King failed to foresee was that by arbitrarily matching a foreign concept of "socialism" with utopian Thai (non)equivalents, however derogatorily, he inadvertently naturalized or Thaified a radical signifier and opened the floodgates of the Thai language to it. Once made Thai and committed to the future and to strangers, it could and would develop a politico-cultural life of its own in the hands of other hegemonic and anti-hegemonic groups, acquiring autonomous and pluralistic meanings over which its original naturalizer had only some initial influence but no absolute control.[49]

Finally, some words should be said about the direct role western governments and advisers played in anti-communist activities in Siam. The British, French, German, and Dutch governments actively cooperated with the Siamese authorities in suppressing communists in Siam by providing intelligence information and advice on anti-communist measures, tracking and intercepting communist suspects abroad, and accepting deported immigrant communists from Siam.[50] And foreign advisers like Raymond B. Stevens, the American adviser in foreign affairs, René G. Guyon, a French legal adviser in the Ministry of Justice, and Sir Robert E. Holland, an English expert on communism, played a significant role in shaping the Siamese official definition of communism from the late 1920s to the early 1930s.[51] We will discuss this more in later chapters.

How Thai a Lookjin Communist Could Be

All studies of the early development of communism in Siam agree that communist activities in the pre-1932 period were limited almost entirely to the Chinese and Vietnamese communities, that the main thrust of their politics was externally oriented and anti-imperialist, and that their major political concern was politics in their respective home countries, not in Siam. Hence, it follows naturally that most of the communists at that time were not Thai, but Chinese or Vietnamese immigrants and their descendants.[52] Again, this third characteristic of the early communist movement in Siam had much to do with the non-colonial situation of the country. If strategic location and the absence of direct colonial policing drew Chinese and Vietnamese communists to Siam, and her underdeveloped, elitist, Thai-language education and Western-educated, conservative, translating class obstructed the flow of Western communism to the Thai people, then, one could argue, the absence of western colonial rulers, in contrast with colonial neighbors such as Burma, Indochina, or Indonesia, in effect sterilized Siam of a nationalist mass movement and its possible radicalization. To put it simply, a western colonial government in colonized Siam could perversely have contributed to the politicization and conversion of many more Thais to nationalism and even communism.[53]

But the fact that the early communist movement in Siam had an overwhelming Chinese and Vietnamese majority also produced some interesting effects. Politically, it made the specter of communism less menacing but also more alien to the Thais, adding the estranging force of racial prejudice to the government's portrayal of communism as utterly un-Thai. Conceptually, it prematurely shut or blurred researchers' eyes to the possibility that a person could arguably be

Chinese or Vietnamese, communist or socialist, and also Thai at the same time, as the lookjin communists turned out to be.[54]

The objective condition of Siam's non-colonial status aside, subjective factors on the part of the early communist movement in Siam also contributed to its largely un-Thai ethnic composition. During the 1923–1927 period of the first Kuomintang-CCP alliance, Chinese communists in Southeast Asia operated under the Kuomintang organizational umbrella.[55] The Comintern, having China within its fold and India as its eventual major target in the Far East, seemed intent on dealing a heavy blow to its main enemy, the British Empire, in this in-between region and rushed ahead with the mobilization of the overseas Chinese rather than wasting time on the natives of those countries where they were politically less accessible, such as Siam and Malaya. Hence the Chinese communists' deliberate limitation of their initial activities in Siam to the Chinese immigrant communities.[56] Likewise, during this period, the Vietnamese Thanh Nien cadres in Siam confined their propaganda and organizational work to the Vietnamese immigrant communities and sent some new recruits to China for further training.[57]

However, both foreign and domestic political developments after 1927 compelled the Comintern and the Siamese communist movement to revise this inclination towards the overseas Chinese. For the Chinese communists in Southeast Asia, the collapse of the Kuomintang-CCP alliance from 1927 meant that their Kuomintang organizational cover was lost, their Chinese-oriented, moderate, united-front policy was obsolete, and their mass base among the overseas Chinese was no longer secure. The Comintern's answer to this new situation was the establishment of the South Seas Communist Party in early 1928 to reorganize and supervise a new communist organizational network in the region, with a more radical, domestically-oriented program, and, it was to be hoped, a more native mass base.[58] Nonetheless, due to the South Seas Communist Party's own lingering Sino-centrism and the customarily Chinese base of the redeployed existing CCP channels, this proved a failure, and it was still a deliberate policy of the Chinese communists in Siam under the direction of the South Seas Communist Party in practice to limit their initial propagandistic and educational activities to ethnic Chinese peasants, small merchants, and poor students. Only after this first step bore fruit would they "persuade oppressed *foreigners* [*khontangchat thi thook kodkhi*, non-Chinese, Southeast Asian nationalities, including Thais; in other words, *locals*] to join the same rank."[59]

Shortly afterwards, from July to September 1928, the Comintern convened its Sixth Congress in Moscow, ushering in the so-called "Third Period" of ultra-leftism which lasted until 1935 in this region.[60] Meanwhile, the Siamese government, out of alarm at increasing communist activity and consideration for

British and French colonial interests, had begun to crack down severely on communist activities in 1929. In response to all this, the Chinese communist groups in Siam began to reorient their policy emphases, propagandistically from radical nationalism to communism, politically from externally-oriented anti-imperialism to internally-oriented anti-absolute monarchy, and organizationally from the Chinese immigrant communities to the Thais, commencing in 1929.[61] The upshot of this process, which happened to coincide with the Comintern's reorganization drive in the region, was the founding of the Communist Party of Siam and the disbandment of the Singapore-based Nan Yang or South Seas Communist Party in April 1930.

And yet, long after priority had been given to party works concerning the "natives," hardly any Thai leaflets were issued by the CPS.[62] This negligence severely hampered the Party's access to ethnic Thai people and prompted the unlikely advice from two visiting foreign communists, a Japanese and a Cantonese, sent on a fact-finding mission from Singapore in June 1931, that the Party should persuade more Thais to become members so as to live up to its "Communist Party of Siam" name.[63] According to a British-intercepted letter from the CPS Executive Committee to the supervisory Communist Party of Malaya, dated September 20, 1932, the CPS's total membership at the time was 325; not one was Thai.[64] Pinpointing this ethnically un-Thai character as the Party's fundamental weakness, a November 1932 issue of *Jitao Bao* (The guide), a CPS monthly journal, self-critically admitted that:

> Our Party is called the Communist Party of Siam, but in truth our Party has only Chinese....The basis by which we can change Siam comes down to a method by which we can bring Siamese into the Party. This is not a new problem. The same measure was discussed at our meeting last year...where we decided that the first step was for members to study Siamese in preparation for contacting Siamese. It was decided to seek results in six months, but from that time to the present it has been a year and not a single branch has announced progress.[65]

Nevertheless, other developments prevented the CPS from carrying through this self-Thaification resolution. Owing to the typical careless ineptitude of its members and the government's increasing suppression, nearly two hundred mostly Chinese party members were arrested in the early 1930s, including supervisors from abroad and members of the central and local committees. This seriously disrupted the communication lines of the party, prevented organizational expansion, severed contact between upper and lower party organs, temporarily suspended political activities, and limited important operations to only three provinces.[66] Severely damaged, the CPS lost contact with the Communist Party of Malaya for a long time, while the Southern Bureau of the Comintern in Hong Kong, responsible for liaison with communist parties in Southeast Asia, had been eliminated by the British authorities in 1930.

However, the CPS seemed to have enjoyed a brief high-profile revival from 1934 to 1936, during which the Vietnamese wing assumed a salient, active role in propaganda and organizational work in many northeastern provinces of Siam and neighboring Laos.[67] Though reportedly small in number, inadequately qualified, and nationalist rather than class-oriented,[68] they were very effective in propaganda work due to provocative, attention-grabbing, daring, and adventurous tactics which allegedly led to conflicts with the more cautious, Bangkok-based, Chinese comrades who, according to a 1934 Special Branch report of the British Straits Settlements Police, were "quite unconnected" with their Vietnamese counterparts. The CPS also managed to re-establish contact with the Comintern through the latter's Far Eastern Bureau in Shanghai some time before January 1935 and sent three members there for training. It was also represented at the Seventh Comintern Congress in Moscow by Rashi in August 1935.[69]

And yet, as a result of their audacious and oft-reckless attempt to convert the Thai masses, the Vietnamese wing of the CPS suffered heavy losses. Following the crucial arrest of fourteen communists at a meeting in Bangkok in April 1936, among whom were a Comintern agent from Shanghai and four CPS Central Executive Committee members including Le Manh Trinh, a top Vietnamese communist leader, communist activity in Bangkok quieted down. On October 31 of the same year, in the aftermath of the arrest of eleven Vietnamese in a secret meeting in the northeastern province of Khon Kaen, about fifty of their comrades held an unprecedented, peaceful, openly communist, anti-government demonstration which was violently broken up by government troops, police, and administrative officials, resulting in two deaths and ten casualties among the demonstrators. Of the 193 Vietnamese, one Laotian, and seven Thais arrested in connection with this incident, a large number were indeed communists, though several were not. Subsequently, the activity of the Vietnamese group in the Northeast began to wane.[70] With over eight hundred of their migrant compatriots and almost all of the CPS's main cadres arrested in Siam and with the beckoning revival of revolutionary activity inside Vietnam, the remainder became increasingly skeptical of the Comintern's unrealistic internationalist exhortations to promote a Siamese proletarian revolution at the expense of the Vietnamese nationalist one and gradually slipped back across the border to fight for the latter cause in their own homeland. After that, the Communist Party of Siam or whatever was left of it appeared to wither away.[71]

The Vietnamese communists did leave one enduring legacy in the form of certain individuals who were radicalized by their propagation of Marxist-socialist ideas. These people, such as Tiang Sirikhan, Yuang Iamsila, Jamlong Daoreuang, and Pan Kaeomat, would later become leading progressive politicians from their native northeastern region of Isan during the parliamentary regime. But as far as the subsequent Communist Party of Thailand was concerned, only one member of its top leadership would come from the Vietnamese group, namely Thong Jamsri.[72]

Thus, upon the decline and eventual demise of the CPS in 1936, only remnants of the pre-existing Chinese communist group were left. They resumed their former organizational form from around 1927 as the Thai branch of the Chinese Communist Party (CCP-TB) or the Siamese Overseas Chinese Communist Party (SOCCP). The structure of the SOCCP was divided into two departments: the older "Chinese Department," which consisted of immigrants from China, and the newly organized "Thai Department," which consisted of lookjins.[73]

But who were these lookjin communists? Where did they come from? They came mostly from the ranks of coolies and students in Chinese schools who were politically educated and recruited into the SOCCP at a tender age by fellow coolies and teachers who were Chinese communist immigrants.[74] As a rule, after finishing Chinese school—cultural-political strongholds and main bases of the Siamese communists since the 1920s, along with Chinese newspapers[75]—they went on to study at local western-established mission schools such as Assumption College, Bangkok Christian School, and St. Gabriel College. None reached tertiary education, and yet their knowledge of English learned in mission schools was good enough for speaking and translation.[76] However, a few of them were sent by their wealthy parents to China for education during the 1920s and were converted to communism there, by no means an unlikely outcome given the cultural commotion following the May Fourth Movement in 1919.[77] These lookjin communists as a group would later form the core of a new Thai communist party and dominate its top rank almost continually from its inception during World War II to its dissipation in the 1980s.[78]

For the Siamese government, the peculiar trouble with these lookjin communists was that they were in a legal sense "Thai" and hence could not be easily expelled. It was the Nationality Act of 1913, a legal invention of none other than the arch-anti-communist King Vajiravudh himself, which, while furnishing the government with the power to banish Chinese and Vietnamese communist immigrants, precluded deportation of the arrested lookjin communists, for it claimed as Thai "every person born on Thai territory."[79] As a consequence, for example, in 1931 the police found a Thai-born Chinese named Lim Sitiang who was a communist, yet they could only put him under surveillance since he had legitimate Thai nationality and could not be deported.[80]

In another interesting instance, from December 1929, a Chinese communist named Piatoe was arrested along with twenty-one others while holding a meeting in a Chinese school called Jintek in Phichit province.[81] As the official investigators found him politically knowledgeable, he was told to write a testimony on communism and Siam, with which he duly complied. The translation of his testimony, originally written in Chinese, was sent to Prince Boriphat, then minister of interior. Having read the testimony, the Prince concluded that Piatoe was a full-fledged communist, that given a chance he would certainly incite the Thais against foreigners, and that he should be banished as a *persona non grata*. However, this was easier said than done, for Piatoe also testified that he had been born in Phichit and sent to study at Datong University in Shanghai from his childhood, and that after his return to Siam, he had married a Thai woman.[82] Therefore, even though this "full-fledged communist" could only write his testimony in Chinese, legally speaking he was a Thai national and could not be deported. Unable to bring himself to believe that a Thai could also be a communist, the Prince, in a report sent to King Rama VII along with the testimony, registered his incredulity at Mr. Piatoe's alleged Thai nationality and suggested that he be exiled. Agreeing in reason with the report, the King added that "the author of this statement is of the half-baked type, and speaks in such a way as to make it seem no one were happy. But where could a paradise on earth be found?" [83]

It is worth pondering what it would have taken to convince these Siamese royal rulers that people like Mr. Piatoe or Lim Sitiang were Thai. Obviously, it went beyond simple legal criteria. Nor was it merely a matter of blood or racial pedigree, for race, as a rule, was invoked in Thai cultural politics only selectively and contextually. It was forgotten as often as it was remembered, depending on the demand of a given situation.[84] Therefore, in the final analysis, what was at issue here was neither a legal nor a racial meaning of Thainess, but an ethno-ideological one. To King Prajadhipok and Prince Boriphat, Mr. Piatoe did not seem to be a Thai because he did not fit the presupposed ethno-ideological identity of Thainess constructed by ideologues of the Thai ruling royalty. In a lecture given to the Samakkhayajan Samakhom (Society of United Teachers) in 1927, Prince Damrong, one of the King's uncles, a key architect of the modernization of the Thai absolutist state, the acclaimed founding father of Thai national historiography, and a member of the Supreme Council of State, authoritatively listed as virtues in the disposition of the Thai nation "Love of

National Independence, Toleration, and Power of Assimilation," characteristics not very conducive to class consciousness and radical politics, to say the least.[85] And in an essay written during the First World War, "Asvabahu" (alias King Vajiravudh, "the founder of modern nationalism in his country"[86]) categorically announced as the essence of the Thai nation knowledge of the Thai language and loyalty to the King. Hence,

> In order to determine the real nationality of whoever, one must consider to whom he pays his allegiance. If he pays his allegiance to the King of Siam, then he is a real Thai.

With that allegiance came an implied willingness, on the part of every "real Thai," to sacrifice personal comfort, independence, legitimate autonomy, and the right to "argue with the helmsman," all for the sake of the Thai nation.[87] Precisely the opposite of what Piatoe and his comrades were doing.

In this royalty-constructed, ethno-ideological sense of Thai national culture, the lookjin communists were of course not Thai, regardless of their ethnicity or birthplace. But from the lookjin communists' perspective, these three factors might be related. A Thai could have a harder time fighting off the conservative, royalist claim on his or her submissive allegiance based on an imputed ethnic identity, whereas a lookjin, by virtue of Chinese or mixed ethnicity and Siamese *patrie*, could have greater freedom or space to mediate between the two ethno-ideological poles—at the same time Thai enough to be committed to Thai politics but Chinese enough to be alien to the royalist ethno-ideology of Thainess. From the radical point of view, to be lookjin was not altogether a political disadvantage, at least initially.

However, to make a political and social revolution in Siam, mere lookjins were not enough. The mass participation of the Thai people, the majority of the Siamese population, was imperative. Hence it fell upon the lookjin communists to bridge communism and the Thai people, first and foremost in the cultural sense, by learning, reading, and writing the Thai language so as to translate communism from Chinese into Thai.[88]

So when Mr. Piatoe, having successfully claimed his Thai nationality and prevented his deportation, walked into jail—sentenced by the criminal court to fifteen years imprisonment and a fine of 5,000 baht—he was actually taking the first step, along with his many lookjin comrades, in a long and arduous Promethean mission of the Thaification of Chinese immigrant communism.[89]

3

Institutions of Thaification: How The Lookjin Communists Turned Thai Patriots

I aim a Chinik nationnaew, holing alieng papers. Whi ong eark they arleg and chark me wik being ang "Inglepengleng Thai" I hef no ilea. How cang a Chinik be ang "Inglepengleng Thai"? How come?

Teachers Qing and Long[1]

Detour to Thainess

For lookjin communists in and out of prison, to become a Thai, as far as the non-legal, ethno-ideological aspects of the matter were concerned, was by no means easy. Ideologically speaking, they were "red," not "blue" or "green."[2] Racially speaking, their blood was Chinese or mixed, not pure Thai. But after the overthrow of the Chakri absolute monarchy in 1932, the continually anti-communist and increasingly anti-Chinese policies of successive People's Party governments did not make it any less difficult for them to remain Chinese, especially under the rule of the militarist-nationalist prime minister Plaek Phibunsongkhram, who came to power in 1938.[3] Therefore, the lookjin communists had no alternative but to take a detour to Thainess and, when an opportunity arose, blast it open to their kind of politics and pedigree. If, in the eyes of the Siamese rulers, they were too racially half-bred and ideologically ill-disposed to ever become proper Thais, they might as well try, as a first step, to imitate the way of life of ordinary Thais, by learning the Thai language and working and living with them. Building on that, they could attempt to think critically in the Thais' cultural terms and act radically on their political side.

Traditionally, for a multitude of historical, social, and cultural reasons, the Chinese in Siam tended to specialize occupationally as merchants, artisan-craftsmen, and laborers, whereas ethnic Thais were to be found mainly in government and agriculture.[4] This sociological fact, coupled with the linguistic basis of ethnic identity, formed what may be called a socio-linguistic notion of Thainess, as distinct from the ethno-ideological one. According to this notion, a lookjin could become Thai by moving linguistically from Chinese to Thai, occupationally from a typically Chinese job to a Thai specialty, and socially from the Chinese to the Thai community.[5]

And so traveled the lookjin communists during the 1930s and 1940s, along a detour that cut through various social institutions, chief among which were prison, schools, factories, trade unions, and newspapers, which were used and transformed functionally by them in the service of self-Thaification and political radicalization. At the end of 1941, though, their journey would take a dramatic turn with the advent of the Pacific War and the emergence of the clandestine anti-Japanese and anti-Phibun government movement in Thailand, which opened new political opportunities and legitimate space for them in the Thai national polity.

Prison

Whereas political prisoners were by no means unprecedented in Siam under Chakri dynastic rule—Thianwan and K.S.R. Kulap, journalists and essayists of commoner origin, were jailed in the reign of King Rama V, and the defeated Khana Kekmeng (Revolutionary Party) junior army officers were jailed in the reign of King Rama VI[6] —"political prisoners" as a state-administrative category seemed to emerge only in the 1930s after the People's Party took power and crushed the royalist, anti-People's Party Bowaradej Rebellion.[7] From the early 1930s until the end of World War II, all people who were convicted of political crimes and sentenced to jail by the Siamese authorities, including Chinese and Vietnamese communists, served most if not all of their time in Area 6 of Bangkhwang Penitentiary. Usually called by its English abbreviation "B.K." by political prisoners, Bangkhwang Penitentiary was located on the east bank of the Chaophraya River in the province of Nonthaburi and linked to Bangkok by road. It was conceived in 1906 by King Rama V to relocate the then existing penitentiary away from the flourishing capital. However, actual construction began only in 1927 during the reign of King Rama VII, and it was finally opened for operation in 1931 with over three thousand prisoners. It is noteworthy that in the original blueprint of Bangkhwang Penitentiary drawn in the late 1920s, there was no area designated for "political prisoners," only one for "alien prisoners." But since most "alien prisoners" happened to be Chinese and Vietnamese communists, that area was turned perforce into one for "political prisoners," especially after the Bowaradej rebels were brought there.[8]

Bangkhwang Penitentiary was divided by walls into six *daen* (areas) to sort out the different categories of prisoners. Area 6 had the best environment. It was clean and spacious, with freshly green grass lawn and various flowers planted beneath the wall. The large canteen could accommodate up to eight hundred people, and the cement bath tank was over thirty meters long. The jail itself was a massive, two-storied building with a corrugated-tile roof and a huge, thickset, iron-barred front door. Altogether, there were fifty cells in the building, twenty-four on each floor and two under the stairs. The cells were arranged in two parallel rows, their iron-barred doors facing each other, with a path in between. In this way, inmates in opposite cells could see and shout to one another. Each cell was four meters wide and six meters long, clean, roomy, and livable. It contained about eight to twelve prisoners at a time.[9] Commenting favorably on these cells, M.R. Nimitmongkhol Nawarat, a member of the royalty and former air force wing commander who was imprisoned there twice on political charges, said: "The cells in Area 6 were like rooms in a house."[10] Furthermore, the Area 6 prisoners were allowed to choose their preferred cell and cellmates freely. Personal books, newspapers, magazines, in both Thai and foreign languages, and stationery were as a general rule either completely forbidden or heavily censored. However, the rule was not always vigorously enforced and these items were made largely available by means of smuggling, hiding, and bribery. These intellectual essentials were subject, of course, to occasional search and confiscation.[11]

The more than one hundred communist prisoners[12] were the sole occupants of Area 6 from its opening until 1933, when the defeat of the Bowaradej Rebellion sent some 318 captured rebels to join them. Eventually, 250 of these were convicted and sentenced, bringing the total population of Area 6 to approximately 350.[13] Their division of living quarters was as follows: "the politicos" (*phuak kanmeuang*), as the Bowaradej political prisoners came to be called by the communists, got the whole first floor and half of the ground floor; the communists got the remaining half.[14] Later, they were joined by a small group of non-commissioned army officers who had been found guilty of plotting the oft-forgotten Kabot Naisib (NCO Rebellion) in 1935.[15] Most of the Bowaradej politicos were gradually released on parole until the remaining seventy non-communist prisoners of both the Bowaradej and NCO rebellions were sent into internal exile on the Tarutao and Tao Islands in the Gulf of Thailand in September 1939.[16] Three new groups of political prisoners would soon replace them. They were: twenty-five alleged conspirators against the government and Phibunsongkhram's life in the notorious Yuk Thamil (Dark Age) case of 1939; scores of Catholic country folks and merchants accused of being fifth columnists for the French during the Thai war with French Indochina in 1940/41; and nine anti-Japanese Thai-issara (Independent Thai) members imprisoned in 1942. But in stark contrast to the lenient and liberal treatment of political prisoners under the former governments of Prime Minister Phahonphonphayuhasena, these new prisoners were subjected by the militaristic and authoritarian Phibunsongkhram government to such harsh measures as universal solitary confinement, time allowed out of cells for washing and going to lavatories limited to twenty minutes twice a day, and eating in cells. Therefore, they had much less freedom and opportunity to socialize with the communists on the ground floor. And their prison accounts, in contrast with those of the Bowaradej politicos, contained almost nothing about the communists who remained the noisy but otherwise indiscernible multitude in the background.[17]

During the up to six years the communists and Bowaradej politicos spent together in jail, these 350 prison inmates were indeed strange bedfellows in both figurative and literal senses.[18] Ethnically, the communists were Chinese and Vietnamese while the politicos were mostly Thai. Sociologically, the former were teachers, merchants, and coolies while the latter were mostly senior or junior civil servants and military or police officers, and therefore considered of low and high status, respectively, by contemporary Thai social standards. Perhaps most important of all, ideologically, the two groups were poles apart—communist revolutionaries versus conservative or liberal royalist counter-revolutionaries.[19] There was even a good chance that some Bowaradej politicos themselves might have been directly or indirectly involved in the original arrests and prosecutions of the communists. Nevertheless, they now shared quite a few things in common. They were suffering the same ordeal, living in the same jail, bound in similar chains, doing the same menial work, eating the same unsavory food, wearing the same blue uniforms, and in the grip of the same hostile government and jailors. Leading a life that was perforce largely collectivized and maddeningly leisured, they were gradually drawn to one another, especially the better-educated and more experienced among them. After all, different as their backgrounds were, they were a politicized thinking breed alike whom the government saw fit to put together behind bars.[20] Therefore, it was not beyond possibility that they would find it convenient to share a cell as they pursued their diverse intellectual activities together.[21]

Initially, they began their relationship by teaching foreign (i.e., non-Thai) languages to one another. The communists taught Chinese, Cantonese, and French to the politicos and the latter taught English and Japanese to the former.[22] The communist teachers of Chinese and Cantonese were Liao A-ngow and Chaiphin. Born in 1904, Liao A-ngow, alias Ngow Sengchin or Ngo Diji, was a Chinese alien and Teochiu by speech group. Said to have been a teacher in Siam for some time, he had returned to China, become a member of the Chinese Communist Party, and risen to the post of secretary-general of the Party Committee in the Sua Thao area. Upon Chiang Kaishek's wholesale crackdown on the communists in China in 1927, Ngo and his wife fled to Siam in January 1928 and worked as teachers at a Chinese school named Kianseu in the northeastern province of Nakhon Ratchasima. Having reestablished contact with his Chinese comrades and been reassigned as propaganda chief of the newly-established Central Committee of the Communist Party of Siam, he moved to Bangkok and opened a grocery store named Sengjua in a row house on Rajprarop Road, Makkasan, where the communist headquarters in Siam were allegedly located. Acting on intelligence information, including a photograph of Ngo provided by the British Legation, police raided his store in August 1930 and, two months later, apprehended him with the help of local Kuomintang informers. His arrest was followed by a major police operation at fifteen locations in Bangkok and three other provinces in which thirty more communists were captured. The Siamese court sentenced him to fifteen years in jail and exile thereafter.[23]

Chaiphin was a Chinese Hakka and graduate of a university in north China who taught Mandarin reading and pronunciation in Bangkhwang. His knowledge of Chinese greatly impressed Dr. Linbing, a Ph.D. graduate from the United States and an emissary of the Chinese government to Siam, on one unlikely occasion when the communist prisoner reluctantly agreed to revise and deliver an official welcoming speech in Chinese to this emissary of the reactionary Kuomintang regime on behalf of the prison authority during Linbing's visit to Bangkhwang.[24] As for the communist teacher of French, he was a Vietnamese who had graduated from a university in Paris. He helped brush up many politicos' French with his superb knowledge of that language and was said to have had a personal connection with a French minister who reportedly wrote to thank his lawyer for defending him at his trial.[25]

The teaching went on for several years, and, judging from the circumstances, the linguistic medium of teaching must have been Thai. Then they moved on to politics, discussing, in both Thai and Chinese, communist ideology and doctrine, the strategy and program of communist revolution in Siam, the "correct" view and evaluation of labor, especially menial, the communists' personal feelings about imprisonment, ideological commitment, past experience, and future plans. There was one particularly fascinating episode in the Chinese communist-Thai royalist relationship in Bangkhwang that is worth some elaboration. When the communist teacher Liao A-ngow volunteered to clean the lavatories in Area 6, he became a laughing-stock among the politicos. So he complained to Leuan Saraphaiwanich, a Bowaradej political prisoner and his pupil in Chinese, that he could not comprehend the politicos' disparaging attitude towards lavatory cleaning. After all, if no one volunteered to do it, there would be filthy dirt all around and society as a whole would suffer. As a matter of fact, this kind of person should be paid handsomely for what he did. He went on to talk his pupil into joining him in the cleaning. Pupil Leuan need only carry the water, he said, Teacher Liao would do all the foul work. Partly persuaded by these unheard-of arguments but largely out of regard for his Chinese teacher, Leuan, who had been a Phraya (second highest rank of nobility) and secretary to four princes before resigning from government service upon the Revolution of 1932 to become a leading anti-People's Party opposition journalist, applied for the job to the Area chief jailor who, in laughter, steadfastly refused to allow such a former big shot to do such stinking work.[26]

The argument and exchange of ideas between the two groups of prisoners were serene, pleasant, instructive, and fruitful enough when the communist interlocutors were senior people of "leader or teacher ranks" (*chan huana* or *chan ajan*), with their mature, educated, polite, and refined manners. But they tended to get rather ideologically charged, passionate, and heated when the younger communists, especially the Vietnamese with their extremist policy, joined the fray.[27]

Notwithstanding occasional clashes, the Chinese and Vietnamese communists and the Thai politicos got on very well. As Leuan Saraphaiwanich testified:

> The B.E. 2476 political prisoners had got along so well and intimately with the communists that some communists came to stay in the same houses with the '76 political prisoners after their release from prison. Several communists had done me a favor in particular by teaching me knowledge of various subjects. I would like to express my thanks to them here.[28]

Personally, the communists managed to win from some politicos not only friendship and trust, but also admiration and respect for their resolute commitment and selfless devotion to the cause they believed in, and for their firm perseverance in face of hardship and persecution. Retrospectively, Leuan later conceded: "Well, it might as well be admitted that as far as the ethos [*jittarom*] of the communists was concerned, I found it without blemish."[29] He also told of an instance in 1937 when he and five other politicos were charged by the prison authority with the criminological investigation of a group of prisoners, including two female communist inmates. Contrary to their presupposition that the two were ignoramuses duped into committing political crimes, they found to their surprise that they knew more about communism than some of their jailed male comrades and were counted among the best propagandists. And yet, though firmly convinced that the implementation of the Comintern program would bring great happiness to the poor the world over, the two alleged that they would give up communist activities after their release, not because they lost their belief in the doctrine, but because they knew they would be kept under such strict surveillance that any party activity would fail and only land them back in jail. Despite the forced ending of their active political life, they vowed never to marry a non-communist.[30]

This favorable impression also seemed to extend, more or less, to the political realm. Of course, it by no means resulted in any of the politicos converting to communism under the influence of their communist inmates in Bangkhwang.[31] But the striking thing was the unusual degree of open-mindedness and attention, sometimes even understanding and sympathy, accorded to communism by, of all people, these intransigent "True Blues."[32] Leuan Saraphaiwanich, for instance, who described at some length the Bolshevik-modelled strategy and program of Siamese revolution he learned from the communist inmates, concluded that since it was difficult to pass judgement on such controversial issues as the comparative worth of contending political ideologies, one had better listen skeptically, read extensively, and argue peacefully about their real principles and practices.[33] And when Leuan resumed his active political life after the war, he would usually take a pro-union socialistic stance along the line of the British and Australian labor parties in his public statements and writings, often referring to Karl Marx and giving a reformist reading of his doctrine.[34]

Or, in another case, disapproving of an anti-communist novel of Siamese dystopia under communist rule entitled "Pho.So. 2481" (B.E. 2481), written in jail by Bowaradej political prisoner and later foremost English-Thai dictionary compiler So Sethaputra, another Bowaradej inmate, M.R. Nimitmongkhol, responded with a fictional rejoinder about an imaginary attempted communist coup d'état in Siam entitled "Bunthamkamtaeng" (By the forces of merits and karma), which treated communism and other political ideologies in a more neutral manner. Regrettably, neither novel was published. The manuscript of "Pho.So. 2481" was smuggled out of Bangkhwang and either lost or burnt, while that of "Bunthamkamtaeng" later fell into the hands of police and earned its author, alas, a charge of communist propagation. The unrepentant Nimitmongkhol went on to write another utopian novel—in Bangkhwang, of course!—entitled "Meuangnimit" (The sight of future Siam), whose pro-tagonist, "Rung Jitkasem," was the only character in modern Thai literature to read Marx's *Capital* (in English and in jail). Rung Jitkasem considers himself a member of the wretched "proletariat" (again, in English), but opts to dream up, by himself, a scientistic ideal of an organicist world state with a strictly natural division of labor, rather than accept the help of the communist party.[35]

Considering that these politicos were likely the first politicized Thai intellectuals the Chinese and Vietnamese comrades had close contact with, this ideological appeal and influence was no small feat.

Amongst themselves, the communist prisoners lived a highly politicized and well-organized collective life. They had communist doctrine and Chinese language classes. They provoked and held work stoppages and hunger strikes among prisoners in and out of Area 6, often with significant success, on such issues as the bad quality of food or the arbitrary transfer of a female communist inmate to another prison. And when any of their comrades passed away, they arranged for the deceased a plain but respectable funeral by standing in two rows and laying a garland of mourning at the body before carrying it away. The unity and discipline of these comrades, male and female alike, in their forceful collective action served as commendable examples to other Bangkhwang prisoners.[36]

The foregoing might not sound like things that should happen in a political prison but this was exactly what "functional transformation" was all about— doing things one was not supposed to within a particular institution. One must add, though, that there seemed to be a peculiar objective dimension to the transformation in this case. Paradoxically, perhaps it was because they were in prison that the communists could and did choose to behave in this open, defiant manner. As one veteran Thai communist who spent twenty-five of his forty-one politically active years behind bars pointed out, once in "the special conditions of prison," there was really no point in concealing one's political identity and beliefs from the government and secret police any longer. Instead, one might as well take this rare and hard-earned opportunity to express oneself freely and audaciously as a real communist in so far as the limits of prison life allowed.[37] Given a lenient government policy and a humane prison governor, these limits could be fairly broad. Fortunately for the Bangkhwang political prisoners, this was the case up to 1939, as the Phahonphonphayuhasena government and the first four governors of Bangkhwang Penitentiary adopted a considerably liberal and benevolent policy towards political prisoners in general, and the Bowaradej prisoners in particular.[38] The rationale behind this policy, in the words of Major Khun Jamnongphoomiwet, the second governor of Bangkhwang (1935–1937) and a member of the People's Party, was as follows:

> ...political prisoners are considered more honorable than prisoners in general. After their release, people all over the world do not despise them for company because political prisoners are regarded as those who mean very well to their nation but hold dissenting views, and hence must be repressed and detained for a while to make them repent. When the

government becomes stable, then they can be set free. I am of the opinion that the government which is like the father of the people of the whole nation should exercise sympathy and kindness in dealing with those who are repentant. This will also make the political prisoners see that the government bears no grudge against the losers, and try to help the government reciprocally. [39]

The fact that many Bowaradej prisoners were once members of the royalty and nobility, even former colleagues, superiors, or personal friends of government ministers and prison governors themselves, certainly contributed much to this policy. At times, it led to such wild exploits as brief unauthorized "leaves of absence" from Bangkhwang to Bangkok for some Bowaradej prisoners for the purpose of savoring ice cream, seeing a Walt Disney animated cartoon, or shopping for a radio. One of them even ran into the Bangkhwang governor on such an occasion![40] Failing all else, there was the last resort of bribery, which worked like a charm to ease things with the jailors, provided one had enough money.[41] However, prison was still prison, and for too wild or rash an action, one sometimes paid dearly. For example, Leuan reported the case of a communist prisoner who embroidered his blue uniform with the words "Fourth International" in Thai. Perhaps the first documented Trotskyist ever to emerge in Siam, he was severely whipped twenty times until he bled for "damaging government property."[42]

There are simply no substantial data on the activities of communist prisoners in Area 6, Bangkhwang during the Second World War. A reasonable guess is that they were active doing and saying anti-Japanese things. Neither is it clear when and in what circumstances they were released. Some seemed to have served their full sentence; others might have been set free after the abrogation of the Anti-Communist Law in 1946.[43] In any case, some of them emerged from jail rather changed from the people they were before, and changed in many a Thai way. Now they spoke, read, wrote, and translated into Thai, learned how to live, work, and argue with Thais, and gained some experience in instigating and organizing Thais. Owing paradoxically to Bangkhwang, the lookjin communists and their "alien" doctrine had become in no small measure Thaified.

Again, the transformation of Mr. Piatoe serves as a perfect illustration of this process. Remembered by Leuan Saraphaiwanich as "a good friend," "of teacher rank," and "polite and well-mannered," Piatoe, whose other Chinese names included Chou Shoulim, Mongji, the derogatory Jek Tow, and simply Toe, not only acquired sufficient knowledge and skills of the Thai language in prison, but also found it politic to have Leuan coin him his first Thai name. "Toe Jutharak" (Big Protector of the Crown or Head) cleverly reflects both the sound and meaning of his Chinese names, that is, the sound of "Piatoe" and the meaning of "Chou Shoulim," with Shoulim (Shouling in Mandarin) denoting head, leader, or chieftain.[44] Moreover, he would later invent for himself such fanciful Thai *noms de plume* and *noms de guerre* as "Phayap Angkhasing" (Northwest Leonine), indicating his regional homeland in Siam, "Phichit na Sukhothai" (Conquest at Sukhothai), sometimes abbreviated to "Pho.No. Sukhothai," refering to his mother's home province, and "Prapanta Virasakdi" (Writing with Honor of Courage), which he used in public as the spokesman of the Thai Communist Party.

One need only read a typical anti-Chinese politico-cultural essay of King Vajiravudh entitled *Priab namsakul kab cheusae* (A contrast of family names with clan names, 1913) to gauge the immense political significance of these nominal changes by Piatoe. In that essay, the King aggressively called for the replacement of Chinese clan names (*sae* in Teochiu, *xing* in Mandarin), still widely in use among Chinese immigrants and lookjins in Siam, with Thai family names. He linked clan names with belligerent gangster solidarity, archaism, barbarism, group inclusion, national division, and political insubordination, while associating Thai family names with blood ties, love, modernity, civilization, social hierarchy, national unity, and political obedience.[45] It followed from this fantastic Vajiravudhian cultural logic that a lookjin communist with a Thai family name could not but be a living political contradiction in terms.

And yet, there he was, Toe Jutharak, alias Phayap Angkhasing, alias Phichit na Sukhothai, alias Prapanta Virasakdi, a lookjin communist with not one but many Thai family names, stepping out of Bangkhwang, probably sometime in the late 1930s, going to Yanan to help with the Chinese Revolution, bringing Mao's thought back to Siam, publishing books on communism and the Thai revolution in Thai, and becoming the first spokesman of the Thai Communist Party![46]

The Siamese Communists versus the People's Party

To Piatoe's comrades outside prison, the constitutionalist Revolution of June 24, 1932, brought no new hope for radical change whatsoever. According to their illegal Thai, Chinese, and English leaflets, which continued to be distributed unabated after the Revolution, as well as their Chinese internal party documents and publications seized by the authorities, the Siamese communists regarded the People's Party as self-styled, that is, fake "people" and "revolutionaries," actually representing the bourgeoisie in alliance with some military leaders and disgruntled bureaucrats, who took power out of self-interest and conflict with the royalty rather than for the poor people who gained little benefit and no power from the whole revolutionary charade. Basically preserving and continuing the old pattern of oppression and exploitation of the people by preventing a socialist revolution of the masses, the new regime was essentially a dictatorship that still served the interests of the monarchy, the rich, and the foreign imperialists as before, but which simply replaced one oppressor with many. The first "permanent" Constitution of Siam, proclaimed on December 10, 1932, was only a cunning deception of the people and in fact amounted to shackles on the poor and a source of wealth for the capitalists. They went on to call for a rejection of the new Constitution, the propagation of communism, the rallying of the Siamese people to the side of the revolution, the overthrow of the constitutional government, and the establishment of a Soviet Government of Workers, Peasants, and Soldiers of Siam.[47]

Thus committed on principle to opposing the new "bourgeois" constitutional regime, the Siamese communists largely ignored emergent signs of radical beckoning from its leftish elements.[48] Shortly after the 1932 Revolution, two radical newspapers alleged to be closely associated with the left wing of the People's Party under Pridi Banomyong's leadership started publication: *24 Mithuna* (June 24), owned and edited by Sanguan Tularak, then right-hand man of Pridi, civilian member of the People's Party, and appointed member of the legislature; and *Sajjang* (Truth), owned by Thongkham Rohittasiri. As a staunch advocate of radical socio-economic change, Sanguan also translated and published in February 1933 a pamphlet entitled *Latthi sochialism mai khwam wa arai* (What is the meaning of socialism?), by J.W. Kneeshaw, in an unusually large edition of ten thousand in the hope that it would be useful for both candidates and voters in the upcoming general election. However, one month later, copies of that socialist pamphlet on sale in the northeastern province of Ubon Ratchathani so upset its governor that he would have banned it outright but for its author's formidable political position. Eventually, it was banned and its copies confiscated by the conservative royalist government that took power in early April of the same year in the aftermath of the first serious political crisis of the new constitutional regime.[49]

Soon, over the heads of the communists, there erupted on the national political scene an unprecedented and fateful conflict among the ruling classes that would determine the future course of the country's socio-economic development. After a long intellectual gestation and energetic preparatory ideological agitation, in March 1933, Pridi Banomyong, leader of the civilian left wing of the People's Party and then minister without portfolio, proposed to the new government of the conservative royalist Prime Minister Phraya

Manopakornnitithada[50] a radical comprehensive plan for restructuring the
national economy along the socialistic, statist-cooperativist line which he
considered the essence and fulfillment of the 1932 Revolution's democratic
principles.[51] Published and widely known as *Samud pokleuang* (Yellow-
covered book), Pridi's Economic Plan was prefaced by a scathing criticism of
those who misrepresented and assailed a particular doctrine, "such as
socialism," out of feigned ignorance, self-interest, or sheer pride, for example,
someone who stuck fast to the delusion obtained from marketplace slander that
"a certain doctrine promotes killings, the confiscation of the rich's wealth and
its equal sharing among the poor, community of women." These "Evil Scum of
the Earth" (*phuak ubat kalilok*, a very strong curse in Thai), as Pridi labeled
them, were the source of bias and confusion that marred rational public debate
on a national economic plan.[52]

Then, he went on to lay out the main components of his plan: forced but
compensatory collectivization of key economic resources (land, labor, and
capital) and activities (primarily agricultural production, exchange, and
consumption, which could extend into industry and commerce); the state as the
dominant owner and entrepreneur, operating through cooperatives in a
command economy; and severe limitation of market mechanisms, private
property, and private enterprise in some economic sectors and their complete
abolition in others. The revolutionary character of this plan could be gauged
from the fact that its implementation would have largely marginalized the
capitalist commodity economy on which the wealth of the royalty and
bourgeoisie was based and totally eliminated the petty peasant production
which had from time immemorial been the economic foundation of the country
and population.[53]

Appositely, Pridi ended his economic plan by invoking, again, the
politicized Buddhist myth of "Sri Arya," this time not to utopianize socialism
as King Vajiravudh had, but to lend popular imagery, familiarity, credibility,
legitimacy, and persuasiveness to his socialistic economic plan by virtue of the
myth's roots in Thai Buddhism and folklore, thus simultaneously de-
utopianizing the Sri Arya myth.[54] He called on fellow Promoters of the
Revolution to drop their hesitation, lead the people forward into the Age of Sri
Arya, and let them reap the fruits of the Kalpa Phruksa (Magic Wish-Granting
Trees), rather than "fall back into the canal" (*thoilang khaokhlong*) of the
antiquated pre-Buddhist Era.[55]

As expected, stiff resistance to Pridi's Economic Plan was mounted both in
the cabinet and in public by conservative and liberal royalists, the more
conservative senior army leaders of the People's Party, and, most importantly,
by King Rama VII himself, who was the alleged author of a candid and rousing,

if caustic and crafty, critique of the plan upon Pridi's forced departure from Siam in April 1933. Dubbed the *Samud pokkhao* (White-covered book), the royal critique followed the well-worn but effective Vajiravudhian style of anti-radicalism by castigating Pridi's Economic Plan as an authoritarian and communistic (three times)[56] copy of the alien Russian Stalinist original (thirty-two times)[57] that would enslave the nation (*pen thas*) and turn it disastrously un-Thai (eleven times)[58] if ever implemented in full. For example:

> Since this is the same as the economic plan used in Russia, as has been said, if our government follows it through, then that will amount to our government helping the Third International, which aims at changing the world into communism, achieve its aim easily. Because, undoubtedly, for us to carry out this plan will eventually land us in communism for sure. Communism here entails a communist economy, not the so-called government-arranged community of women. Be that as it may, Thailand shall thence become the second communist country in the world after Russia...[59]

> But one important point that can be clearly seen without doubt is that this plan is certainly the same as the one being used by Russia. As to who copied whom I don't know. Whether Stalin copied Luang Pradist [Pridi], or Luang Pradist copied Stalin can't be answered. The only answer that can be given is that these two plans are completely the same right down to the minute details about the methods to be used and their forms. The only difference is that "Russia" is changed to "Thailand" or "Thailand" to "Russia."...[60]

> Probably, Thainess will become *thas*-ness [slavery] because, as has happened in Russia where the same method of insurance was used, the people there have to insure welfare with their freedom and submit to the government as its slaves.[61]

> Can it be said that the aim of this plan is to prevent people from becoming beasts when it will turn them into slaves of pre-King Chulalongkorn's Abolition of Slavery times? And instead of becoming so-called "royal servants," it is likelier that they will turn into state slaves...[62]

Artfully refuting Pridi's all-too-frequent conjuration of the Sri Arya myth, the King pointed out that, in accordance with the original Buddhist tale, the Age of Sri Arya would arrive only in the year B.E. 5000. Since the time then was just B.E. 2475, why the hurry? Rather than deliver Siam to the Paradise of Sri Arya, Pridi's untimely plan would rush her into the Sri Arya's Inferno (Aweji Sri Arya) instead![63]

There was, however, a slight but significant shift in King Prajadhipok's arguments from those of his predecessor. Whereas King Vajiravudh said that socialism, like the ancient Thai utopias of "Uttarakuru" and "Phra Sri Arya," was paradisiacal but impossible, King Prajadhipok argued that communism was possible but infernal (Aweji Sri Arya) and therefore un-Thai. The world-historical watershed that made heaven and hell change places in Thai royal anti-radical discourse was, of course, "the Great October Proletarian Socialist Revolution of 1917" in Russia.[64]

This first great contest of ideas and policies in modern Siamese history was fought in every newly established major political institution in the country. It was divided into two rounds, each side taking turns gaining the upper hand. In the first round, after four stormy debates in a special government committee and the cabinet, Pridi's Economic Plan was finally voted down in a cabinet meeting on March 28, 1933, by eleven votes to three with five abstentions. Then in April, the National Assembly dominated by Pridi's followers was prorogued, certain provisions of the Constitution suspended, and Pridi relieved of his ministerial post, branded a "communist," and sent into paid unofficial exile by the Phraya Manopakorn government.[65] Actually a compromise between the royalists, military moderates within the People's Party, and Pridi himself to avoid a violent show-down between the Manopakorn government and Pridi's devout friends and followers, Pridi's well-arranged exile was handsomely paid (one thousand pounds sterling annually from the government treasury), unofficial ("an economic study trip abroad"), and not really an exile (said to be "temporary"). Moreover, much pomp and circumstance attended his departure from a Bangkok port, where two thousand people, five cabinet ministers, and many members of the National Assembly showed up to bid and kiss him goodbye.[66]

But most important to our comrade spectators was the enactment of the first Anti-Communist Act of Siam by the government on April 2, 1933. Said to have been drafted with the help of Raymond B. Stevens, the American adviser,[67] the Act defined "communism" and "communist doctrine" in Article 3 as follows:

(1) Communism means the economic method or principle that consists of a complete or partial abolition of private ownership of property, and its common ownership by the country or the people.
(2) The Doctrine of Communism means any doctrine which advocates *Nationalization of land or industry or capital or labor* [phrase in italics appeared in English in the text of the Act].[68]

The rather superfluous and pointless differentiation between "Communism" and "the Doctrine of Communism," as well as the inclusion of the equivalent

English phrase in the text of the Act, a very unusual practice in Thai law-drafting convention, which generally avoided foreign-language terms or used Thai transliterations, indicates both conceptual confusion on the part of its draftsmen and the inadequacy of the Thai language to cope with the new terminology.[69] Needless to say, these idiosyncratic and sweeping definitions covered all manner of socialists, social democrats, agrarian reformists, and even advocates of monopolistic state enterprises. They were all denied legal status and political space in state institutions along with actual communists. Therefore, ironically, the first Anti-Communist Act of Siam was veritably not anti-communist at all, but anti-socialist, or more specifically, anti-Pridi, anti-left wing of the People's Party, and anti-Economic Plan.[70] As was the case with so many other foreign-derived entities in Thai politics, words were fitted to things other than they had been intended for in their homeland, thus changing both the meaning of words and the identity of things.

The conservative royalists did not have long to enjoy their political dominance, however. The tables turned barely three months later with the decisive shift in political alignment of a junior military faction of the People's Party away from the government. Fearful of losing power and offices newly won in the Revolution and of resurgent monarchical clout, they successfully staged a second coup d'état under the pretext of "protecting the Constitution and the National Assembly," forcing the resignation of the Phraya Manopakorn government on June 20, 1933, and founding a new one on the morrow, led by Prime Minister Colonel Phraya Phahonphonphayuhasena, top leader of the army section within the People's Party.

The Phraya Phahon government then proceeded, step by step, to partially undo what the conservative royalists had done. Immediately, the National Assembly was reconvened and the previous government's constitutional suspension rescinded.[71] Badly in need of the versatile policy-making and administrative expertise of Pridi, widely acknowledged as "the Brain of the People's Party," and also out of personal friendship and sympathy, the Phraya Phahon government began a shuttle diplomacy in mid-August 1933 between the exiled Pridi and the still suspicious King to negotiate his return and reinstatement. The political deal was at last struck with Pridi's acceptance of eight conditions set by the government (responsible for six) in consultation with the King (who added two—no forced purchase of land and no forced labor), which amounted to a permanent shelving of his Economic Plan. With the most explosive issue defused, Pridi was recalled from exile on September 29 and reinstated as a government minister on October 1.[72]

Subsequently, the National Assembly proceeded to clear its favorite leader of Phraya Manopakorn's damaging communist charge by appointing a special commission to investigate the matter. Chaired by M.C. Wan Waithayakon Worawan, prolific and influential Thai neologist of Western-derived political terms, the commission included two western experts on communism, René G. Guyon and Sir Robert E. Holland, who were jointly responsible for preparing a report on the unique principles of communism, based not on the all-inclusive Anti-Communist Act of 1933, but strictly on Karl Marx and Friedrich Engels' *Manifesto of the Communist Party* and on the programs of the Comintern and the British and French communist parties. Significantly, the commission agreed from the outset that the nature of the communist charge was political, not legal, and that its object of investigation was solely Pridi, not his Economic Plan. Therefore, having verbally denied harboring any of those principles, Pridi was triumphantly absolved on March 10, 1934.[73]

Meanwhile, on September 15, 1933, the increasingly dishonored and disgruntled King Prajadhipok was unprecedentedly and irreverently sued for libel in a criminal court by the secretary of the Tramway Workers Union, Thawat Riddhidej, on the basis of a passage in his *Samud pokkhao*, in which he blamed the tramway workers' strike on certain opportunistic people who just wanted to savor a union head's salary.[74] Soon, Thawat was arrested and counter-charged with rebellion and *lèse-majesté* by the Department of Public Prosecution. In October, Thawat appealed to the National Assembly for a ruling on the constitutionality of his litigation against the King, but the National Assembly rejected his appeal on the technical grounds that he was not its member. Nevertheless, one month later, upon the King's and government's request, it agreed to discuss the issue and ultimately ruled against Thawat.[75] Even though the issue was resolved in the King's favor, the damage to his personal honor and the throne was done. Amidst growing estrangement from the Phraya Phahon government, he left Siam for medical treatment abroad in January 1934 and finally abdicated in Britain on March 2, 1935 over the government's and National Assembly's repeated rejections of his political demands.[76]

The second round ended, befittingly enough, on October 1, 1935, with a revision of the definition of communism in Article 3 of the 1933 Anti-Communist Act so as to exclude socialist reformists, including Pridi and his left-wing followers, from its purview. The drafting of the amendment was done by Phraya Thepwithoon, a former minister of justice under the constitutional regime, who reportedly copied most of the new definition of communism from *The Encyclopedia Britannica*. Consequently, thenceforth:

> Communism means any doctrine that aims at the abolition of an existing social order by the use of force as the only means to bring about the

transfer of all land, other properties and big businesses from private to state or social ownership.[77]

At the end of this big political battle, there appeared to be no clear winner. Although Pridi and his radical supporters won the power and legal games, they did lose the policy game to King Prajadhipok and his conservative retinue who were able to block Pridi's socialistic Economic Plan for good.[78] This was the first instance of what would become a recurrent pattern in Thai politics: at a moment of life-and-death political crisis for Thai capitalism, when an alternative presented itself clearly and audaciously, it was always the monarchy that came in decisively to save it.

But there were clear losers—the Siamese communists who stood rather passively by and got the worst of it through and through. From February to July 1933, throughout the Economic Plan controversy, the conservatives' "anti-communist" backlash, and the second coup, there was a marked hiatus in public communist activity.[79] Why? Perhaps for two main reasons. First, the communists might have realized that they were not the real target of this anti-communist drive; and second, even though they distinguished Pridi and his left-wing faction from the rest of the People's Party, they did not treat them as a possible ally.[80] In the meantime, the Phraya Phahon government vowed from the beginning that it would never implement any communist policy and would work rigorously to eliminate communism.[81] It complied with the King's wish, in September 1933, to grant amnesty to all political prisoners except communists.[82] And when the National Assembly voted to vindicate Pridi, it made clear that it would tolerate no communist among its membership as a matter of principle.[83] The 1935 Amendment to the Anti-Communist Act also left no doubt that it targeted the communists.

After continual and severe government suppression forced the dissipation of the Communist Party of Siam around 1936, as described in Chapter 2, the remaining Chinese communists fared no better after the Phibunsongkhram government took over in 1938, as a result of the new government's "Thai nationalist" onslaught against the Chinese community's economic dominance, cultural autonomy, and political movement. It put state pressure on some Chinese economic interests to give way to the building of both state enterprises and personal economic bases of People's Party leaders under the pretext of "economic nationalism"[84] and hit hard at Chinese anti-Japanese political organizations supported by both the local Kuomintang and CCP.[85] Chinese schools, printing presses, newspaper offices, association headquarters, and secret societies throughout the country were raided by the police. Several thousand Chinese community leaders and political activists were arrested and sentenced to jail or deported. Chinese aliens were banned and driven away from six strategic "prohibited areas" in the provinces of Lop Buri, Prachin Buri, Chon Buri, Nakhon Ratchasima, Ubon Ratchathani, and the district of Warinchamrap. All but one Chinese newspaper and all but two Chinese schools in the country were closed. Chinese commercial signboards were taxed out of display while the lookjins were mandated by the state to use Thai. It is evident that the government deliberately took the opportunity to provoke anti-Chinese racism among the general public, from which it stood to gain both economically and politically.[86] Thus, whether under King or bureaucrats, due to ideology or race, the communists still remained sequestered from the legal-political institutions of Siam. Over five hundred of its members, the communist movement would later claim, languished or perished in prison from 1935 to 1945.[87]

Would Pridi have dealt with the Siamese communists differently in this period if he had not been hampered by conservative opponents and military colleagues? On the day after his unofficial exile in April 1933, his arch-enemy, Prime Minister Phraya Manopakorn, held a press conference in which he alleged that Pridi had been sympathetic to the arrested Chinese communists and had asserted that only the use of force against the law was a crime and that a belief in communism was not.[88] While the allegation itself does not sound far-fetched, one should take it with a grain of salt, given its source. One should also consider the largely amicable relationship between Pridi and the Kuomintang. This dated back to 1929 when Pridi, then a junior official in the Ministry of Justice, was reported to have paid an enigmatic visit to Y.S. Cheng, an envoy of the Kuomintang government visiting Bangkok.[89] In the decade after the 1932 Revolution, when he held various ministerial offices in successive governments of the People's Party, he never let the nationalism and radicalism of his policies and public statements go so far as to alienate the Kuomintang in the way Phibunsongkhram's version of fascist-modelled Thai nationalism did.[90] Later, when he was denied an American visa during his escape from Thailand in 1947, he was offered welcome hospitality in China by none other than Generalissimo Chiang Kaishek.[91]

All in all, the best way to describe relationship between the Siamese communists and the People's Party before the Second World War, so far as the Thai national polity was concerned, is as a case of the outsider unwilling and unready to enter, the insider refusing to let him in. For not only did the Siamese communists' unacknowledged but actual constituency remain by and large the immigrants, but their political frame of reference was still in large part overseas. As Hoang Van Hoan, a contemporary Communist Party of Siam Vietnamese cadre in charge of propaganda, who later rose to join the Party Executive Committee, reminisces in his memoirs, his job consisted largely of translating documents and pamphlets written by fellow party members from Chinese into Thai, documents whose contents had to do with such un-Thai landmarks as the commemoration of International Woman's Day on March 8, the anniversary of the Russian Revolution on November 7, and other important international workers' dates. And the target groups of his translated propaganda tracts were rice millers, tramway workers, rickshaw drivers, and railway workers, most of whom were Chinese. The upshot was that, throughout its approximately six-year existence (1930–1936), the CPS managed to recruit only five to seven Thais into its rank and file, all of whom occupied low-level positions.[92]

Nothing encapsulates this fact better than one CPS leaflet, most likely translated from Chinese into Thai and issued on December 11, 1934, one day after the second anniversary of the promulgation of the Siamese Constitution, to commemorate the CCP's overthrow of the local Kuomintang government in Guangzhou in 1927[93] and to oppose the Siamese Constitution. It urged Thais and Chinese to take up arms and topple the falsely Buddhist Phraya Phahon government and the hypocritically monarchist People's Party![94] A wonderful show-piece of half-cooked political mixed grill, neither very Thai nor strictly communist.

Translation of One Radical Nationalism to Another

The menacing rise of Japanese militarism and German Nazism subsequent to its 1928 Sixth Congress prompted the Comintern at its Seventh Congress, in July and August 1935, to abandon its aggressive ultra-leftist line and adopt a conciliatory "united people's front" tactic in order to seek alliance with the western imperialist powers against international fascism. Consequently, at its August 1, 1935 party meeting, the Chinese Communist Party also passed a resolution to shift its policy emphasis from armed struggle against the Kuomintang class enemies to building up an anti-Japanese national united front. The outbreak of the Second Sino-Japanese War at the Marco Polo Bridge on July 7, 1937 added a further sense of urgency to the implementation of this new policy for the Chinese comrades both in and outside China.[95]

The remaining post-CPS Chinese communists in Thailand, then regrouped as the Thai branch of the Chinese Communist Party (CCP-TB) or the Siamese Overseas Chinese Communist Party (SOCCP), also took part in this worldwide Chinese nationalist drive and redirected their political attack from local Siamese class enemies to the Japanese aggressor against their far-away imagined homeland, as good long-distance nationalists. Following the direct instructions of the CCP's Eighth Route Army office in Hong Kong, which were sought and brought back by two SOCCP agents sent from Siam in 1937, the SOCCP dissolved its earlier affiliated ultra-leftist or anti-western imperialist organizations and divided them into many smaller "study groups." Further, it created a central organ called the "All Siamese Overseas Chinese United Front for Anti-Japanese Resistance and National Salvation," also known by its Chinese abbreviation of "Kang Lian" (United Resistance), to co-ordinate and direct the activities of other newly-created, affiliated, sectional united front-type organizations such as "Wen Kang" (Cultural Resistance), "Shang Kang" (Commercial Resistance), "Fu Kang" (Women's Resistance), "Gong Kang" (Worker Resistance), and "Xue Kang" (Student Resistance). Based mainly in the communist strongholds of Chinese schools, the Chinese press, and factories, Kang Lian reached out across political and class divides to Chinese newspapers, business tycoons-cum-community leaders, merchants, workers, teachers, students, and even heads of Angyi gangs or triads, be they pro- or anti-Kuomintang, in its burgeoning, aggressive, and oft-times violent anti-Japanese campaign.[96]

Kang Lian solicited various forms of symbolic, material, and manpower support for the cause of the CCP's anti-Japanese war in China, such as financial collections for the war chest, winter clothes donations for the troops, the making and shipment of patients' uniforms to military hospitals, and the recruitment of over three hundred overseas Chinese volunteers to join the Chinese Communist New Fourth and Eighth Route Armies or to work in their Yanan base area. But the most important, effective, and widely-feared activity of Kang Lian, given the fact that Japan was by then Siam's largest trading partner, was an extended public campaign among the local Chinese and Indian merchants to boycott Japanese imports and impose trade sanctions on Japan. For that purpose, a secret intelligence and terrorist organization called the "Siamese Overseas Chinese Nation-Seller-Eliminating Association for Anti-Japanese Resistance and National Salvation" or "Chu Jian Tuan" was created out of eighteen existing Chinese triads to operate in co-ordination with and under the direction of Kang Lian. [97]

Its operational procedure went something like this: Chu Jian Tuan would gather intelligence from dock coolies already under triad control to find out which local merchants were connected with export and import shipments to and from Japan. Based on that information, Kang Lian would issue a letter of warning to each of those merchants, giving detailed and precise records of the Japanese shipments concerned, and demanding that they place an advertisement for their personal apology and repentance in local Chinese newspapers within three days, as well as pay a fine to the anti-Japanese cause by transferring money through a Bangkok-based Chinese bank into a CCP-owned bank account in

Hong Kong. Usually, one such letter was enough to bring about instant compliance. Otherwise, a second letter would be sent. Further procrastination or refusal to comply on the part of the recalcitrant nation-selling merchants would result in their serious injury or elimination by Chu Jian Tuan agents. Given the booming, lucrative nature of this respectable anti-Japanese, nationalist extortion racket, up to ten other less, or differently, principled movements and gangs soon emerged, some Kuomintang-led, or non-partisan and self-organized, others simply criminal and opportunistic. At one point, the racket ring became so crowded and chaotic that Kang Lian decided to impose some order and discipline with its own newly-created armed force, the "Overseas Chinese Anti-Japanese Vanguard" or "Min Xian" (People's Vanguard). Min Xian inspected, selected, and pressured only quality organizations among the mixed lot into joining an umbrella organization called "Sahasamakhom Prasan-ngan Koochat Totan Yipun" (Coordinated Anti-Japanese Resistance and National Salvation United Association) or "Nine Parties."[98]

The effectiveness of the Kang Lian and Chu Jian Tuan-imposed anti-Japanese boycott and trade sanctions in Siam can be gauged from contemporary Japanese and Thai official reports. By the end of August 1937, all Japanese goods in the Siamese market, from cloth to pottery, were totally boycotted by Chinese merchants. By the end of October 1937, all Chinese merchants completely refused to trade either openly or secretly with Japan. By January 1938, Indian merchants followed suit. And by the end of March 1938, the voluntary boycott of Japanese goods by local Chinese consumers had markedly increased; there were more reported cases of Chinese merchants who traded with Japan being subjected to violence, including exporters of rice, salt, and buffalo leather to the Japanese market; and the shipping of Japanese imports came to a complete halt as local coolies and boats refused to handle goods from Japanese-related ocean liners. Never before had Japanese merchants in Siam suffered so much, a March 1938 issue of the journal of the Japanese Chamber of Commerce in Siam concluded gloomily. However, this bore no comparison at all with the tragic fate of their Chinese trading partners. As of July 30, 1940, sixty-one of them had been killed in the ongoing, violent boycott and trade sanctions campaign, according to a Thai government committee report.[99]

The Siamese authorities regarded the widespread Kang Lian-instigated extortion and violence as a growing, serious threat to domestic law and order and soon moved against them in earnest. On February 12, 1938, the whole leadership of Kang Lian and Chu Jian Tuan was rounded up by the Thai Special Branch police and deported *en masse* one month later. Further major police crackdowns on Chinese political activists, for example, in September 1938 and April 1939, led to the arrest of two top SOCCP leaders and disrupted the anti-

Japanese campaign.[100] Their leadership severely weakened and their organizations fragmented and disunited, in 1940 or 1941 the remaining Chinese communists in Thailand again sought advice from the CCP's Overseas Chinese Committee in Hong Kong, which now included Ngo Diji, formerly of Bangkhwang. They were instructed to set up a special committee to reconnect and reunify the scattered organizations in preparation for the re-establishment of a communist party of Thailand.[101] Around 1941, a Chinese Comintern agent named Li Qixin (Li Kising in Teochiu) was sent from Penang to Thailand to head the operation, and a veteran SOCCP lookjin leader named Qiu Ji (or Khoo Kib or Jit Lekhawat) also re-entered Thailand from Laos to serve as his deputy, while a Chinese SOCCP named Li Hua returned from Hong Kong to rebuild and lead Kang Lian.[102]

As members of the newly organized, so-called Thai Department of the SOCCP, the lookjin communists were presumably involved in the Kang Lian-directed, radical Chinese nationalist movement, as well as in the subsequent reconstruction and reconstitution of the communist movement in Siam.[103] One of them was Si Anothai, who, years later, drew a picture of a number of young, radical lookjins from well-to-do families who, while getting a good multi-lingual education in upper classes Christian mission or Thai schools like Assumption College, St. Gabriel College, Thepsirin, Suankulap, and Rachini in the course of the 1930s, also read communist and radical literature in English and Chinese and protested against the authoritarian school regimes as a political sideline. After graduation, unperturbed by the lure of university education or inherited business enterprise and guided by political consciences most likely nurtured in early Chinese school years by overseas Chinese communist teachers, they joined the ranks of low-paid menial laborers in such places as the Bangkok Dock, the Banmai and Saphanleuang tobacco factories, the Makkasan Railway Maintenance and Repair Factory, the Bangyikhan Distillery, and other large sawmills and rice mills, undoubtedly to the amazement and despair of their parents.[104]

Undoubtedly, these selfless radical youngsters were among the first contingent of lookjin communists, probably affiliated with Xue Kang or Student Resistance, dispatched to reach, propagate to, and organize the largely ethnic Chinese proletariat,[105] their imputed class constituency, for the anti-Japanese resistance and (up till then still Chinese) national salvation cause as dictated by Kang Lian.[106] Besides their productive and political work in the factories, they set up a library of political books, monitored news of wars in Europe and Asia, and in 1940 formed an underground organization called Klum Rakchat Nakrian Nakseuksa (Patriotic Students' Group) in anticipation of a possible Japanese invasion of Thailand.[107]

The long-expected Japanese troops finally invaded central and southern Thailand by land, sea, and air at nine points at 1 a.m. local time, December 8, 1941. Two days later, their mission to occupy Thailand was successfully completed.[108] Following a government-sponsored bill passed by the National Assembly in September of that year, which stipulated the duty of Thai citizens to fight any foreign invader to the last man, stiff resistance was mounted against the Japanese by Thai soldiers, police, and civilians in several localities, resulting in 183 people killed and 158 injured on the Thai side, and 141 killed and 45 injured on the Japanese side.[109] The resistance was called off by the Thai government six and a half hours later in view of its suicidal futility. This opinion was voiced most strongly in the emergency cabinet meeting by Deputy Prime Minister Police Major General Adul Aduldejjaras and Prime Minister Phibunsongkhram, who cut short Pridi's plea for a careful discussion before taking any decision, saying: "But a cease-fire should be ordered first because to fight on will be disastrous." Persistently goaded by the prime minister, who was himself under intense Japanese pressure, the cabinet, including Pridi, voted for a cease-fire at 7:30 a.m. the same day, a resolution which was read by the Japanese ambassador to Thailand as a "surrender."[110]

Later that day, an agreement granting right of passage through Thai territory to Japanese forces was concluded by the Thai and Japanese governments. However, Prime Minister Phibunsongkhram and his cabinet supporters soon changed their minds and were no longer satisfied with that kind of cautious, at-arm's-length relationship between the two countries. Partly out of concern for the preservation of the Thai armed forces, and partly carried away by the whirlwind of early, rapid Japanese military success and the prospect of expanding Thai territory into Burma and turning Thailand into the Cultural Center of South Asia, Phibunsongkhram proceeded to make a virtue out of Japanese-imposed necessity. He brought Thailand, in quick succession, into a military alliance with Japan on December 11, into a further political pact with her on December 21, into war against the United States and Great Britain on January 25, 1942, and almost into the pre-existing Rome-Berlin-Tokyo Axis![111] In fact, it was later revealed that the Japanese embassy had informed Prime Minister Phibun of Japan's need for military passage through Thailand, and proposed an alliance with her as early as November 20, 1941.[112] Consequently, in the cabinet meetings on November 25 and December 3, Phibun allegedly tried unsuccessfully to persuade the cabinet to agree to the proposal.[113] In view of this earlier attempt and his very swift adaptation to the overwhelming presence and apparent omnipotence of the Japanese imperial armed forces, the actual Japanese invasion might have played the role of a de facto policy instrument that pushed the cabinet in the direction he might have wished in the first place but for the opposition of his more cautious colleagues.

Meanwhile, the non-cooperative members of the cabinet, chief amongst them Minister of Finance Pridi Banomyong, who steadfastly objected to the Japanese request for a huge loan, were removed from ministerial offices to idle ones by the prime minister, acting on the demand of the Japanese. Pridi himself was "promoted" to the Council of Regency for the absent King Rama VIII on December 23. It was by no means coincidental that the Declaration of War against the Allies, which the Phibunsongkhram government rushed through one month later, did not have his endorsing signature.[114] It should be pointed out, however, that this was not simply a matter of the "bad," pro-Japanese, anti-Chinese Phibunsongkhram versus the "good," pro-Chinese, anti-Japanese Pridi, as it has sometimes been portrayed. Rather, it was a conflict between two Thai nationalists with different political inclinations, understandings of the international situation, foreign policy visions, and diplomatic methods, who happened to bet their own and the nation's fortunes on opposite sides in the Second World War in the hope of achieving political power and national survival. Where Phibun was inclined towards a military autocratic regime, an expansionist policy, and a bellicose, militaristic diplomacy, Pridi was for a parliamentary regime, a neutral policy, and a peace-making diplomacy. Their prefered alliances with foreign powers were short-term tactical decisions rather than long-term ideological commitments and should be taken to reflect primarily the respective folly or wisdom of their political leadership rather than the vice or virtue of their personal morality.[115] What is so astonishing, even fascinating, about them is not the set images of hero and villain portrayed by their respective followers and detractors, but the passive inaction of Pridi and his supporters to mount any serious and genuine resistance to Japan for fifteen long months (December 1941 to February 1943),[116] and the flexibility of Phibun who tried to switch sides behind the suspicious backs of the Japanese in early 1944.[117]

One has to bear in mind how persistently, before the invasion, the Phibunsongkhram government had called on Thais to defend their country against foreign invasion, using all imaginable weapons, including centipedes, scorpions, and stinging cowhages, and, in case of defeat, to burn down their dwellings and storehouses so that "the enemy can seize only a barren land," to appreciate how widespread was the feeling of disillusionment, cynicism, and indignation among Thai people and government officials alike at the government's shameless about-face.[118] Phibun himself was well aware of this public sentiment; he told the Japanese early on of the need to turn long-standing anglophilic Thai public opinion against Great Britain and later ordered all Thai government officials to swear allegiance to the new pro-Japanese policy of his government.[119]

The Phibunsongkhram government's strategy in dealing with its "Big Brother" ally and the actual military occupation was to bend with the wind and reap any windfalls therefrom. It took an easy and low-cost ride on Japan's military advance into British Burma and Southeast Asia, but at the same time, tried as much as possible to prevent the expansion of Japanese power and influence inside Thailand and to retain whatever sovereignty, legally speaking, that remained. It thus created a bilateral coordinating agency called "the Joint Thai-Japanese Committee" (later renamed the "Allied Coordinating Department") to serve as the institutional body for negotiation with the Japanese military authorities. Regarding its ally's uneasy relationship with the local Chinese community, it insisted on its sovereign right to intervene as mediator and broker between the two, claiming the Chinese to be under Thai jurisdiction. Nevertheless, when push came to shove, it was prepared to sacrifice the Chinese population to Japan's exacting demands, especially for thousands of laborers to build the Thai-Burmese strategic railway, in order to protect the Thai people, its perceived real political constituency.[120]

The Japanese military, in turn, had prepared and actually adopted a policy of control and co-optation of the Chinese in Thailand as an economic instrument of national interest, based on the mutual exchange of benefits. Thus, although they were resolute and severe in capturing, torturing, and eliminating Chinese and Indian spies and saboteurs, often acting unilaterally in violation of a standing police-coordination agreement with the Thai authorities and notwithstanding the latter's repeated protests, they remained mostly discriminating and circumscribed in their suppression of the local Chinese. By the end of the war, only about three hundred people had been arrested by the Japanese military police for anti-Japanese activities in Thailand, and only eleven out of eight hundred Japanese military police officers and their associates were identified by local Chinese witnesses as torturers of Chinese prisoners. This was because their main objective was to win local Chinese business and community leaders over to their side through the alternating use of threats and patronage. While presenting themselves to the local Chinese elite as an alternative patron to the discriminatory and uncaring Thai government and bureaucracy, the Japanese military also pressured them, directly and indirectly (through the Thai government), to utilize their extensive local networks and money to recruit scarce Chinese labor in return for lucrative business deals. There was thus an oblique class differentiation built into the Japanese strategic relationship with the Chinese community, resulting in the reactive ire of the Chinese coolies being directed not only at "the Japanese bandits" who invaded their distant homeland and present country of residence and conscripted their labor, but also at the war-profiteering, Chinese-eating-Chinese, capitalist nation-sellers.[121] In contrast, the Phibunsongkhram government's ethnic discrimination against the Chinese, manifest in labor recruitment for Japanese railway construction, in reserving certain professions for the Thais, and in forcibly removing "aliens" from prohibited areas, earned it the contempt and hatred of the whole local Chinese community, which came to regard its erstwhile patron as no longer helpful or dependable, but merely a feeble and subordinate mediator-cum-broker for the Japanese.[122]

Among the general Thai populace, the attitude towards the Japanese was remarkable for a lack of passion, either for or against. Part of the explanation may lie in the fact that, apart from some fighting upon the initial Japanese invasion, there were only two reported cases of subsequent serious armed clashes between the two sides.[123] Both were random and isolated incidents, the casualties not heavy, and the conflicts quickly and decisively resolved. Those who opposed the Japanese occupation and the Phibunsongkhram government's alliance with Japan were mostly the better-educated Thais, such as some lookjin, Thai journalists and politicians associated with Pridi or the Thai-issara group, and the 145 Thai diplomats and students who launched Khabuankan Serithai (Free Thai Movement) in the United States and Great Britain in early 1942.[124] The other strategic group among the Thais who showed growing impatience and discontent with the Japanese were government officials. A Japanese navy attaché, instructed by his ambassador to sound out many high-ranking Thai government and military leaders on their opinions about the Japanese, concluded in mid-1942:

> At present, there is no pro-Japanese group in the Thai bureaucracy. The young government officials in particular oppose Thailand's dependence on Japan. The anti-Japanese atmosphere is on the rise. This is the real situation that is happening.[125]

In the opinion of the Japanese ambassador, Thai government officials, though made to swear allegiance to Phibun's pro-Japanese policy, felt contrarily for the following five reasons. First, with the support of Japanese military might, Japanese trading companies were using Chinese and Indians to invade Thailand economically, exporting Thailand's basic necessities, and creating economic havoc. Second, Japanese soldiers looked down upon Thai officials and civilians alike, did not really observe Thai law, and when undisciplined, were not firmly punished. Third, the Japanese interfered in Thai domestic policy, obstructing Thai public administration. Fourth, Japan had yet to transfer the property of enemy nationals to the Thai government, despite Thailand's absolute authority over it according to international law. And fifth, Japan treated Thailand like a colony. On top of that, the Japanese had yet to formally grant the occupied Burmese Shan States to Thailand as promised.[126]

Upon assuming his newly-created office in February 1943, the commander of Japanese troops in Thailand, well aware of these issues, had tried to improve Thai-Japanese relations by yielding to some key demands of the Phibunsongkhram government for the transfer of property of enemy nationals and the formal annexation of the Shan States. It did placate Phibun for a while but it came, as it were, too little, too late. With the tide of war turning progressively against the Axis powers in the European theater, Phibun started perceptibly to distance himself and his government from Japan's Greater East Asia Co-Prosperity Sphere in mid-1943 and tried clandestinely to switch to the winning side in early 1944, to his ally's growing but inconclusive suspicion and mistrust.[127] The Thai bureaucratic elite, fearing post-war Allied reprisal, wanted to follow suit. They did this furtively and cautiously, first by turning a blind eye to the resumption of underground anti-Japanese activity by the Pridi group (as requested by Pridi sometime in the first half of 1944), then by supporting Pridi after his successful parliamentary maneuver to remove Phibun from power in July 1944, and finally by joining Pridi's underground resistance and creating at long last the domestic Free Thai Movement in September 1944.[128]

Being essentially the Thai state bureaucracy's movement to save its own skin with a modicum of bureaucracy-organized but politically hollow adjunctive popular participation, the domestic Free Thai Movement was nevertheless integrated with anti-Japanese groups among Thais in the United States and Great Britain and actively assisted the Allied war effort in Southeast Asia behind enemy lines during the remaining eleven months of the war. Contributing considerably to the Allies' success, it earned the latter's crucial and priceless official recognition as the sole Thai resistance organization. That, in turn, helped salvage Thailand from the disadvantageous status of a defeated country after the war and, of course, saved the conservative Thai bureaucracy and its instinctively ever-adaptable and opportunistic elite as well. In addition, the whole Free Thai Movement episode underlines the nature and limitations of Pridi's political career as a democratic, nationalist revolutionary of the Thai bureaucracy.[129]

This breathtaking and complex turn of events presented an unprecedented opening in the Thai political opportunity structure for the Siamese communists. For the first time in twenty years of activities in Siam, to be a Chinese or Vietnamese nationalist (opposing the Japanese invaders of their homelands)[130] and a communist internationalist (making a world proletarian revolution and obeying the Comintern's dictates) coincided politically with being a Thai patriot and anti-government rebel. This in no way implies that by being the latter they stopped being the former—culturally speaking, how could that possibly be?—only that under these new circumstances they could be both at one and the same time. At long last, after years of being left out in the cold, came a golden opportunity for the Siamese communist movement to be naturalized in the Thai polity.

At a deeper cultural political level, through this opening or window of political opportunity, so to speak, the Siamese communists could and did come to see political parallels between Japanese-occupied, dictatorial China and Japanese-occupied, dictatorial Thailand, making a leap of imagination from one to the other. If before the occupation, they saw long-distance and hence invisible China in visible, tangible Thailand, and acted out their Chinese nationalist part in the Thai theater, now they came to imagine Thailand herself in the image and with the radical discourse of China. It was precisely in this dimension of cultural political imagination, rather than in organizational or ethnic or political dimensions,[131] that the translation between one radical nationalism and another took place, in which a radical anti-Japanese Chinese nationalist could possibly turn into a radical anti-Japanese Thai nationalist, and vice versa, through "the Spectre of Comparisons," as the lookjin communists did.[132]

Thus, while Li Qixin's original purpose, as instructed by the Comintern, was to reorganize the Chinese comrades, probably owing to a combination of factors—the new political opportunity, the much-weakened Chinese Department of the SOCCP in the aftermath of Phibunsongkhram's anti-Chinese suppression campaign, and the already existing SOCCP Thai Department—he soon focused on lookjins and Thais in his recruitment efforts. The upshot was the founding of a new communist party at its First Congress on December 1, 1942, in which Li Qixin played a key role. With a membership of fifty-seven at its inception, the Party was essentially a naturalized reincarnation of the simultaneously disbanded SOCCP's Thai Department, the latter's lookjin members being automatically Thaified and transferred.[133] Even though, in principle, the TCP and the SOCCP's Chinese Department were henceforth separate organizational entities, in practice their organizational structures were very close and in the initial period often confusingly overlapping, with mutual policy and functional cooperation. In any case, by all accounts, the real wartime leadership of both parties lay in the hands of Li Qixin and Qiu Ji.[134] The SOCCP continued to exist until it was formally dissolved in 1953.[135] After the Second World War, the Party's official newspaper, *Mahachon*, named Prasong Vongvivatana (alias Phairaj or Song Nopphakhun or Eu Song) as its secretary-general.[136] Song was a lookjin whose father was a Chinese rice-mill owner and mother was a Thai. His appointment as Party secretary-general after its founding congress was said to be the Comintern agent's handiwork.[137]

The Party originally called itself Phak Khommunit Thai (Thai Communist Party or TCP), translated into English as "Communist Party of Siam." Since the Party's official translation fails to capture the ethnic-Thai nuance in the original Thai name, it will not be used here. The name was changed to Phak Khommunit Haeng Prathet Thai (Communist Party of Thailand or CPT) at its Second Congress in February 1952, allegedly to stress its "national" as opposed to "ethnic" character.[138] It was ironic, then, that the Party adopted an "ethnic-Thai" name when it was overwhelmingly composed of lookjins, perhaps to create a Thai-ethnicity effect in compensation for a missing reality, but chose to drop it at precisely the time when it approached the reality.

The Party's ten-point policy statement, issued December 8, was essentially anti-Japanese and anti-Phibun government, democratic and Thai-patriotic, with an obvious Chinese slant:

(1) Drive the Japanese bandits away from Thailand. Restore Thailand's independence and sovereignty.

(2) Confiscate all enterprises and property of the Japanese bandits. Capture the Thais who sell the nation out and put them on military trial.

(3) Overthrow the Luang Phibun government which gangs up with and sells out the national interests to the Japanese bandits. Establish an anti-Japanese, democratic government.

(4) Practice democratic politics. The people have the right to assembly, association, speech, writing, publication, election, and being elected. Release all anti-Japanese political prisoners.

(5) Improve the living conditions of the people. Increase salaries. Help the unemployed. Reduce rents and taxes. Relieve natural disasters. Improve the living conditions of soldiers and teachers. Abolish trifling taxes. Collect supplementary taxes.

(6) Expand national industry and commerce. Welcome foreign investors. Abolish the present active policy of trading monopolies.

(7) Cooperate with China, Britain, America, and the Soviet Union in a joint war against Japan.

(8) Cooperate with all aliens against Japan. Stop the discriminatory policy against the Chinese.

(9) Various nationalities in Thailand have equal rights. Various nationalities have freedom of worship and education.

(10) Rally the whole nation, funds and force, all out to resist the invasion
       of Japanese imperialism.[139]

Note the obviously Chinese-derived conceptions of Japanese bandits, Japanese
imperialism, nation-selling Thais and government, anti-Japanese democratic
politics and government, independence and sovereignty, and rights and
freedoms, which were employed by the TCP to articulate and imagine a
Japanese-occupied and a soon-to-be liberated Thailand in parallel with China.
It was through these translated lexical media that radical values and
imagination and the analytical-critical concepts associated with the Chinese
communists' notion of China were transposed into the lookjin communists'
new and properly imagined national community called Thailand. Provided with
such good ideological reasons, they could come to share and love, identify
with, and fight and die for *their* Thailand, in contrast and contestation with
other, differently-imagined versions of Thailand.

Similar imaginings seem to be at work in another text. Here Qiu Ji, one of
two top wartime communist leaders in Thailand, in a conversation with the local
Thai, Chinese, and English press on September 12, 1945, described the
emergence of Thai and Chinese nationalist movements against Japan in Thailand:

When Japanese troops moved to the South, Chinese and Thai nationals had
jointly and continuously mounted anti-Japanese resistance everywhere in
Thailand. The reason for this cooperation was because Chinese and Thai
nationals wanted independence and freedom for their own nations as well
as liberation from the conditions of slavery. Therefore, Chinese and Thai
nationals had risen up...

As to the fact of this matter, for example, in the Ranong Incident, Thai
soldiers and police had resisted the Japanese with the eager support of
the Chinese. When the Sahasamakhom Totan Yipun (Anti-Japanese
United Association) and the Volunteer Force waged a war against the
Japanese in the South, they received unending cooperation from the Thai
military and civilians. Thai and Chinese workers had also risen up to join
the anti-Japanese resistance everywhere, and destroyed a Japanese
army's godown, for instance.[140]

What is remarkable about the above is not Qiu Ji's all-too-obvious ex-
aggerations, but his translated imagination of the two nationalist movements
against a common external enemy merging into one.

So, shortly after the Japanese occupation, Si Anothai and his lookjin
comrades launched their underground anti-Japanese activities.[141] In 1942, they

formed a series of Workers' Welfare Associations (Samakhom Songkhrao Kammakorn) in various industries in Bangkok, beginning with tobacco and spreading to shipping, land transportation, rice-milling, timber, railways, tramways, and naval docks. Overtly, these welfare associations organized mutual aid among workers and others who suffered from Allied air raids, but clandestinely, they led workers in strikes, slow-downs, and sabotage of Japanese war-related industries and military equipment. A CPT source later claimed that during the Japanese occupation, there were more than 150 strikes involving workers in 220 factories. Among the workers' acts of sabotage were: producing defective boots, contaminating canned food, throwing away war materials, stealing vehicle parts, damaging factory machines, booting supplies out of goods wagons, and perforating or unloosing cargo boats from their convoy.[142]

In mid-1945, on the basis of these Workers' Welfare Associations, then numbering between thirty and forty and comprising both Thai and Chinese workers, a semi-clandestine central organization embracing all of them was created and named Sahasamakhom Kammakorn Krungthep (Bangkok Workers' United Association) or Sahabal Kammakorn Krungthep (Bangkok Workers' Union).[143] During the previous year, the TCP had also taken the initiative in bringing together various underground anti-Japanese groups, including the Thai-issara Movement, under an umbrella organization called Sahasamakhom Totan Yipun (Anti-Japanese United Association), with a claimed total membership of eleven thousand.[144] In the process, the Party's cadres had come into contact with such anti-Japanese local leaders as Tiang Sirikhan, an elected member of the National Assembly from the northeastern province of Sakon Nakhon and head of the Free Thai Movement in that area, and Lieutenant Colonel Phayome Julanond, a key army staff officer responsible for planning the country's defense along the eastern line.[145] According to Phin, contact was made with the Free Thai Movement at the highest level as well. The TCP agent who met with Pridi during the war was Wiroj Amphai. As a smart, amiable, articulate, and tactful lookjin Bangkokian from a well-to-do family with extensive pro-Pridi political connections, he was regarded by the Party as an ideal candidate for this diplomatic job. His access to Pridi was made possible by Vas Sunthornjamorn, a pro-Pridi veteran journalist and labor activist who acted as intermediary, and by the Party's underground anti-Japanese press, especially the Thai-language *Mahachon*, the like of which the Free Thai Movement did not produce but needed to show to the Allies as evidence of resistance activities in Thailand.[146] Being essentially a bureaucracy-based organization, the Free Thai Movement itself had no need for such a popular propagandistic organ, in contrast with a popularly-based, strongly ideological mass movement like communism.[147]

Besides building up an alliance with other anti-Japanese, anti-Phibun political forces, especially among the Thais, the TCP also planned to launch an armed struggle against the Japanese military in rural areas in the South, Northeast, and Central Region of the country. The Party's leader in charge of anti-Japanese armed resistance during the war was none other than Song Nopphakhun. Preparations included cooperating with local anti-Japanese forces, stealing Japanese ammunition and bayonets, mobilizing workers to produce weapons and other military equipment, and recruiting students and active members of the Workers' Welfare Associations to form a Kong Asasamak Totan Yipun (Anti-Japanese Volunteer Force) in 1944.[148] A veteran of the Anti-Japanese Volunteer Force in the South claimed that the first shot of the TCP's partisan warfare was fired in Kuboo Village, Sadao District, Songkhla Province in 1944. Armed with four and a half rusty rifles (one had no butt) and a number of firecrackers, they noisily but bloodlessly took over a local police station and captured eleven rifles and some ammunition.[149] Nevertheless, the whole endeavor was too little, too late. No sooner had the Anti-Japanese Volunteer Force engaged the Japanese in a few skirmishes than the war ended.

Meanwhile, on the domestic political scene, Khuang Aphaiwong, a liberal civilian member of the People's Party and a Free Thai sympathizer, replaced Phibun as prime minister on August 1, 1944. From then until shortly after the war, governmental power fell for all practical purposes into the hands of Pridi and his underground Free Thai followers.[150] By virtue of their timely turn-about and self-serving contribution to national salvation during the war, some leading members of the Free Thai Movement were widely acclaimed as national heroes while Pridi was granted by King Rama VIII the honorary title "Ratthaburus Awuso" (Senior Statesman) in December 1945. Reaching the zenith of his power and influence, Pridi was de facto prime minister maker and unmaker, and took the premiership himself for several months.[151]

But the Pridi-Free Thai group was not the only one to gain politically from the war. Their credentials for Thainess guaranteed by their wartime anti-Japanese, patriotic action,[152] the lookjin communists emerged triumphantly from prison and from the underground, not only with their immediate foreign and domestic enemies vanquished, but also with a Thai *phak* (party), a lot of Thai *phuak* (followers), and many Thai *pheuan* (friends). Among their Thai friends were some royalists (Leuan Saraphaiwanich), progressive northeastern MPs (Tiang Sirikhan, Pan Kaeomat), former members of the Workers' Party (Police Second Lieutenant Vas Sunthornjamorn, Sun Kijjamnong), socialist politicians (M.C. Sakol Wannakon Worawan),[153] and Pridi and his leftist followers. The most striking sign of the communists' new strength was the establishment of a nationwide central labor organization called Ongkan

Sahaachiwa Kammakorn Haeng Prathet Thai (generally known in English as the Central Labor Union) on April 25–28, 1947, with twenty-three local labor organizations under its umbrella and a membership of sixty to seventy-five thousand throughout the country.[154] Although the great majority of the communist Central Labor Union's membership was Chinese and its curiously oft-neglected vice-chairman was a Chinese named Zangqi, the listing of Central Labor Union leadership clearly indicates its configuration of communist-led alliance with the Thais: Thianthai Aphichatbut (Sahachip Party), chairman; Damri Reuangsutham (TCP), secretary; Si Anothai (TCP), head of education; Sun Kijjamnong (ex-Workers' Party), head of welfare and reception; Vas Sunthornjamorn (ex-Workers' Party, Sahachip Party, and later TCP), legal adviser; and M.C. Sakol Wannakon Worawan (Sahachip Party), adviser. The communist Bangkok Labor Union (the core of the Central Labor Union) was actually divided into two departments, each with its own leadership, the Thai led by Damri Reuangsutham and the Chinese by He Kikai (He Digai).[155]

In addition to recognition, credibility, and legitimacy, the TCP also received its hard-won legality in the Thai polity when Prasert Sapsunthorn, an elected MP for the southern province of Surat Thani, submitted a bill to the legislature calling for the abrogation of the 1933/35 Anti-Communist Act. The story of how Prasert, after a long detour, became the foremost advocate of legal communism after the war and the first and only self-proclaimed communist MP in Thai history is fascinating. After previous political flirting with Phibun's nationalism and the Prachathipat (Democrat) Party's conservative royalism, Prasert found his own way to communism and planned to submit legislation abrogating the Anti-Communist Act and to form a communist party. Through his old friend Tiang Sirikhan, he succeeded in winning the understanding and support of the initially suspicious Pridi, whose written personal message to him on this issue he included in his opening speech to the parliamentary debate on the bill. Meanwhile, the TCP, anxious that Prasert's plan for another communist party might split the burgeoning Thai communist movement, managed, through Wiroj Amphai and Udom Sisuwan, to persuade him to drop it and enroll in the Party instead. A deal was struck whereby Prasert pushed for the repeal of the Anti-Communist Act in the House of Representatives in exchange for an exceptional instant admission into the TCP.[156]

Under international pressure from the Soviet Union and with the active domestic support of Pridi, the government, and the leftists in general,[157] the House of Representatives finally approved the bill by a vote of forty-nine to thirty-seven on September 12, 1946, over the strong opposition of conservative MPs. The Senate, which was dominated by pro-government members, approved the bill on October 18, 1946.[158] This brought to an end the first thirteen-year life of the notoriously problematical, Thai-style Anti-Communist Act, under whose provisions 991 persons had been arrested but only sixteen convicted.[159]

Could it be said that this was the completion of the lookjin communists' Thaification process? That they had thereby been thoroughly naturalized as Thai patriots? Perhaps legally, but not in terms of cultural politics. In the less-than-free democratic polity Siam was from 1932 to 1946, laws hardly reflected real cultural life, as the Nationality Act of 1913 and the Anti-Communist Act of 1933/35 had shown. Culturally speaking, the legally Thaified Thai Communist Party still had to win the hearts and minds of the Thai people, especially of their intellectuals. Furthermore, it still had various ethno-ideological notions of Thainess (conservative royalist, militarist racist, and otherwise) to transform. For the Thaification of immigrant communism, had it been finished, would at any rate have been only half the process, the other half being the radicalization of the ethno-ideology of Thainess, to make "Thainess" necessarily entail "radicalism." This would involve the reconstruction of Thai history, political discourse, poetry, novel, and symbolism, in short, the re-imagination of the Thai community in those cultural areas essential to the kind of politics it wanted to carry out.

One such area was the officially standardized Thai speech, roughly based on the Central Thai and especially Bangkok dialect and promoted as part of the state centralization of education and radio broadcasting under Phibun's nationalist regime. The political significance of clear Thai speech for the recruitment of the Thai elite, "reactionary" and "revolutionary" alike, can not be stressed strongly enough.[160] However, for a Chinese of the Teochiu dialect group (which has been predominant in Thailand), this represents a particularly tough challenge. His or her inability to speak Thai clearly and articulately (*phood thai mai chad*) has a typical Teochiu characteristic—the inherent absence of certain consonants (d and r) and vowels (-euan, -n) in Teochiu speech and hence their replacement by other consonants (l for d and r) and vowels (-ian for -euan, -ng for -n) in Thai speech.

Contrary to their expectations, for the lookjin communists, the Gramscian "war of position" in Thai speech, as in other areas of Thai cultural politics, was indeed the hardest part, taking much longer than serving time in Bangkhwang or fighting the Japanese. Piatoe, alas, could testify to this. He might have been elected secretary-general at the Second Congress of the Party in February 1952 in place of the rerun Song Nopphakhun, but for one seemingly trivial but politically damaging blemish on his Thainess to which the majority of party delegates objected: he spoke unclear Thai with a Chinese accent.[161] Aiya, ik wok nok easie ak all to become a Thai khommunik!

4

Marxism as Commodity: Prefiguring Demand

A specter is haunting Siam, the specter of Stupidity!

Intharayut [1]

What is *Marxism*? What is *Leninism*? These are questions whose answers I would like to know for a very long time. And my agonizing curiosity grows even stronger with the turning of the tide of the Chinese civil war in Mao Tse-tung's favor…The wave of the October Revolution, which had reconstructively transformed Russia into a socialist country, has now hurled its enormous swell into Asia. And I wonder when it will reach Thailand. But there is one thing I am sure of: definitely it must arrive. Hence a desire which I have always cherished in my heart, namely, how I can come to own a book that at least sheds some light on or solves these questions of mine with sufficient clarity [words in italics appeared in English in the original].

Udom Udakan [2]

The Market for Marxist Cultural Commodities

Communism, once legalized, entered the post-war Thai cultural market with unprecedented freedom in the form of considerable numbers of printed commodities. Radical newspapers, magazines, books, printing houses, publishing houses, and bookstores occupied the newly won democratic space, along with communist and socialist political parties, members of parliament, trade unions, and youth and other front organizations. And indeed, it was precisely through print capitalism and the capitalist market that the anti-capitalist cultural commodities of Marxism-communism thrived, disseminating their radical ideas and language throughout the central political and cultural domains of the country and forming the main counter-hegemonic discourse during the years 1946 to 1957.[3]

But prosperity in a capitalist cultural market came at a cost to Marxist printed commodities, not least of which was being inexorably subjected to the economic logic and ideological profanation of capitalism that bore on any cultural product offered in its market. Simply put, those that did not sell well enough perished regardless of their inherent intellectual and political merits, while ideological purity could not but be compromised for the sake of business survival.[4] Besides, the fact that Marxism was a foreign cultural product, having originally been manufactured in foreign lands, accounted for the peculiar nature of its market in Thailand, namely, that it was a cross-cultural and pluralistic market with several competing importing agents and translating suppliers and a medley of customer groups with distinct and even conflicting interests and demands. On top of that, during most of the aforementioned decade, this market existed under a conservative military authoritarian regime that fell increasingly under American anti-communist Cold War influence, especially after November 1947, and whose policy towards the radical press varied from repressive tolerance and active suppression to selective patronage and political manipulation. These complex economic, cultural, and political factors intertwined to form a web of contradictions between legality and militancy, business and ideology, community and conflict, and plurality and monopoly that enveloped and greatly affected the production and circulation of Marxist cultural commodities. It is to the specific preconditions and socio-economic setting of the development of this market in post-war Thailand that we now turn.

Potential Readership

Not all Thais were so fortunate as to have a chance to be enlightened by the Thai radical printed commodities on sale in the market. To be able to consume them directly, one had, first of all, to be literate, and literacy then was by no means pervasive. According to government statistics, out of the total 1947 Thai population aged ten years and above of 12.32 million, 5.7 million or 46.3 percent were illiterate and hence had no earthly use for radical printed material.[5] As for the 5.1 million who, in addition to literacy, also had some formal education and hence constituted the pool of possible buyers and readers, only a tiny fraction of them might be prone to do so.[6] A breakdown of the educated population by level of education (see Table 4-1) shows that those with pre-university, university, vocational, adult, or Buddhist education numbered only 262,450 or 5.11 percent of the educated population (2.13 percent of the total population) aged ten years and above. It was these educational groups that had a discernible relationship with the radical press.

Pre-university education as a separate two-grade educational stage, generally called Triam Udomseuksa, had been introduced by the government and administered by Thai universities and military academies since 1938. It was incorporated by the Ministry of Education into the normal curriculum of secondary education as its final part in 1946. During the 1940s and 1950s, pre-university schools and crammers were primarily located in Bangkok and had as their students young people in the seventeen-to-twenty-year age range from all over the country. Among them were the seventeen-year old Phin Bua-on from Phetchaburi, the twenty-year old Phichit Dijai from Si Sa Ket, and the young rebellious lookjin Miss Kanlaya from Chachoengsao. They came to Bangkok for Triam Udomseuksa after the war, soon joined the ranks of avid readers of the radical press, and later joined the communist movement.[7]

Of the five universities and two vocational colleges in Thailand in the decade after 1947,[8] Thammasat and Chulalongkorn were the two leading and, politically speaking, most active ones. The Chulalongkorn student population during that period numbered between two and four thousand, while Thammasat's registered student population was between twelve and twenty thousand. However, as Thammasat was then an open university, only six hundred to one thousand of its students spent their daily lives on campus.[9] It was presumably among these twenty-six hundred to five thousand resident students of the two universities that the radical press found its keenest readership.[10] Readers of the radical press

Table 4-1

Educated Population over Ten Years of Age by Level of Education, 1947

LEVEL OF EDUCATION	NUMBER OF PEOPLE	PERCENT OF TOTAL POPULATION
Primary (grades 2–6)	4,466,768	36.23
Secondary (1–6)	402,447	3.26
Pre-university (7–8)	26,183	0.21
University (1–5)	3,691	0.03
Thai university graduate	4,793	0.04
Foreign university graduate	1,379	0.01
Vocational certificate holder	12,018	0.10
Adult education graduate	210,189	1.71
Buddhist degree holder	4,197	0.03
Total	5,131,665	41.62

Source: Adapted from Thailand, Department of Interior, Ministry of Interior, *Kansamruaj sammanokhrua thua rajanajak-kanseuksa* [Whole-Kingdom census survey—education] (Bangkok: Department of Interior, Ministry of Interior, [n.d.]), 233.

among domestic and foreign university graduates ranged from a bachelor of science who graduated with First Class Honours from London University[11] to a drop-out from Siriraj Medical School.[12]

Vocational, adult, and Buddhist educational programs produced two key professions with respect to readership of radical literature and membership in radical movements. These were the school teachers and Buddhist monks who together constituted the moral and cultural leadership of Thai rural communities. In 1947, there were 71,920 school teachers in the country and, judging from their average rate of increase, their number must have risen to nearly 100,000 by 1957.[13] Readership of the radical press among members of this profession was widespread (especially among those originating in the Northeast), instances of which were reported in Bangkok,[14] Si Sa Ket,[15] Ubon Ratchathani,[16] Udon Thani,[17] and Nakhon Ratchasima.[18] It is noteworthy that teaching in provincial private schools seemed a favorite job among communist escapees, probably by virtue of its status in the local community, easy access to potential recruits among colleagues, students, and villagers, and ease of application. Requiring only an educational certificate and no background check, provincial teaching was a relatively safe haven from government surveillance.[19]

The conditions of monkish readership of radical literature were similar to those of school teachers, with several reports of "red" books unexpectedly turning up from under yellow robes and being lent to radical novices, particularly in the Northeast.[20] The cause might be that entering the monkhood was the cheapest way for lower class people to get an education, especially in the rural areas. Presumably, literate monks from lower-class backgrounds might be especially susceptible to radical leftist ideas. Particularly interesting was the TCP's ill-fated attempt to organize some Buddhist monks, who were readers of the radical press, into a peace committee and a monkish branch of the Ongkan Thai Koochat or Tho.Ko.Cho. (Thai National Liberation Organization, a communist front organization of peasants focused in the Northeast, set up by the TCP at the end of 1949).[21] The episode ended disastrously with some of the monks conscientiously adhering to the Buddhist precept against lying on the witness stand![22] The upshot was that, owing to their peculiar reading tastes, school teachers and Buddhist monks figured prominently alongside students, writers, and journalists among suspected communists rounded up by police in the 1952 and 1958 crackdowns on the leftist opposition.[23]

However, if geographical distance is also taken into consideration, the above-mentioned estimate of possible readership of the radical press might still be grossly inflated. For readers' place of residence in the country considerably affected their access to the radical press, with those in the capital city of Bangkok having far greater, safer, and convenient access to the readily available radical press than their counterparts in the provinces, who usually had to subscribe by mail. Among the hazards and hindrances encountered by provincial readers were higher prices (generally by about 20 percent), inadequate distribution, and unreliable provincial sales agents, especially for the weekly newspaper *Mahachon*, the *Aksornsarn* magazine, and the *Karnmuang Weekly*. Arbitrary censorship by conservative local public librarians saw the banning of *Aksornsarn* in Ratchaburi's public library; and Ubon Ratchathani and Nakhon Si Thammarat readers' subscriptions and mail orders prompted suspicion, interrogation, house search, and arrest by local and Special Branch police.[24]

Being the center of the nation's publishing business, journalism, education, bureaucracy, and politics, Bangkok was by far the most literate and best educated city in the country. In 1947, of the 885,068 Bangkokians aged ten years and above, 601,172 or 67.9 percent were members of the reading class, while the national average was 53.7 percent. In addition, all universities, as well as the majority and the best of pre-university schools and crammers in Thailand, were located in Bangkok.[25] The capital city was thus a natural home to the radical press' "core readership," namely pre-university and university students and graduates, both domestic and foreign, who in all numbered approximately 36,000 or roughly 0.3 percent of the whole population aged ten years and above in 1947. An allowance should also be made, however, for the practice of collective "reading aloud," reportedly fairly common among organized workers, which could raise the number of the radical press' actual audience to several times that of their core readers.[26]

The Pull of International Communism

But why would these 36,000 or so "core readers" be so interested in Marxism-communism or, more precisely, the Thaified version of it, as to spend their money and reading time on radical printed commodities? The answers are manifold. Their demand for a new, comprehensive, militant political discourse was generated by various strands of socio-economic and politico-cultural development in Thailand and the world after the war. Across broad segments of the Thai population, there was great fascination for and curiosity about the emerging communist camp and particularly the apparently powerful ideology and wonderful doctrine that inspired and guided it. Actually, this should have come as no surprise, for the Second World War had greatly shifted the global balance of power in favor of the Soviet Union and remarkably altered its international image and reputation. Having heroically resisted and forcefully vanquished the bulk of Hitler's Wehrmacht, the Soviet Union emerged triumphantly from the war as the dominant power in Eastern Europe and the second most powerful country in the world; it would soon become an atomic power in its own right, obviously an indispensable pillar of global (in)security. Formerly shunned and boycotted by Thai absolute monarchs as a subversive pariah in the world community,[27] it now sat in the Security Council of the United Nations in judgment over Thailand's application for U.N. membership, which it finally approved in exchange for Thailand's abrogation of the Anti-Communist Act in 1946 and the establishment of a Soviet legation in Bangkok in 1948.[28] The extent of the Soviet cultural presence in Thailand and the Thai public's interest in it during that time are attested to by the substantial number of Soviet books in English available in certain Bangkok bookstores and the many Soviet films shown in Bangkok movie theaters (especially the Chinese Saiboothai Theater and the Nakhornsanuk Plaza), bearing such titles as "Queen of Lizards," "Bright Road," "Youth Sports," "Peter the Great," "The Napoleonic War," "Paradise of Love," "God of Horses," "The Fall of Berlin," and "The Third Offensive."[29] According to one leftist reviewer, they compared favorably with their Hollywood counterparts in attracting a Thai audience. Moreover, when, during their showings, Uncle Joe appeared on the screen, he was allegedly welcomed with applause and the murmuring of his name all over the theater![30] A more serious reason for the Thai public's new interest in the USSR might have been hit upon by the owner/editor of a bourgeois leftist newspaper trying to justify the continuous barrage of articles on the Soviet Union the paper had been running.[31] He explained that the USSR, despite the fact that it was a major player in post-war world politics, was still "a mystery." The paper thus took it as a duty to report on this mysterious country, by no means out of sympathy for communism, but in order to provide its readers with the information necessary to analyze world politics.[32]

Much nearer in terms of geography, social conditions, and ethnicity, and hence even more interesting and appealing to the Thai public, was the communist revolution in China. About 11 percent of the total population and 45.7 percent of Bangkokians in the early 1950s were of Chinese descent, and the politics within these Chinese communities were still predominantly China-oriented and concerned with such issues as which Chinese national flag, the Communist or the Nationalist, to fly on Double Tenth.[33] Thus the rapid growth and continuing success of the Chinese Communist Party could not but be a great attraction for them and one with potentially grave consequences for Thai politics, especially when the CCP's experiences and lessons were considered "universal" and therefore reproducible outside China.[34] The catastrophic drama of rampant hyperinflation in the post-war Kuomintang-mismanaged economy and the irresistible southward advance of the Chinese People's Liberation Army at the average rate of one major city per month from late 1948 unfolded daily on the pages of contemporary Thai newspapers, capturing the interest and firing the imagination not only of Chinese but also Thai audiences.[35] Anticipating the impending victory of its Chinese comrades, the TCP dispatched a message to the CCP in August 1949, expressing its hope that the liberation movements in Southeast Asia would receive support from China under communist rule. And upon the CCP victory in October 1949, congratulation messages were sent to the new regime by the Chinese Workers Department of the Bangkok Labor Union and the Central Labor Union, as well as by various Chinese immigrants' associations.[36] These were soon followed by the pilgrimages of several Chinese community leaders, including a loyalty mission to Peking.[37] Among the attentive Thai readers of the radical press who sought a comprehensive understanding and theoretical interpretation of "this very great change" were, for example, Thaweep Voradilok, a rising young poet, and many other Thammasat students.[38] The Chinese Communist Revolution also inspired Atsani Phonlajan (alias Intharayut, Naiphi, or Specter), a talented poet of the TCP, to compose two *khloong* poems of eulogy to the CCP.[39] Nor was its influence limited to the Thai radicals; the revolution so saddened Phrakhroo Naphisi, a merciful and internationalist Buddhist monk of the Khirimekkhalaram School, Sarika Hill Falls Village, Nakhon Nayok, that the Reverend announced his wish to travel there to accomplish through his good Buddhist offices what American ambassador Patrick Hurley and General George Marshall had repeatedly failed to do—mediate an end to the internecine Chinese war.[40]

Chinese Communism also affected Thai politics in a more direct and tangible way, as reflected in the personal fortunes of the two top Thai political figures of the decade 1947–1957, who found themselves temporarily on opposite sides of the Cold War barricade. Field Marshal Phibunsongkhram, disgraced after the war as "Siam's Number One Quisling" and military dictator,[41] managed to stage a political comeback in March 1947 and work his way back to the premiership in April 1948, partly by playing on the fear and loathing of Chinese Communism among Kuomintang Chinese businessmen in Thailand.[42] Senior Statesman Pridi Banomyong, chased out of the country following the military coup led nominally by Phibun on November 8, 1947, and failing in his attempted counter-coup in the Royal Palace Rebellion of February 26, 1949, ended up heading an unofficial Thai delegation, the only foreign one aside from that of the Soviet Union, to the inauguration ceremony of the People's Republic of China on October 1, 1949. Pridi remained in exile in China with his family and dwindling entourage for another twenty-one years and from there stirred Thai politics with his occasional radio-broadcast statements, open letters, and philosophical treatises.[43]

Eventually, the fascination for Communist Russia and China among Thai readers found its most startling public manifestation in a series of well-publicized pilgrimages to both wonderlands behind the iron and bamboo curtains made by throngs of well-known Thais, at risk of arrest upon return, during the short period of political liberalization from 1955 to 1958. Five left-leaning politicians—Thep Chotnuchit (Setthakorn [Economist Party] MP for Si Sa Ket), Khlaeo Norapati (Setthakorn MP for Khon Kaen), Thim Phooriphat (Setthakorn MP for Ubon Ratchathani), Sawang Trachoo (Setthakorn Party), and Praphas Khongsamai (Liberal Democrat MP for Trang)—visited the PRC with four journalists and three merchants in early 1956. They were put in jail by Police General Phao Sriyanond upon their return.[44]

Many journalists traveled to the USSR—Kulap Saipradit, Utthorn Phonlakul, Thanong Satthathip, Sanit Ekkachai, Samut Surakkhaka, Udom Sisuwan, and Chat Bunyasirichai; and to the PRC—Kulap Saipradit, Suchat Phoomborirak, Chaloem Khlainag, Thongbai Thongpao, Karuna Kusalasai, Issara Amantakul, Wet Buranakij, Luan Pannoi, Prayoon Julphamorn, Jaroen Kanokrat, and Ari Suchatoe.[45] The visits of writers like Kulap Saipradit, Suwat Voradilok, and Thawan Voradilok had direct literary results.[46]

Two famous singers, Phensri Phumchoosri and Suthep Wongkamhaeng, were among a troupe of forty-eight Thai performing artists who "sneaked" into China in April 1957, performed there for two months, and returned to Thailand in August.[47] In September 1957, movie producer "Phaen Pracha" took part in the Asian Film Week in Peking, where a Thai film was shown.[48] In August and September 1958, Thae Prakatwutthisan, a producer, and Phairaj Kasiwat, a famous cameraman, were observers at an Afro-Asian film festival in Tashkent, Republic of Uzbekistan, during the screening of another Thai movie, "Song phinong" (Two brothers).[49] And the Daeng Leuang (Red-Yellow) basketball team, headed by Adul Phamaranond, went to play in China in early 1957.[50]

Labor leaders Thongyoi Palkawong (Sawmill Union), Prakob Toelaklam (Kammakorn [Worker] Party), Suwit Niamsa (Sixteen-Unit Workers), Thongbai Thiangsoongnoen (Rice Mill Union), San Ungtrakul (Wat Soithong Thread-Spinning Factory Union), Khajorn Wajjanadilok (Private School Teachers Union), Sompong Jitjinda (Construction Labour Union), and two other unnamed leaders were invited to attend the 1957 May Day celebration in China.[51] With official permission and pocket-money from Prime Minister Phibun himself, the following student activists traveled to Moscow in 1957 to attend the Sixth International Youth and Students' Festival for Peace and Friendship and visited both the PRC and North Vietnam on their way back:

Suwit Phadoemchit, Anukul Rattanaphan, Bunsin Jaturaphreug, and Wijit Siriroj from Thammasat University; Phasom Pechjamras from Kasetsart University; Niphon Masawisut from Chulalongkorn University; and Kamjorn Sukphongsri from the Fine Arts University.[52]

And four monks—Phra Maha Sangwian Miphaophong (alias Tejatharo Bhikkhu), Phra Maha Manas Phuanglamjiak (alias Jittathamo Bhikkhu), Phra Maha Nakhorn Phayungyat (alias Khemapali Bhikkhu), and Phra Maha Ophas Wianglek (alias Ophaso Bhikkhu)—were invited by the Chinese Communist government to visit China on a religious mission in 1957 or B.E. 2500 (traditionally held to be the Mid-Buddhist Era Year). After their return to Thailand, the first three were arrested, defrocked, and jailed on communist charges, while Ophas, expecting arrest on his arrival home, decided instead to go to Laos, where he disrobed and became an internationalist revolutionary à la Che Guevara.[53]

But preceding all these people's diplomats was a secret diplomatic mission sent to China by Prime Minister Phibun and Field Marshal Phin as early as December 1955.[54] In return, during 1957, Peking expressed growing approval of the Phibunsongkhram government and a Soviet troupe visited and gave a performance in Bangkok.[55] Meanwhile, many communists and pro-Pridi leftists who had gone into exile in China also took this opportunity to come back to Thailand and, in some cases, resume their political activities either openly or covertly (for example, Jaroen Wanngam, Phin Bua-on, Phayome Julanond, Prasert Sapsunthorn, Chiab Chaisong or Amphunan, Sanguan Tularak, Suri Thongwanich, and Nongyao or Nongphot Praphasathit).[56]

Together with the rise of the communist camp, the post-war world saw the decline of the European powers, which after devastation and/or defeat in the war, lost much of their capacity and determination to govern their colonies. Especially in Southeast Asia, where less than four years of Japanese "liberation"-cum-occupation provided colonial peoples with both inspiration and opportunity for some degree of self-government, the western colonial masters' attempts to re-impose their rule met with stiff resistance everywhere. With a wave of anti-colonial nationalism sweeping through the region, Thailand saw the rise of national liberation or revolutionary movements against the colonial and/or indigenous authorities in one neighboring country after another, usually under the direct leadership, domination, or strong influence of communist or radical leftist parties. In Vietnam, the communist-led Viet Minh (Vietnamese Independence Brotherhood League) fought a brilliant and heroic people's war against the French and the puppet State of Vietnam from 1946 to 1954, culminating in the spectacular fall of Dienbienphu in May 1954.[57] In Laos, the French and the French-installed Kingdom of Laos were resisted first by the nationalist Lao Issara (Free Lao) and then by the communist-dominated Pathet Lao (Lao Nation) from 1946 to 1954; the joint military offensive between the latter and the Viet Minh resulted in the liberation of Sam Neua and Phong Saly in late 1953.[58] In Cambodia, Khmer Issarak (Khmer Independence) guerrilla fighters battled the French and the Sihanouk government from 1946 to 1954, bringing more than half the countryside under its control in 1953.[59] In Burma, "Red Flag" and, two years later, "White Flag" communists as well as ethnic minorities rebelled against the British and then the AFPFL (Anti-Fascist People's Freedom League) government from 1946 onwards, leaving only a few urban centers under government control by the end of 1948.[60] In Malaya, the communist-led Malayan Races Liberation Army (MRLA) launched an armed insurrection against the British and then the Alliance government beginning in 1948, ushering in a twelve-year period of "Emergency" rule in the country.[61] In Indonesia, the Revolution that lasted from 1945 to 1949, and especially the concomitant militant and spontaneous *pemuda* (youth) mass movement in Java and Sumatra, helped bring about the end of Dutch colonial rule, challenging and sometimes destroying traditional local elites in the process. And despite the debacle of the communist Madiun Rebellion of 1948, the PKI (Communist Party of Indonesia) made a remarkable recovery and enjoyed rapid growth in the 1950s, becoming the second largest communist party in Asia after the CCP, with a membership of at least three million.[62] Finally, in the Philippines, the communist-led HMB (People's Liberation Army), which had begun in 1946 as spontaneous, armed self-defense by former Hukbalahap (People's Anti-Japanese Army) peasant members against the U.S.-supported government and the landlords' violent repression, raged from 1948 until 1956, involving up to fifteen thousand guerrilla fighters at its peak in 1951.[63]

So breathtaking and so close to home, these communist-related developments, particularly those in Indochina, must have furnished spectacular reading for the Thai public, not to mention for Laotian majorities and Vietnamese and Khmer minorities in Isan or the Northeast of Thailand, who shared more culturally with the communities on the other side of the Mekong River than with the generally more affluent and powerful Central-Thai-speaking population of the central plains of the Chaophraya River.[64] Besides, Thailand was no passive spectator to all this but was increasingly drawn in as an active participant, becoming in turn a base of revolutionary support and solidarity for Southeast Asian national liberation movements under the Pridi and Thawan regimes, and then one of colonial reaction and repression under the second Phibunsongkhram regime.

Thus, under the internationally far-sighted if domestically inopportune auspices of Pridi, sanctuary, official recognition, and a substantial number of

Free Thai (originally Allied) firearms were provided to the Vietnamese, Laotian, and Cambodian nationalist movements, communist and non-communist alike. For instance, among the then or subsequently well-known Southeast Asian freedom-fighters who took refuge or resided in Thailand at the time were Prince Phetsarath and Prince Souvanna Phouma of the Lao Issara Movement and Son Ngoc Minh and Long Reth (Nuon Chea) of the Khmer Issarak Movement. The (first) Khmer Issarak Committee and its successor, the Committee of National Union (Khana Ruam Chat or Ko.Ro.Cho.), both of which had been manipulated and dominated by the Thais, were also based in Bangkok.[65] A Southeast Asian delegation of the newly founded Democratic Republic of Vietnam (DRV) was allowed to open in Bangkok in early 1946 and, in September of the following year, the Thawan government recognized a "Free Cambodian Government" in exile.[66]

Covert Thai military cooperation and supplies were also extended to these nationalist movements. Reportedly, a certain Bang-i Forest in Isan near the Cambodian border was the gathering place of three hundred Khmer Issarak guerrillas co-commanded by Son Ngoc Minh. On August 7, 1946, facilitated by Thailand, they briefly seized the city of Siemreap and killed seven French officers.[67] And in response to solicitation by "Vietnamese patriots," Pridi arranged for a freight train loaded with weapons and a barge carrying twenty tons of carbines to be delivered to the Viet Minh, for which Ho Chi Minh wrote him a thankful letter and named the two Vietnamese battalions armed with these Free Thai weapons the "Siamese Battalions." Tiang Sirikhan, a leading Isan MP and one of Pridi's close aides, was quoted as saying that he was involved in supplying arms to the Viet Minh. But the Thai authorities were not always open-handed internationalist philanthropists and could be good businessmen when they chose to be. It should be noted that Thailand was then considered the best place to buy bootleg weapons in the region and was much frequented by purchasing agents of the nationalist insurgent movements of neighboring countries.[68]

Pridi's effort led eventually to the founding of the Southeast Asian League, his own brainchild, a regional organization for the co-ordination of the independent states and/or nationalist movements of Thailand, Vietnam, Laos, Cambodia, Burma, Malaya, Indonesia, and the Philippines, in Bangkok in September 1947. Significantly, the League's leadership comprised Tiang Sirikhan as president (pro-Pridi, ex-Free Thai, ethnic Laotian, leftist former cabinet minister, and Isan MP of the Sahachip Party), Tran Van Giau as vice-president (senior Vietnamese communist leader), Prince Souphanouvong as secretary-general (chief of staff of the Lao Issara army and future Pathet Lao leader), Thawin Udon as public relations officer (pro-Pridi, ex-Free Thai, ethnic Laotian, leftist former cabinet minister, former Isan MP, and senator of the Sahachip Party), and Le Hi as treasurer (Vietnamese communist).[69]

The TCP was, of course, extremely enthusiastic about this mission of "proletarian internationalism" in support of fraternal revolutionary movements and parties in nearby lands. Its active support ranged from organizing a public rally (through the Bangkok Labor Union) to celebrate the founding of the Southeast Asian League and providing the League with wide publicity and coverage in its newspapers,[70] to setting up the Ongkan Thai Koochat or Tho.Ko.Cho. (Thai National Liberation Organization) in northeastern Thailand in preparation for a co-ordinated military operation with the Indochinese communists against both the French and American imperialists.[71] Moreover, hundreds of young ethnic Laotian and Khmer "Thais," fired with a strangely mixed imagination which might be called "ethnic interstate-nationalism" as against "class internationalism,"[72] had over the years left the Thai state to fight against the French colonials in and for the Indochinese nations, either on their own initiative or upon the urging of the TCP.[73] The influence the Indochinese nationalist cause had on the Thai public was reflected in the variety of people who became in one way or another Thai "internationalist fighters." They included communists (Phichit Dijai from Si Sa Ket in Vietnam and Laos, Phornchai Santawasi from Si Sa Ket in Laos, Maha Ophas Wianglek from Udon Thani in Laos, Long Reth from Thammasat University in Cambodia), political innocents (Lieutenant Thawan from Chumphorn in Vietnam), opportunistic mercenaries (Sergeant Dap Chhuon from the Thai Army in Cambodia), and pan-Thaists who wished to recover and retain control of Siemreap and Battambang, which the Phibunsongkhram government had seized from the French in November 1940 (the Aphaiwong family from Bangkok in Cambodia, Yat Hwaidi from Surin in Cambodia).[74]

In contrast, during his second term in office from 1948 to 1957, Prime Minister Field Marshal Phibunsongkhram, with a shrewd instinct for political survival and rather militaristic adventurism in international affairs, gradually committed Thailand to the anti-communist cause of the western capitalist nations in exchange for their political recognition and support, as well as military and economic aid and cooperation.[75] His government widely exchanged intelligence on alleged communist activities, knowledge of anti-communist propaganda techniques, and experience of anti-communist political measures with Laos,[76] South Vietnam,[77] Hong Kong,[78] Taiwan,[79] and the Philippines.[80] He cooperated with the British to suppress the communist MRLA in Malaya and a large-scale Muslim rebellion in southern Thailand in 1948/49.[81] He condoned the Dutch "Police Action" against the young

Indonesian Republic when it attacked Yogyakarta in 1948.[82] And he recognized the three French-supported puppet regimes in Indochina.

At home, Phibun publicly invited the United States to set up military bases and station troops in Thailand in March 1950,[83] concluding a military assistance agreement in October.[84] He imposed on the Vietnamese community new and tighter restrictions on movement and residence, harassing and arbitrarily arresting many of its members in 1950/51.[85] He expelled Nguyen Duc Quy, president of the DRV's Southeast Asian delegation in Bangkok and effectively shut down the delegation in late 1951.[86] And he built strategic highways throughout the Northeast to prepare for joint military intervention with western powers in the Indochinese war against the national liberation movements.[87] Regionally, Phibun despatched four thousand infantrymen and an unspecified number of ancillary naval and air forces, as well as forty thousand tons of rice, to the United Nations forces fighting the Korean War in 1950,[88] set up a glaringly interventionist government committee called Khana Kammakan Chuaileua Prathet Pheuanban Totan Latthi Khommunit (Committee to Help Neighboring Countries Resist Communism) in December 1953,[89] and co-founded the multilateral SEATO (Southeast Asia Treaty Organization) in September 1954 as part of U.S. global strategy to contain the spread of communism.[90] Given such varied and deep involvements in the communist-nationalist affairs of her neighbors, whether for or against, interest in communism and demand for a radical press in Thailand could not but be unusually high.

The Push of Domestic Socio-Economic Crisis

Aside from international causes, there were ample domestic factors in the aftermath of the war that contributed to the Thai reading public's interest in the radical press. The immediate post-war years were a time of grave economic hardship, serious social problems, and, extending throughout the following decade, severe and often violent political strife and instability. The wartime issuance of hundreds of millions of yellowish "Kongtek" baht notes[91] to finance increasing government budget deficits[92] and, against yen credit, to underwrite an export surplus vis-à-vis Japan and local expenditures of Japanese troops,[93] had left over two billion baht notes in circulation, practically without cover from precious metals and foreign exchange. This combined with an acute shortage of manufactured goods both for investment [94] and consumption [95] to make inflation rampant after the war. And while prices of staple foodstuffs and other essential items soared as high as ten to fifteen times their pre-war levels,[96] pushing the overall cost of living up over 1000 percent (see Table 4-2), incomes lagged far behind, including the salaries of minor and senior government officials, even after raises of 650 percent and 150 percent, respectively, in 1946.[97]

If people earning 700–800 baht per month, who had previously been considered among "the very-high income group," found themselves short of money,[98] undoubtedly clerks and minor officials earning a meagre 30–60 baht per month simply could not survive on their salary when food alone for one person cost 10–15 baht per day.[99] The shortage of rice, the basic Thai staple, was especially acute because of steady population increase,[100] occasional declines in rice production due to natural disasters,[101] Thailand's obligation to export 600,000 tons of rice to the British at a low fixed price,[102] and widespread, lucrative smuggling of rice out of the country in response to strong foreign demand and a much higher price on the world market.[103] The upshot was that after the war, there was often less rice available on the domestic market than previously (see Table 4-3) resulting in inflated prices,[104] shortages,[105] rationing,[106] and queues for rice purchase, historically a potent sign in rice-rich Thailand that things were going terribly wrong.[107]

Such dire economic conditions, coupled with the effects of social uprootedness and easy acquisition of arms through the black market, made the immediate post-war period the heyday of the "Seua," literally "tiger," a prefix used before the names of notorious bandits to denote their personal attributes of ferocity, cunningness, daringness, and cruelty. Banditry, robbery, petty crime, and piracy abounded, from which not even the Royal Palace or a

Table 4-2

Estimated Cost of Living and Purchasing Power of the Baht, 1938–1947

YEAR	COST OF LIVING	(1938 = 100) BAHT PURCHASING POWER
1938	100.00	100.00
1939	102.60	97.47
1940	112.70	88.73
1941	132.90	75.24
1942	175.99	56.50
1943	221.92	45.06
1944	466.89	21.42
1945	904.66	11.05
1946	1,071.57	9.33
1947	1,247.11	8.02

Source: Thai government statistics cited in Thongchai, "Latthi khommunit," 246–247.

general's house were secure.[108] Portrayed and romanticized in two well-known contemporary popular novels, *Seua Dam* and *Seua Bai* by Po. Intharapalit, the Seuas performed many legendary exploits, including a spectacular battle in Ratchaburi between three hundred of them and two hundred police in February 1947. The police authorities tried to cope with this problem in various ways, including setting up a specially trained and well-equipped five-hundred-strong Special Crime Suppression Squad and distributing one hundred Thompson sub-machine guns to local authorities in Seua-ridden provinces. They even called on the author of the two "Seua" novels to moderate the feats of his protagonists, who so outmaneuvered, outfought, and outshone their police opponents that their real counterparts-cum-readers might be inspired to imitate them.[109] These measures might have worked better to stop the crime wave but for the fact that many people in uniform, both khaki and green, were themselves breaking the law. For instance, the Thai police on the Siam-Burma railroad were so busy looting that the British had to arm Japanese troops to guard the property.[110] As for the military, a Lieutenant General Jira Wichitsongkhram commented in April 1947 that "banditry is like a contagious disease which spreads from the outside into the military ranks."[111]

As a matter of fact, this was only to be expected. Reportedly, even lowly hawkers and street vendors earned many times more than respectable second-grade government officials, leaving the latter, be they military, police or civilian, few alternatives to financially maintain their traditional dignity and lifestyle as "royal servants." They and their family members could either make do with odd jobs and the sale of personal valuables, or make good with *sengli* (Teochiu for "business," here denoting official corruption and abuse of power for personal gain).[112] Notorious cases of official *sengli* became so ubiquitous

Table 4-3
Annual Rice Output, Export, and Domestic Supply, 1946–1950

Year	Rice Output	Rice Export	(in million tons) Rice Supply
1946	2.86	0.09	2.77
1947	3.39	0.78	2.61
1948	4.22	0.81	3.41
1949	4.12*	1.21	2.91
1950	4.18*	1.49	2.69

* The official figures of rice export have been doubled to account for estimated smuggled rice.
Source: Calculated from data in Prachoom, "Thailand," 131, 132.

and commonplace, and the reportage and complaints about them in the press so frequent and voluminous, that "it sounds as if all eighteen million Thais were embezzlers."[113] Under the long-standing system of institutionalized official *sengli* built by the People's Party regime since the late 1930s, in which state enterprises, government-owned trading corporations, privileged private banks, and companies were created with the help of certain Chinese business groups to provide political rewards and economic bases for members and supporters of the ruling party,[114] the dividing line between official and unofficial *sengli* was not very firm to begin with, and lower officials were undoubtedly tempted to cross that line by the inglorious example of their superiors.[115] Alleged and/or proven perpetrators of (un)official *sengli* included politicians and bureaucrats of almost all ranks, branches, categories, and localities, who infested the cabinet, the House of Representatives, the Senate, the ruling parties, the army and police, the Royal Crown Property Bureau, the Bank of Thailand, the Department of Railway, the Food Organization, the Tobacco Factory, the Government Purchasing Bureau, Siriraj Hospital, and many provincial administrations.

The fact that corrupt politicians seemed all too willing to "sell" themselves for just a few hundred thousand baht prompted a political commentator to hypothesize anxiously that should any secret organization or foreign nation wish to buy Thailand and her democratic system, it could do so easily with 600 million baht—500 million to pay the legislators and the rest to pay the ministers.[116] A rather far-fetched but, come to think of it, actually practicable and fairly economical idea.[117]

The glaring socio-economic distress, anomie, and inequality of the time was succinctly described by a liberal columnist in the following manner—the middle and lower classes were so impoverished and needy that they had to cheat, steal, rob, and sell their bodies just to survive, while high society enjoyed a lavish life-style, evaded taxes, hoarded commodities, gave birthday parties, and danced in night-clubs.[118] Under these conditions, an oppositional discourse geared toward economic-based and class-oriented explanation, as propagated then by the radical press, had a special attraction. It seemed to make sense of the bewildering post-war socio-economic chaos and provided its readers a ready set of verbal tools to conceptualize their plight and articulate their discontent and resistance—*chonchan* (class), *naithun* (capitalists), *khoodrid* (exploit), and *suankoen* (surplus). The most crucial point, though, was that it suggested a possible political solution to all these and other social problems, a real and yet Uttarakuru-like, becoming-less-distant and yet mysteriously appealing, alternative system of government which most Thai people had still had little chance to know about, let alone be disillusioned with—communism.

5

Marxism as Commodity:
Precipitating Demand

"Maybe this is what the big nobs were blowing about at election time.
What did they say, Professor? Cracy, cracy something."

"Democracy, nut! Not cracy," Kerhn said severely, "They call it a
democratic coup d'état, see. You have to have a lot of coups d'état.
Otherwise it isn't democracy."

Khamsing Srinawk (Lao Khamhawm), "The Politician"[1]

The treasure-hunters must consist of two kinds of people—one is the
laboring diggers who are certainly the proletariat and the other is the
map-decipherers and magicians responsible for driving off those
treasure-guarding cobras and Grandpa Soem—these are the students.
As the diggers must follow the map-decipherers in the map-guided
treasure-hunt, so the proletariat must follow the directing and self-
sacrificing students in the search for the bliss of Uttarakuru. And if the
students are in any danger, the proletariat must try their best to save
them. When this is done, heaven on earth will be right before us all.

Sri-Intharayut (Atsani Phonlajan)[2]

Political Violence and Contested Legitimacy

Even though the country's economy began to improve in 1947/48 and, a couple
of years later, was given a boost by the Korean War boom,[3] its domestic politics
took a violent turn and deteriorated steadily during much of the decade.
Signalled by the mysterious death by gunshot of King Rama VIII in his palace
bed on June 9, 1946, and followed by a coup d'état by retired and active middle-
ranking army officers calling themselves Khana Ratthaprahan (the Coup
Group), with Field Marshal Plaek Phibunsongkhram as figurehead, on
November 8, 1947, modern Thai politics entered a period of transition from the
authoritarian constitutionalism of the People's Party (1932–1947) to the military

absolutism of the Khana Patiwat (Revolutionary Group) under Field Marshal Sarit Thanarat and Thanom Kittikachorn (1958–1973).[4] This decade-long transition (1947–1958) was characterized most notably by the unprecedentedly routine use of force to solve political conflict, especially within the ruling circles, and the decline and/or loss of legitimacy of each alternative system of government the country had hitherto experienced.[5] It meant, in Gramscian parlance, that the post-1932 constitutionalist political order based on an anti-royalist, nationalist bloc under People's Party hegemony and maintained by the purged, hence politically loyal, active armed forces and police had essentially, if not formally, come to an end. That historic bloc was shattered by drastic political division, realignment, and rapprochement during the war, with the once dominant army losing political clout to and deeply estranged from the new civilian political leadership.[6] Thus, the ensuing political violence and legitimacy crisis of hitherto systems of government were primarily symptoms of an organic crisis of the state in which coercion was used in compensation for the inability of any one political group to exercise leadership by consent and of a failure to reach a consensus on the basic premises concerning the continuation of the constitutionalist order.

If a longer view is taken of the pattern of modern Thai state power and apparatus after 1932, the following observations can be made. Two of the most crucial political innovations introduced by the People's Party upon the 1932 overthrow of absolute monarchy were the use of regular armed forces to effect political change and the attempt to establish the principle of rule of law over and above absolutist personal rule. These two innovations often conflicted with one another but it was to the People's Party's credit that most of its members maintained a workable balance between the two during the Party's fifteen-year rule, making state coercion largely legal-constitutional and keeping Prime Minister Field Marshal Phibun's autocratic inclination in check. (He was, after all, deposed by constitutional means by the National Assembly.) However, these political legacies were increasingly eroded and dismantled by the Coup Group during the transitional period when state power was exercised more and more through unlawful coercion and became based less and less on contractual consent (the constitution), while the rule of law was selectively and arbitrarily applied along personal and clique patronage lines or ignored altogether. These developments were accompanied by an overgrowth and strengthening of the state security apparatus (especially the army, air force, and police), coupled with a severe weakening and instability of representative institutions such as parliament and the political parties. Looked at in this light, Sarit's "revolutionary regime" was therefore both a formalization and extension of the pre-existing informal practices and limited tendencies of the transitional period, that is, from unlawful to dictator-authorized coercion, expanded from within the ruling circles to among the people at large. So developed, such a regime would later prove strong enough in its repressive capacity to contain rural insurgency but too weak in its political legitimacy to appease or win over urban mass demonstrators.

Political violence in the post-war decade took two major forms: private murders of personal political opponents within the ruling circles by statepower holders[7] and armed putsches. The growth and spread of political violence was caused by the ready availability of leftover firearms from the war and easy access to them through both official and black market channels. Of particular relevance were the substantial number of firearms delivered by the Allies for anti-Japanese purposes near the end of the war, which, in the possession of the Free Thai Movement, facilitated its emergence as a rival to the Royal Thai Army.[8]

A relatively small national resistance movement in a country of over seventeen million people, the eight-thousand-strong Free Thai Movement did little actual fighting against Japanese troops in Thailand, though it greatly assisted the Allies in the underground subsidiary tasks of intelligence gathering, communication and transportation, hiding and helping Allied secret service officials, rescuing and protecting Allied POWs and nationals, and sabotaging Japanese war supplies and installations.[9] Nevertheless, the Free Thais were generally credited with saving the nation from defeated country status and were officially honored by being called to parade triumphantly before the regent, cabinet, and Supreme Allied Commander of Southeast Asia in the center of Bangkok on September 25, 1945, and being awarded a "Santi Mala" (Flower of Peace) medal by the National Assembly on March 12, 1946.[10] And though the Movement was repeatedly declared disbanded after the war by Pridi (its head) as a gesture of patriotic selflessness and good faith towards other political groups and parties, its residual personal ties and organizational network continued to function informally and loosely as an alternative to the much weakened monarchy and split People's Party as a base for political association and source of political loyalty. Amid reports of frequent Free Thai get-togethers, a conservative opposition newspaper alleged in December 1946 that the Movement was being revived and reorganized. These activities, as well as the political rise of some former Free Thais in the Pridi-Thawan governments, provided grounds for the Phibun group's opportunistic grumbles about the political eclipse of the People's Party.[11]

Aside from political camaraderie, former Free Thai leaders could provide one another with financial and military resources in times of need as they had at their disposal the remains of the Free Thai wartime coffers and arsenal supplied to them by the Allies during the war. Free Thai wartime expenses amounted to around eight million baht, including nearly $50,000 provided by the United

States government. A Special Committee appointed by the National Assembly to investigate Free Thai finances concluded in May 1946 that the money had been fully accounted for. However, it appeared that not only were election campaigns of MP candidates from the two Free Thai-related political parties (Sahachip and Naeo Ratthathammanoon)[12] financed with loans from Pridi-controlled commercial banks, but that ten former Free Thai leaders had sums totaling more than twenty million baht in their personal accounts at these two banks.[13]

The Allied arms supply began to flow to the Free Thai Movement only after April 1945, quite near the end of the war.[14] Tiang Sirikhan, a wartime Free Thai Isan leader, was quoted as saying that the Allies had furnished the Free Thais with enough firearms to equip eight army battalions but with little ammunition. A quarter of these firearms were later given to the two Viet Minh "Siamese Battalions," while Free Thai-affiliated army units took another part, enough to equip several battalions. The rest remained in the possession of various former Free Thai leaders around the country.[15] These formidable stores of weapons, which, according to a U.S. diplomatic observer, amounted to "a private arsenal for his [Pridi's] private army,"[16] were located at Thammasat University,[17] the Military Police Headquarters,[18] the Special Branch Police,[19] and the houses and/or hiding-places of several Isan MPs and other Free Thais.[20] Their semi-public, semi-private status and absolute sanctity were de facto prescribed by the authority of Prime Minister Pridi himself, who, responding to persistent inquiries by opposition Prachathipat MPs in March and April 1946, rejected outright their demand for a parliamentary investigation into the Free Thai arsenals as "irrelevant" and questioned the purity of their motives.[21] In one especially revealing incident on August 3, 1947, not even the presence of the director general of the Police Department, nor the written permit of the minister of defense could open the gate of the Military Police Headquarters for a police search due to the existence of a Free Thai arsenal therein. The consequences of that confrontation were the resignation of the police chief, his replacement by the Free Thai military police commander, and a public admission by the minister of defense of the limit of his power.[22] It was this jealously guarded private political capital of Free Thai arms and men that the less scrupulous among Free Thai leaders abused to intimidate and terrorize their conservative political opponents and that Pridi later mobilized and squandered in his two abortive counter-coup attempts in late 1947 and February 1949.[23]

Undoubtedly, these post-war developments made the army, which had become accustomed to political dominance and social prestige under former Prime Minister General Phahon and Field Marshal Phibun, feel unappreciated, slighted, and increasingly restive, for it was in effect deprived by the civilian Free Thai governments[24] of the basic resources, security, and prerogatives it once enjoyed. Firstly, not only did it lose political power to new civilian power centers such as the Free Thai Movement and various political parties, but it also found itself constitutionally excluded from political office altogether by the new Constitution of 1946, which barred active military officers and active government officials from serving in the cabinet, Senate, and House of Representatives.[25] The Ministry of Defense under the Pridi government explicitly reinforced the ban, ordering soldiers to stay clear of any political association, organization, party, or electioneering.[26]

Secondly, the military's established legal monopoly of war weaponry was brazenly broken by the Free Thais, who were widely condemned as "arms-holders for private interests outside the National Army." And while the Free Thais were brandishing brand-new, modern, American-made weapons, the army found its own stock of arms old and obsolete by contrast. The army's subsequent request for these modern weapons was flatly rejected on the grounds that the Allies had lent them to the Movement on the condition that they not fall into army hands.[27]

Thirdly, the left wing of the Free Thai Movement—socialist followers of Pridi and the Isan MPs, who together formed the core of the ruling coalition Sahachip Party—advocated reducing the role of the army, cutting its budget, and diminishing its size to something more appropriate for a small country like Thailand. Sanguan Tularak, an appointed member of the National Assembly and Sahachip leader, stated in parliamentary debate on February 7, 1946, that:

We should know well that now people fight one another with atomics [sic]. Our country cannot build an atomic [sic] therefore the military are there to help the police maintain internal order only. [28]

Even though other Free Thai factions disagreed with this extremist policy and the civilian Free Thai governments never adopted it explicitly, the end of the war and resultant budgetary squeeze led perforce to the demobilization of a large number of army soldiers.[29] For instance, during the six-month period from October 1945 to March 1946, two army divisions, four infantry regiments, four artillery battalions, two machine gun battalions, eight infantry battalions, and one cavalry battalion were disbanded.[30] Especially hard hit was the army officer corps, one fifth of which was discharged from 1945 to 1947 (see Table 5-1), though the government did find other jobs for some of them.[31]

But sometimes the army's privations and dishonor were caused by the government's own careless mistakes and inept handling of military affairs, as when the expeditionary Kongthap Phayap (Northern Army), which had been dispatched by Phibun to take over parts of the Shan States in Burma in 1942, was ordered to withdraw and demobilize. Not only was proper military procedure not followed, but the troops were provided with neither adequate means of transportation nor food and other supplies. Thus, in stark contrast with the triumphant parade of and heroic welcome for the Free Thais, Northern Army soldiers were left to fend for themselves and make their own journey back by bus or on foot in abject destitution, bitter humiliation, and complete disarray. Losing discipline and morale and wearing tattered uniforms, many broke ranks and turned to looting to feed themselves, while others were robbed, attacked, wounded, or killed on their way home.[32] And while the Free Thais were proudly showing off their "Santi Mala" medals, the soldiers had shamefacedly to take off their "Chai Samoraphoom" (Victorious Battle) medals because the government had neglected to publish the awarding act in the Government Gazette.[33] These incidents left so deep a scar on the government-army relationship that any subsequent chance event could easily be used to provoke the army's resentment. Hence, the natural decay of the urns at Phra Sri Mahathat Temple, which exposed the cremated soldiers' bones to the elements, made the sensational headline "Dogs To Eat Soldiers' Bones" in the pro-Phibun opposition *Kiattisak* of October 2, 1946. This prompted another columnist to give the government a friendly warning that the soldiers who had gone to war in compliance with the order of the old-time politicians might not obey that of the new ones who paid them no care or attention.[34]

And, indeed, the army officer corps had a good professional reason for discontent because, fourthly, the army hierarchy was being invaded by political appointees. Right after Phibun's fall from power in July 1944, around forty Phibun men among the army top brass had been replaced by Pridi/Free Thai men, and since then transfers and promotions were based primarily on loyalty

Table 5-1
Discharged Army Officers, 1945–1947

RANK	TOTAL	DISCHARGED	PERCENT OF TOTAL
General	81	11	13.5
Colonel	1,035	303	29.3
Captain	3,845	1,455	37.8
Sergeant	2,577	730	28.7
Corporal	24,544	3,905	15.9
All ranks	32,082	6,404	19.96

Source: Based on Sornsak, *Khabuankan serithai*, 255.

to Pridi and the Free Thai Movement. This caused particular resentment among middle-ranking officers who found themselves commanded by men whose professional merit they doubted and whose political connections they resented. As in the case of the minister of defense's public submission to the authority of the Free Thai military police commander, which turned chain of command upside down, the army hierarchy was plagued with heterodox ideas put forward by leftist Pridi/Free Thai politicians, such as the proposal by Sanguan Tularak to replace the conventional military commander with a joint military-civilian commanding committee.[35]

Finally, adding insult to injury, the leftist Pridi/Free Thai politicians, including some cabinet ministers, subjected the army to a barrage of abuse that trampled on its traditional sense of military honor. The accusations included: "the army lost the war"; "the army could not maintain Thainess [national independence] and military expenses were simply wasted"; "in the army's fifty-year long existence, it could not accomplish what the Free Thai Movement did in two years"; "the army's greatest hero and wartime leader [Field Marshal Phibunsongkhram] is a war criminal"; "the army will one day become a dictator's instrument again"; and "there is no use in having an army anymore."[36] Lieutenant Colonel Krit Punnakan, then commander of the First Cavalry King's Bodyguard Battalion, commented bitterly that while post-war Bangkok was swarming with merry Free Thais, the disgraced regular soldiers were regarded as "millipedes and worms" by the public.[37] Colonel Sarit Thanarat, commander of a key army unit in Bangkok, complained: "The soldiers were badly humiliated. The Free Thais ordered their discharge in the worst manner. When the King passed away, I, as commander of the First Infantry King's Bodyguard Regiment, could not even enter the Royal Palace."[38] Another army officer, Major General Net Khemayothin, himself a Free Thai, neatly captured the army's general mood: "...[the soldiers] were humiliated by some Free Thais. The underlying sense of hurt turned to frustrated anger. With little prodding and invitation, they reacted."[39]

That "little prodding and invitation" was duly and zealously extended by pro-restoration members of the royalty, the conservative opposition Prachathipat Party,[40] the Phibunsongkhram group, and the Coup Group, both before and after the 1947 coup. The more pernicious of their allegations were that Pridi and his Free Thai gang were communists and that they committed regicide, plotted a revolt against the throne to set up a republic, and were hatching a separatist scheme to establish a Golden Peninsular Confederacy in the Northeast.[41] Far-fetched as these allegations might have sounded, once planted in the fertile soil of the military's "frustrated anger," they could easily nourish seeds of rebellion, as evident in the cases of several army officers who attributed their participation in the 1947 coup partly to the Pridi-Thawan governments' alleged involvement in, or at least failure to deal with, the communist peril and King Rama VIII's mysterious death.[42]

Consequently, the initial reaction of the army to the anti-Pridi/Free Thai smear campaign was to withdraw loyalty from its legal and constitutional clients—the current political regime and government. The 1946 Constitution was thus criticized as "not good, not correct" by Group Commander Luang Katsongkhram, a Coup Group top leader-to-be, who alone cast his vote against the Constitution in the National Assembly.[43] The civilian Free Thai governments were accused of being "detrimental to the nation's Armed Forces."[44] And taking part in a coup came to be regarded by some army officers as "our duty to defend the three institutions of nation, religion, and monarchy" from communism.[45] Especially after a gruelling, week-long censure debate in parliament, called by the opposition Prachathipat Party and broadcast live by radio from May 19 to 27, 1947, the coalition Thawan government, though still constitutionally secure with a parliamentary majority, had become so unpopular,[46] disreputable,[47] and disunited[48] that most Free Thai military and police officers were no longer willing to defend it from being deposed by unconstitutional means. This left only a few ardent Pridi men in the Special Branch Police and Ministry of Interior as well as some Isan MPs to worry about a coup and try helplessly to thwart or resist it. In the end, the army,[49] navy,[50] and air force commanders-in-chief,[51] and the director general of the police who was concurrently commander of the military police,[52] all received prior warning of the November 8, 1947 coup, but they either showed indifference, promised cooperation, indicated non-interference, or waited until it was too late to counter it.[53]

The alternative candidate for the army's clientship was none other than Field Marshal Phibun, who cautiously emerged from the political ghetto of war criminality with a newly found, anti-communist, royalist voice.[54] He perfectly timed his public announcement of political comeback and call for revision of anti-Phibun wartime historical records shortly after President Truman's "Block Communism" speech to the U.S. Congress in March 1947.[55] Phibun's shrewd political move was preceded by graffiti on an approach to the King Rama I Memorial Bridge—"We the Military Reserve Want the Field Marshal"[56]—and followed by pro-Phibun statements by Prachathipat leaders and retired senior army officers, "friendly chats" between Phibun and the latter, the establishment of a pro-Phibun, anti-communist, royalist Thammathipat Party, the publication of the politically compatible *Newsweek*, and the revival and public rallying of the militaristic wartime Ongkan Yuwachon Thahan (Military Youth Organization).[57]

These efforts paid off handsomely on November 9, 1947, as Phibun was quite literally carried back to power at the Ministry of Defense amidst loud applause and a hero's welcome by the Coup Group as its titular head, the supreme commander of Thailand, and the commander-in-chief of the army, in short, the army's new client.[58] The Coup Group did not assume direct governmental power right after the coup, but let its Prachathipat co-conspirators set up an "independent" government under Prime Minister Khuang Aphaiwong to lend a more acceptable civilian facade to the new regime and win international recognition. But there was never any doubt about who held the reins. As a contemporary situation report from the American Embassy in Bangkok put it: "...[any] surface act by Khuang's government would not materially alter the fact that the army is always 'on hand' and at present at least devoted to Phibun. Just a nod from him—and any government could be thrown out in a few days. Phibun is the key to the stability of the Khuang government..."[59] And nod Phibun did, barely five months after the coup and one month after U.S. and British recognition of the regime. Thus, on April 6, 1948, four Coup Group army officers called on the helpless Prachathipat prime minister at his house and "ji"— told him to "stick 'em up." The air force and navy commanders-in-chief were implored but declined to stick up for him, and off Khuang went.[60]

Thai politics in the subsequent decade of Phibun's second premiership, from April 8, 1948, to September 16, 1957, followed much the same pattern of political instability and violence, murder and rebellion, but with far greater tension and frequency, due to the complex tangle of conflicts between individuals—Pridi versus Phibun; Pridi versus Khuang; Pridi versus Seni and Kukrit; Phibun, Phin and Phao versus Kat; Phao versus many Free Thai leaders and Isan MPs; and Phao versus Sarit; between groups—Pridi/Free Thai versus Phibun group; Pridi/Free Thai versus royalists; Pridi/Free Thai versus Coup Group; army, navy and Bangkok versus Isan politicians; Kuomintang versus Communist Chinese; southern Muslims versus local government officials; and radical workers, students, and journalists versus police, army, anti-communists, and conservative royalists; between parties— Sahachip and Naeo Ratthathammanoon versus Prachathipat; Sahachip versus Naeo Ratthathammanoon; and Prachathipat versus Thammathipat; between institutions—army versus navy; police versus navy; army versus police; Thammasat University versus army; and parliament versus government; and between ideologies—"royalism versus democracy"; "military dictatorship versus civilian democracy"; "bourgeois democracy versus new democracy"; "patriotism versus imperialism"; "nation, religion, and monarchy versus communism"; and "communism versus capitalism."

The period can be roughly divided into two phases according to the shifting balance of power among different groups within the ruling circles. The first phase was from 1948 to 1952, during which Coup Group governments under

Prime Minister Phibunsongkhram tried hard by all kinds of unscrupulous means to quell the various sources of political opposition in the country, namely, the Prachathipat Party (with a dwindling minority in the House of Representatives and a controlling majority in the Senate), southern Malay ethnic insurgents, communist-influenced Chinese in Bangkok, mutinous army general staff officers, the Pridi/Free Thai group, the navy, Thammasat University students, the free press, the peace movement, the Thai Communist Party, and dissension within the Coup Group itself.

The second, so-called "triumvirate" phase was from 1953 to 1957, during which political rivalry within the Coup Group itself, between the army wing headed by Field Marshal Sarit Thanarat and the police wing headed by Police General Phao Sriyanond, came to the fore and dominated the scene. Prime Minister Phibun acted as both mediator and manipulator of this conflict, trying to maneuver it to his own political benefit by playing off one side against the other, meanwhile liberalizing and reorienting his government's domestic and foreign policies in search of a new popular power base and ally.[61] As can be seen in Table 5-2, this was the most violent and bloodiest period in modern Thai politics prior to the beginning of the communist guerrilla war in 1965.

The recurrent bloodshed and chaos could not help but strongly affect the politically conscious and civic-minded among the reading class, causing deep concern among them for the political plight of the country. And in their different ways, they reacted. Some took up arms, others their pens. There were, for example, fifty or so ex-Free Thai Thammasat students and faculty members who took part in the "February 26 Democratic Movement" against the Phibun government.[62] Others, better at rhyming than shooting, made political poems a favorite daily staple in the radical and popular press, such as Naiphi (alias Atsani Phonlajan), the mysterious master of caustic and esoteric political poetry from 1946 to 1952, and Thaweepvorn (alias Thaweep Voradilok), Thammasat sophomore and rising poet, moved by the political assassination of four Free Thai ministers on March 4, 1949, to compose a eulogy to the four "fighters."[63] That many of them also took up radical books and publications was owing to the other characteristic of Thai politics in that period: the decline and/or loss of legitimacy of the country's pre-existing systems of government, past and contemporary.

In the terms of post-war Thai political discourse, Thailand had undergone three main types of political regime during her recent history—absolute monarchy (before the 1932 People's Party's seizure of power), nationalist military dictatorship (from 1938 to 1944 under Prime Minister Field Marshal Phibunsongkhram), and constitutional democracy (from 1946 to 1947 under the 1946 "fully democratic" Constitution).[64] Judging from past and contemporary

Table 5-2

Political Murders and Rebellions in Thailand, 1946–1958

POLITICAL MURDERS	
June 9, 1946	King Rama VIII shot dead
August 4, 1946	Thangai Suwannathat (Prachathipat MP candidate) crippled by a grenade which killed one, injured nine
Mid-1946	Khunying Phanga shot at, but missed
Early 1947	Cheun Rojjanawiphat (editor, Prachathipat) shot dead
July 13, 1947	Suwich Phanthuset (Prachathipat MP, editor) shot at but missed
1947	Police Captain Chiab Chaisong (Pridi/Free Thai, Santibal) shot at, but missed; poisoned, but survived
February 27, 1949	Major Phone Inthorathat (Free Thai, Naeo Ratthathammanoon) arrested and shot dead
February 28, 1949	Police Colonel Banjongsak Chippensuk (Free Thai, Phao's personal foe) shot dead by police
March 4, 1949	Dr. Thongpleo Chonlaphoom (Free Thai, Naeo Ratthathammanoon), Thongin Phooriphat (Isan, Sahachip), Thawin Udon (Isan, Sahachip), and Jamlong Daoreuang (Isan, Sahachip) shot dead in police custody
March 31, 1949	Dr. Thawi Tawethikul (Free Thai, Naeo Ratthathammanoon) surrendered, but shot dead by police
Early 1949	Manas Wijanphoothorn Amorndit (journalist) fatally wounded in Minister Liang Chaiyakal's residence
December 12, 1952	Tiang Sirikhan (Free Thai, Isan MP), Chan Bunnag and Lek Bunnag (Free Thais), Phong Khiewwijit (Chan's apprentice), and Sanga Prajakwong (Tiang's chauffeur) strangled, cremated, and buried by police
March 9, 1953	Ari Liwira (owner of many independent newspapers and magazines) shot dead by police
March 24, 1954	Phorn Malithong (Naeo Ratthathammanoon MP, Police General Phao's personal foe) and Phong Suwannasin (civilian police informer) strangled and thrown into river by police
Other victims:	Army Lieutenant Uthis Chaisaengjan (Free Thai), Hayi Sulong (southern Malay Muslim religious leader), Commander Phot Jitthong, Suwit Phumchoosri, etc., killed by police

REBELLIONS	
Late 1945, July 1946	Alleged royalist coup plots
November 8, 1947	Army coup by the Coup Group under Phibun
November 15, 1947	Alleged "30 November 1947 Revolution Plot" or "Establishing the Republic Project" by Free Thai/Sahachip Party
February–March 1948	Alleged "Separatist Rebellion" by Isan MPs
April 1948	Insurgency of Malay Muslims in the south
April 6, 1948	"Stick'em Up" coup against PM Khuang by the Coup Group
October 1, 1948	Abortive "General Staff Rebellion" by army general staff officers and some Free Thais
February 23, 1949	Abortive "U Aung San Assassination-Style Rebellion" by Free Thai army officers

February 26, 1949	Defeated "February 26 Democratic Movement" or "Royal Palace Rebellion" by the Pridi/Free Thai group
1949	Clashes between police and protesting rickshaw drivers resulting in arrests and charges of rebellion in the so-called "Jaroenkrung Rebellion"
January 27, 1950	Alleged "Luang Kat Rebellion" by Luang Katsongkhram, a Coup Group dissident leader
June 29, 1951	Defeated "Manhattan Rebellion" by the naval Khana Koochat (National Liberation Group)
November 29, 1951	"Radio Coup" by the Coup Group renamed; royalist constitution abolished; parliament and parties dissolved
March 21, 1952	Police arrest of seven railway strike leaders in the "Makkasan Rebellion"
November 10, 1952	Government crackdown on leftist opposition in the "Peace Rebellion" incident
August 26, 1953	Arrest of twelve military officers and civilians for plotting the "Flood Rebellion"
February 21, 1956	Government crackdown on hunger strikers for democratic reform in the "Hunger Striking Rebellion"
February 21, 1956	Arrest of twelve politicians, journalists, and businessmen for unauthorized trip to China in the "Touring Red China Rebellion"
September 16, 1957	Army coup against the Phibun government and Police General Phao led by Khana Thahan (the Military Group) under Field Marshal Sarit Thanarat; constitution suspended; parliament replaced
October 20, 1958	Army coup against constitutional regime led by Khana Patiwat (the Revolutionary Group) under Field Marshal Sarit with government consent; constitution, parliament, and political parties dissolved; martial law declared

Sources: Compiled from Chai-anan Samudavanija and Phirasak Janthawarin, comp., *Khomoon pheunthan keung satawas haeng kanplianplaeng kanpokkhrong thai* [Basic data of half a century of Thailand's change of regime] (Bangkok: Social Science Association of Thailand, 1982); Chit, *Phao saraphap*; Kittisak Sriamphai, *Prachathipatai samai Phol.T.O.Phao Sriyanond: Yuk assawin phayong thamil khrong meuang* [Democracy under Police General Phao Sriyanond: The age of overbearing knights and evil rulers] (Bangkok: Prakasit Law Office, [n.d.]); Niyom Sukrongphaeng, *Thahanreua kabot manhattan* [The Navy's Manhattan Rebellion] (Bangkok: Sinlapawatthanatham Press, 1986); Prasert, *Ratthasapha*; Prathip, *Kabot wangluang*; Sornsak, *Khabuankan serithai*; Sungsidh, *Prawat*; Suthachai, "Kankhleuanwai"; Sawai, *Dr.pridi*; Thak, *Thailand*; Thaweep Voradilok, "Naknangseuphim kab thoraraj" [Journalists and tyrants], *Matichon* 9 (January 9, 1986): 18–21; Wiwat, "Kabot santiphap"; *Karnmuang*; and declassified reports from the period from the American Embassy in Bangkok.

experiences, none of them seemed to work satisfactorily. The Phibun regime had visited upon the nation a dubious Special Court-Martial, an unprecedentedly large number of political executions, the high-handed and disdainful treatment of the National Assembly, a series of repressive and annoyingly fussy "Cultural Mandates of the State" on all kinds of daily manners, a personality cult, two costly but futile wars, and the risk of being mistreated as a defeated country after the war. Among liberal and radical intellectuals and those who, in one way or another, had suffered politically under his rule, opposition to the return of nationalist military dictatorship was very strong and vocal since in their view such a regime had already been proven a catastrophic mistake the country could not afford to repeat.[65] The former "Leader," caricatured together with his "Lady" as "Nai Plaek-Nang Laiad,"[66] was acidly ridiculed as a petty, despicable, cowardly, and untruthful war criminal in contrast with the brave and candid Hideki Tojo,[67] and rather prematurely dismissed as a political nonentity with no chance of reclaiming the premiership.[68] Phibun's brand of militaristic nationalism was irreverently criticized as a mere delusion of grandeur and source of divisive racism, its crooked preachers condemned as "a nation of thick-skinned demons" that should be exterminated once and for all.[69] The military was generically regarded as unfit for politics and government by training, inclination, and expertise, and its rule denounced as a "dark age," "evil age," or "brutal dictatorship."[70] And despite the potentially great negative impact of inherent conflict in a parliamentary democracy, its demise would spell, in the cryptic and poetic prose of Atsani Phonlajan:

> ...the default of the Angel of Fire. Instead, Darkness, Evil, Ignorance, Crudity, Bitterness, and Suffering would undoubtedly prevail. And hence would arise the Angel of Death, who is, certes, the Rajah, the Dictator.[71]

But to the dismay of many opponents of military dictatorship, the "fully democratic" post-war regime did not function very well either. The 1946 Constitution differed from the "semi-democratic" 1932 document by barring permanent government officials from assuming any political office (Articles 24, 29, 66), allowing royalty from the Serene Highness rank (*momchao* or M.C.) and upwards to take part in politics (abrogating Article 11 of the 1932 Constitution), and abolishing the government-appointed, second-category membership of the National Assembly which had guaranteed the People's Party a virtual monopoly of power for almost fourteen years (abrogating Article 56 of the 1932 Constitution). It created in its place a bicameral parliament, with the powerful Phreutthi Sapha (Assembly of the Seniors or Senate) to be elected by members of the popularly elected House of Representatives.[72] Such an indirectly elected Senate might appear more participatory than a monarch- or government-appointed one but it still could be and indeed was manipulated by the ruling parties to continue their political dominance. Electorally packed with ruling parties' members and supporters, and with none from the opposition regardless of qualification, the Senate became not only the constitutional mainstay of the government in office but also an assembly of political beneficiaries and, according to Prachathipat leader M.R. Seni Pramoj, of mediocrities as well. Hence the title "Phreus Sapha," a pun on Phreutthi Sapha, coined by Seni and meaning "the Assembly of Buffaloes."[73]

The Senate issue caused an uproar among liberal journalists and cast serious doubt on the whole democratic project of the People's Party going back to 1932 itself. They attributed all the nation's troubles to "democracy" and its "Promoters," the People's Party, which, after taking absolute power from the monarchy under the pretext of passing it on to the people, had instead jealously kept that power for itself for the past fourteen years by means of the temporary provisions of the 1932 Constitution and now wished to perpetuate it through the new institution of "Phreutthi Sapha."[74] This simplistic but sensible argument against democracy as Thailand had known it gained increasing credibility with the Pridi-Thawan governments' persistent inefficiency and failure to solve government corruption and other pressing socio-economic problems, with the ongoing shamelessly unscrupulous "Ngew Kanmeuang" (Chinese political opera) of bickering over power and personal gain in the face of national decline and popular suffering, and with the apparent impossibility of driving the corrupt and unpopular Thawan government out of office by constitutional means. In the end, the legitimacy of constitutional democracy itself was called into question. Yai Sawitchat, Prachathipat MP for Nakhon Sawan, warned that large-scale corruption in a newly democratic country like Thailand risked alienating people from "this weird democratic regime":

> ...and people may mistake the taking away of their money to create the wealth of an oligarchy for democracy. Then other regimes will win over the people, such as communism, nationalism...[75]

Naturally, with "democratic progress" so much in doubt, someone was bound to call for a return to the good old days of absolute monarchy. That "someone" appeared in the form of certain conservative royalty, old-time aristocrats, royalist ex-political prisoners, and turncoats from the People's Party who coalesced to form and lead the conservative royalist Prachathipat Party.[76] They regarded the People's Party Revolution of 1932 not as a genuine "people's revolution," but as a premature "theoretical revolution" in which the Promoters had cut down "the majestic Bo and Banyan trees" and planted "an itchy nettle" in their place. Thai politics during the subsequent fourteen years became simply "a mortar tumbling downhill into dictatorship," "a dark or evil age," "a dark night" awaiting "the new national daylight."[77] And what was that "daylight" to be? Barring some intransigent historical oddities and vindictive avengers among the late King Prajadhipok's kin and former retinue, the majority of Prachathipat members no longer seriously contemplated the restoration of absolute monarchy since such a regime was by then world-historically obsolete and, in any case, most senior ruling members of the royalty under the *ancien régime* had already joined their Chakri ancestors.[78] Rather, what these self-proclaimed "democrats in the head but royalists in the heart" had in mind was a royalist constitutional monarchy controlled by the politically privileged royalty and nobility in which the principle of democratic majoritarianism was subordinate to the wisdom of aristocratic elitism. Leading advocates of what has come to be called "the Democratic Form of Government with the King as the Head of State" were the two Pramoj brothers, M.R. Seni and Kukrit.[79] In 1947, under the pen-name "Malaengwi" (Fruit Fly), M.R. Seni wrote:

> Democracy does not simply mean majority rule because if five hundred bandits hold a meeting with five monks and a motion as to whether or not there should be a robbery is proposed, each time it is put to the vote, those five hundred bandits will surely always vote it through against the monks. But this by no means signifies that the majority opinion in favor of robbery is morally right....The government by the majority which is called democracy must not hold as its sole criterion a greater number of votes but also take into account greater knowledge, greater allegiance to the nation, and greater honesty to the people. Only so will it become a good government for the full benefits and happiness of the people and deserve the name of democracy.[80]

But behind these solemnly proclaimed royalist principles, less lofty motivations may have been at work. Since both the late King Rama VIII and his brother-successor King Bhumibol were very young (the former only twenty-one years old on his death in 1946, the latter nineteen when he ascended the throne later that year) and had spent most of their lives abroad while the People's Party ran the kingdom, the royalty itself had little or no power base, influence, or connections.[81] The real power in a royalist constitutional monarchy, were it to be established, would naturally fall into the hands of senior Prachathipat advisers like M.R. Seni and Kukrit, who could play the wise and experienced "uncles" to the green monarch.

Their semi-restoration scheme finally came to fruition by means of their cooperation with the Coup Group in toppling the Thawan government, eliminating the Pridi/Free Thai regime, abolishing the 1946 Constitution, and setting up a sham civilian government in November 1947.[82] Its concrete manifestations were the provisional, so-called "Under Waterjar Constitution" of 1947, drafted by the Coup Group, and the 1949 Constitution, drafted by the Prachathipat-dominated constituent assembly.[83] Under the 1947 Provisional Constitution, the King had the prerogative to delay passage of a bill by refusing to sign it into law (Article 30), to appoint members of the Senate (Article 33), to dismiss any member of the cabinet or the whole cabinet by royal command (Articles 78 and 79), to pass laws in case of emergency in the absence of parliament, later to be submitted to parliament for information but not review (Article 80), and to pass emergency fiscal laws even during parliamentary session (Article 81).[84]

But even these measures did not go as far as the Prachathipat Party wished. Hence the need for a new, unadulteratedly royalist "permanent" constitution which was proposed by the Khuang government in January 1948 and passed by the Prachathipat-dominated parliament one year later.[85] The lengthy 1949 Constitution further enhanced the king's formal power by granting him the prerogative to create titles and confer royal decorations (Article 12), to appoint and dismiss members of the privy council (Articles 13 and 14), to veto any legislation approved by the parliament unless overruled by a two-thirds majority of the total membership of both houses (Article 77), to personally select and appoint members of the Senate (Article 82), to receive a pledge of allegiance from members of the privy council, cabinet, and both houses of parliament (Articles 16, 102, and 141), and to call for a national plebiscite on any vital constitutional amendment already passed by the parliament (Articles 174–176). Most importantly, in view of the recent resumption of a political role by the military, it tried to depoliticize and keep the armed forces in check. The 1949 Constitution stated unequivocally that "the Armed Forces belong to the nation and are under the supreme command of the King" (Article 59), that they could mobilize only "by royal command except in the case of declaration of martial law" (Article 60), and that "no individual, group of persons or political party may directly or indirectly use the Armed Forces as a political instrument" (Article 61).[86]

While the Pridi/Free Thai group was virtually alone in opposing the mildly royalist 1947 Provisional Constitution,[87] the staunchly royalist 1949 one met with almost universal condemnation from the Coup Group, the Phibun government, the pro-Phibun Sahaphak (United Front) MPs, the liberal press, and the TCP, in addition to the Pridi/Free Thai opposition. It was accused of "falling back into the canal of absolute monarchy" and restoring the "old power of the Khana Jao" (Royalist Party, referring to the king, royalty, and nobility).[88] Furthermore, by involving the king "too much" in politics and military affairs, it was attacked for violating the principle of democratic constitutional monarchy and probably damaging the king's honor and status itself.[89] Far from being a "fully democratic" constitution as M.R. Seni Pramoj claimed, it was, remarked Pridi Banomyong, "bureaucratic through and through" and would lead to "a government by bureaucrats, the retinue, and advisers whose appointments were made by the king either on his majesty's own or as proposed by the government or his majesty's advisorial privy council."[90] And in the opinion of his arch-rival, Prime Minister Field Marshal Phibun: "As a 1932 Promoter, I still love the 1932 Constitution."[91]

Although the Prachathipat Party had underestimated the residue of anti-royalist sentiment, whether genuine or opportunistic, from 1932, it still managed to pass the 1949 Constitution owing to its well-installed majority in parliament. Later, despite the loss of more and more of its MPs in the lower house to the Sahaphak Parties through Phibun's maneuvering,[92] the Prachathipat Party continued to hold onto the powerful Senate, whose one hundred members the Khuang government had carefully screened and handpicked in November 1947.[93] The Prachathipat Senate used its power from January 1949 to October 1951 to send thirty-four of sixty bills back to the lower house, to substantially amend twenty-two others, and to grill the Phibun government with thirty-five questions concerning opium smuggling by police, the Ministry of Defense's purchase of substandard armored vehicles, and the government's violent handling of recurrent rebellions.[94] Presumably, Phibun nodded again and gone was the royalist Constitution of 1949, together with the hostile Prachathipat Senate, in the Radio or Silent Coup of November 29, 1951, just three days before the return of the young King Bhumibol from his long study and convalescence in Switzerland to resume what could have been formidable constitutional powers. Most of them were thus snatched away by the military through the reinstatement of the 1932 Constitution, Phibun's favorite.[95]

The point of this lengthy digression is not to argue that the aforementioned political ideals—absolute monarchy, military dictatorship, and constitutional democracy—had lost all their legitimacy in Thai public opinion (obviously, they had not), but rather to point out that the dismal performance of the successive regimes instituted in their names had rendered each downright unacceptable, as a political system, to one major group or another in the Thai political spectrum, thus creating an opening for an untainted-because-untried political system. And, in fact, it became normal or even fashionable for people, to think, read, talk, and perhaps practice politics in terms of "system," that is, as "democrats," "royalists," "nationalists," "socialists," or "communists." It is against this cultural-political background that we can better appreciate the strong allure of a self-proclaimed, radically new, alternative political system which was communism, as well as the popular demand for information about it, amidst the staleness and waning appeal of hitherto underachieving political systems in post-war Thailand.

Mass Movements and Intellectual Vanguard

Besides the two major characteristics of Thai politics during the post-war decade explored above, there was one other which, although of comparatively minor consequence overall, played a significant role in arousing popular interest in leftist ideas and firing many radical intellectuals' imagination of leftist political activism. This was the emergence of "mass politics," in form if not in substance. It was the tender age of the multi-party system, labor organizations, student activism, and mass movements which, for the first time, were legally permitted and officially recognized in modern Thailand. The legal landmarks in this development were the Constitution of 1946 (Article 14),[96] the Constitution of 1949 (Articles 37–39),[97] the Political Parties Act of 1955,[98] the Labor Act of 1956,[99] and the official establishment of the elected Student Committee or autonomous student union in Thammasat University in 1948.[100] From this open legal opportunity structure arose a number of political parties and mass organizations, as well as a wide array of foreign-borrowed and Thai-modified forms of mass political activity, namely, rallies, marches, work stoppages, hunger strikes, sleeping protests, public lectures, debates, plays, and fancy dress shows, used alone or in combination, mostly in Bangkok and Thonburi but also in other provinces. The peculiar character of Thai-style mass politics is exemplified by a typical election rally of the Prachathipat Party in the central square of Thonburi on July 14, 1946, which included "a morning market fair, numerous speeches, a boxing contest and music," which, in the opinion of an American diplomat, resembled nothing more than a "traveling circus."[101] But not all political rallies were so merry or peaceful. Many incidents of assault,[102] fistfight,[103] stabbing,[104] scuffle,[105] stampede,[106] and even bombing[107] were reported during some of them.

As contemporary accounts and later studies show, these forms of mass politics were used at one time or another by virtually all political parties and groups regardless of ideology. They seemed to function in three ways: first, for immediate practical purposes based on the demands and interests of the parties and groups involved, be they economic, educational, electoral, or political; second, for long-term ideological propagation, leftist or rightist, communist or anti-communist; and third, and most interestingly, for supplementing crucial political moves by a party or group in parliament or from the barracks with a legitimating, palpable, and spectacular manifestation of *mati mahachon* (public opinion) in their favor. Thus, an anti-Thawan government rally of the hitherto largely defunct Military Youth Organization at the King Rama I Memorial Bridge was called by one of Phibun's cronies just six days before the November 1947 coup, and a pro-Phibun rally was called by a certain "Workers' Group" about a week before Prime Minister Khuang was forced out of office in April 1948.[108] Rallying supplemented parliamentary action in the case of the Basic Textbooks Act, which was sponsored by General Mangkorn Phromyothi, minister of education and deputy head of the ruling Seri Manangkhasila Party under Phibun's leadership; a rally staged at Sanam Luang by party secretary-general Police General Phao Sriyanond's henchmen shortly before the Act came before parliament in August 1955 was an attempt to defeat it, humiliate General Mangkorn, and pave the way for Phao's rise to the top of the Party.[109] In March 1957, four days after the Phibun government's victory in a general election, university students and others, instigated by opposition Prachathipat politicians and some leftist students, marched in protest against the "dirty election" from Chulalongkorn University to the Government House, with the connivance of Field Marshal Sarit Thanarat. The protest ended with the marchers' storming into the Government House, Sarit's successful call for calm, and the building of his image as the people's "hero."[110] Finally, an anti-Phibun, anti-Phao, and pro-Sarit rally was mounted at Sanam Luang by the Hyde Park group on the very eve of the army coup by Field Marshal Sarit in September 1957, culminating triumphantly in a cheerful march to Sarit's residence at Sisao Thewes and another daring attack on the gate of the Government House by the demonstrators.[111]

Of course, the Thai communists and radical leftists also tried to make full use of mass political activism to achieve their propaganda and political aims as far as opportunities, legal or otherwise, allowed. Roughly speaking, their post-war mass political action can be divided into three subperiods according to the changing legal/political circumstances and their tactical adaptation.[112]

From 1945 to 1947, owing to the abrogation of the Anti-Communist Act in 1946 and the leftist inclination of the Pridi/Free Thai governments, the TCP operated freely and openly either by itself, jointly with the social democratic Sahachip Party, or through its many front organizations, the more important being the Central Labor Union (CLU), the Bangkok Labor Union (BLU), the Student Group of Thailand, and the Thai Youth Organization.[113] In the second subperiod, from 1948 to 1952, with the fall of the Pridi/Free Thai group and the return of the authoritarian Phibun regime, the TCP operated for the most part covertly through the widely-based Peace Committee of Thailand,[114] the increasingly militant Thammasat Student Committee (especially its very active Lecture and Debate Department),[115] and the less active Bangkok Labor Union.[116]

The government crack-down on the Peace Movement and the subsequent passage of a new Anti-Communist Act in November 1952 caused the CPT (the renamed TCP) organization some damage, driving it underground and making it adopt more cautious low-profile tactics for a few years. The third subperiod of the communist and leftist mass political activism was then ushered in by Phibun's liberalization and policy reorientation in mid-1955 and lasted until the establishment of Sarit's military dictatorship in October 1958, during which the CPT resumed its active operation amidst a new flow of mass political movements and a high tide of socialist popularity. Much of its activity was channeled through leftist mass organizations and political parties, the more important of which were:

The Sixteen-Unit Workers' Group. Formed in 1955, the Kammakorn Sibhok Nuai (Sixteen-Unit Workers' Group) was a tactical alliance among pro-Phibun leaders of the government-sponsored Samakhom Kammakorn Thai (Thai National Trade Union Congress or TNTUC), former CLU and BLU leftist labor activists who had perforce become part of the TNTUC, and some independent trade unionists in the Kammakorn (Worker) Party. All of them wanted to pressure the Phibun government to pass a pro-union labor law and revoke the government ban on May Day celebration, but needed a new acceptable umbrella organization to circumvent their respective status as government union, underground organization, and political party. The Group's chairman was Prasert Khampleumjit, a frank and honest rickshaw drivers' leader in the TNTUC, and its secretary was Jamnong Noothong, a former BLU rice mill union leader. However, being mostly staffed, operated, and dominated by the left, it served in essence as a Trojan horse for the left's takeover of the official labor movement and its transformation into a political opposition force. Having achieved its original common purposes, the Group was dissolved two years later.[117]

The Naeoruam Sangkhomniyom (Socialist United Front). This was an electoral alliance of four legal socialist, leftist, populist, and anti-imperialist opposition parties—the Setthakorn (Economist) Party, the Sangkhom Prachathipatai (Social Democratic) Party, the Sangkhomniyom (Socialist) Party, and the Khabuankan Hyde Park (Hyde Park Movement) Party.[118]

The Setthakorn (Economist) Party. A party of veteran independent socialist Isan MPs, the Setthakorn Party was headed by Thep Chotnuchit (ex-Prachathipat, former minister, MP for Si Sa Ket). Thim Phooriphat (relative of the murdered ex-minister Thongin Phooriphat, himself MP for Ubon Ratchathani) was deputy head, and Khlaeo Norapati (MP for Khon Kaen) was secretary-general. It had a close unofficial working relationship with the CPT.[119]

The Sangkhom Prachathipatai (Social Democratic) Party. Led by Suthep Sajjakul as party head and Prakhong Minpraphal as secretary-general, the

Social Democratic Party appears to have been a small group of self-styled, muddle-headed Bangkok socialists.[120]

The Sangkhomniyom (Socialist) Party. Led by Wisit Sriphatthra (former BLU railway workers' union leader) as party head and Bunsong Wijarana (former BLU rice mill workers' union activist) as deputy head, the Socialist Party seems to have been a party of CPT-influenced professional labor organizers. By far, it was the most radical partner in the Socialist United Front and the only one that called for a total, long-term, socio-economic "revolution" by legal means "in the Thai way."[121]

The Khabuankan Hyde Park (Hyde Park Movement) Party. Formed by regular speakers at the Hyde Park forum at Sanam Luang, this party was an assortment of populist demagogues, political malcontents, aspirants, opportunists, and leftists who were influenced, manipulated, or perhaps even hired in turn by the Phibun group, the Phao group, and the CPT. This political marriage of convenience lacked real cohesive organization, and the progressive populist platform of the Party did not help much in holding it together, as reflected in the frequent desertions of its leaders and prominent members. The party leadership included Phethai Chotnuchit (former editor of *Karnmuang*, ex-member of the Peace Committee, and MP for Thonburi), first party head, who quit to join the ruling Seri Manangkhasila Party; Prasong Neuangjamnong (member of Chon Buri's provincial council), second party head; and Chuan Rattanawaraha, secretary-general.[122]

The Sri Arya Mettraya Party. According to its head, loyal Pridi follower Police Captain Chiab Amphunan (formerly Chiab Chaisong), he was dispatched by Pridi from Peking back to Bangkok to found this party as an authentically Thai patriotic and mildly socialist alternative to the CPT, which, in Pridi's opinion, was pro-Chinese and theoretically wrong. Presumably, following Pridi's frequent political use of the Buddhist utopian myth of "Sri Arya Mettraya" in the past, the party was so named to express the Thai pedigree of its socialist vision.[123]

The Kammakorn (Worker) Party. Set up and financed by Phibun to garner workers' votes for the government and prevent the left from usurping the "kammakorn" title, the Worker Party was the political offshoot of the two major government-sponsored labor unions, the Thai National Trade Union Congress and the Free Workmen's Association (Samakhom Seri Raengngan). The Party's policy was drafted by Sang Phatnothai, Phibun's labor aide. In practice, however, the Party was led by Prakob Toelaklam as party head; originally a pro-Phibun railway union leader, he was arrested in the Makkasan Rebellion incident, fell out with the corrupt TNTUC leadership, and became an independent labor activist. Other leaders were Khlai Chunhajan (secretary of the TNTUC), party secretary-general; Thongyoi Palkawong na Ayudhya (leftist sawmill union leader), deputy head; and Kran Koednopphakhun, (leftist petty traders' union leader), deputy head. The Party showed an independent leftist inclination.[124]

The Santichon (Peace Fighter) Party. Headed by Utthorn Phonlakul, leftist newspaper editor and former Peace Rebel, this party was mostly a continuation of the suppressed Peace Movement in both policy and personnel, many of its prominent members having "graduated" from Bangkhwang Penitentiary by virtue of the Phibun government's amnesty in 1957. Consisting mainly of famous radical writers and journalists, its anti-war, anti-imperialist, and neutralist foreign policy attracted wide support among university students.[125]

Apart from these, there were, of course, the radical Thammasat Student Committee, progressive student organizations in other universities, and the Student Union of Thailand, a national umbrella organization of major university student unions formed in September 1956.[126] Some of the more important mass political protests and activities engaged in by these leftist organizations from 1946 to 1957 are listed in Table 5-3. Undoubtedly, public curiosity about radical ideas and purchase of radical publications were stimulated by the boisterous election and political rallies of the CPT and other leftist parties, annual May Day celebrations and hundreds of strikes by leftist unions, raucous weekly Hyde Park forums at Sanam Luang, occasional protest marches and demonstrations by

Plate 5-1. Students confronted army soldiers in a protest march against the dirty election (photo taken on 2 March 1957; photo credit: Nitisat Rab Satawas Mai [Journal of law: The new century issue] 7, no.4 [1957])

Table 5-3

Selected Leftist Mass Political Protests and Activities, 1946–1957

TIME	PLACE	ORGANIZER	ISSUE
May 1, 1946	Saranrom Park, Bangkok	Bangkok Workers' Welfare Association and Tricycle Association	First May Day celebration
December 8, 1946	Sanam Luang, Bangkok	TCP	Against return of four annexed Indochinese provinces to France
January 1, 1947	Sanam Luang, Bangkok	Bangkok Labor Union	Celebrating its founding
April 7, 1947	Sanam Luang, Bangkok	Sahachip Party and Student Group of Thailand	Anti-Phibun
May 1, 1947	Sanam Luang, Bangkok	Central Labor Union	Biggest May Day celebration
August–September 1948	Thammasat University	Radical student activists	Against additional training requirements of Bar Association
May–June 1950	Thammasat University	Student Lecture and Debate Department	Lectures on socialism
June 8 and 22, 1950	Ministry of Interior	Thammasat and Chulalongkorn students	Protesting discrimination against Thammasat students in government job application and salary scale
February–March 1951	Thammasat University	Faculty of Economics	Lectures on capitalism
May 1, 1951	Bangkok Labor Union office	Bangkok Labor Union	May Day celebration
May 3, 1951	King Rama I Memorial Bridge	Peace Committee of Thailand	Anti-Korean War
October 11, 1951	March from Ministry of Justice to Parliament	Thammasat Student Committee	Demanding return of Thammasat campus from the army
November 5, 1951	Thammasat University	Thammasat Student Committee	Break-in and sit-in at Thammasat campus to protest army occupation
March 21–29, 1952	Makkasan Railway Maintenance Factory and Government House	Railway Workers' Association	Strike against unfair regulations and protesting arrest of strike leaders
May–June 1952	Thammasat University	Student Lecture and Debate Department	Lectures on Marxist and radical themes
June 13, 1952	Mass demonstration near restaurant where Chinese Chamber of Commerce and Thai officials banqueted	Chinese communists	Protesting twenty-fold increase in alien registration fee
August 21, 1954	March from Thammasat University to Parussakawan Palace	Thammasat Student Committee	Protesting the beating up of a Thammasat student by army cadets
August 1955	Sanam Luang, Bangkok	Hyde Park Movement	Weekly open forum for anti-government speeches
November 8, 1955	March from Sanam Luang to Democracy Monument	Hyde Park Movement	Demanding dissolution of the Coup Group and appointed membership of the National Assembly

December 10, 1955	March from Sanam Luang to Democracy Monument	Hyde Park Movement	Demanding dissolution of appointed National Assembly and abrogation of temporary provisions in constitution
February 1956	Sanam Luang, Bangkok	Hyde Park Movement	Hunger strike for democratic reform
1956–1957	Thammasat Univeristy	Student Lecture and Debate Department	Weekly discussions and lectures by radical speakers
1956–1957	Bangkok and nearby cities	Various labor organizations	New wave of strikes and unionization
May 1, 1956	March from Sanam Luang to Sanam Seuapa	Sixteen-Unit Workers' Group	Resumption of May Day celebration
Mid-1956	Ministry of Culture's Meeting Hall and Sri Ayudhya Movie Theater	Sixteen-Unit Workers' Group	Open discussion of pending labor legislation
October 11, 1956	Parliament Building	Sixteen-Unit Workers' Group	Pressing for passage of labor law
December 9, 1956	Ministry of Culture	Sixteen-Unit Workers' Group	Celebrating passage of Labor Act
December 31, 1956	Sanam Luang, Bangkok	Sixteen-Unit Workers' Group	New Year celebration and anti-imperialist demonstration
January 6, 1957	March to Government House	Pedicab drivers	Submitting six demands to the prime minister
March 2, 1957	March from Chulalongkorn University to Ministry of Interior and from Sanam Luang to Government House	Chulalongkorn students	Protesting "dirty election"
April 23, 1957	Sanam Luang, Bangkok	Socialist United Front	Anti-imperialist, anti-SEATO, pro-China rally
May 19, 1957	Sanam Luang, Bangkok	Radical students	Anti-SEATO and demanding government expansion of education
June 24, 1957	Sanam Luang, Bangkok	Sanga Neuangniyom or "Chang Ngadaeng" (Red-Ivory Elephant, member of Hyde Park Movement)	Gesturing that King Rama IX was responsible for the death of the late King Rama VIII
September 15, 1957	March from Sanam Luang to Sarit's residence and Government House	Hyde Park Movement	Calling for Phibun government's resignation, Phao's resignation and exile, and Sarit's coming to power
September 23, 1957	Rally in Chulalongkorn University Auditorium	Chulalongkorn students	Submitting three-point demand for policy change to the new government
Late 1957–early 1958	Countrywide	Socialist and leftist parties	Election rallies
May 1, 1958	Bangkok	Radical labor unions	Last May Day celebration before Sarit's military dictatorship

Sources: Compiled from *Mahachon*, *Karnmuang*, and *Pituphoom* weekly newspapers and the following secondary sources: Charnvit et al., part 2 of *Prawat thammasat*; Damri and Jaroon, chapters 3 and 4 of *Khabuankan*; Kanya, chapter 3 of "Prawat"; Kittisak, *Prachathipatai*, 35–93; Skinner, chapter 9 of *Chinese Society*; Sungsidh, part 2 of *Prawat*; Suthachai, chapters 5 and 6 of "Kankhleuanwai"; and declassified reports from the American Embassy in Bangkok.

university students and the people, and countless public lectures and debates on Marxist theory and socialist issues organized by radical student activists.

University students closely observed, directly participated in, and even planned and led some of these political activities themselves. But why on earth should these well-educated youth, relatively free from occupational burden or particular socio-economic interest, have become interested in leftist mass movements, or in radical literature for that matter? The answer, I believe, lies somewhere between the sociologically generic condition and the historically specific situation of students in institutions of higher education.

The first factor derives from the fact that university education is a transitional and contingent socio-economic condition in which contradictory processes and practices are at work that may lead to varied political inclinations on the part of the students.[127] In the case of modern Thailand, on the one hand, with formal education under state control, Thai university students had been trained ideologically and technically to staff, first and foremost, the state bureaucracy and, secondarily, private business, both being concentrated in the urban areas. Hence a clear tendency on their part to become state bureaucrats or members of various bourgeois strata in the cities.[128] On the other hand, they were also temporarily detached from their class background and the actual process of economic production, and therefore did not yet enter any definite social relations of production and belong categorically to any specific class. Furthermore, if on the one hand university education was a process of ideological subjection, on the other hand students also acquired a cultural qualification in the sense that they were more or less trained and linguistically equipped to search for and discover new knowledge and ideas from libraries, professors, and friends.[129] That some of these ideas and knowledge turned out to be radical was only normal in the post-war period for the reasons discussed above.

This relative class and cultural autonomy of the university student condition, a kind of liminal state in which they were betwixt and between, provided the basis for a political deviation of some students from state control, making it objectively possible for them to "betray" their classes of origin and the ruling classes. But for precisely the same reasons, they could sway in the opposite direction.[130] Which direction they would actually take seems to have been a function of their immediate social and political experiences and the influence of the repertoire of counter-hegemonic ideas existing in a given cultural matrix. In addition, psychologically speaking, was the fact that the mostly male, teenage students who came from the provinces were tasting personal freedom from parental authority for the first time, while collective living conditions in rooming houses and dormitories greatly facilitated the exchange of ideas and peer influence. This kind of independent life coupled with the mild rebelliousness typical of teenagers was arguably conducive to new ideas and activism.

Leaving aside these generic causes, there were a number of historically and situationally specific ones that led to the initiation of Thai university students into radical ideas and politics in the post-war period. The maelstrom of student activism began at Thammasat University, which was rightly regarded as the most politically active and ideologically radical of Thai universities (its full original name being Mahawitthayalai Wicha Thammasat Lae Kanmeuang, the University of Moral and Political Sciences). It had been founded by Pridi Banomyong two years after the 1932 Revolution in order to educate and train citizens and qualified personnel for the new constitutional regime and reformed bureaucracy. Pridi was Thammasat's sole (and highly prestigious) chancellor since its inception, and the University had played an important role in supporting him on the national political scene, especially during the war, when it sheltered the secret headquarters of the Free Thai Movement and many of its students joined the ranks of that organization. After the war, it continued to house a secret Free Thai arsenal and many Thammasat faculty members and students joined Pridi/Free Thai political parties and governments. Naturally, in the aftermath of the 1947 coup, it was closely watched and frequently harassed by the Phibun government as one of the few remaining domestic political bases of the then-exiled Pridi and the Free Thai Movement. That about fifty Thammasat students and faculty took part in the Free Thai Royal Palace Rebellion of February 1949, engineered and led personally by Pridi, only confirmed the government's suspicions. In its aftermath, many Thammasat administrators, faculty members, and students were summarily arrested, dismissed, and in some cases murdered by government order, while Thammasat graduates were repeatedly subject to unfair and discriminatory requirements and regulations arbitrarily meted out by various government agencies. Finally, the army took the opportunity of the naval Manhattan Rebellion of June 29, 1951, to dispatch its troops to "borrow" the university campus as "a temporary shelter for the maintenance of law and order," forcing faculty, staff, and students to pursue their "homeless" education elsewhere. Three months later, the army had apparently found the campus so homelike that it proposed to buy the whole place for five million baht in order to turn it into permanent barracks. Only by virtue of the concerted and audacious campaign of Thammasat and some other university students, which included marching on parliament on October 11 and storming the campus on November 5, and the strong support of many sympathetic MPs and newspapers, did the Phibun government and army relent and begin to evacuate the university in December 1951. But what the government could not capture physically, it emasculated symbolically, passing a new law on March 13, 1952, removing

"Kanmeuang" (politics) from the university's name in an attempt to depoliticize Thammasat University once and for all.[131]

And a vain attempt it proved to be. Though "Kanmeuang" was cut loose from the title of the university, politics stuck fast to its students. On the basis of their real grievances and actual resistance to the government, scores of Thammasat students became avid readers of radical publications and ready receivers of the Marxist-communist message which not only gave a sense of revolutionary purpose and grandeur to their plight and struggle, but also placed them in the world and national "historical materialist" scheme of things.[132] As it turned out, Thammasat University became the most fertile breeding-ground for student recruits to the CPT in the post-war period, during which about twenty Thammasat students worked as party cadres both in and outside the campus. The university was thus credited with providing the Party a crucial linkage with Thai intellectuals, and through them, with the rural peasant majority of the population, in other words with Thainess and the Thai nation.[133] It did not take very long for the "Red Peril" to spread to other universities and spoil their age-old serenity. By the early 1950s, radical books, party cells, and mass protests (in that order) had infested most if not all of them, turning them into battlegrounds of the publishers and readers of radical books versus their censors and burners.[134]

Last but not least were the comparatively advanced—though not necessarily inherently superior—intellectual and cultural qualities of contemporary Thai radical literature itself. In the historical development of the modern Thai intelligentsia, the decade after the war was a transitional period between the demise and/or eclipse of "palace-temple" and "government-bureaucracy" intellectuals and the rise of "university" intellectuals. During this transition, the center of intellectual and cultural life, at least the most progressive and exciting part of it, fell within the ambit of "journalistic-literary" circles (see Table 5-4). Various factual or realistic fictional accounts of Thai journalism and literary writing from the 1930s to the 1950s stressed two distinctive intellectual advantages these two usually overlapping professions furnished their practitioners, namely, opportunity for free expression of critical thought and easy access to a lot of new and good books, including foreign ones.[135] But the domestic educational background of most journalistic-literary intellectuals also made their access to the original sources of foreign culture and ideas mostly indirect and hence limited, though there were the notable exceptions of those who had been abroad as news reporters, diplomats, or students.

It can be further extrapolated that, as non-government freelancers or employees in the private sector or "civil society," they were less hindered by

Table 5-4
Social Status, Education, Occupation, and Audience of the Four Groups of
Modern Thai Intelligentsia

	SOCIAL STATUS	EDUCATION	OCCUPATION	˙AUDIENCE
Palace-Temple	Royalty/nobility	Domestic, informal, traditional; foreign, formal	Royal servants	Peers and masters
Government-Bureaucracy	Middle-class commoners	Domestic and foreign, formal	Public officials	Colleagues and bosses
Journalist-Literary	Middle-class commoners	Domestic, formal	Freelancers and private employees	Buying and reading public
University	Middle-class commoners	Foreign, formal	Public officials	University students and colleagues

official regulations from delving into what the government considered dangerous ideas than their counterparts in the state sector. Finally, unlike other groups of intellectuals, they had a wider audience beyond their immediate surrounding community who were under no professional or educational obligation to pay either money or attention to their work. This fact itself necessitated a lively literary style of writing and facilitated free-thinking, humanistic, universal interest, unhampered by the dry, narrow, and pedantic styles of bureaucratic officialdom and academic disciplines.

When, for the reasons that have been elaborated above, many and especially the best of Thai journalistic-literary intellectuals turned leftist after the Second World War, they brought with them to the new political cause an advanced degree of intellectual sophistication and versatile literary skills. And with the giants of the "palace-temple" and "government-bureaucracy" intellectual groups either dead or past their prime, the cultural center stage was invaded and, in certain fields, dominated by these young and vigorous leftists.

In poetry, for example, Chit Burathat (d. 1942), "Khroo Thep" (Chaophraya Thammsakmontri, d. 1943), and "No.Mo.So." (Prince Phitthayalongkorn, d. 1945) were replaced as top-notch poets by "Naiphi" (Atsani Phonlajan, b. 1918), "Thaweepvorn" (Thaweep Voradilok, b. 1928), "Ujcheni" (Prakhin Chumsai na Ayudhya, b. circa 1920), "Naisang" (Pleuang Wannasri, b. 1923), and "Srinakhorn" or "Khwannara" (Jit Poumisak, b. 1930).[136] In historiography, the "Royal Chronicles" of Prince Damrong (d. 1943) and the "Thai National Epic" of Luang Wijitwathakan (in his fifties) were challenged and rewritten by "Aran Phromchomphoo" (Udom Sisuwan, b. 1920) and "Somsamai Srisootphan" (Jit Poumisak) following a class struggle approach.[137] In political economy, the Economic Plan of Pridi (in permanent exile from 1949) and various economics textbooks written by Phraya Suriyanuwat, Dr. Thawi Tawethikul (d. 1949), Dr. Thongpleo Chonlaphoom (d. 1949), and Dr. Uphai Phinthuyothin (repeatedly arrested from 1949 and soon to resign from Thammasat University) were overshadowed by *Khaepitalist*, the singular study of Marx's *Capital* in Thai by Supha Sirimanond (b. 1914) and by *Setthakij nai rabob prachathipatai phaen mai* (The economy in a new democratic system), the translation by Sanan Waraphreug ("So.Wo.Pho.") of the Chinese communist "Textbook on New Economics."[138] In philology, ethnology, and Thai cultural and folklore studies, Atsani Phonlajan and Jit Poumisak were researching and writing works that soon rivaled or surpassed the achievements of the pioneers in these fields—Phraya Uppakitsinlapasan (d. 1941), Phra Sanprasert (d. 1945), Phraya Anumanrajadhon (in his sixties), and Luang Bunyamanopphanit (in his fifties).[139] In literary theory, history, and criticism, the socialist realism and historical materialism of "Banjong Banjoedsil" (Udom Sisuwan), "Seni Saowaphong" (Sakchai Bamrungphong, b. 1918), "Intharayut" (Atsani Phonlajan), and "Thipakorn" or "Sil Phithakchon" or "Bookman" (Jit Poumisak) defied and outflanked the aesthetic formalism and historical empiricism of Prince Phitthayalongkorn, Prince Wan Waithayakon (busy with diplomatic duties), and the Chulalongkorn professors of literature, such as "Nai Tamra na Meuangtai" (Pleuang na Nakhorn).[140] In the natural sciences and philosophy, the deaths of Dr. Tua Laphanukrom, Dr. Luang Phrotphitthayaphrat (both around the end of the war), and Saen Thammayos (in 1952) left these fields free for Samak Burawas (b. 1916) to display his wide-ranging knowledge and Marxist-slanted interpretation.[141] And finally, in prose fiction, the most popular genre of contemporary Thai literature, the post-war decade was the heyday of Thai "Literature for Life." The social and political novels, short stories, and plays of "Seni Saowaphong," Kulap Saipradit (b. 1905), Issara Amantakul (alias Abrahim Aman, b. 1920), Suwat Voradilok (b. 1923), "Or. Udakorn" (Udom Udakan, b. 1925), "Lao Khamhawm" (Khamsing Srinawk, b. 1930), "Kulish Indusakh" (Atsani Phonlajan), and Srirat Sathapanawat (b. 1918) were counted among the best of their kind and largely dominated the market.[142] By and large, it could be said that if a reasonably informed member of the post-war Thai reading class went shopping for a good book, the chances are good that he or she would end up buying one written by a leftist intellectual with a fair amount of Marxist-communist ideas didactically or subtly inserted into it, thus inadvertently boosting the aggregate demand for Marxist printed commodities through the individual demand for good literature.

Treasure Map to Uttarakuru

Two contemporary short pieces of literature by leftist intellectuals best illustrate the multiple and problematic politico-cultural context in which the readership of Marxist printed commodities found themselves. The first is a short story written in 1950 by Or. Udakorn (Udom Udakan), newly equipped with elementary knowledge of Marxism-Leninism from the monthly *Aksornsarn*, entitled "Karl marx, klin dinpeun lae nanthiya" (Karl Marx, gunpowder smell, and Nanthiya), which portrays most of the things discussed in this chapter in a strangely improbable way.[143] It is the story of a proud young master of economics graduate with first class honors named Set Phatthanand (certainly from Thammasat University, though not so specified), who has been unfairly dismissed from his government job for political reasons (Suphat Sukhonthaphirom?)[144] and hence decides to vent his anger and frustration through revolutionary agitation on a group of impoverished and haggard peasants (in response to the TCP's call for university students to go to the countryside and mobilize the peasantry in its 1948 booklet *The New Year Present?*).[145] He delivers a ferocious two-hour speech on "the economic doctrine of Karl Marx" (Thammasat Summer Special Lectures?) to the murmuring, commending, but rather bewildered country folks (victims of un-Thaified intellectualism) in the hot summer sun, standing on a pile of broken red bricks in a run-down temple (religious decline?). However, his didactic lecture against capital is cut short (Thank God!) by his worldly-wise socialist-reformist former professor, a retired supreme court judge, who manages to sway him from "un-Thai" violent revolution to the path of peaceful evolution. At this point, the police arrive to arrest him on "communist" charges (Police General Phao's "Knights"?).[146] The ex-judge himself, knowing police arrest for what it was (kangaroo court), cautions him to flee immediately (so much for "the rule of law" and "human rights"), but the poor, proud lad is incited instead to surrender to the police by the professor's beautiful daughter Nanthiya, his own college sweetheart, who thoughtlessly wants to "entrust him temporarily to the police" in an attempt to prevent him from joining the spreading clandestine revolutionary organization (TCP?). To her great shock and sorrow, he is summarily shot dead by the police soon after (obviously modeled on the police murder of seven members of the Pridi/Free Thai group in 1949).[147]

As the story ends, though the socialist reformer might get the upper hand in the argument, it is the police who win the fight. And although the smell of gunpowder puts an abrupt end to the unfinished debate on Karl Marx, it seems Nanthiya's Marxist revolutionary-to-be boyfriend speaks the last and loudest word on the issue with the sheer silence of his death. Meanwhile, the peasants, backbone of Thailand and embodiment of Thainess, go on toiling and living their miserable lives unheard.

The other work is an essay written by "Sri-Intharayut" or Atsani Phonlajan, widely hailed as the most talented and craftily iconoclastic among Thai communist poets. Atsani usually adopted another pen name for his poetical works, "Naiphi," by which he became best known and which also turned him ingeniously into a kind of Hinduized "Mr. Specter" of Communism. Though seemingly simple (*nai* means "mister" or "master," *phi* means "ghost"), the pen name contains many ambiguous connotations of which Atsani made full use. Said to have angrily denied that "Naiphi" meant "Mr. Ghost," Atsani himself explicated on several occasions that it denoted "Master of the Ghosts." That term alluded to Shiva, mighty Hindu God of Death, Destruction, and Purgation, who, according to certain Hindu texts, was even more powerful than Vishnu, Hindu God of Universal Order Maintenance and Police, of whom the Siamese monarchs traditionally claimed to be avatars. In fact, Shiva was also called, among hundreds of other names, "A-sani," which was lexically identical with "Atsani" and might have been the very reason he chose this pen name in the first place. However, when occasion arose to render "Naiphi" into English, Atsani chose to translate it as "Specter," the key word in Marx and Engels' famous opening dictum in the *Manifesto of the Communist Party*, of which Atsani was certainly well aware and which he himself sometimes used in that particular sense in his poems. Thus, it is arguable that, by calling himself "Naiphi," Atsani cunningly placed the "Specter of Communism" at a central divine position one rung above the Siamese monarchy in the traditional Hindu theological universe, thus promoting a radical alien idea (and his own poetic self) using a Thai conservative discourse and radicalizing the latter with the former in one stroke![148]

In August 1948, four months after Prime Minister Phibun retook power and launched a new campaign against "the Specter of Communism," our Hinduized "Mr. Specter" published a highly allusive and intriguing essay[149] in which he returned to the age-old Hindu myth of "Uttarakuru," obliquely picking up the debate with the late King Vajiravudh, who had first invoked this myth in his diatribe against socialist "Utopia" in the 1910s.[150] With no qualms, Atsani simply took over the myth, de-utopianized it, and turned it against the anti-communist forces by retelling and reinterpreting its story.

The differences between the two versions reflect not only the disparate political stance and power of the two authors, but also what had transpired in Siam and the world in the intervening thirty years. Unlike the late King, who had explicitly identified the real ideological referent of "Uttarakuru" as socialism and constantly compared and condemned the two "Utopias" of East and West, Atsani filled his essay with lengthy extracts from two original Hindu treatises describing the blissful life in Uttarakuru, adding only a brief introduction and short epilogue of his own. Not once was the real referent of Uttarakuru explicitly identified by him, though he took care to provide readers with enough clues. Moreover, the former had written as the Lord of Lives while the latter wrote as a columnist under the surveillance of an anti-communist regime. And while the late King, writing in English, had had to labor at great length the point that socialism was Uttarakuru and hence utopian, Atsani, writing in Thai, simply stated that Uttarakuru was no Utopia and did actually exist in this world as "a country to the north which is the Union..."[151] Well, there was no need for Atsani to say more since the real existence of the socialist camp spoke louder than words and the Thais surely could not help hearing it. Alluding to Marxism-communism as the "treasure map to Uttarakuru," Atsani elaborated on his conception of the revolutionary "treasure-hunting" movement:

> The treasure-hunters must consist of two kinds of people—one is the laboring diggers who are certainly the proletariat and the other is the map-decipherers and magicians responsible for driving off those treasure-guarding cobras and Grandpa Soem—these are the students. As the diggers must follow the map-decipherers in the map-guided treasure-hunt, so the proletariat must follow the directing and self-sacrificing students in the search for the bliss of Uttarakuru. And if the students are in any danger, the proletariat must try their best to save them. When this is done, heaven on earth will be right before us all.[152]

How convenient it was that the treasure map to Uttarakuru happened to be on sale then in the market!

Read together and in contrast, these pieces of writing help illuminate the plight of Thai readers of radical literature in their confusing and sometimes contradictory relationships with different kinds of discourse, different sorts of reality, different types of revolution, different classes of people, and different styles of radical cultural politics. We can begin to understand this by first noticing a stark and paradoxical contrast between the two: though largely based on contemporary factual events, the overall character of Or. Udakorn's "Karl marx" story was that of a political fantasy, while Sri-Intharayut's "Uttarakuru" essay, despite its mythical basis, was actually a rallying cry to real, organized social forces. The fantastic quality of Or. Udakorn's story resides in the fact that Set Phatthanand, the story's main character, seeks "the rule of law" and "human rights," two principal legacies of the 1932 constitutionalist Revolution then being jeopardized by Phao's rampant police rule. It is the absence of these liberal democratic principles that costs Set his government job and eventually his life. But with the military, originally chief force of the 1932 Revolution, now betraying that Revolution by turning its back on legal-constitutional rule and civil rights, Set has to look for a new social force to continue the unfinished Revolution. And he did not look among his own educated, literate, and articulate kind in the city, but among the mostly ignorant, illiterate, and inarticulate folks in the countryside, whom he tries thoughtlessly to rouse to revolutionary action with a pedantic and rather un-Thaified lecture on Marx's economic theory, which it is highly doubtful any of them could understand![153] Given so malapropos a method, no matter how many separate factual events were strung together to form the plot, they did not in the least bring closer to reality Set's political mission—to stir up a millenarian uprising of the peasantry with an unadapted modern discourse.

But while Or. Udakorn was trying to make use of a new Marxist-communist discourse to finish the old bourgeois democratic Revolution, Sri-Intharayut was doing the opposite, employing the old Hindu millenarian discourse to start a new socialist revolution. The realistic quality of Sri-Intharayut's rallying cry lies in the fact that, unlike Or. Udakorn's peasants, who, as a matter of fact, were mostly apolitical and unorganized, a large number of his "laboring diggers" and "map-decipherers" were both radicalized and organized into labor and student movements. The trouble, however, was that it was becoming increasingly risky to address them in the police-recognizable modern discourse of Marxism-communism. Hence the recycling of the vintage Thai religious utopia of "Uttarakuru." And yet, what appeal could this ancient millenarian myth still hold for his worker and student readers who, with their modern education and urban ways of life, were worlds apart from their religious peasant compatriots in the village community and thus unlikely to believe it, let alone to launch a socialist revolution upon it?

It was through this maze of misplaced modernism and recycled tradition, rural backwater and urban modernity, bourgeois cause and socialist movement, peasantry and proletariat, "un-Thai" millenarianism and "ur-Thai" Marxism that our Thai readers had to find a way to their potential roles as political actors, radical agitators, and Marxist-communist revolutionaries.

6

Marxism as Commodity: Supply

AMERICAN MILITARY ATTACHÉ BRINGS FAKE "RED" TEXTS: A special news item which we have received from a person close to diplomatic circles says that Mr. Bullwit, the new American military attaché who used to work with General MacArthur, has already arrived for his posting. His arrival was accompanied by a large number of communist texts most of which were written by Karl Marx. But it so happens that the content therein has been modified and revised from the original. Hence they are fake or unauthorized [*theuan*] texts. As to the aim of this person, it is not yet clear.

Headline news of the communist Mahachon¹

Communists are just human beings but I don't know who they are. We must judge people by their activities. If there is no such activity, then they are not communists. Those who make a one-sided assault or propaganda, or launch a [parliamentary] debate against the government, or commit the same activities as Ho Chi Minh's "koochat" [national liberation] are all communists. Lieutenant Commander Manas and Group Commander Anond used the term "koochat" so they were communists.

Prime Minister Field Marshal Plaek Phibunsongkhram²

Pre-Market Scarcity

For real or fictional Thai intellectuals who reached maturity during the war, like Or. Udakorn, Set Phatthanand, and Suphat Sukhonthaphirom, openly available sources of knowledge about Marxist-communist doctrine in Thai were rare. After the passage of the first Anti-Communist Act in 1933, Pridi Banomyong's voluntary shelving of his 1933 state socialistic Economic Plan, the self-imposed exile of the Plan's arch-opponent, King Prajadhipok, in 1934, and the incarceration of most royalist anti-communists and Chinese-Vietnamese communists in Bangkhwang Penitentiary, there was hardly anyone left to continue the public debate on Marxism-communism outside of prison. Apart from those few who were lucky enough to obtain underground communist publications or old copies of Pridi's *Yellow-Covered Book* or of King Prajadhipok's *White-Covered Book*, most Thais who knew anything about Marxism-communism learned it indirectly, either in a few academic courses taught in universities or from a handful of published translations of foreign books on political and economic subjects.

Notably mentioned in various personal accounts of this period were the requisite undergraduate and graduate courses on "Latthi Setthakij" (economic doctrines), given successively by Professor J.F. Hutcheson, Dr. Thawi Tawethikul, and Dr. Uphai Phinthuyothin at Thammasat University.[3] A substantial proportion of their lectures and published lecture notes, which were used as textbooks and bought by tens of thousands of Thammasat students, especially those living in the provinces and unable to attend classes regularly, was devoted to the explication of various schools of socialist economic doctrine, including Marxism (roughly 60 percent in the case of Hutcheson and Thawi's textbook and 50 percent in Uphai's).[4] Although most students had difficulty understanding the abstract and complicated subject matter of economic theory, their teaching did leave a deep impression on the few who comprehended it and appreciated its importance.[5] Consider Kulap Saipradit, for example, a committed democrat and veteran oppositional journalist and novelist who, after graduating from Thammasat University during the Second World War, developed a growing interest in socialist doctrines and translated an English lecture on Marxist theory by Professor C.E.M. Joad in October 1946.[6] Or Suphat Sukhonthaphirom, a master of economics graduate from Thammasat University and later independent Marxist writer and theoretician, whose ardent interest in Marxism-communism was kindled by Dr. Uphai's lectures on socialist economic theories in 1941 and became a lifelong intellectual pursuit. Forty-four years later, he could still showily recite in tolerable French Marx's dictums on economic principles under socialism and communism, which he had learned from his francophone lecturer.[7] As for non-academic sources of ideas on Marxism-communism, one oft-mentioned book was a popular biography of Indian nationalist leader Jawaharlal Nehru, translated by Liang Chaiyakal, an opportunist Prachathipat MP for Ubon Ratchathani. Weirdly enough, Liang's garbled rendering of Nehru's own fairly sympathetic and favorable reflections on Marxism-communism in that book was frequently quoted by many writers of the time as a credible comment on the doctrine and an inspiration of their interest in it.[8]

But however sympathetic or favorable to Marxism-communism, these sources were relatively narrow and limited, simply mentioning it in passing or reducing it to one alternative academic approach or research method among many others of comparable validity. They might be sufficient to rouse intellectual curiosity but were no substitute for the partisan propagandists' committed advocacy and methodical explication of Marxism-communism as the most revolutionary world-view, social theory, and program for collective political action. With the upsurge in interest in the "alien" doctrine among the reading public after the Second World War, the resultant demand was amply and directly satiated with a great variety of foreign, outright "red" printed commodities by four different groups of suppliers. They were private bookshops, public libraries, individual Thai intellectuals who had been abroad, and foreign diplomatic delegations.

Supply of Foreign "Red" Books: Bookshops

Taking advantage of the state legalization of Marxism-communism and the rising market demand for it, many bookshops in and around Bangkok began to import and sell foreign Marxist-communist publications in the late 1940s, mostly from the Soviet Union and China but also from the United States, Britain, and India, and soon became the principal source of them in Thailand. Among these bookshops, those that ran their businesses solely on a commercial basis with no known political motivation or association included Charnvit Bannakhan (2/4 Nares Road Corner, some distance from Bangrak District Office), Silom (on Silom Road), Nibondh (40-2 Jaroenkrung Road), and Sairung (Jaroenkrung Road, near the Central Post Office). Based on advertisements published in the contemporary radical press and the accounts of several radical bookworms, Charnvit Bannakhan appears to have been the first commercial bookshop to publicly sell foreign-language periodicals from the Soviet Union, beginning in 1947.[9] Silom followed suit, while Nibondh, as a book importer and exporter, specialized in ordering books and periodicals by mail from abroad for selected customers rather than in open sale.[10] Thus, whereas Charnvit Bannakhan and other bookshops drew customers by advertising in Thai radical newspapers and magazines long eye-catching lists of English Marxist-communist titles with selective Thai annotations, or by organizing seasonal book sales (on May Day they discounted up to 30 percent), Nibondh expanded its clientele unnoticed by word of mouth.[11] Later, these different marketing approaches proved crucial as Nibondh managed to continue importing foreign "red" books discreetly long after other bookshops, in the face of increasing pressure and censorship, either stopped selling them or were closed down by the police.[12] Sairung seemed to be an ordinary

commercial bookshop that made use of the business opportunity arising from
Phibun's political liberalization in 1955 and lifting of trade restrictions against
the People's Republic of China the following year to import Marxist-
communist books from China. This business opening lasted until the arrival of
Field Marshal Sarit Thanarat's anti-communist dictatorship in 1958.[13]

Much more significant and interesting in terms of their cultural-political
roles were the "political" bookshops, those whose business was not only
motivated by radical ideology but also backed, managed, or even owned by
radical leftist organizations. The most widely known and biggest among them
was the Dazhong Wenhua Gufen Youxian Gongsi (Mass Culture Company
Limited, located at 647 near the entrance of Kalantan Alley, Jaroenkrung Road,
Sam Yaek) or Dazhong Wenhua for short.[14] Growing out of the Chinese
communists' extensive clandestine anti-Japanese propaganda apparatus in
Thailand during the war, it was formally founded in October 1945, part of the
public emergence, legalization, and renaissance of the wartime underground
Chinese press, with a remarkably substantial registered capital of one million
baht, which could perhaps be attributed to the Chinese communists'
widespread post-war practice of squeezing large financial contributions out of
rich Chinese war merchants-cum-collaborators with the Japanese.[15] True to its
name, Dazhong Wenhua had an unusually large number of shareholders, over
three thousand, the overwhelming majority of whom were Chinese laborers in
the rice-milling and sawmill industries as well as in transportation and port
services. And, according to the company's curious statute, the unequal number
of shares in their possession made no difference in terms of representation at
the annual shareholder meetings, where the egalitarian principle of "one man,
one vote" prevailed.[16]

Although commercially speaking Dazhong Wenhua was in the common
business of newspaper publication, printing, selling books and printing
equipment, and importing and exporting, its communist-controlled board of
directors evidently geared the key part of the company's activities towards the
uncommon business of radical politics and ideology. Thus, Dazhong Wenhua's
daily Chuanmin Pao (October 10, 1945–December 1952), which cost the
company over half its annual expenditure, quickly became the foremost
Chinese radical newspaper in post-war Thailand.[17] Likewise, the Dazhong
Wenhua Bookshop, located at the company's headquarters, was from all
accounts built into the foremost bookshop of foreign radical literature in post-
war Bangkok. In contrast with its purely commercial competitors, Dazhong
Wenhua widely extended the range of imported foreign Marxist-communist
publications from the Soviet Union and China to cover the orthodox Marxist
classics by Marx, Engels, Lenin, Mao, and others, as well as theoretical and

literary works by modern and contemporary communist writers in both English and Chinese. Furthermore, it greatly reduced prices and advertised regularly in all the leading Thai radical periodicals, such as *Mahachon*, *Aksornsarn*, and *Karnmuang*, not only making foreign communist literature known and affordable to potential Thai readers as never before, but also contributing financially to the advertising revenue of the Thai radical press.[18] In addition to these overt functions, Dazhong Wenhua served covertly as an active link between Chinese communists and the Thai radical intellectuals who browsed frequently on the premises and as a "travel agency" for Thai political dissidents and young lookjins who sought refuge and/or education in the PRC.[19]

Dazhong Wenhua's role as the most effective Chinese mouthpiece of the PRC and the chief supplier of foreign Marxist-communist printed commodities in Thailand brought it moderate business success. For example, in 1950, at the peak of communist influence on the Chinese community in Thailand, the value of the company's assets rose to 1.7 million baht and its annual sales reached 3.5 million baht, yielding a net profit of 48,978.20 baht.[20] However, given the ideological character of its printed commodities, the growth of Dazhong Wenhua's business could not but entail growing political troubles under the increasingly anti-communist Phibun government. Consequently, three of the company's founders and top executives—Lao Jekmeng (company founder and director and *Chuanmin Pao*'s registered owner), Ngow Kiangtong (*Chuanmin Pao*'s publisher and advertiser), and Chua Jihong (company founder and *Chuanmin Pao*'s chief editor)—were subjected to recurrent police harassment and arrests, leading in February 1951 to Chua and Ngow's banishment for anti-American propaganda.[21] The office of *Chuanmin Pao*, located in the company's printing house (576 Saphanleuang, Rama IV Road, Mahaphreuttharam, Bangrak), became a favorite target of police raids, while the Dazhong Wenhua Bookshop was put under constant police surveillance.[22] By July 1951, the Special Branch Police had asked the Department of Commercial Registration, Ministry of Commerce, for a complete list of Dazhong Wenhua's board of directors and shareholders.[23]

Perhaps aware of the impending danger, the Dazhong Wenhua Bookshop changed its trade name to Hua Chiao (Overseas Chinese) Book Store around April 1952, the company was sold to private entrepreneurs, and the affiliated *Chuanmin Pao* taken over by a certain Yongfa Company. But the real control and operation of the legally split business remained in the hands of the same communist cadres, and police investigators were not deterred.[24] The government crackdown came in November 1952 during the Peace Rebellion incident when scores of company executives and employees in various departments were arrested. The bookshop shut down quietly soon afterwards, while the *Chuanmin Pao* was ordered closed by the police in December 1952.[25]

On a much smaller scale, the TCP's functional equivalent of the Chinese communists' Dazhong Wenhua in 1951 and 1952 was the Bangkok Witthayakhan Bookshop, located on the premises of a drugstore called Bangkok Osot (52-4 Yaowarat Road, at an approach to Phanuphan Bridge, near Wad Teuk Crossroads). Amiably advertising itself as "your book counsellor to help solve your book problems," the nature of its counsel was betrayed by the radical ideological orientation of most English books and periodicals on sale and by the cheap prices, as low as half a baht to two baht.[26] Apart from providing foreign-book-ordering services, Bangkok Witthayakhan acted as a TCP front publishing house and sales agency of Thai literary books by communist and radical authors, under the control of Udom Sisuwan, head of the Party press and literary publication department.[27]

Not surprisingly, Bangkok Witthayakhan's business ended in the same way and around the same time as Dazhong Wenhua—at police hands in late 1952. The Anti-Communist Act of November 1952, opportunistically rushed through parliament by the Phibun government three days after the suppression of the Peace Movement and the leftist opposition, combined with the tightening police ban on radical literature to bring the inflow of foreign Marxist-communist publications to a halt.[28] But this did not last long. Following Phibun's political liberalization and the revival of commercial and cultural ties with the socialist camp, especially with China in 1955/56, foreign Marxist-communist books and periodicals, especially in English, from the Soviet Union and China again surfaced in and around Bangkok, announcing themselves, if more cautiously, on the advertising pages of radical leftist periodicals.[29]

At the forefront of foreign radical book-selling in this liberalization period was the Aksornwatthana Bookshop (126 at the approach to King Rama I Memorial Bridge on the Thonburi side), then CPT front book importer, publisher, and seller, much like its forerunner, Bangkok Witthayakhan.[30] It served as part of the CPT-engineered legal cultural apparatus that included the political *Pituphoom (La Patrie) Weekly*, the economic *Sethasarn Biweekly Magazine*, the literary *Saithan Monthly Magazine*, the Pituphoom Publishing House, the Sahaban Publishing House, and the Busbaban Publishing House. These were aimed at spearheading a resumption of public radical cultural activities by exploiting the worsening conflict within the Phibun-Phao-Sarit triumvirate and by relying upon the fresh blood of CPT graduates of the Marxist-Leninist Institute in China, as well as Peace Rebellion convicts granted amnesty by the government on the occasion of the Mid Buddhist Era Year of 2500.[31] The product of their combined efforts, besides replenishing the shelves of some bookshops with foreign radical publications, was a second stream of Thai leftist newspapers, periodicals, and books of literature and criticism, political travelogue and memoir, commentary on foreign politics and policy, and politicized moral advice on private matters from a radical ideological perspective. A relative dearth of Thai books dealing explicitly with Marxist-communist theory and the parallel disappearance of Marxist-communist classics and theoretical works from the lists of advertised foreign radical books during this period reflects the fact that this second radical cultural renaissance was engineered under the threatening authority of the 1952 Anti-Communist Act and the police censorship whose list of banned books was ever lengthening.[32]

Public Libraries and Private Collections

Not all Thai readers who sought foreign radical books needed to buy from bookshops; there were other sources from which they could purchase them more cheaply, obtain them for free, borrow, or even steal them. These sources were of comparatively less importance and access to them was for the most part personal and limited to well-educated, middle-class intellectuals in the diplomatic, educational, journalistic, and literary circles. The more public of them were libraries in some universities and leftist trade unions. For instance, the communist-controlled Bangkok Labor Union had set up a Kammakorn (Worker) Library at its office (24 Trok Wet, Silom Road, Bangrak) containing hundreds of Thai and Chinese radical books to serve its rank and file in mid-1947.[33] Similar efforts by other leftist unions with substantial Chinese or lookjin membership could be reasonably expected given the widespread practice of individual or collective oral reading of radical books among leftist organized labor and school students.[34] It could be safely presumed that most foreign radical books in the union libraries were in Chinese; it was unlikely that many ordinary workers could read other foreign languages.

In university libraries, the availability of Marxist-communist books in English or other western languages in their collections was uncertain in most cases and rather scanty at any rate. Consider, for instance, the Thammasat University Central Library, which reputedly has had the best and largest collection of English books in the country. Several contemporary radical Thammasat student activists found it of no use in satisfying their demand for foreign Marxist-communist literature.[35] My own survey of the Library's collection of all western-language books by key orthodox communist authors (Marx, Engels, Lenin, Trotsky, Stalin, Mao) or on communism in general indicates that only a dozen or so could possibly have been available before 1958. Of these dozen books, those written by orthodox communist authors are Marx's *Capital, On the Founding of the First International* (ed. L.E. Mins), *Theories of Surplus Value: Selections*, and *On Revolution and Counter-Revolution* (ed. Eleanor Marx Aveling), Engels' *The Condition of the Working Class in England*, and Lenin's *On Trade Unions and Revolution, 1893–1917* (ed. Thomas Taylor Hammond).[36] No other university library fares better in this regard as none of them figured prominently in the reading experience of contemporary radical students and intellectuals. To make matters worse, some of the few Marxist-communist books available were put out of circulation by a certain radical student who, acting in direct contravention of his professed ideological tenets, privatized public property by appropriating them. It was thus that Jit Poumisak got hold of two copies of Marx's *Das Kapital* by "jik-king" (filching) them from the Chulalongkorn University Central Library, according to Prawut Srimantra, his fellow student and a member of the CPT. One could always argue, of course, that Jit did this to salvage the books and popularize them through his literary medium rather than leave them "to the gnawing criticism of the mice," unused and unappreciated in conservative Chulalongkorn.[37]

But there were less deplorable ways than theft to get hold of a foreign radical book, such as receiving it as a personal gift or loan. These cerebral gifts and loans normally came from certain radical intellectuals and some of their friends who had been abroad to western or socialist countries after the war. The usual occasion for their travel was an official diplomatic mission, advanced study in a foreign institution of higher education, or a journalistic-literary professional delegation. Only a small number of radicals were blessed with the chance to go to the fount of printed Marxist-communist "truth" and buy it first-hand. There were several known cases of such Thai radical bookworms' dreams coming true. For example, Supha Sirimanond, future founder and editor of *Aksornsarn*, worked as the press attaché to the Thai embassies in the Soviet Union, Switzerland, and France from May 1947 to May 1948. Supha had bought some used English books on Marxism during his six-month visit to Tokyo in 1938 and had begun his independent study of Marx's *Capital* (ordered by mail from the United States) around 1943. No sooner did he arrive in Moscow, on May 5, 1947, than he and his close colleague, Sakchai Bamrungphong (a celebrated radical journalist-novelist under the pen-name "Seni Saowaphong"), with the help of a rough street map and a bellboy's advice, sought out a bookshop of foreign-language Soviet publications on Kutnezski Mosk, the second premises they acquainted themselves with after a restaurant.[38] To his great delight and excitement, Supha found the cost of buying and shipping English books so cheap that he bought up and sent about a hundred copies home to give freely to his friends.[39] Back in Thailand, his personal collection of English Marxist-communist books became a treasure trove for young and curious students and intellectuals such as Samak Burawas and Thaweep Voradilok.[40] Apart from lending these books generously to his junior friends, Supha also insistently urged on them the necessity to study English or at least one foreign language so as to expand their horizons beyond the narrow limits of the Thai press and textbooks.[41]

A similar case is Kulap Saipradit, who, financed by a loan from the Bank of Asia which he obtained through Pridi Banomyong's personal recommendation, went to Australia to pursue an informal study of "politics and political practice" at the University of Melbourne from July 1947 to February 1949.[42] Kulap was not an enrolled student but had access to the university library and a weekly private meeting with then junior lecturer in Australian politics Alan Fraser Davies (1924–87), a special arrangement "facilitated through officials in the [Australian] Department of External Affairs…[and] Professor William Macmahon Ball," a specialist in East Asian affairs and then head of the University's Department of Political Science.[43] Kulap's keen interest in Marxism and association with local leftist and Asian-community activists led to the nagging but inconclusive suspicion of the Commonwealth Investigation Service (C.I.S., the Australian internal intelligence agency of the time) that he might be a closet communist. "A stack of Marxist books and pamphlets [were found] in one corner of [the] living room" of his flat, reported a visiting and interviewing C.I.S. agent, and the Department of Immigration reached the premature conclusion that Kulap was indeed a communist and denied his and his wife's application for an extension of their visas. The threat of immediate deportation was averted through the timely intervention of both Alan Davies and Professor Macmahon Ball, who appealed to the Australian authorities on his behalf that the Marxist literature was part of the required reading.[44] Finally, the Saipradits decided that enough was enough and packed up and left Australia in January 1949.

Accusations by his Thai and Australian detractors to the contrary, there was simply neither evidence nor reason to doubt Kulap's profession that "neither my wife nor myself is a Communist…If I were a Communist (or any other 'ist'), I would not wait till I was found out by anybody. I would profess my beliefs publicly."[45] He might not have been " a dangerous radical," as the C.I.S. agent reported, or "a radical ideologue," as Barme opines, but radical he was indeed in his humanistic view against racial discrimination and for the disadvantaged.[46] And it was this ingrained lifelong humanism that moved a decent gentleman like him step by step from the position of a radical democrat to that of a radical socialist intellectual sympathetic to the Marxist-communist doctrine and movement. The increasingly left turn of the content and political posture of his writings subsequent to his unceremonious return from White Australia strongly indicated that Kulap must have become favorably disposed towards the doctrine, at least theoretically or intellectually, while studying in

Melbourne.[47] And, of course, among the English books on political theory and parliamentary democracy that he and his wife brought back from Australia were volumes on trade unions, socialism, and Marxism-communism that they later translated or used as data in their writings, the most popular of which was Kulap's translation of Emile Burns' "very simple exposition" of Marxist-communist theory, *What Is Marxism?*[48] Not "content to sit back and play the typewriter radical," as David Smyth points out, Kulap chose to live what he authentically believed, stuck his neck out, and worked with the communists in the Thai chapter of the International Peace Committee in 1952.[49]

Through channels like this a lot of rare and/or prohibited foreign radical books reached a limited circle of Thai leftist intellectuals who then reproduced them in one form or another for the general Thai public, as Supha did with a four-volume set of Charles A. Beard and Mary R. Beard's *The Rise of American Civilization*, which he received by mail in early June 1949 from a friend studying in the United States.[50] And with the dramatic increase in air traffic from Bangkok across the "dollar curtain," as Jit Poumisak sardonically put it, to Peking and Moscow in the late 1950s, members of many Thai cultural delegations took the opportunity to smuggle back not a few "red" volumes for themselves or their radical friends. One such smuggler was Kamjorn Sukphongsri, a radical student activist from the Fine Arts University who was invited to participate in the Sixth International Youth and Students' Festival for Peace and Friendship in Moscow in August 1957. Among those seeing him off at the Donmeuang Airport was Jit, then a lecturer in English at his university, who reportedly shouted impetuously "mir-drujba!" ("peace-friendship" in Russian) as the plane took off. Jit had several good reasons to feel so excited about the trip: not only had Kamjorn helped take the heat off him by assuming the authorship of Jit's own controversial pseudonymous essay, "Sinlapa pheua chiwit" (Art for life), published in a 1957 Fine Arts University "Welcome to Freshmen" book, but he also agreed to buy Jit many radical books in Moscow, especially ones by Howard Fast.[51]

The Soviet Legation and the Dark Parody of Anti-Communism

Sometimes foreign Marxist-communist books seemed to make their own way miraculously into the hands of Thai radical intellectuals in extraordinary circumstances without the latter having to part any "curtain," be it "iron," "dollar," or otherwise. This unusual convenience was made possible through the good offices of the Soviet Legation and the American Embassy in Bangkok.[52] Initially, the Soviet Union did not appear to value the strategic and political importance of Thailand as highly as it did Southeast Asian countries like Indonesia, showed marked indifference to the resumption of diplomatic relations, and took more than a year after mutual official recognition to dispatch its envoy, Sergi Nemtchina, to Thailand to open an official legation on Silom Road in March 1948.[53] Then, far from plotting a campaign of ideological propaganda and political conspiracy against the Thai government, as hyperbolic anti-communist officials and media, both foreign and Thai, would have it, the fifty-two Soviet nationals in Bangkok, many of whom were spouses and children and all of whom were under constant police surveillance, took an interest in trading rather than politics and largely limited their Thai social contacts to formal official occasions and publicity moves, such as inviting Bangkok's mayor to visit Moscow on the occasion of the two-hundredth anniversary of its founding or distributing information bulletins to the Thai press.[54]

It was in connection with the Soviet Legation's publicity routine that another outlet for foreign Marxist-communist books was opened through a Thai radical intellectual named Suphat Sukhonthaphirom. Having served faithfully in the wartime Free Thai Movement as a close aide to Pridi and his family and taken a staunchly anti-military dictatorship stance in his own frequent newspaper articles, Suphat became a marked man under the post-1947 coup rightist governments. Following the "Political Classification of Newspapers" scandal at the Ministry of Foreign Affairs in December 1947, Suphat, who had been working at the Ministry as head of the Thai Embassies Comptroller Section, was suspected of having leaked information to the press and was unfairly dismissed two months later.[55] Despite his outstanding educational qualifications and occupational experience, his subsequent employment at both the Bank of Sri Ayudhya and Krung Thai Bank was cut short because of persistent political pressure put on his employers by the deputy director general of the Police Department, Phao Sriyanond, and his henchmen. Unrelentingly persecuted and tailed, and repeatedly picked up by the police, he was desperate for a job but unable to find a Thai boss willing to pay the price of hiring a pro-Pridi political pariah. Finally, Suphat took a chance on the Soviet Legation's advertisement for a Thai translator, reasoning that Phao would not dare bother the Soviet diplomats. His gambit was right and from 1949 to 1952 he translated for the Soviet News Agency.[56]

The job turned out to be an exceptional stroke of luck for Suphat; it afforded him a handsome salary, a convenient working schedule, ample free time to pursue his journalistic and political sidelines, and unlimited access to the Soviet Legation's library of foreign books.[57] This allowed him a unique opportunity to acquaint himself further with "authentic" Marxist-communist doctrine directly from the motherland of the first great proletarian revolution and socialist system through books, some of which he was encouraged by his Soviet boss to keep as his own, such as Engels' *The Origin of the Family, Private Property and the State* and Lev Abramovich Leontiev's *Political Economy: A Beginners' Course* (1935). Using the Soviet publications in the Legation's library as his sources, Suphat wrote or translated a series of articles on the U.S.-dominated world capitalist economy, the Soviet and Polish socialist economic systems and, in consultation with his Soviet employer, the status of the individual in the socialist system. The last was written to counter a main theme of official anti-communist propaganda, originally borrowed from the Philippines and then disseminated in Thailand, that socialism would completely abolish individual freedom.[58]

Meanwhile, regional and domestic political developments were leading to greater tension between Thailand and the Soviet Union. With the Thai government adopting a more pro-American, anti-communist policy with each successive coup, Thai expeditionary troops fighting in Korea, and the Thai police rounding up Chinese and Vietnamese communist sympathizers, the Soviet Union began publicly to support the TCP and its burgeoning anti-war and anti-American Peace Movement by providing them wide publicity and frequent coverage in its mass media. Although Soviet "internationalist" support in itself was inconsequential with regard to Thai domestic politics, it sufficed to frighten the Phibun government, already persuaded by a flood of hyperbolic intelligence from the U.S. and its regional allies of the Soviet Legation's extensive subversive activities, into ordering its police, customs, and educational officers to tail all Soviet diplomats and nationals, arrest all Thais who made contact with the Soviet Legation, and ban or block all imported Soviet goods and films.[59]

At one point, the relationship between the Phibun government and the Soviet Legation became so strained that even diplomatic formality could no longer be maintained. During a big welcoming state banquet for a team of visiting American military assistants and advisors in February 1951, the Soviet minister and his colleagues found the performance of a Thai play, "Thamma thamma songkhram" (Just and unjust wars) so outrageous that they walked out in protest. Written by the late King Vajiravudh in justification of his controversial decision to dispatch Thai troops to Europe to fight on the Allied side in the First World War, the play was suited on this particular occasion to Phibun's Korean War policy by having the "unjust" party wear a red uniform instead of the original black. To make sure that the intended message got across to the foreign audience, Major General M.L. Khab Kunchorn, the arch-anti-communist secretary of the Prime Minister's Office, was there to provide instant English interpretation of the provocative dialogue.[60]

The most alarming thing Phao's police informers found out about the Soviet Legation was the secret political sideline of its paid translator—a small and rather loose conspiratorial underground of largely pro-Pridi leftist journalists and dissident military officers called Khabuankan Koochat (National Liberation Movement),[61] which was founded on an "anti-fascist, anti-imperialist, new democratic/socialist" platform, and led by Suphat and Squadron Leader Phrangphej Bunyaratphan. Suphat, the chief theorist of the group, was the author of its Bolshevik-type organizational statutes and New Democracy program, while Phrangphej, who had a peculiar obsession with political conspiracy, was the group's key plotter. A domestically trained air force officer, former Free Thai, and dilettante socialist, Phrangphej was a rising star in the air force officer corps who, ironically, had made his name sinking the rebel-controlled battleship *Sriayudhya* with a bomb during the government suppression of the naval Manhattan Rebellion by Khana Koochat in mid-1951. He was an occasional contributor to the newspaper *Kiattisak* under such pen names as "Intelligentsia," "Phonlalok," and "So.So.Ro." Angered by a newspaper article attacking his daring exploit, he published a rejoinder explaining the necessity of the air raid. The exchange led him to know and befriend Samut Surakkhaka, the article's author, and, through him, Suphat and Suphot Dantrakul. Together, the four founded the Khabuankan Koochat.[62] It was Suphat who chose the "koochat" name for the group and his reasons for doing so help explain the term's contemporary currency, that is, partly to appeal to disgruntled naval officers who longed to avenge the Khana Koochat's defeat of 1951 and partly to keep in line with the "national liberation movements" then prevalent in Southeast Asia.[63]

Since its inception between November 1951 and early 1952, members of the Khabuankan Koochat had been busy holding not-so-secret meetings with like-minded leftist dissidents, drafting the movement's political program and plan of action, distributing anti-American and anti-government leaflets in public places, and, like a wolf in sheep's clothing, scouring armed forces barracks for new recruits to its military wing, "The Revolutionary Soldiery," under cover of the Peace Movement's signature campaign. All these were preliminary to the still distant seizure of governmental power, as technically, the Movement considered itself in the first phase of the first stage of its plan of action. According to the plan, the whole process was divided into the Primary Stage and the Revolutionary Stage. The Primary Stage was subdivided into the Preparatory Phase, consisting of the Organization of the People's Army Project, the Propaganda Project, the Intelligence-Gathering and Counterintelligence Project, the Fund-Raising Project, and the Political Project; and the Operational Phase, consisting of the Military Plan and the Civil War. The Revolutionary

Stage was subdivided into five Revolutionary Projects: governmental, economic, social, military, and cultural/religious.[64]

However, the TCP-dominated Peace Movement was not at all happy about the Khabuankan Koochat's unauthorized intrusion and unsolicited overtures of unity. So in response to a statement of support from the Khabuankan Koochat's Soldiery and its request for participation in a secret Peace Movement meeting, Dr. Jaroen Seubsaeng (alias Khun Jaroenworawej), president of the Peace Committee of Thailand and former Sahachip MP for Pattani, publicly denied any relationship or shared objectives between the two movements. Moreover, the Committee issued a statement implicitly denouncing the Khabuankan Koochat's action.[65] And although a few known TCP members were involved in the Khabuankan Koochat—Pan Kaeomat (former pro-Pridi, Sahachip-Isan MP for Nakhon Phanom and TCP member since May 1952), Pleuang Wannasri (former Thammasat student activist and poet-journalist), and Bunmi Latthiprasat (writer-translator)—their involvement in this instance appeared to have been spontaneous and individual, based on their own ideological conviction as well as personal friendship, professional acquaintance, and regional background, rather than organized or designated in any specific way by the TCP. This is confirmed by the Peace Committee's spurning of the Khabuankan Koochat's advances and also by the latter's independent foreign policy thinking which, unlike the TCP's simplistic pro-Soviet formula, rejected the prevailing Cold War/two camps framework, the rigid application of the "class analysis approach" to international politics, and the facile identification of the Soviet and American camps as political representatives of any particular class. Instead, the Khabuankan Koochat advocated a neutral, non-aligned foreign policy which could not but jar on the TCP's creedal nerves.[66]

Given Pan's close cooperation with Suphat in forming the Khabuankan Koochat,[67] it was only normal for the Thai political police, prone as they were to conspiracy theory and constantly misinformed and prodded by their western "colleagues," to extrapolate from a series of incidental individual associations an imaginary, organized network of international communist conspirators intent upon overthrowing the Phibun government and making a New Democratic revolution; they imagined a formidable network stretching from Moscow through Peking to Bangkok and linking the Soviet Legation, the Chinese communists, the Pridi/Free Thai group, the Thai communists, the Ongkan Thai Koochat, the Peace Movement, and the Khabuankan Koochat together.[68] That was the immediate reason for a police sweep of all known members of the Khabuankan Koochat and other communist/leftist opposition groups, including Suphat, on November 10, 1952, and the subsequent hasty passage of the new Anti-Communist Act. These reasons were spelled out in

detail by the deputy minister of interior and director general of the Police
Department, Police General Phao Sriyanond, in an official memorandum dated
November 11, 1952, to the foreign minister, Prince Narathipphongpraphan
(alias M.C. Wan Waithayakon Worawan), to be relayed to foreign diplomatic
circles.[69]

There is no reason to doubt Suphat's sincerity when he insisted that, being
steadfast to his nationalist principles, he never so much as revealed the
existence of his Khabuankan Koochat sideline to his Soviet bosses, let alone
received any guideline or money from them for the movement.[70] Yet it is highly
improbable that the latter, in furnishing him with generous pay, a leisurely work
schedule, and easy access to Marxist-communist books, did not take into
account their translator's sensational political past, radical ideological
inclination, and active literary-journalistic writing. Be that as it may, the police-
jumbled "Soviet-Peking-Pridi-Suphat-CPT" plot proved too tempting for the
criminal court to resist. And so, on March 15, 1955, of the fifty-four accused
brought to trial in three separate criminal lawsuits (divided into three "mutually
supporting and cooperating" groups—the Khabuankan Koochat, the peace
activists, and the communists), forty-nine were convicted of "rebellion in and
outside the Kingdom" and sentenced to twenty years' imprisonment. However,
owing to their cooperative testimonies during the trial, all except one had their
sentences reduced by a third to thirteen years and four months' imprisonment.

The more important and better known among these forty-nine convicts were:
Suphat Sukhonthaphirom; Squadron Leader Phrangphej Bunyaratphan; Suphot
Dantrakul (pro-Pridi journalist of *Siam Mai Newspaper*); Suchat Phoomborirak
(journalist of *Kiattisak*, close friend of Kulap's family during their future exile
in China); Bunmi Latthiprasat (Kulap's classmate, leftist writer and translator,
former TCP member expelled from the Party for unruly personal behavior);
Pal Banomyong (Pridi's son); Lieutenant Commander Manas Jarupha (leader
of the defeated Khana Koochat); Jaroen Seubsaeng (reported CPT member,
popular philanthropic physician in Pattani, elder brother of People's Party
member Jaroon Seubsaeng); Sun Kijjamnong (last president of the BLU, CPT
member); Kulap Saipradit; Samak Burawas; Utthorn Phonlakul (editor of
Khaophap Newspaper); Chat Bunyasirichai (editor of the communist-
controlled *Puangchon Weekly Newspaper*); Khrong Jandawong (Isan school
teacher, Ongkan Thai Koochat leader); Ari Imsombat (Thammasat student
activist, editor); Prasit Thiansiri (CPT leader in the South); and Sawai
Malayavej (southern businessman, CPT member, writer). The five accused
who were later released were: Pleuang Wannasri (CPT member, Thammasat
student activist, poet, journalist); Samphas Pheungpradit (CPT member,
Thammasat student activist, journalist, lawyer); Mongkhol na Nakhorn (local

southern politician, CPT affiliate if not party member); Singchai Bangkhadanara (Thammasat student, poet); and Ngow Hanghao (employee of the CCP-TB-controlled Anta Company).[71]

Once in jail, this odd assortment of radical intellectuals, junior military officers, Isan peasants, and Chinese clerks could not avoid taking up the illustrious scholarly tradition of their communist and royalist predecessors. Whether initially at the Khlong Prem Light-Sentence Prison in Bangkok or later in Area 6 of the Bangkhwang Penitentiary in Nonthaburi, they took to the intellectual pastimes of book and manuscript-smuggling and -hiding, teaching, lecturing, learning, reading, writing, translating, and, occasionally, singing and drinking. Under the administration of an "Educational Committee" chaired by Kulap Saipradit, "Khlong Prem and Bangkhwang Universities," as they loved to call the places, offered unofficially to the political inmates lectures and/or tutorial classes in Marxist philosophy (taught by Samak Burawas), historical materialist social science (by Kulap), socialist political economy (by Suphat), English (at the elementary, intermediate, and advanced levels by Squadron Leader Phrangphej), Chinese (by Prasit Thiansiri and Ngow Hanghao), French (probably by Utthorn Phonlakul), journalism (by Kulap and Utthorn Phonlakul), literary composition (by Kulap), geology and natural history (by Samak), navigation (by Lieutenant Commander Manas Jarupha), and Buddhist doctrine and meditation practice (by Phra Phimoltham, a senior progressive monk of Mahathat Temple, who initiated the program from outside with official permission).[72]

As if by providence, it was Suphat's English-language Soviet books that fulfilled the fantastic plot imagined by the police: they accompanied their rightful owner from the Soviet Legation right through the strong, thick prison walls under the very noses of the largely friendly, ignorant, and at times drunken guards and jailors, further diffusing the seditious message of international communism behind bars.[73] Consequently, besides learning the Chinese language, "German" (i.e., Marxist) philosophy, and Buddhism, and writing a comprehensive Maoist class analysis of Thai society,[74] Suphat had the opportunity to translate Leontiev's *Political Economy*, which he also used in his prison lectures on capitalist and socialist economic systems. He gave his copy of Engels' *Origin of the Family* to Kulap, who made similar use of it. Kulap's rendering of Engels' work turned up on the pages of the weekly *Piyamit* in 1954 under the titles "Kamnoed khrobkhrua khong manussayachat" (The origin of the human family) and "Rabiab sangkhom khong manus" (The human social order), whereas, unfortunately, Suphat's over one-hundred-page translation of Leontiev's book, together with Samak's philosophical manuscript and Sawai's record of daily conversations with Kulap on literature and literary composition, fell into the hands of the overzealous head of the Prison's Control Section, M.C. Woraphong Thassanaworawut, never to see the light of day. However, Prince Woraphong made one too many searches for his own good. While rummaging through the inmates' cells for banned materials, His Serene Highness stumbled on something that terribly upset him, a drawing of "Ai Khik" (the linga or phallus) drawn and hung in ambush by the inmates' teacher of philosophy, Samak Burawas.[75]

More than half of the forty-nine convicts were not members of any communist party or affiliated organization, while at least three of the five released were, and no contemporary top-ranking CPT leader was to be found in either group. These odd facts attest to the accuracy of the inmates' favorite joke: true to his name, Police Lieutenant General Phra Phinij*chonkhadi* (alias Seng Intharathoot), deputy director general of the Police Department and, as chairman of the Investigation Committee for these cases, chief architect of the "Soviet-Peking-Pridi-Suphat-CPT" plot, did indeed *chon khadi* or jumble up the cases.[76] As it turned out, the only relatively big communist fish caught in this little pond was Prasit Thiansiri, a CPT leader in the South of Thailand, who was arrested by chance on an express train to the South at the Thonburi railway station on November 7, 1952. His possession of sixty copies of the CPT's Second Congress Statutes, forty leaflets about the tenth anniversary celebration of the CPT's founding, and seven Chinese communist books frightened the police authorities into immediate drastic action against the "communists" three days later.[77] Moreover, the uncanny wording of subsequent official announcements relating to anti-communist legislation and measures revealed that the "chon khadi" complication was typical not only of Phra Phinij but of the Phibun government in general. In a statement issued November 14, 1952, concerning the purpose of the new Anti-Communist Act, the government warned: "If any organizations or groups of people or individuals have been engaged in activities forbidden by this Act prior to the date it came into effect, they should immediately disband those organizations or groups, or withdraw their cooperation there from..."[78] Five days later, reacting to news that a congratulation message had been sent by the CPT to the Nineteenth Congress of the CPSU, Prime Minister Phibun ordered the Department of Public Relations to broadcast an announcement that "...if there is really such a communist party committee, then, as a communist organization, it will be in violation of the Constitution and those persons involved in this organization will be guilty according to the Anti-Communist Act of 1952."[79] Betraying both uncertainty and hesitation, the "if's" cited above strongly indicate that the government was actually in the dark about the real communist movement. So Suphat, himself far from being a CPT member, who characterized his relationship with the CPT as "mutual shunning" occasioned by the CPT's mistrust of his close association with Pridi and his contempt for the CPT's intellectual and theoretical inferiority, recorded:

> During the era of Field Marshal Po. [Plaek Phibunsongkhram], the suppression of communists or leftists was targeted mainly at Ajan Pridi's group because it was the main political antagonist. As to the real left, be it the CPT or CCP, they were merely by-casualties of the suppression. But they [the authorities] did not know. They had no idea that some of the people they suppressed were CPT or CCP. They just hit them by chance.[80]

There were many factors that led to the Phibun government's ignorance of the Thai communist movement and doctrine, some being objectively given, others subjectively willful. On the objective side, the state agency responsible for keeping track of communists and other opponents of the current government, the Santibal or Special Branch Police, had undergone several purges of key personnel and drastic reversals of policy during the volatile and violent decade after the Second World War. As the internal eyes and ears of the government, so to speak, it was particularly vulnerable to shake-up each time an opposition party or group forcibly replaced its adversary in power.[81] For instance, shortly after the end of the war, the new deputy director general of the Police Department, himself a one-time detainee of the Santibal under the previous government and seeing no use for it, proposed dissolving the Santibal Police altogether, thus sending shock waves through the rank and file.[82] Although his proposal was not realized, the Santibal Police did experience the rapid turnover of four commanders in three years: Police Major General Khun Chalo Srisarakorn (appointed by the Phibun government), replaced by Police Lieutenant Colonel Luang Samrit Sukhumwat (by the Pridi government in 1946), replaced by Police Lieutenant Colonel Prasong Limaksorn (by the Thawan government in August 1947), replaced by Police Colonel Banjongsak Chippensuk (by the Khuang government in late 1947), who was in turn removed by the second Phibun government in mid-1948.[83] More importantly, the Santibal unit directly responsible for the labor and communist movements (Section 4, Division 2) was purged of political undesirables twice in the same period, first by the Pridi government in 1946 and then by the Coup Group in November 1947, in line with government policy toward these movements changing from age-old mistrust and constraint to help and cooperation (under Prime Ministers Pridi and Thawan), and back again to outright hostility and suppression (under Prime Ministers Khuang and Phibun).[84]

All these developments, needless to say, bewildered the Santibal, disrupted its operations and dislocated its resources, leaving the government's intelligence faculties severely impaired. It was perhaps only sometime in mid-1948 that the Santibal could resume its anti-communist operations in earnest. In the early 1950s, several middle-ranking police officers were sent abroad (to the United States, Britain, Australia, and the Philippines) to train as experts on (anti-)communist doctrine and methods, such as Police Major Chat Chawangkoon to Britain and Police Colonel Chai Suwannasorn to the Philippines, while the domestic surveillance of leftist dissidents and communist suspects was pursued more vigorously and aggressively than before.[85] Nevertheless, the Santibal's knowledge of communism in general and the Thai communist movement in particular did not improve much until after 1952 when the foreign-trained police experts began to return home and at least five leftist/communist suspects in the Peace Rebellion case gave way under police interrogation or torture, providing useful information and, in some cases, turning King's evidence, namely Phra Maha Dilok Suwannarat (the Peace Committee), Samut Surakkhaka (Khabuankan Koochat), Siriphorn Worachat (Khabuankan Koochat), Prajuab Amphasawet (CPT Youth League), and Phong Phanthurothai (Khabuankan Koochat). It is important to keep in mind, however, that the testimonies of these and other suspects in this case were given under extreme duress and so could not be taken for granted. Unused to physical pain and mental torment, many of them agreed to sign whatever the police interrogators put forward to avoid further battery and death threats. A notable exception was Prasit Thiansiri (CPT), whose endurance at the hands of Phao's police thugs was legendary. Another was Supha Sirimanond, arguably the foremost Marxist intellectual of the time, who steadfastly and adroitly refused Phra Phinij's repeated attempts to recruit him as an anti-communism expert for the police.[86]

Meanwhile, the Phibun government relied heavily upon anti-communist intelligence and news reports from friendly neighboring and western governments, Thai embassies abroad, and a medley of foreign press, news agencies, and radio stations. The foreign governments that energetically offered this service to Thailand included those of the United States, Great Britain, Hong Kong, Singapore, Taiwan, South Vietnam, Laos, and the Philippines. Thai embassies or consulates in Hong Kong, South Vietnam, the Philippines, and the USSR were active in this regard. Other sources of information about communist activities tapped by the Phibun government were an odd selection from foreign press and radio broadcasts.[87] Calculated to induce an actively anti-communist foreign policy on the part of the Thai government, most of these reports placed undue and exaggerated emphasis on alleged subversive activities of the Soviet Union, Communist China, and the Pridi group against Thailand.[88] That the thrust of this hyperbolic (un)intelligence happened to coincide perfectly with the traditional ethno-ideological bias of the Thai ruling classes against radical politics and ideology could not but contribute to the Phibun government's will to believe in the misinformation, for it seemed to console and confirm the government in its conviction that the "communists" remained by and large "un-Thai."[89]

In addition, there was the simple fact that, with few exceptions, Prime Minister Field Marshal Phibun and his ruling circle never knew or met any members of the CPT leadership personally, let alone served, sat, or socialized in any top political, bureaucratic, or military institution with them.[90] Consisting mostly of lookjin, *lookyuan* (Thai-born Vietnamese), and Thai students, workers, journalists, writers, lawyers, teachers, and petty merchants of the middle and lower classes, almost all CPT top leaders spent the best part of their active political life underground or in prison, thus outside the Thai legal, official polity, and usually far from the Thai ruling circles (except for those unlucky few who were temporarily behind bars). Therefore, unlike the leaders of most other opposition parties and groups, who belonged to the same social background and milieu as the Phibun group and with whom they used to consort, converse, confer, conspire, and clash,[91] the CPT leaders were so socially and politically distant that, to all intents and purposes, they represented an obscure petty nuisance.

And yet, the already obscure and distorted picture of the aggressively Thaifying communist movement and its doctrine was further willfully misrepresented and manipulated by the Phibun government itself. This was a case of realpolitik *par excellence* in which western anti-communist discourse was pragmatically adapted and opportunistically abused to suit the Thai rulers' own practical purposes in typical Phibunsongkhram style. Simply consider some of Prime Minister Phibun's public statements concerning the Thai government's policy on the global Cold War conflict between the communist and democratic camps. At a meeting of provincial governors and officials at the Government House on January 15, 1951, for example, Phibun gave four revealing reasons for his decision to side with the western democracies:

1) We are a member of the United Nations Organization; 2) we are an agricultural country that has to depend on industrial products; 3) the oceans that are the main routes of transportation are in the hands of the democratic camp and 4) in terms of the economy, we still have to depend on the democratic countries.[92]

Unlike other less wise anti-communist zealots, Phibun's motives for opposition to the communist camp and alliance with the West were plainly non-ideological—nothing here but cool, calculating *raison d'état*. Another example was a notorious investigation of two alleged communist politicians by the Phibun government during the peak of McCarthyism in the United States. In February 1951, U.S. ambassador Edwin F. Stanton delivered a scandalously interventionist letter to Prime Minister Phibun questioning the wisdom of retaining the head of the newly formed social democratic Ratsadorn Party and MP for Si Sa Ket, Thep Chotnuchit, in the cabinet as deputy minister of commerce. Pressed to appease his generous American donors, ever allergic to "reds" and "pinks," and yet in need of the Ratsadorn MPs' support in parliament, Phibun stage-managed a witch-hunt of Thep and his younger brother, Phethai Chotnuchit (MP for Thonburi, former editor of *Karnmuang*, and secretary-general of the Ratsadorn Party) in radio-broadcast hearings *à la* HUAC for Thai and American audiences. However, if the American original was a serious tragedy, the Thai copy was a shallow farce in which the Chotnuchit brothers were simply asked to denounce and swear to resist "the evil doctrine of communism" in front of the deputy prime minister without any in-depth probing or questioning. When asked to account for his authorship of a book entitled *Soviet russia kab khommunit* (Soviet Russia and communism), Thep explained that he had written the book to condemn the cruelty and mistakes of communism, not commend it. If by chance, however, what he had written happened to promote communism, he deeply regretted it because he had not intended to do so! The inquisition wound up with these solemn words:

> Thep: If I ever believe in this evil doctrine of communism, I am ready to be deprived of everything even my life.
>
> Phethai: Let me swear to Phra Thai Thewathiraj [the Thai Guardian Angel] that I am willing to sacrifice everything to resist communism and will join hands and hearts with others in eliminating and opposing it in every possible way.
>
> Deputy Prime Minister: Thank you two brothers for proving yourselves and submitting your statements to me as evidence.

That done, the presiding inquisitor facilely declared himself satisfied and absolved both from the "red" taint.[93] Put simply, Phibun played along with the anti-communist West as far as it served his own and Thailand's immediate interests as he perceived them.

In the same vein, Phibun and his group unscrupulously (or creatively, if one wishes) overextended the meaning of "communism" and "communists" into a catchall for all types of domestic political opponents regardless of ideology, be they Chinese workers, the Pridi group, Sahachip-Isan politicians, parliamentary oppositionists, dissenting cabinet ministers, the Peace Movement, the Khana Koochat, the Khabuankan Koochat, or the opposition press. Apart from Phibun's own jumbled definition of "communists" cited at the beginning of this chapter, Police Lieutenant General Phra Phinijchonkhadi, who admitted under cross-examination in court that he knew absolutely nothing about the socialist economic system or Marxism-Leninism, provided another official "chon khadi"-type characterization of communists.[94] Referring to the recently aborted Flood Rebellion of Luang Katsongkhram and company, which was anything but communist, Phra Phinij explained in September 1953 that:

> The authorities hold that any rebellions whatsoever in the present are all communist activities. The communists have a policy to keep on staging a rebellion in order to provoke unrest, weaken our internal strength and create difficulties so that they can eventually seize power and turn the country into communism.[95]

The pinnacle of the Thai parody of anti-communism was, of course, the new Anti-Communist Activities Act of November 13, 1952. No sooner had Phibun resumed his premiership in 1948 than he ordered the Juridical Council to begin drafting a new anti-communist law. However, his order met with repeated, principled objections from senior members of the Council, especially Phichan Bulyong and Serm Winijchaikul, on legal-constitutional grounds. The slow bureaucratic process was further interrupted by domestic unrest and the outbreak of the Korean War, while six different drafts were considered, rejected, and revised one after another so as to incorporate not only communists but other growing opposition groups such as the Peace Movement. Eventually, after four years in the making, the final draft was completed less than ten days before it was adopted by the National Assembly.[96] The Act defined "communist activities" as follows:

(a) The overthrow of the democratic form of government with the King as the Head of State, or

(b) The changing of the national economic system whereby private ownership or means of production is expropriated to the State by forfeiture or otherwise without payment of just compensation, or

(c) Any act of intimidation, sabotage or deceitful means such as to foment hatred among members of the public if calculated to enforce, assist, support or prosecute the object described in (a) or (b). [97]

If its 1933 predecessor had set a notorious precedent for the arbitrary definition of "communism" by covering a wide variety of collectivisms indiscriminately, this version went much further in its potential to sweep sundry political doctrines into the same category. No less an authority on Thai anti-communist juris-prudence than Mr. Thanin Kraivichien, future Supreme Court judge and prime minister, pointed out afterwards that even absolute monarchists, republicans, and military dictators would fall into the pigeonhole of "communist" and become culpable for "communist activities" according to the letter of the 1952 law.[98] The outcome of its practical application bore witness to its underlying absurdity: from 1952 to 1958, 190 "communist" suspects were locked up under this law; thirty-three cases were dropped during pretrial investigation, twelve cases came to trial, and only five (11.11 percent of all cases initiated) resulted in conviction. All "communist" convicts were released in any case under a general amnesty in 1957, along with those of the earlier Peace Rebellion cases.[99]

Not all episodes in this parody were so funny or light-hearted. Its dark, odious side was revealed when the "communist threat" (internal and external) became firmly established as the standard and almost automatic excuse for the military's seizures of power from constitutionally elected governments (in 1947, 1951, 1958, 1971, 1976), as well as a spicy and sometimes deadly ingredient in the recipe for political mud-slinging.[100] Suffice it to note that just before Police General Phao's right-hand butcher, Police Colonel Annop Phukprayoon, had Tiang Sirikhan (pro-Pridi, Sahachip-Isan MP for Sakon Nakhon) and four other people strangled for their intransigent opposition to Phibun and Phao on December 12, 1952, he accused them to their faces of being "communists." Having initially feigned ignorance of Tiang's disappearance, Phao announced on December 16 that the treacherous Tiang was a "communist" and had fled the country via Kanchanaburi to Victoria Point in Burma. This was followed by wild rumors in the press of his whereabouts in various neighboring countries, including a story showing an alleged picture of him with communist chief Ho Chi Minh. Fabricated though it was, Phao's announcement did contain an element of truth. The "communist" Tiang and his fellow "comrades" had indeed been hauled to Kanchanaburi, where their remains lay crudely cremated and buried in a remote old charcoal-pit.[101]

The American Embassy and the Manufacture of Communist Specters

As part of an ongoing effort to inculcate the communist threat into the Thai authorities, the American Embassy had over the years brought a quantity of

English-language communist books into Thailand to use in what may be called the manufacture of fake "communist specters." As early as July 1948, there was a curious report on the front page of the TCP's *Mahachon* of the arrival of the new American military attaché, Mr. Bullwit, suspiciously accompanied by a large number of "fake or unauthorized" "red" texts.[102] The exact use of these books, about which *Mahachon* was left wondering, became apparent when, sometime in 1953, the American Embassy, under incoming ambassador and former OSS chief General William Joseph Donovan, offered to commission William J. Gedney, an American linguist on a research grant from Cornell University, to translate Marx and Engels' *The Communist Manifesto* into Thai. Gedney accepted the offer provided the American Embassy also pay a native Thai assistant translator to help him.[103]

Gedney's chosen Thai assistant, who was to have a seminal Marxist-communist classic delivered to him by the American Embassy, was the young, cocky, brilliant, and wayward junior in the Faculty of Arts at Chulalongkorn University, Jit Poumisak. By that time, besides starting a Thai-Khmer dictionary and a Thai philological encyclopaedia, Jit had already published in established literary, popular, and student periodicals several fine, old-style poems and erudite, well-argued articles on Thai linguistic subjects, which had received very enthusiastic commendation and earned him the reputation of a promising "jewel" in literary circles.[104] Greatly impressed with the extraordinary knowledge and talents of this student prodigy recommended to him by two Chulalongkorn professors, Gedney had employed Jit from 1950 to 1951 and again in 1953 as a live-in tutor in Thai language and literature and occasional assistant translator at the handsome rate of three hundred baht per month for tutoring, plus forty baht per hour for translating. Earning much more than enough for his usual needs, Jit began to develop a taste for a comfortable "bourgeois" lifestyle, lavishing upon himself such luxuries as foreign cigarettes, a pipe, a Zippo lighter, a Mido wrist-watch, a Parker fountain pen, polished leather shoes, and pedicab rides to the campus, to the envy of many other students.[105]

But Jit also put his money and brains to other, shall we say, "anti-bourgeois" uses of which neither Gedney nor his American patrons were aware: the purchase and reading of Thai and foreign Marxist-communist books and periodicals. Nourished by the ready availability of these publications and easy access to some of their authors in Bangkok during the early 1950s and encouraged by a few progressive fellow students in the Faculty of Political Science at Chulalongkorn, Jit's initial curiosity about Marxism-communism had grown into serious, full-fledged, self-educated radicalization by the time the American Embassy put *The Communist Manifesto* into his hands. For example, Jit was said to have bought himself a complete set of the erudite, radical monthly *Aksornsarn* (1949–1952) and to have visited its editor, Supha Sirimanond, at his home twice, the second time by himself. Jit's private collection of books at his own house was reportedly very large and extensive. And his progressive friends in the Faculty of Political Science, having been interested in radical ideas for some time before Jit, were active in getting him foreign Marxist-communist books as well as affording him the opportunity to become involved in student activism.[106]

When, with their help, Jit was elected 1953 editor of the prestigious Chulalongkorn University yearbook, published annually on October 23 in memory of the university's namesake, the late King Rama V, he was eager to put his newly acquired radical ideas into editorial and literary practice. Refurnished with colorful, *waek naeo* (unorthodox) design and novel, leftish symbolism, the 1953 yearbook was to contain among its forty or so articles and poems many radical, anti-government items, including three significant pieces from Jit's own pen: a Marxist critique of Buddhist philosophy and practice entitled "Phi tong leuang" (The spirits of the yellow leaves) under the pen-name "Nakhorn That" (City Slave);[107] a short story about an ideal woman who devotes her life to progressive political and historical causes entitled "Khwan meuang" (The city's pride); and a *klon* poem condemning sexually promiscuous and maternally irresponsible women entitled "Thoe kheu ying rabjang thae chai mae khon" (You are really a hired woman not a mother).[108]

However, Jit's mutant brainchild never saw the light of day. Alerted by an employee of the Thai Watana Panich Printing House as to the yearbook's "communist" content, the university and police authorities moved to confiscate all the coverless copies shortly before they were due to come out. Jit was then "requested" by the university administration to give up his editorship and appear on October 28, 1953, before an assembly of the entire student body in the university's main auditorium to argue his case. Organized in the lingering hysterical McCarthyite atmosphere of the general crackdown on "communists" one year earlier, the student meeting soon degenerated into something much graver than the witch-hunt of the Chotnuchit brothers, though less brutal than the kangaroo court's condemnation of Tiang and his friends. As Jit was proving himself too persuasive a public speaker, a lynch mob of rightist engineering students rushed to cut short his self-defense speech by *yoenbok*, or throwing him off the stage onto the floor, thereby knocking him out.[109]

Although Jit suffered no serious injury in the incident, he was suspended from the university for one academic year while Gedney, because of his subsequent newspaper interview in defense of Jit, was presumed by the Santibal Police to be the imaginary foreign communist brainwasher and mastermind behind the green Thai student. The indispensable un-Thai villain in the "communist conspiracy" plot, he was pressured into leaving the country.[110] With the commissioned translator gone and his assistant in hot water, the American Embassy had to scrap the translation of *The Communist Manifesto*. Yet the unfinished project seemed to have over-accomplished its goal. Its attempt to forge a printed "communist specter" contributed in some ways to the manufacture of two effectively "real" ones, at least as they were perceived by the Thai authorities.

But the game of communist-ghost-playing was by no means one-sided, for the Phibun government had its own career conjurers. The Thai censorship authorities under Phibun and Phao's control focused their censorship effort on foreign-language radical publications, rather than Thai ones, even though the latter were amply available in the market most of the time.[111] Thus, from 1950 to 1957, 251 items of printed matter, due to their "probable contrariety to public order and morality," were prohibited from being ordered, imported, sold, or distributed, and were subject to confiscation by eighty-one different orders of the director general of the Police Department and press officials in the provinces of Bangkok, Thonburi, Si Sa Ket, Nan, Lampang, Chumphorn, and Phangnga in accordance with Sections 8 and 9 of the Press Act B.E. 2484. Of the 251, 129 were in English, 113 in Chinese, and one in French; only eight were in Thai.[112] Although most of the banned foreign-language publications were indeed on Marxism-communism, several of them were not in any reasonable sense and seem to have been banned simply because of their Soviet or Chinese publishers, for example, Ivan Turgenev's *Fathers and Sons*, *Sheying Yishu De Zaoxing Jiqiao* (Modelling techniques in the art of photography), and *Shibanhua Jifa Yanjiu* (A study of block-drawing techniques and methods).[113] Moreover, the paraphrased, summarized, or translated Thai versions of many banned foreign Marxist-communist books had been previously, or were later, published without being subjected to the same censorship, such as the *Constitution of the Soviet Union* (already translated from Chinese by Prasit Kanjanawat and published in *Karnmuang* in 1948), Stalin's *Problems of Leninism* (already translated by "Bamrung Phairachwathi," alias Lom Loetpricha, in *Mahachon* in 1948), Stalin's *Dialectical and Historical Materialism* (already translated by Samak Burawas in *Aksornsarn* in 1950–1951), Mao's *On Practice* (already translated by "Or. Pho.," alias Udom Sisuwan, in *Aksornsarn* in 1951), and Engels' *The Origin of the Family, Private Property and the State* (later paraphrased by Kulap Saipradit in *Piyamit Weekly Magazine* in 1954).[114]

Of the eight Thai publications listed in the orders, three were pornographic magazines: *Thai Phim Weekly Magazine*; *Thai Phim Phises Magazine*, published every ten days; and *Tai Phim Weekly Magazine*. Three were criticisms of the official Buddhist establishment: Ki Thanissorn's *Prab marn lem 1* (Conquering the demon, volume 1); Ki Thanissorn's *Patiwat khana song thai kab thammayutikprahan* (The revolution of the Thai sangha and the liquidation of the Thammayutika sect); and a leaflet entitled *Tham di dai di tham chua dai chua* (Those who perform good deeds will be rewarded, those who perform evil deeds will be punished). Another was a pictorial representation of the Thai suppression of the Khmer minority (actually, a student notebook with a drawing of the execution of Phraya Lawaek, a Khmer king, on its front cover. This left only a single Thai book on Marxism-communism out of a total of 251 publications banned, namely *Pratya prayuk* (Applied philosophy), Thatri Niwatthanathamrong, alias Phornchai Saengchaj's translation of Howard Selsam's *Handbook of Philosophy*.[115]

Such incongruously "un-Thai" book-banning orders, which seemed designed for application in the U.S. or China, may actually have been intended, according to Craig J. Reynolds' perceptive observation, for the "easy reading of foreign analysts in Bangkok embassies" as "a sign of the Thai government's orientation."[116] For all the ignorance, bias, and misinformation of the Phibun government which might have contributed to the obvious imbalance between the active banning of foreign radical books and the sluggish neglect of Thai ones, there is both reason and evidence to believe that another motive was at work. This anomalous practice may well have been a conscious effort to evoke a local communist specter for the Thai public and the American ally so as to dupe them into giving it political support and financial aid for urgent but unending exorcism, an effort which called, ironically enough, for the surreptitious maintenance, furtherance, and even replacement of the Thai radical press within controllable limits. Consequently, as fighting the reds was becoming a politically fashionable and financially lucrative career in the Cold War world, a group of Phibun and Phao's cronies[117] formed a number of anti-communist "popular" organizations for that purpose, such as the Sannibat Seriphan (League of Free Assemblies), the Samakhom Kammakorn Thai (Thai National Trade Union Congress), the Samakhom Seri Raengngan (Free Labor Association), the Laeng Wingworn Santiphap Khong Phoomi Sassana (Peace Appeal Center of Religious People), and the Ongkan Songserm Seriphap Thang Sassana (Organization for the Promotion of Religious Freedom).[118] Over the years, these organizations resorted from time to time to the fabrication and circulation of various Thai "red" publications, including a number of TCP leaflets and pamphlets and an issue of *Mahachon*, in order to stimulate demand for their services, prove their necessity and worth, and frighten some red-scared Thai capitalists and American aid-donors out of their wits and money.[119]

Given these precedents, it was only normal that, in the Mid-Buddhist Era Year of 1957, when the Phibun-Phao group was involved in exacerbated conflict with the opposition parties, the press, the leftist student movement, the Americans, the monarchy, and the army, it would try to pull the same old trick by conjuring up yet another printed "communist specter."[120] Thus, a sum of thirty thousand baht was extended by Phibun and Phao through Sang Phatnothai to radical student activists at the Faculty of Law, Thammasat University, for the publication of a historic, 532-page special issue of the faculty journal *Nitisat rab satawas mai* (Journal of law: The new century issue). Apart from two stately pictures of the Thammasat University Rector (Phibun) and Vice-Rector (Phao) and a short pro-government speech by Sang, the issue was filled with fifty-four pieces of overtly anti-government, anti-American, Marxist-communist writing.[121] Setting aside the bizarre fact that the government subsidized and co-committed this gross violation of Sections 5 and 9 of the 1952 Anti-Communist Activities Act,[122] what made the document unique and indeed monumental in Thai cultural politics was that it contained five seminal contributions by Jit Poumisak and one by Suphat Sukhonthaphirom, especially Jit's renowned paradigmatic 136-page historical essay on Thai "feudalism" entitled "Chomna khong sakdina thai nai pajjuban" (The real face of Thai feudalism today) that has since immortalized the term "sakdina," along with its author, in Thai radical discourse.[123]

For both Suphat and Jit personally, the publication of their mature Marxist-communist works in *Nitisat rab satawas mai* must have been sweet revenge. Suphat, who had just been released from prison under the government's Mid-Buddhist Era general amnesty in May, now saw his made-in-prison Maoist class analysis of Thai society into print through the financial support of those who had put him in prison in the first place.[124] Jit had been working as a book and art review columnist for several leftist newspapers and periodicals, as well as teaching English in the Fine Arts University and actively plotting, organizing, and guiding student activism as a recruit of the secret CPT-affiliated youth organization in Chulalongkorn University. He now succeeded in publishing the harshest and most sweeping historical critique to date of the antiquated Thai system of "sakdina" beliefs and practices that had so barbarically thrown him and his "waek naeo" ideas out to begin with.[125] Their fates seemed to have turned around completely, their persecutors becoming patrons, their accusers standing accused, and their powerful anti-communist adversaries becoming, legally speaking, "communist assistants."

Whether the Americans fell for Phibun-Phao's latest trick and, if so, how long these mutually deceiving partners of convenience would have continued the paradoxical game of setting out to catch real communists but getting mostly non-communists (like Suphat) and trying to manufacture fake "communist specters" but ending up producing real ones (like Jit), we will never know. What we do know is that most Thai leftists and one influential wing of the Thai communists did fall for the manufactured image of Field Marshal Sarit Thanarat as a "patriotic and democratic military commander," showering his personality and actions with such eulogistic tributes as "resolute," "prudent," "timely," "courageous," and "patriotic," and cheering him on as he craftily manipulated the press and public's accumulative anger at the corrupt and brutal Phibun-Phao regime in his own bid for power.[126] On September 16 of the same fateful year, Sarit unleashed his army tanks amidst popular cheers of support and off went Prime Minister Phibun and Police Director General Phao to the far-away lands of Japan and Switzerland, respectively, never to return.[127] There followed a brief honeymoon period during which the two successive governments installed by Sarit adopted a number of popular policies, such as holding a relatively less "dirty" general election, prosecuting Phao's police butchers for murders, and facilitating the visits of various Thai delegations to socialist countries.[128]

But the initial euphoric hurrahs of the communist and leftist crowd soon turned into howls of sour disappointment and then stunned silence as censorship was again tightened. Only one year after the first coup, following a visit to the Walter Reed Army Hospital in the United States for major surgery as well as alleged conversation about further aid, and a subsequent convalescence-cum-study tour of Europe for some brief tutorial in comparative constitutionalism, Sarit came home and took power from himself (that is, from the puppet government under his control) in a second, this time avowedly "anti-communist," coup on October 20, 1958. He then proceeded to establish the most absolutist regime Thailand had ever experienced since the end of absolute monarchy, turning on his former communist-leftist allies with a comprehensive nationwide crackdown that was much more violent and sweeping than anything accomplished by Phibun and Phao. Hundreds were rounded up on "communist" charges and thrown into the new Ladyao Central Penitentiary, still under construction, for an indefinite period of detention. Four were later summarily executed, namely Suphachai Srisati (engineering graduate from Japan and labor leader, on July 6, 1959), Khrong Jandawong (Tho.Ko.Cho. leader, on May 31, 1961), Ruam Wongphan (CPT politburo member, on April 24, 1962), and Thongphan Sutthimat (CPT member, on May 31, 1961).[129]

Among this third generation of suspected "communists"-cum-political prisoners, later known as the "Ladyao Communists," were Suphat Sukhonthaphirom, Jit Poumisak, and Sang Phatnothai. That the first of this trio was a non-communist, the second a communist, and the third an anti-communist, indicates the political diversity of the inmates, the mixed motives of their persecutors, and the perennial ambiguities of the terms "communism," "non-communism," and "anti-communism" in Thai political discourse. Be that as it may, one thing was reassuringly predictable about their imprisonment—the usual covert accompaniment of an abundant supply of foreign Marxist-communist books. Banished as these printed "communist specters" were from the free book market, they were destined to show up no where else but in the unfree habitat of prison. Lying hidden in odd corners of cells to be read, studied, discussed, and translated by the "Ladyao Communists" were such best-sellers as Plekhanov's *The Role of the Individual in History*, Lenin's *The Collapse of the Second International*, Stalin's *Problems of Leninism*, *The History of the CPSU (Short Course)*, *Selected Works of Mao Tse-tung* in four volumes, the CCP's *Long Live Leninism!*, Emile Burns' *What Is Marxism?*, and Maurice Cornforth's *Dialectical Materialism, Historical Materialism*, and *Theory of Knowledge.*[130] In a manner typical of the whole tragicomic business of foreign Marxist-communist printed commodities in Thailand, the former government's anti-communist law and censorship orders had made Ladyao perhaps the only remaining public sanctuary where demand could still meet supply and imprisoned Thai radical intellectuals could still read banned un-Thai communist books.

7
Marxism as Commodity: Reproducers

I made use of many party people without acknowledging their party
membership or otherwise...I am an individual outsider. I sent manpower
to the Party without telling it, making it acceptable to the kids.

Supha Sirimanond[1]

Important as foreign Marxist-communist publications were to the development
of radical culture in post-war Thailand, they constituted but half its story, and
the less consequential and interesting one at that. The reason is obvious:
objectively speaking, only a very small percentage of the whole population had
physical and/or cultural access to them,[2] and one absolutely needed to
reproduce their message of "universal truth" culturally in Thai before one could
dream of the Thai masses politically reproducing a Marxist-communist social
revolution. Subjectively, there were understandably strong motives on the part
of foreign-language-reading radical intellectuals for precisely that kind of
cultural reproduction, namely, missionary zeal to preach Marxist-communist
truth to their compatriots and a dire economic need to publish, either to earn
their living as career writers/journalists or to supplement the inadequate
income of their main jobs.[3]

But who were these Thai cultural reproducers of foreign-derived Marxism-
communism? The conventional way of categorizing them, according to their
contemporaries and recent researchers, is to divide them into two main groups:
first, the communist group, which refers to leading ideologues and propagandists
of the Thai Communist Party (later Communist Party of Thailand), the Chinese
Communist Party-Thai Branch, and the remaining Vietnamese group of the
defunct Communist Party of Siam; and second, the Pridi or *Aksornsarn* group,
which denotes Thai socialist or Marxist intellectuals outside the communist
movement, most of whom were followers or sympathizers of Pridi Banomyong
(or regarded as such), former members of the Free Thai Movement, and largely
associated with the *Aksornsarn* monthly magazine.[4]

Originally, the first group was centered around the weekly *Mahachon* and
generally dominated by people of Chinese and Vietnamese descent outside

government and bureaucratic circles with a lower than tertiary level of formal Thai education, like Song Nopphakhun (TCP secretary-general, lookjin); Phayap Angkhasing or Piatoe (TCP spokesman, lookjin-Khamu); Thong Jamsri (*Mahachon*'s first editor, lookyuan), Wiroj Amphai (*Mahachon*'s owner, lookjin); Sak Suphakasem (*Mahachon*'s second editor, lookjin); Uthai or Sangob Thiambunloet (owner of the TCP's Uthai Printing House, lookjin); Udom Sisuwan (head of the TCP press and literary publication department, lookjin-Ngiew-Shan);[5] Jaroen Wanngam (*Mahachon* reporter, Laotian); Damri Reuangsutham (head of the TCP labor and student movement, lookjin); Si Anothai (leader of the TCP labor movement, lookjin); Wirat Angkhathaworn (TCP Bangkok, lookjin); Lom Loetpricha (*Mahachon*'s English-Thai translator, teacher at Uthenthawai Construction School); Miss Nith Phongdapphet (head of the TCP student movement); Sujin Akharasamit (journalist of TCP's *Sethasarn*, lookjin); and Sanan Waraphreug (editor of CCP-TB's *Maitrisarn*, lookjin).[6]

By contrast, the second group consisted mostly of well-educated Thais who had served in senior positions in the government and/or bureaucracy. They included M.C. Sakol Wannakon Worawan (former adviser to various government agencies and the Sahachip Party, public speaker, and pamphleteer); Sanguan Tularak (former cabinet minister and secretary-general of the Sahachip Party, first ambassador to nationalist China, owner of *Chon Kammachip* newspaper); Suri Thongwanich (editor of *Lok Mai* and *Siang Thai* newspapers and owner of Choochon Publishing House); Thianthai Aphichatbut (lookjin senator); Jaroen Seubsaeng (Sahachip MP for Pattani); Pan Kaeomat (Sahachip MP for Nakhon Phanom and secretary to the minister of education); Police Second Lieutenant Vas Sunthornjamorn (journalist, trade union lawyer and activist, co-founder of the Khana Kammakorn or Workers' Party and of the Sahachip Party); Police Captain Chiab Chaisong (former Santibal officer, owner of *Sangkhom Samakkhi*); Mrs. Nongphot Praphasathit (novelist); Supha Sirimanond (former Prime Minister's liaison officer with the army, press attaché to the Thai Embassy in Moscow, editor of *Aksornsarn*); Kulap Saipradit (veteran leading journalist and novelist, student of political science at Melbourne University); Samak Burawas (bachelor of science from London University's Imperial College of Science and Technology, Royal School of Mines, member of the prestigious Royal Institute in the discipline of philosophy, director of the Division of Mineral Science at the Department of Mines, director of the Research Division at the Naval Signal Corps, lecturer in mineralogy and philosophy, prolific writer and translator), Suphat Sukhonthaphirom (master of economics from Thammasat University, former head of the Thai Embassies Comptroller Section at the Ministry of Foreign Affairs, translator for the Soviet Embassy, leader of the Khabuankan Koochat); Suphot Dantrakul (journalist of *Siam Mai* newspaper);

Sakchai Bamrungphong (diplomatic official at the Thai Embassy in Moscow, novelist and columnist); Chat Bunyasirichai (editor of *Siang Thai* newspaper); Thaweep Voradilok (Thammasat student activist, poet, and editor of *Phimthai* newspaper); and Thongtoem Samerasut (caricaturist, partner of *Aksornsarn*).

In the late 1940s and into the 1950s, while the Pridi/*Aksornsarn* group was progressively shrinking due to severe government suppression and internal dissension,[7] the communist group was able to penetrate the wider circles of educated and cultured Thais and substantially expand its ranks and those of its myriad affiliate front organizations, often at the expense of the Pridi/*Aksornsarn* group. It recruited politicians—Prasert Sapsunthorn (MP for Surat Thani), Pan Kaeomat (MP for Nakhon Phanom), Khrong Jandawong (MP for Sakon Nakhon), Jaroen Seubsaeng (MP for Pattani), Lieutenant Colonel Phayome Julanond (MP for Phetchaburi), and Mongkhol na Nakhorn (municipal councillor and member of Provincial Council of Trang); trade unionists—Vas Sunthornjamorn (Khana Kammakorn), Suwit Niamsa (railway workers' union), and Jamnong Noothong (rice mill workers' union); journalist-writers—Kulap Saipradit, Atsani Phonlajan, Issara Amantakul, Utthorn Phonlakul, Corporal Roeng Mekphaiboon, Bunmi Latthiprasat, Suchat Phoomborirak, and Luan Pannoi; and student activists—Jit Poumisak and Prawut Srimantra (from Chulalongkorn University), Ruam Wongphan, Prajuab Amphasawet, Somkhuan Phichaikul, Phin Bua-on, Sanao Phanichjaroen, Pleuang Wannasri, Phichit Dijai, Waithoon Sinthuwanich, Winai Phoemphoonsap, Athorn Phutthisomboon, Somphong Pheungpradit, Samphas Pheungpradit, and Sanong Mongkhol (all from Thammasat University). By 1957, Udom Sisuwan, himself a lookjin party leader, was able to claim emphatically that communists, far from being the "monsters" anti-communists portrayed them as, were definitely "Thais," "patriots," and "lovers of the Thai way of life."[8]

This conventional, two-group categorization comes in handy because it underlines a crucial fact about post-war Thai radical cultural politics. The communist group, especially the TCP, stood alone on the Thai Left as a full-fledged, organized, mass political movement with the solid organizational strength and coherent political direction to withstand government repression, market fluctuation, and prolonged periods of political inactivity underground, in prison, or in exile; its resilience was unmatched by other leftist groups and parties. However, as with all systems of categorization, this pairing of "communist" versus "Pridi/*Aksornsarn*" is useful in so far as we are aware of its limitations as an approximation of a far more complex and dynamic reality and not that reality itself. In this case, the limitations are threefold, as the groups were neither all-embracing, homogeneous, nor mutually exclusive.

First, there were a number of prominent advocates and publicists of socialist or socialistic ideas and systems who belonged to neither group. These included: Leuan Saraphaiwanich (MP for Thonburi, minister of education for the Prachathipat Party); Prasit Kanjanawat (MP for Chachoengsao, founder and owner of *Karnmuang* prior to its communist take-over, and Police General Phao's henchman); Thep Chotnuchit (MP for Si Sa Ket, deputy minister of commerce, founder and head of the Ratsadorn and Setthakorn Parties); Khlaeo Norapati (MP for Khon Kaen, secretary-general of Setthakorn Party); Ari Liwira (Chinese journalist and translator, proprietor of the giant Thai Phanitchayakan Press and newspaper chain, Chinese nationalist democrat); Kanda Liwira (Ari's widow, later Thaweep's spouse, Chinese translator); Suwat Voradilok (romantic novelist and playwright, Santichon Party); Thanong Satthathip (journalist and editor-in-chief of *Sanseri*, protégé of Field Marshal Sarit); Khamsing Srinawk (novelist and assistant manager of Kwianthong Press, protégé of Kulap); Thongbai Thongpao (writer and journalist of *Thai Mai*, lawyer for communist political prisoners); and Jintana and Chankhun Kotrakul (Chinese translators, owners of Thewawes Press).

Second, neither group was ideationally or politically homogeneous. Not surprisingly, this characteristic was especially pronounced within the Pridi/ *Aksornsarn* group. This was because, aside from their common socialist-Marxist ideological orientation, members of this group were essentially united by personal loyalty to Pridi and the joint effort of publishing *Aksornsarn* and other radical publications. A modicum of formal organization and discipline was represented by such failed political ventures as the February 26 Democratic Movement (1949), the Khabuankan Koochat (1951–1952), and the Sri Arya Mettraya Party (1957). Given their personal and editorial nature, these bonds proved too loose to hold the group together in the face of growing personal discord and political differences among its members. There were many such issues, ranging from the pivotal to the trivial.

One recurrent disagreement was over the method of seizing power. While Pridi was plotting and engineering an armed uprising against the Phibun government in 1949 (the February 26 Democratic Movement), Supha refused to lend anything more than moral support because of his "personal aversion to the use of force." The reckless adventurism of that armed uprising also alienated Nongphot Praphasathit, another faithful follower. Later, Pridi's insistent instructions from China to his disciples in Thailand to re-attempt a similar fatal "koup-de-ta" provoked the poignant criticism of Chinese officials that Pridi seemed to care less about the sufferings and lives of his disciples than his persistent bid to regain power.[9]

Other points of contention stemmed from the group's dealings with communist China. Pridi alienated his hosts with his principled refusal to promise to grant privileged political and cultural autonomy, as a "national minority," to the Chinese and lookjin population in Thailand in exchange for Chinese aid. Pridi's refusal even to pay lip-service to this demand, and his indignant condemnation of the "pseudo-communist chauvinism" behind it and of covert inspection of the exiles' private mail stalled negotiations between the two sides from 1950 to 1954 and resulted in China's worsening treatment of its Thai guests. Pridi's intransigence and the consequent long delay led to the desperation and desertion of many of his disciples in China.[10] However, when the Chinese later dropped their "chauvinistic" demands, initiated a rapprochement with Pridi, and broadcast his article attacking "the reactionary Phibunsongkhram Government and American Imperialism" on Radio Peking in July 1954, this in turn prompted many of his liberal disciples in Thailand, like Direk Jayanama, Wijit Lulitanond, and Thongyen Lilamian, to denounce him as a "thoughtless red."[11]

The issue of leadership of the international communist movement also sparked angry debate. One such began in a study session between the "internationalist" Sanguan Tularak, who zealously supported the Moscow-Peking leadership of the movement, and the "isolationist" Nongphot Praphasathit and Police Captain Somsak Phuawes, who were distrustful of any form of foreign domination of their homeland. The debate ended with Somsak's threat to break Sanguan's head had they only been in Thailand.[12]

Over time, disagreements arose over the historical significance of the People's Party's overthrow of the absolute monarchy in 1932 and the historical stature of Pridi himself. Swayed by the Thai and Chinese communists' standard belittling interpretation, Sanguan Tularak turned against Pridi's long-held views on the 1932 overthrow as "the unfinished and betrayed democratic revolution," the People's Party as "the party of revolution," and Pridi himself as "a revolutionary." To the resentment of Pridi, the turncoat now derided the 1932 undertaking as "a coup d'état," the People's Party as "a group of power-grabbing aristocrats," and his own master as "a reformer" of lesser historical stature than even the revolutionary King Rama V.[13]

Finally, Pridi's personal privileges in exile were divisive. In the early days of the group's exile in China, the communist authorities allowed Pridi alone the exclusive right to private correspondence with his family in Thailand. Later, the enviable happy reunion of Pridi with his wife and two daughters in Peking amidst the universal separation of his exiled disciples from their spouses and children, and hence their generally unfulfilled concupiscence, became an especially controversial issue.[14] In view of the accumulated bitterness caused by these frictions and quarrels and the evident inexperience of the Pridi group in leading an organized collective life, it is little wonder that, by the end of the 1950s, the Pridi/*Aksornsarn* group had basically broken up.[15]

What was less noticeable or, at any rate, less publicly discussed, owing to the clandestine nature of the subject, is the fact that the communist group was not nearly as homogeneous as it claimed or understood itself to be, according to the ideal of a monolithic Stalinist party of iron discipline.[16] After all, the TCP was a newly-founded party, formally established only in 1942, and the post-war period was a time of rapid expansion when the Party admitted, at times hastily, a host of new recruits marked by young age, political rebelliousness, higher education, intellectual independence, personal arrogance, and different native ethnic and cultural backgrounds. Nothing illustrates this point better than the images of Sanao Phanichjaroen and Corporal Roeng Mekphaiboon, two self-educated Thai Marxists whose initiation into the doctrine owed nothing to the Party. Udom Sisuwan described his first meetings with each of them at the *Mahachon* office. Similarly smoking pipes and exuding a cocksure air, Sanao and Roeng walked into the then Thai Communist Party propaganda headquarters and introduced themselves to Udom with the respective purposes of showing off a red-covered, self-translated-and-published Thai version of Marx and Engels' *The Communist Manifesto*, entitled *Kamnodkan khommunit*, and of discussing the philosophy of "watthuniyom wichakajcha" or "dialectical materialism." It was Sanao's independent translation and Roeng's persistent discussion that served as their passport to membership in the TCP.[17] Similar was the case of Prasert Sapsunthorn, MP for Surat Thani, who won shortcut admission to the Party in exchange for his successful sponsorship of the abrogation of the Anti-Communist Law in the House of Representatives in 1946.[18]

Obviously, these were precisely the kind of people one could least expect to shut up and kowtow tamely to flimsy logic, inferior argument, flawed theory, and the unreasonable imposition of centralized command and discipline by anyone, let alone senior lookjin party cadres whose compliant familiarity with democratic centralism was matched only by their unpliant unfamiliarity with the Thai language and culture. This unpliant unfamiliarity, though inadvertent in cases such as Phayap Angkhasing's unclear Thai pronunciation, was willful in others, such as the recurrent opposition of Song Nopphakhun, Uthai Thiambunloet, Prasert Aeuchai, and Wirat Angkhathaworn to Phin Bua-on's proposal to Thaify the CPT.[19] Put together in a collective, revolutionary organization in the midst of the violent and volatile political turmoil that was Thailand and the Far East in the 1950s, it would be a wonder indeed if these people could work in perfect harmony, much less think and act in unison. As it turned out, they did neither. Therefore, like the discordant Pridi/*Aksornsarn* group, the communist group was plagued during the post-war decade with various major internal disputes of both a theoretical and political nature. Some of these conflicts were waged over the Party's position on the "coup line," the importance of united front, peaceful parlimentary struggle, Titoism, and the Party's "national character."

In the late 1940s, certain TCP leaders (like Song Nopphakhun and Udom Sisuwan) were briefly interested in the seizure of power by coup d'état and collaborated with the Pridi group in planning and arranging the deployment of forces in the February 26 Democratic Movement or Royal Palace Rebellion of 1949, with Pan Kaeomat acting as go-between. The collaboration did not come to much since Pridi regarded the TCP as only a minor force in the whole operation; in any event, the Rebellion was put down before the Party's armed force could take any action. Those party leaders involved were later attacked by Wirat Angkhathaworn, Thong Jamsri, and Jaroen Wanngam for "day-dreaming about the Coup Line."[20]

The dispute over the united front began as a debate in China during a theoretical education and training program for twenty leading Thai communist cadres which was sponsored by the CCP, co-taught by Soviet and Chinese teachers, and run by a CPT Educational Committee consisting of Wirat Angkhathaworn, Thong Jamsri, and Jaroen Wanngam, from 1952 to 1957. The debaters were Prasert Sapsunthorn, Vas Sunthornjamorn, Pan Kaeomat, Phayome Julanond, Phin Bua-on, and Sanao Phanichjaroen on one side and the Educational Committee triumvirate on the other. Prasert, the leader of the faction, argued that building a united front between the CPT and the Pridi/Free Thai group was essential to the success of the Thai revolution, whereas the triumvirate regarded such a united front as not only dispensable, but also tending dangerously towards the "Coup Line" and neglect of the masses and party work in the countryside. In sum, it amounted to "ham wo hai chonchan naithun" (carrying the capitalist class' palanquin) or "foolishly helping the Pridi/Free Thai group to power." Equipped with insubstantial argument and weak logic to support his pro-united front proposition, Prasert lost the debate and his idea was condemned as antithetical to the Maoist Second Party Congress' line of peasant-based revolutionary armed struggle in the countryside.[21]

Though defeated in the first round, Prasert was still convinced of the correctness of his idea and spent the following five years refining and developing it in a new direction. Encouraged by Khrushchev's idea of a possible non-violent path to socialism presented in 1956, he submitted to the

Party Central Committee in early 1958 an over one-hundred-page critique of the Maoist Second Congress line and an attendant proposal for an alternative line of peaceful parliamentary struggle, aiming first to establish a bourgeois democratic form of government and then to win state power by legal-electoral means. The CPT's rejection of his proposal *in toto* led to Prasert's final break with the Party and return to Thailand.[22]

The conflict over Titoism also occurred in China in 1953 during the education program mentioned above. Sanao Phanichjaroen, one of the program's students who had once authored an article attacking Tito's policy of independence from the Soviet Union in *Aksornsarn*, now had a change of heart and unyieldingly defended Tito against the standard Soviet condemnation parroted by the Wirat-Thong-Jaroen triumvirate. Sanao's pigheaded "Titoism" resulted, by order of the Educational Committee, in his expulsion from the Party and almost forty-year exile in Chongqing, where, married to a Chinese woman, he worked as a librarian and raised a family until his return to Thailand in the early 1990s.[23]

The dispute over the Party's "national character" centered on Phin Bua-on's proposal to Thaify the still largely ethnic Chinese CPT by recruiting more ethnic Thais, especially Thai peasants in the countryside, to party organizations at every level. He first raised this proposal during the theoretical education and training program in China. It met with strong objections from several senior lookjin party members, including Uthai Thiambunloet, and its author was branded a "nationalist." However, Phin got the upper hand when, unexpectedly, the Chinese comrades came out in favor of his idea, with special emphasis on its organizational aspect. Yet the CCP's fraternal advice led to further controversy, for Uthai and other CPT students of both lookjin and Thai ethnicity, like Suri Sisuwan and Atsani Phonlajan, were incensed by what they perceived to be Chinese "intervention in the internal affairs of the Thai revolutionary movement." Their criticism at this instance of "intervention," directed rather indiscreetly at their Chinese hosts, was considered by the triumvirate to have gone too far. As punishment, a severe, written condemnation of their "anti-organization" behavior, with their names fully listed, was publicized to humiliate them and serve as a warning to others.[24]

Another example was the issue of pursuing a tactical alliance with Phibun-Phao or Sarit. From 1954 onwards, the CPT tried to take advantage of the burgeoning strife between Police General Phao Sriyanond's faction and General (later Field Marshal) Sarit Thanarat's faction within the ruling Coup Group by playing off police against army in an effort to revive the leftist popular movement after the 1952 set-back. This was evident in various political tactics adopted by Thammasat and Chulalongkorn student activists under CPT leadership at that time.[25] However, the CPT found itself on the horns of a dilemma when Prime Minister Phibunsongkhram introduced liberal and pro-labor reforms with Phao's support over Sarit's objection in 1955 and the conflict between the government and army worsened in 1957. The question was whether to support Phibun-Phao in anticipation of further reform or to cheer on the ambitious Sarit to replace the decade-old brutal authoritarian regime once and for all.[26] In the event, the CPT did both or, more accurately, different factions of the party leadership made different choices. Roughly speaking, the trade union faction led by Party secretary-general Song Nopphakhun and Damri Reuangsutham allied itself with Phibun-Phao, while the more vocal and influential intellectual-student faction led by Udom Sisuwan, some of whose members and collaborators were strategically placed on the editorial staff of several major newspapers, sided with Sarit. The resolution of this tactical difference was made more difficult and belated by the general lack of co-ordination, of even a simple meeting, between the factions. It persisted even after Sarit's second coup of 1958 and the ensuing imprisonment of many CPT leaders, including Udom himself.[27]

Be that as it may, in contrast to the disorganized Pridi/*Aksornsarn* group, the communist group, as a mass party with pretensions to Stalinist principle, had various organizational and disciplinary measures to cope with or dispose of individual dissidents and "alien" elements without too much disruption to the Party's overall structure and functioning. These ranged from censorship (Atsani Phonlajan, Corporal Roeng Mekphaiboon, Mongkhol na Nakhorn) and public censure (Uthai Thiambunloet, Atsani Phonlajan, Suri Sisuwan) to discrimination (Song Nopphakhun, Udom Sisuwan, Atsani Phonlajan), demotion (Prajuab Amphasawet, Atsani Phonlajan, Lieutenant Colonel Phayome Julanond), and purges (Bunmi Latthiprasat, Sanao Phanichjaroen, Prasert Sapsunthorn, Phin Bua-on).[28] Plainly, no comparable control mechanisms were available to Pridi, Supha, or Suphat for reining in the intensifying centrifugal forces within their amorphous group and avoiding final disunion.

The final limitation of the "communist" versus "Pridi/*Aksornsarn*" categorization is that the two groups were not mutually exclusive. Un-doubtedly, they were deeply divided by numerous serious disagreements and mutual reservations, such as their interpretation of the 1932 overthrow of the absolute monarchy,[29] their respective roles in the anti-Japanese resistance, their rival claims to pioneering Marxism-communism in Thailand,[30] and the relative expediency of supporting the socialist camp versus pursuing a neutralist foreign policy.[31] More directly, Pridi denounced the CPT as an alien-established and -commanded, pseudo-communist satellite party of Chinese ultra-nationalism,[32] Suphat was contemptuous of the CPT's inferior and second-hand knowledge of Marxist-communist theory,[33] and Supha disapproved of the CPT's "phasa sontaphai" (leading-people-by-the-nose language) and "siang lae klin takiab" (chopsticks' voice and smell).[34] These last remarks were aimed at the CPT's typical use of didactic propaganda that tended to stupefy readers rather than encourage critical thinking and autonomous rational judgement and at its cheap imitation of the Chinese communists' crude and rude polemical style and content. In return, the CPT was mistrustful of Supha's independent, open-minded, and scholarly brand of Marxism and editorial practice.[35] These disputes led to several instances of discrimination and exclusion, especially on the part of the CPT, when sectarian mistrust overrode ideological solidarity, as when the Peace Movement rejected the Khabuankan Koochat's offer of cooperation and the CPT insisted on removing Khamsing Srinawk from a 1958 delegation of Thai writers and journalists led by Kulap Saipradit to Peking on account of Party suspicion that Khamsing was a CIA agent.[36]

And yet there were many instances of cooperation and joint action between the two groups, such as their indirect cooperation through Prasert Sapsunthorn on the 1946 passage of legislation abrogating the Anti-Communist Act and the Pan Kaeomat-mediated abortive joint uprising in the 1949 Royal Palace Rebellion.[37] Individual members of both groups also took part in political and cultural movements organized and led by the other. For example, the communist side arranged for M.C. Sakol Wannakon Worawan, Thianthai Aphichatbut, and Police Second Lieutenant Vas Sunthornjamorn to participate in the communist-dominated trade union movement[38] and for Jaroen Seubsaeng, Pan Kaeomat, Chit Wejprasit (former Sahachip MP for Phuket), Kulap Saipradit, Samak Burawas, Sanguan Tularak, Suri Thongwanich, and Thaweep Voradilok to be involved in the communist-engineered Peace Movement and its press organ, *Karnmuang*.[39] Radical works and translations by non-communists were published by communist-operated publishing houses. For example, the *Mahachon*-connected Yuk Mai (New Age) Press published Prasit Kanjanawat's translation of the Chinese version of the 1947 revised Soviet Constitution, along with appended commentaries by Suphat Sukhonthaphirom and Udom Sisuwan.[40] And TCP-affiliated publishing house Saha Bannakorn Press published a travelogue, a novel, several literary essays, and translations of Soviet fiction by Sakchai Bamrungphong.[41]

Sizable funding was provided to *Aksornsarn* through private financial contributions and paid regular advertisements taken by communist-owned companies.[42] One noteworthy communist private patron of *Aksornsarn* was Sawai Malayavej, a well-to-do southern Thai businessman and member of the TCP. Dissatisfied with the low quality and inadequate quantity of inner Party theoretical education and publications, Sawai headed for Bangkok, spent a large sum of money on higher education, and finally found the kind of knowledge he looked for in *Aksornsarn* and the writings of Supha. Gradually, he befriended the initially suspicious Supha and donated about two thousand baht to the magazine by buying remainders of *Aksornsarn* and Supha's *Khaepitalist* and giving them freely to public libraries and his acquaintances, especially in the South. Likewise, Supha knowingly enlisted several communists, namely Sanao Phanichjaroen, Atsani Phonlajan, Sanan Waraphreug, Pleuang Wannasri, Udom Sisuwan, and Sak Suphakasem, to write for and help edit *Aksornsarn*, while Suphat involved Pan Kaeomat, Bunmi Latthiprasat, and Pleuang Wannasri in organizing the Khabuankan Koochat.[43]

Apparently, the two main reasons for this "cross action" were the open, fluid, and varied characters of the two groups and the underlying commonality of their cause, immediate shared goals, and universal theoretical horizons,[44] both of which made them willing to reach out to each other in times of need. As Udom Sisuwan explained, since the CPT was then largely underground, its members did not lightly reveal their membership; what was more important than party membership was to achieve the Party's goals. Hence, the broad involvement of non-CPT radicals in various activities of the Party.[45] Reciprocally, for all his harsh judgement of and aloof attitude toward the CPT, Supha occasionally described his relationship with it in remarkably amicable if sardonic terms: "I made use of many party people without acknowledging their party membership or otherwise…I am an individual outsider. I sent manpower to the Party without telling it, making it acceptable to the kids."[46] Significantly, as a consequence of the ongoing cross action, members of both groups were notably open and indeed susceptible to ideas of the other, for example, Sanguan Tularak, Pridi's so-called "Phra Mokkhalla" (right-hand man), who came under the influence of by-then CTP member Vas Sunthornjamorn and clashed with Pridi over the interpretation of the 1932 change of regime,[47] or Sawai Malayavej of the TCP, who confessed much later that, theoretically, "I got nothing from the Party. Supha was my first teacher of Marxism."[48]

Therefore, although the binary categories of "communist" and "Pridi/ *Aksornsarn*" do highlight the important and instructive politico-organizational context of post-war Thai radical cultural practice, it is advisable not to make a fetish of the group dichotomy, especially when dealing with such a diffuse entity as culture. It is preferable to conceive of the Thai reproduction of Marxism-communism as a cross-group cultural process, with special emphasis on how Marxism-communism was transferred and transformed across authors (or "reproducers"), languages, and literary genres from the core to the periphery of Thai cultural spheres. About this cultural process the following preliminary observations can be made:

First, as far as "authors" are concerned, Thai Marxism-communism spread from bilingual lookjin communists and Thai leftist bureaucrats ("core reproducers") through politicians, writer-journalists, and university students, to rural teachers, monks, and peasants ("peripheral reproducers").

Second, Marxism-communism was disseminated in Thailand through the linguistic medium of Chinese/English, then Thai, and finally through various languages and local dialects such as Laotian, Pak Tai, and Kham Meuang.

And third, the literary genres in which Marxism-communism was introduced and propagated in Thai were, in rough sequence: political leaflets, pamphlets, statements, and programs; translations of theoretical and philosophical works, usually accompanied by a glossary; historical and sociological analyses of Thai society; prose fiction, plays, poetry, and songs; literary essays and reviews and self-help handbooks;[49] and simplified pamphlets and handbooks for new recruits to party organizations, often written in local languages.[50]

In the post-war decade, this cultural process of Thai reproduction of Marxist-communist discourse took place mainly on the printed pages of Thai radical periodicals. Table 7-1 is probably the most comprehensive list of them compiled. However, it makes no pretension of being all-embracing. Covered are all known radical periodicals of the period, be they commercial, student, or underground. Left out are those that did not have the propagation of radical ideology as their standing editorial policy or practice, and thus published radical writing only occasionally or in special issues, such as the newspapers *Siam Nikorn*, *Thai Mai*, and *Sanseri*, the weeklies *Siam Samai* and *Piyamit*, the journals *Nitisat* and *Euangfa*, and *23 Tula*, the Chulalongkorn University yearbook.

Given the stated purpose and limited scope of the present study, our focus is on the culturally crucial junctures in the reproductive process where Marxism-communism was received by writer-journalists, translated into Thai, and rhymed into poetry on the printed pages of three key radical periodicals of the post-war decade, which will be examined in detail in the next chapter. These are *Mahachon*, *Aksornsarn*, and *Karnmuang Weekly*. These three publications are chosen on the basis of their relative cultural-political significance and the extent to which they represented the major groups of Thai radical cultural reproducers: the CPT, the Pridi group, the left-wing Kuomintang, Thammasat University-related independent leftists, and the Peace Movement.

Table 7-1
Thai Radical Publications, 1946–1957

TITLE	DATES OF PUBLICATION	AFFILIATION	OWNER(S)/EDITOR(S)
Mahachon	August 1942–1951	TCP	Thong Jamsri, later Wiroj Amphai/Sak Suphakasem
Karnmuang Weekly	c.1944–1951	Independent, later the Peace Movement (TCP)	Prasit Kanjanawat/ Phethai Chotnuchit, later Jaroen Seubsaeng/Jamras Sapthanawin
Chon Kammachip	August/September 1945–?	Pridi group	Sanguan Tularak
Lok Mai	November 1945– March 1949	Pridi group	Suri Thongwanich
Dome (monthly)	September– December 1947	Pridi group	Thammasat students
Thammajak	September 1948– 1952	Independent, later TCP	Thammasat Student Committee/ Prajuab Umphasawet, later Thaweep Voradilok, Wichian Watthanakhun, Phiphat Phatthanophas, Suwit Phadoemchit
Sangkhomniyom (weekly)	November 1948–?	TCP and Prasit Kanjanawat?	Khana Sangkhomniyom
Aksornsarn	April 1949– October 1952	Pridi group	Supha Sirimanond
Maitrisarn Biweekly	1949–1951	CCP-TB	Somphong Phawichit
Siang Thai	1939–1952	Pridi group	Prasit Kanjanawat and Phethai Chotnuchit/Chat Bunyasirichai, later Suri Thongwanich
Thammajak (biweekly)	1950–1951	independent	Ari Imsombat
Puangchon (weekly)	c.1951–1953	TCP	Chat Bunyasirichai
Thang Mai (monthly)	May 1951–1952	TCP	Wichian Sariman
Yuk Mai (biweekly)	May 1951–?	TCP	Central Labor Union/unknown
Sajjatham	c.February– September 1952	CPT	Phin Bua-on
Issaraphap	1953–?	CPT	Unknown
Thammasat Journal	1953–1957	independent	Thammasat Student Committee/Jamras Chomphoophol, Suraphorn Phejwisai, Issara Nitithanpraphas
Sethasarn Biweekly Magazine	June 1953– October 1958	CPT	Luan Pannoi
Pituphoom (La Patrie) Weekly	December 1955–1958	CPT	Pleuang Wannasri and Samphas Pheungpradit
Naeo Nakseuksa (biweekly)	1956	unknown	Rome Bunnag
Siang Nisit (biweekly)	1956–1957	CPT	Phinij Nanthawijan
Sangkhom Samakkhi Monthly Magazine	1957	Pridi group	Sri Arya Mettraya Party/Police Captain Chiab Amphunan
Saithan Monthly Magazine	May–October 1958	CPT	Thongtoem Samerasut/Chao Phongphichit

8
Marxism as Commodity: Reproduction

No. MAIJEUD (alias) Thongyoo Yoskrit the fortune-teller, a meticulous expert in life and travel palmistry who is popular with VIPs and big officials and whose signature appears in many visitors' books, would like to predict that no matter whether there will be a change or not, the lives of three VIPs, namely Field Marshal Po. Phibunsongkhram, Luang Katsongkhram, and Lieutenant General Phin Chunhawan, will never be down on their luck and always do well, adventurous though they are. Speaking about the character of the country, it owes its continued existence to their sociability. It is guaranteed that change is most difficult to happen. Master Thongyoo would like to warrant you that his prediction of your life will be accurate to the utmost. He is now scheduled to go on a fortune-telling tour to the southern provinces accompanied by two female secretaries.

Advertisement in the communist weekly *Mahachon*[1]

Mahachon

The *Mahachon* (the People or the Masses)[2] weekly newspaper (August 1942–1951) was the first and principal official propaganda organ of the TCP during its First Congress period (December 1942–February 1952).[3] The paper was launched as an anti-Japanese, anti-Phibun government underground publication under Japanese occupation on August 20, 1942, that is, more than three months before the founding of the TCP.[4] In this regard, it probably served as part of the preparations for the Party's actual founding. *Mahachon*'s first editor, staff writer, proofreader, typesetter, pressman, and deliverman during the war was Thong Jamsri,[5] who almost single-handedly ran the whole operation, manually printing the paper sheet by sheet with a roller on plates. Thong's jack-of-all-trades working style was admiringly inherited by the later editorial staff of *Mahachon*, whose members conscientiously performed all the technical printing tasks involved.[6]

In the latter half of 1944, probably sometime after the fall of the Phibunsongkhram government in July, *Mahachon* emerged from clandestineness as a legal commercial weekly publication with a newly expanded, competent, and versatile editorial staff. Based on available primary and secondary sources,[7] Table 8-1 provides an incomplete list of the names, brief backgrounds, and editorial roles of *Mahachon*'s staff. Other well-known progressive writers and journalists who published their work periodically in *Mahachon* were Sod Kuramarohit, Issara Amantakul, Sanit Ekkachai, Po. Booranapakorn (Pakorn Booranapakorn), Ko. Surangkhanang (Kanha Khiangsiri), So. Assanajinda (Somchai Assanajinda), and Thida Bunnag.

Sold cheaply at one baht per copy, *Mahachon* advertised itself as follows: "Read the *Mahachon* weekly newspaper and you will be informed of the workers' activities, know political problems definitely, and understand the situation clearly." Outwardly, *Mahachon*'s format looked no different from any ordinary Thai newspaper, complete with editorials, domestic and foreign news reports and analyses, articles, features, poems, novellas, and advertisements. Its communist slant showed up in the many TCP manifestos, statements, policy documents and interviews provided by the Party spokesman, expositions of communist theory and history, translations of communist classics, and glossaries of Marxist terms. In addition, the news reports, analyses, and features it carried were always presented from the standpoint of communist ideology and the Party's policies, while the short stories and poems attempted in their own ways to be politically radical.

In content, *Mahachon*'s post-war political emphasis shifted from anti-Japanese, anti-Phibun united front to the propagation of communist doctrine, opposition to western imperial powers, especially American imperialism, and support for the socialist and New Democratic camp and communist-led national liberation movements in colonial countries, especially in Siam's Southeast Asian neighbors. Domestically, it emphasized anew an urban, grass-roots-based, united-front-oriented struggle for "true democracy and independence" through socio-economic and political reform within the existing political framework in opposition to conservative royalist political forces and the pro-Phibun military. These new emphases reflected the TCP's path-breaking strategic adoption, immediately after the war, of a non-insurrectionary parliamentary route to state power, or perhaps to the sharing of power in a coalition government of leftist forces. Socio-economically, the Party's revised post-war ten-point immediate policy was remarkably more moderate than Pridi's aborted National Economic Plan of a decade earlier.[8] All these mirrored the TCP's partial adaptation to a new, open, and approachable political regime and the degree of its newly acquired legitimacy. In the words of a CPT official history:

Table 8-1

Mahachon's Editorial Staff

NAME	BACKGROUND	EDITORIAL RESPONSIBILITY
Wiroj Amphai	Lookjin son of a well-to-do family; chief "united front" cadre of the TCP	Owner, and publisher, mostly making contact with outside people rather than writing
Sak Suphakasem	Lookjin graduate of Chulalongkorn University at the end of World War II; fluent in Chinese and Russian owing to his temporary refuge and work as the first teacher of the Thai language in Moscow in the early 1950s	Editor, poet, and short-story writer
Uthai (Sangob) Thiambunloet	Lookjin owner of Uthai Printing House, which published *Mahachon* and housed its office	Key writer and superb translator, presumably from Chinese; regular writer of editorials and special features
Phayap Angkhasing	Party spokesman	Most likely supervised the whole *Mahachon* organ
Thong Jamsri	*Mahachon*'s original editor and key operator	Editorial responsibility unknown
Udom Sisuwan	Lookjin-Ngiew-Shan and former Christian from the northern province of Lampang; educated at local American Protestant mission school, fought Japanese in Yan'an in 1938 and applied for CCP membership there; admitted into the TCP with Phayap's sponsorship in 1946; head of TCP press and literary publication department in the 1950s; fluent in English and Chinese (also studied some Esperanto in Yan'an)	Accomplished political columnist, literary essayist, and Party theorist
Jaroen Wanngam (and his wife)	Ethnic Laotian and former Christian of middle peasant family background from the northeastern province of Ubon Ratchathani; came to Bangkok for vocational education, working part-time in a meat factory, where he met party cadres; anti-Japanese agitator and saboteur among workers in a Japanese factory; recruited into the party near the end of WWII	News reporter but not much of a writer; nothing definite known about the background and editorial role of Jaroen's wife
Prasert Sapsunthorn	Sole communist MP	Wrote poetry and the enormously popular "Chiwathas" (Life Conception) column, a communist guide to correct conduct
Atsani Phonlajan	Ethnic Thai of old aristocratic family in the central province of Ratchaburi; graduate in law of Thammasat University (1940); audacious state prosecutor better known as an extremely knowledgeable and wildly iconoclastic poet, fiction writer, literary critic, and political and legal essayist of genius; allegedly (perhaps exaggeratedly) fluent or literate in Latin, English, French, Chinese, Hindi, Pali, Sanskrit, Urdu, Malay, Javanese, etc.; member of the TCP from 1950	Regular contributor of poems and short stories
Lom (Bunlom) Loetpricha	Teacher at the Uthenthawai Construction School	Regular translator from English of communist theoretical writings

Plate 8-1. Udom Sisuwan (1920–1993), columnist and chief propagandist of the Communist Party of Thailand during the 1950s (photo taken circa 1950s; photo credit: Matichon Press)

Under such [partially democratic] circumstances, the party had to readjust its policy and tactics to conform to this new development. It did this by operating both clandestinely and openly and both legally and illegally. It used legal and practical forms of struggle and organization to consolidate and lead the people of all strata in the struggle against the imperialists, feudalists and bureaucratic capitalists, to grasp the due rights and interests for the people and to heighten the people's consciousness for the benefit of the country's revolution.[9]

Thus, in stark contrast to the later, resolutely insurrectionary stance of the CPT, there was no facile talk in *Mahachon*, at least prior to the 1947 military coup, of a violent overthrow of the current government or political order, despite a still vaguely revolutionary rhetoric.[10] Rather, trade unionism and legal-constitutional politics were the name of the game.[11] Moreover, although the paper was keenly and increasingly interested in the Chinese Communist revolution, it was still predominantly Soviet-oriented and not yet strongly pro-Chinese, as the Party would subsequently evolve to be.[12]

In practical terms, this stance meant, on the one hand, TCP support for Pridi and his former-Free Thai followers, organized into the social democratic Sahachip (Unionist) Party and liberal Naeo Ratthathammanoon (Constitutional Front) Party, and, on the other hand, opposition to the conservative royalist Prachathipat (Democrat) Party "of the big landlords" and the anti-communist, royalist Thammathipat (Right Is Might) Party of the militaristic Phibunsongkhram group.[13] Although with only a single seat in the 178-member House of Representatives the TCP's political weight did not count for much in parliamentary politics, the Party-led and -organized labor and student unions were a significant extra-parliamentary force. Usually in cooperation with the leftist Sahachip Party, they were capable of launching extensive, coordinated strikes, such as the joint strikes at sixty-nine private and public rice mills along the Chaophraya River in 1945 and 1947 which effectively paralyzed the industry.[14] And they could rally tens of thousands of people in Bangkok on such occasions as the demonstration celebrating peace and supporting the punishment of war criminals at the end of 1945,[15] May Day and other worker celebrations in 1946 and 1947,[16] protest against the return of the four Phibun-annexed provinces to the French on December 8, 1946,[17] and the anti-Phibun rally on April 7, 1947.[18]

This political posture worked well enough for the TCP and *Mahachon* while Pridi and his followers were in power, even if the Party's friendly if unrealistic coalition proposal went largely unheeded,[19] its vote cast for the pro-Pridi-Thawan government in a vote of confidence was not much appreciated,[20] the

Workers' Protection Legislative Act which it and the Sahachip Party co-sponsored was rejected in the House by pro-Pridi liberals,[21] and communist labor leaders and strikers were occasionally subject to police arrest and brutality.[22] The Party was nonetheless able to continue its many activities, including the publication of *Mahachon*, mostly unharassed and with unprecedented freedom under the auspices of such political notables as M.C. Sakol Wannakon Worawan, adviser to the ruling Sahachip Party, and Thianthai Aphichatbut, a senator who served as honorary adviser and nominal chair of the communist-affiliated and -controlled Central Labor Union.[23] Indeed, shortly after the war, Sanguan Tularak, Pridi's right-hand man and then a cabinet minister without portfolio, assembled government officials to inform them that government policy would henceforth be pro-labor.[24] Santibal Police Captain Chiab Chaisong, then head of Section 4 (labor and communist activities) under Division 2 (political activities in general), to his almost speechless amazement, was summoned and personally instructed by Prime Minister Pridi secretly to help, support, and coordinate with the labor movement, in good faith and in every possible way, above all during strikes. This total reversal of government policy on organized labor from one of mistrust, control, and suppression for the purpose of government stability, was duly followed by Chiab. From 1946 to 1947, he used his influential office to urge employers to make concessions to strikers, applied the law in the strikers' favor, paid monthly living expenses to dismissed strikers out of the Santibal secret service's coffers and found jobs for them, and procured rice for the communist-dominated Central Labor Union to sell to its members in time of shortage.[25]

However, things began to change on November 8, 1947, when the Thawan government was overthrown and Pridi fled for his life following the military coup d'état of the Coup Group, whose deployment of anti-aircraft guns around the Defense Ministry Building that morning sent the surprised, frightened, and militarily simple-minded staff of *Mahachon* scurrying helter-skelter from their nearby office.[26] One of the six reasons given by the Coup Group for taking power was that "the coup will rid the country once and for all of vestiges of Communism and cherish the Buddhist religion forever."[27] In the five-year period of extreme political instability that followed, the TCP came under increasing government pressure and harassment, usually occasioned by drastic domestic and international political developments. It began with Prime Minister Phibunsongkhram's repeated public statements after coming to office in April 1948 that communism was anti-monarchical and hence unconstitutional and that Thailand was being encircled by it.[28] Soon after, in August and September 1948, on the recommendation of Minister of Defense Lieutenant General Luang Chatnakrob, who admitted ignorance of communist literature and TCP policy, and Army Commander-in-Chief Lieutenant General Phin Chunhawan, the cabinet began an internal witch-hunt for "any government officials who are communists or believe in communism" in all government agencies. Those found guilty of the thought-crime were to be demoted or dismissed and their colleagues to be kept under surveillance, urged to inform on each other's "communist activities," and forbidden to read communist newspapers.[29]

The government's "red scare" campaign aimed at the general population included fabricated TCP leaflets and publications which proclaimed alienating ultra-leftist policies against religion and the monarchy, alleged TCP membership of some leftist politicians, and threatened terrorist arson and sabotage. These were usually distributed in Bangkok and their messages further publicized by anti-communist royalist newspapers and government radio broadcasts, especially a regular radio program produced by the Sannibat Seriphan (League of Free Assemblies), an anti-communist organization founded and led by such Phibun cronies as Major General M.L. Khab Kunchorn, Luang Saranupraphan, Sang Phatnothai, and Chai Wirojsiri.[30] The Sannibat Seriphan operated under the auspices of the Publicity Department from July 1950, stressing the value of freedom and private property and the incompatibility of communism with Thai social and political institutions and cultural values.[31]

Most serious of all, the burgeoning nationwide communist-dominated trade union movement under the direction of the Central Labor Union and the Bangkok Labor Union[32] was perceived by the Phibunsongkhram regime as triply dangerous—communist, Chinese, and pro-Pridi—and thus to be nipped in the bud. Trade union offices were repeatedly ransacked, their leaders and activists chased away or arrested.[33] Taking their place were a number of government-backed anti-communist trade unions, set up and controlled by Phibunsongkhram's close political and labor aide, Sang Phatnothai. Chief among them was Samakhom Kammakorn Thai (Thai National Trade Union Congress), affiliated with the anti-communist International Confederation of Free Trade Unions.[34]

Overseeing all these and other aspects of the government's anti-communist crusade was a series of organs established by Prime Minister Phibun specifically for the purpose—Khana Kammakan Raksakan Klang (Central Supervisory Commission, November 1948); Khana Kammakan Obrom Kharajkan Lae Prachachon (Committee for the Instruction of Officials and the People); Krom Pramual Rajkan Phaendin (National Intelligence Agency); Khana Kammakan Phijjarana Hathang Lae Damnoen Kanprabpram Nangseuphim Thi Pen Fai Khommunit (Investigative and Executive Committee for the Suppression of the Communist Press, October

1951); Khana Kammakan Phijjarana Rang Kodmai Waduai Kankratham Thi Pen Patipak To Prathet Thai (Un-Thai Activities Act Drafting Committee, October 1952); Kong Tamruaj Raksa Chaidaen (Border Guard Police Force, 1954); and Kong Asa Raksa Dindaen (Territorial Guard Volunteer Force, February 1954).[35]

But instead of cautiously mincing its words, the TCP bluntly and scathingly attacked the Coup Group, the transitional puppet governments of the Prachathipat Party, and the succeeding Coup Group governments through the *Mahachon* newspaper and various clandestine pseudonymous leaflets.[36] Barely two and a half months after the coup, the paper published a TCP statement calling for the replacement of the Coup Group-installed Prachathipat Party government with a "truly democratic" coalition government of the Communist Party and other democratic, patriotic, and peace-loving political forces. To achieve this goal, the TCP proposed a common struggle waged by a Naeoruam Haeng Prachachat Thai (United Front of the Thai Nation), consisting of "the oppressed classes of workers, peasants, soldiers, students and merchants, including all democracy-oriented organizations, associations and political parties, as well as minorities and patriots."[37] There followed a series of expositions of various aspects of the Party's policies related to the United Front.[38] Then came the resignation at gunpoint of Prachathipat Party Prime Minister Khuang Aphaiwong and his replacement by the Coup Group's own symbolic leader, Field Marshal Plaek Phibunsongkhram, on April 8, 1948. *Mahachon* reacted by publishing daredevil editorials and articles: "Prachathipatai tai tintakhab" (Democracy under the tank's tracks),[39] "Phadejkan thang kanmeuang kheu kanpokkhrong doi amnaj thahan" (Political dictatorship is military rule),[40] "Ratthabal pen tonhet khong khwamseuam" (The government is the source of decline),[41] and "Chak haeng kanphikhat prachathipatai" (The scene of democracide).[42] In timely and prescient fashion, it also anticipated, exposed, and countered the Phibunsongkhram government's "Invoking and Repressing the Specter of Communism" campaign as part of the U.S.-led worldwide anti-communist movement, though apparently to no avail.[43]

This militant bravado on the part of *Mahachon* did not bode well for its continued legal existence under anti-communist military rule. Publication of "Ratthabal pen tonhet khong khwamseuam" (The government is the source of decline) in issue 153 of October 17, 1948, led to Wiroj Amphai, *Mahachon*'s owner, being summoned by police for investigation on a charge of "publishing an article that propagates criticisms of the government."[44] And following the defeated Royal Palace Rebellion in February 1949, *Mahachon* was temporarily closed down along with seven other newspapers for failing to submit news reports to the police for pre-publication censorship. *Mahachon*'s editor, Sak Suphakasem, was also arrested and detained for several months in the Bangkok Light-Sentence Prison for defaming the government and for suspected involvement in the Rebellion.[45]

Censorship was further tightened in the aftermath of the Chinese Communist victory in October 1949 and the outbreak of the Korean War in June 1950, which helped substantiate and heighten the "communist peril," so vociferously invoked to justify repression of the opposition and restrictions on freedom. In March 1950, Prime Minister Phibun issued a secret order to the Police Department to find ways to close all communist newspapers.[46] One month later, he had the Central Supervisory Commission appoint a security subcommittee responsible for the prevention and suppression of communist propaganda. By order of the government in June of the same year, strict prosecution was henceforth to be pursued against any newspaper "publishing lies that are likely to cause disturbances in the land or reporting news intended to provoke unrest in the country in accordance with communist principles."[47] And when the government's decision to participate militarily in the Korean War met with a flood of press criticism, the Police Department issued, on July 20, 1950, a six-month order banning "publications and comments on international politics that may adversely affect diplomatic relations with regard to Thailand." With its scope subsequently expanded to cover news reports on Thai military operations in Korea and meetings of the Thai defense and armed forces' councils, the order was extended many times on a six-monthly or yearly basis until its eventual repeal on June 16, 1956.[48] As a result of these measures, all copies of a November 1950 issue of *Mahachon* were confiscated for "publishing strongly anti-government statements" and its editor again arrested for "committing propagation that provokes internal unrest."[49] This time Sak learned his lesson and escaped to the Soviet Union.[50]

And yet, neither the Prachathipat Party nor the Coup Group governments outlawed the TCP or banned *Mahachon* outright. By contrast, much more violent measures, including police assassination, were meted out to non-communist opposition groups, individuals, and newspapers, especially those that were pro-Pridi.[51] Apart from the previously discussed general ignorance of the Thai communist movement in ruling circles and the Phibun government's willful manufacture and maintenance of visible and manageable Thai communist specters,[52] there were a number of supplementary factors that appear to account for this discrepancy. Political conflicts in this period were fought mainly with soldiers' bullets and voters' ballots (in that order),[53] and the Thai communist movement, lacking physical means for the former and strategic confidence in the latter, might not have figured as a principal menace in the government's perception. Furthermore, with its potentially powerful trade-union wings clipped, the TCP and its mouthpiece seemed capable of noisy barks but only a toothless bite and no longer required the government's primary attention in view of other more urgent threats and the tasks of power consolidation at home and winning recognition abroad.[54]

Therefore, the publication of *Mahachon* was allowed to continue openly and legally until its final cessation, probably sometime after May 1951, and its replacement the following year by the newspaper *Sajjatham* (Truth) of the Second Party Congress, the CPT's intended equivalent of the Bolsheviks' *Pravda*.[55] But because Sak's editorial colleagues had in the meantime dispersed and gone into hiding,[56] *Mahachon* came to be published irregularly, changing from a weekly into an ad hoc newspaper as required by the volatile political situation.[57] So when some issues of *Mahachon* failed to appear at the usual times, the Sannibat Seriphan found it expedient to take "communist" matters into its own hands by publishing a fake issue, number 207, in February 1951, a few copies of which were marketed and mailed to certain printing houses, government officials in the Ministry of Interior, and provincial admin-istrators. The counterfeit *Mahachon* prompted Wiroj Amphai, the genuine owner of *Mahachon*, to publish an open letter firmly disowning the fake issue and indignantly condemning its forgers, while another columnist claimed one motive of the forgery was to "dupe the capitalists who urge a plot against the Communist Party and the people into giving them money."[58] This rather curious incident helps reveal the phantasmal side of the Specter of Communism, in this case conjured up out of thin paper by the witch-hunters themselves.

Aksornsarn

In sharp contrast to *Mahachon* in both style and content was the monthly magazine *Aksornsarn* (Inscribed Advice), published from April 1949 to October 1952 by a group of mostly pro-Pridi and independent Thai leftists and some communists.[59] The magazine's founding fund of 17,900 baht was provided jointly and unequally by ten partners whose names, brief backgrounds, and investment shares are shown in Table 8-2. It is clear from this data that the magazine's main financiers were Supha Sirimanond and his family, who together provided nearly 90 percent of *Aksornsarn*'s founding coffers. Moreover, it was due to their long friendship with Supha that other minor partners joined this publishing venture in the first place. As a matter of fact, it is not wide of the mark to say that the whole *Aksornsarn* enterprise was Supha's "one-man," or more accurately, "one-family," show for not only was he the magazine's chief editor, publisher, and advertiser, but his wife served as general manager and their modest home, Krathom Pakpao (Puffer Cottage), served as its office. Their tough, mostly self-sufficient, and unsalaried working arrangement was such that the couple became, by way of comparison, *Aksornsarn*'s Thong Jamsri, with Supha doing the chief editorial, typing, and design work and Chinda being responsible for all the essential but tedious menial and clerical chores of proofreading, packaging, mailing, delivery, collection of remainders and payments, and accounting. But for the devotion and painstaking efforts of this patient, caring, and intellectually unassuming lady, the highbrow *Aksornsarn* would never have seen the light of day, nor would its founder, who suffered from severe tuberculosis, have survived its publication.[60]

However, unlike the case of *Mahachon*'s editorial staff, Supha and Chinda's jack-of-all-trades working style was not a matter of ascetic self-training but dire necessity. *Aksornsarn*'s income came from two main sources: sales of the magazine at four baht per copy (about 1,200 copies yielded about 3,850 baht per issue, given the booksellers' 20 percent commission)[61] and the commercial

Table 8-2

Name, Brief Background, and Investment of *Aksornsarn*'s Partners

NAME	BACKGROUND	INVESTMENT
Supha Sirimanond	Pro-Pridi veteran journalist and Marxist socialist	5,000 baht
Chinda Sirimanond	Supha's wife and a trained nurse	10,000 baht (the sole partner with unlimited liability)
Luang Suphathep (Toe Sunthararohit)	Supha's father-in-law, wealthy retired civil servant	1,000 baht
Chanid Saipradit	Kulap's wife; a freelance writer and translator	1,000 baht
Uthai Sakhornwasi	Druggist and friend of Supha; family owned a Bangkok pharmacy	300 baht
Thongtoem Samerasut	caricaturist and columnist; old colleague of Supha at *Nikorn Wanathit* during the war	200 baht
Saengarun Ratkasikorn	Painter and lecturer in the arts at Chulalongkorn University; designed and painted *Aksornsarn*'s cover	100 baht
Sommai Huntrakool	Japanese-educated lookjin official at the Bank of Thailand	100 baht
Jaroen Chaichana	Popular historian	100 baht
Thuanthai Bamrasarinphai	Close friend of Supha	100 baht

Source: Thailand, Department of Commercial Registration, Ministry of Commerce, "Aksornsarn Limited Partnership," Registration Profile File no.738.

Plate 8-2. Supha Sirimanond (1914–1986), owner and editor of *Aksornsarn* (photo taken in the 1980s; photo credit: Matichon Press)

advertisements it carried regularly. Printing costs and contributors' fees constituted most of its expenses, the comparatively handsome rates of the latter being 150–200 baht per novelette and short story and 350 baht per article.[62] On average, though the magazine's sales earnings were just enough to cover the contributors' fees (about 3,000 baht per issue),[63] its advertising income failed dismally to meet the high printing bills. This was especially true during the first year of publication, due in large part to the culturally commendable but financially disastrous, unanimous policy of *Aksornsarn*'s partners and publishers to maximize the magazine's "reading space" and minimize its "advertising space." Therefore, while remunerative learned articles and fine fiction and poetry filled each of *Aksornsarn*'s unusually voluminous, 150-page early issues, commercial advertisements occupied only one twenty-fifth of its total printing space, falling far short of a contemporary estimate that at least one sixth was necessary to achieve self-sufficiency.[64]

It took a substantial deficit of 10,000 baht, over 50 percent of the founding capital, as discovered by the magazine's accountant at the end of its first year of publication, to jolt *Aksornsarn*'s partners and publishers out of financial insouciance into the practice of economy.[65] From that point, the number of pages per issue declined, eventually stabilizing at about one hundred,[66] a faster and more efficient printer was sought to economize on printing costs,[67] and the contributors' fees were contained. But all the savings achieved through these measures were consumed by a threefold rise in the price of paper (from 72 to 200 baht per ream) caused by the Korean War in early 1951, a shocking business calamity that occasioned a barrage of outraged condemnations of "capitalist economic dictatorship" from the usually reticent general manager, Chinda Sirimanond.[68]

Meanwhile, the magazine saw no improvement on the advertising front, with the number of ads per issue gradually decreasing from fifteen in the first year of publication to ten or less in the later years. Moreover, the real business situation of *Aksornsarn* was even bleaker than these figures suggest for underlying the gradual decrease was the perceptible tendency of purely commercial advertisers to withdraw from radical publications like *Aksornsarn*, to be replaced by politically motivated ones. Thus, of the approximately five hundred advertisements published in the forty-three issues of *Aksornsarn*, forty-seven were *Aksornsarn*'s own and brought in no revenue, 133 (29 percent of the income-earning advertisements) were placed by *Aksornsarn*'s partners and/or staff members, and fifty-three (11 percent) were placed by Thai and Chinese communist-related companies, leaving only 270 (60 percent) as proper commercial advertisements. Evidently, these were less than sufficient to support the business.

That against all these economic odds, Supha and Chinda managed to turn out issue after issue of the high quality *Aksornsarn* for almost four consecutive years was indeed a testimony to the sincere devotion, painstaking effort, and selfless sacrifice the Sirimanond couple dedicated to the cause of the scholarly study and enlightened propagation of Marxism-communism in Thailand. Be that as it may, they would not have been able to endure and overcome all the hardships and obstacles but for the recurrent timely aid of a personal friend and patron named Bunchoo Rojanasathian, then a rising lookjin accountant and banker of the Bangkok Bank, who would become a top tycoon in the Thai banking and finance industries in the 1960s and 1970s. Credited with being "one of the two main pillars of *Aksornsarn* magazine" by Supha (the other being Kulap Saipradit), Bunchoo helped procure and pay for the scarce and expensive medical prescriptions to cure Supha's critical tuberculosis in 1949; arranged for *Aksornsarn* to be printed by the more competent Rungnakhorn Printing House, of which he was a co-founder and shareholder, in 1950; financed the publication of Supha's magnum opus, *Khaepitalist*, in 1951; and secured a 40,000 baht loan from the Bangkok Bank in 1952 so Chinda could expand her Pakpao Cottage into a thriving Pakpao Nursery to support Supha and *Aksornsarn* financially.[69] Why did this capitalist friend of Supha anonymously finance the publication of a book-length study and critique of "the origins, structure, existence, and laws of motion of the age of capitalism," the first and probably still the best of its kind in the Thai language, as well as play "Engels" so generously and persistently to "Marx" and his brainchild, the radical *Aksornsarn*? Supha explained that it was due to Bunchoo's "profound appreciation of [the need for] progress, security, and education of the masses."[70]

Intended as a "serious political magazine" for "serious readers" (both printed in English in the original), *Aksornsarn* carried in-depth foreign news analyses and literary and theoretical writings. Deliberately designed by Supha to be a direct reaction and liberal alternative to the TCP's didactic propaganda, the magazine had a noticeably more learned, erudite, intellectual, and pluralistic style than *Mahachon*.[71] Overtly vowing as a matter of principle never to become a propaganda mouthpiece of any particular group or school of thought, *Aksornsarn* considered itself a broad platform for various contending ideas serving to enlighten public opinion and the literary and artistic world. It cautioned its readers against blindly accepting what it had to say, or being steadfastly committed to the views, tradition, or faith of any single group or school. Rather, they were advised to keep a pure, just, and open mind in their reading.[72] Hence, during its early years, *Aksornsarn*'s printed pages were liberally apportioned to writings of disparate ideological persuasions, be they anti-communist, conservative, liberal, democratic, Buddhist, Fabian, Marxist, or communist. The rationale behind this, in Supha's words, was as follows:

I did not publish this magazine for the leftists. The progressive people could find their own reading. I wanted to wash [*fok*] the thoughts of the older generation [*khonrunkao*] therefore I had a lot of backward, idealistic stuff in the magazine, hoping that having read it, they might perhaps also glance this way and read...[the progressive writings] little by little.[73]

The ideological composition of *Aksornsarn*'s editorial staff also reflected this open-minded policy, at least initially. Of its eleven members, six were Marxist socialists or communists, while the rest were to their right, ranging from social democrat to liberal. The name, editorial responsibility(ies), and brief background of each are shown in Table 8-3. It should be noted that the alienating effect of this ideological rift was somewhat mitigated by personal, family, and social relationships among individuals of the two groups. Nevertheless, this frictional mélange led to occasional head-on or oblique clashes between ideological opposites on the pages of the magazine. Thus, for example, in 1949, when Colonel Watthana Phayakkhanithi (a graduate of the Diplomatic Academy of Geneva, Switzerland, and commentator on international affairs on the government radio) wrote an article describing the civil war in China as a war of interests rather than of ideology and the Chinese communists as mere followers of the late Sun Yatsen, he was openly challenged and censured by Sanao Phanichjaroen (TCP member since 1949) in another article and by Atsani Phonlajan in a short story for his "belittling," "vulgarization," and "distortion" (English originals) of the Chinese revolution, the CCP, and the class struggle.[74] Later that year, when assistant editor Colonel Sanong Thamangraksat wrote an article discussing the Yugoslav-Soviet conflict over Macedonia from a realist, geo-strategic point of view, his views were countered in article printed next to it by Sanao Phanichjaroen, who, following the Cominform line, took a strongly anti-Tito, pro-Soviet stance.[75] This prompted a final rejoinder by Sanong in a later issue in which he reasserted his realist, non-communist opinions on the Tito regime.[76]

The ideological dispute did not limit itself to political issues but spread to literary ones, as when radical literature editor Atsani Phonlajan repeatedly sniped at senior literary composition editor Pleuang na Nakhorn without mentioning him by name, defiantly titling his own essays on poetry "Kho mai na seuksa thang kanpraphan" (What should be unlearned about literary composition), a pun on the title of Pleuang's regular column, "Kho na seuksa thang kanpraphan" (What should be learned about literary composition). He

Table 8-3

Political Persuasion, Brief Background, and Editorial Responsibility of
Aksornsarn's Staff

NAME	BACKGROUND	EDITORIAL RESPONSIBILITY
THE LEFT		
Supha Sirimanond	Pridi loyalist and one-time personal aide; well-known newspaper editor and reporter	Chief editor; international affairs, entertainment and fiction, and translation editor
Kulap Saipradit	Pridi political ally; renowned and respected veteran journalist and novelist	Political science editor
Atsani Phonlajan	See Table 8-1	Literature editor
Samak Burawas	Brilliant British-educated philosopher and scientist; member of the Royal Institute from 1942	Philosophy and sociology editor
Sanan Waraphreug	Member of the CCP-TB and of the pro-PRC *Maitrisarn Biweekly* editorial staff	Staff writer on international affairs and translator from Chinese
Thaweep Voradilok	Poet, lyricist, Thammasat student activist, and editor of the Thammasat Student Committee's newspaper, *Thammajak* in 1949/50	Literature and poetry editor, 1950–52
THE "RIGHT"		
Direk Jayanama	Former foreign minister; ambassador to Japan during the war and to Great Britain afterwards; liberal follower of Pridi	International affairs editor
Sommai Huntrakool	Master of economics from Japan, where he met Supha in 1938; head of the Research Division of the National Bank	International economy editor
Jaroen Chaichana	Popular historian	Translation and feature editor; international economy editor
Colonel Sanong Thamangraksat	Graduate in military economics (Italy) and in political science (University of Lausanne, Switzerland)	Assistant editor; staff writer and translator in international affairs
Pleuang na Nakhorn	Leading literary historian and critic; lecturer in literary composition and journalism at Chulalongkorn University	Literary composition editor

criticized Pleuang's formalistic, banal, and inadequate teachings on poetry and literary composition,[77] taunted him with a critique of his style of futile, purely aesthetic, as opposed to political, study of traditional Thai literature,[78] and condemned his illustrated books of erotic verse.[79] All these published disputations were plain enough to *Aksornsarn*'s attentive readers, though the disputants were too cautious and courteous ever to engage in face-to-face verbal confrontation.[80]

Nevertheless, if we judge *Aksornsarn* from the political content of the overwhelming majority of its articles, essays, stories, and poems and from the obvious change in its political tone over its four years of publication, it is plain that this non-partisan magazine was firmly committed to radical socialist thought. Supha himself conceded as much in his then unpublished editorial correspondence with the magazine's readers. For example, on November 4, 1949, in reply to a reader's complaint that *Aksornsarn* was "a little too heavy for the brain," Supha wrote: "The *Aksornsarn* magazine is a magazine committed to progressive thought and wishes that every piece of writing it publishes have such a character, including even novelette and short story."[81] Later, admittedly, it grew even heavier.[82] In a letter dated October 4, 1951, he confided to a reader sympathetic to the magazine's radicalism: "Initially, the nature and character of *Aksornsarn* monthly magazine were not as crystal clear as they have later become because we wanted them to be so...Lately, this magazine's nature and character have proceeded more definitely along the designated ideological lines..."[83]

Probably pressured by the criticisms of their leftist colleagues and sensing the progressively radical direction the magazine was taking, by the middle of the second year, all five "rightists" had voluntarily left *Aksornsarn*'s editorial staff and, in some cases, their responsibilities were taken up by others—Direk Jayanama (left after volume 1, number 8, replaced by Supha Sirimanond), Sommai Huntrakool (left after volume 1, number 9, replaced briefly by Jaroen Chaichana), Jaroen Chaichana (left after volume 1, number 11, replaced by Supha), Colonel Sanong Thamangraksat (left after volume 1, number 12, replaced by Sanan Waraphreug), and Pleuang na Nakhorn (left after volume 2, number 6, replaced by Atsani Phonlajan). Thus, the early medley of politico-ideological views expressed on *Aksornsarn*'s pages gradually but surely and increasingly gave way to Marxist, Leninist, Stalinist, and Maoist views in the later years. Marking this change was Supha's addition of the English slogan—"To think freely is good, but to think right is better"—to the contents page of every issue from the third year of publication. It was originally derived from the motto of the Swedish University of Uppsala, which Supha visited in early 1947 on his way to Moscow to serve as press attaché to the newly opened Siamese Embassy.[84] Ironically, "to think right," in the particular context of *Aksornsarn*, obviously meant "to think left."

But although the *Aksornsarn* "right" had now left, this by no means marked the end of internecine friction concerning the magazine, since "to think left" in the peculiar way Supha and the *Aksornsarn* left did, that is, independently and liberally, did not fare well with the *Mahachon* communists. In the event, Supha's individualistic and intellectualistic propagation of Marxism-communism in *Aksornsarn* became a source of recurrent irritation for the TCP, and he himself an unauthorized loose cannon vis-à-vis the ideological authority of the Party. His wayward and outrageous offenses included the publication for the sake of non-partisan appearance of a translated 1948 American anti-communist report prepared by the Foreign Affairs Commission of the United States Congress, entitled *The Strategy and Tactics of World Communism*;[85] the "no good" and "hasty" publication of Samak Burawas' translation of Stalin's *Dialectical and Historical Materialism*;[86] Supha's own "needlessly bogged down in detail" and "dead wrong" interpretation of Marx's *Capital*;[87] and the Marxist-communist neologisms of Supha and Samak that were at odds with the Party's authorized versions.[88] Also refraining generally from naming names and direct confrontation, their usual ways of sniping at each other were opaque allusions and malicious gossip that nonetheless cumulatively nourished bitterness and resentment between them and resulted eventually in long-standing mutual non-recognition of each other's Marxist-communist credentials.[89]

Supha insisted from the beginning on categorically refraining from publishing any factual or analytical articles dealing explicitly with contemporary domestic political and socio-economic events and personalities, as a precaution against state suppression.[90] This is because with the political demise of Pridi Banomyong's leftist forces following the 1947 coup and their subsequent failures to stage a counter-coup, Supha's political fortunes and diplomatic career took a deep plunge due to his long-standing association with, and personal services to, Pridi.[91] Their relationship had begun in the late 1930s when Pridi, then foreign minister, asked Supha to be his personal aide in dealing with foreign guests and news reporters. During the war, Supha was close enough to Regent Pridi to initiate a discussion on Marx's *Capital* with him and Direk. In 1945, when called upon by Pridi, Supha dutifully left his family and the editorship of the leading weekly magazine *Nikorn Wanathit* for India to work as a liaison officer for the Free Thai Movement. After arriving in Bombay via a secret route, Second Lieutenant "Anan" (his Free Thai *nom de guerre*) was sent to receive further military training with Force 136 at a camp in Poona, whose well-stocked library afforded him many days of calm and pleasurable reading. However, four or five months of soldiering and reading later, the war ended abruptly with the atomic bombings of Hiroshima and Nagasaki before he had a chance to take part directly.

Subsequently, he came back to Thailand and briefly resumed his journalistic career. During the National Assembly election campaign of October 1945 to January 1946, he even campaigned for a pro-Pridi liberal candidate in Bangkok, a significant gesture in view of his subsequent shunning of electoral politics.[92] Soon afterwards, at Prime Minister Pridi's request, he gave up journalism again and served the Prime Minister's Office as liaison officer with the army. And in the wake of slanderous attacks on Pridi and the government by the conservative press concerning the mysterious death of King Rama VIII in June 1946, his devotion to Pridi made him go so far as to become a member of the government press censorship committee,[93] an ethically unsavory office for a journalist and one which earned him many enemies in newspaper circles.[94] In any case, soon after the fall of Pridi, in November 1947, Supha was abruptly and arbitrarily transferred from his diplomatic posting in Switzerland to Paris, urgently called back to Thailand in January 1948, investigated by the police about the late King's death in May, and throughout these months viciously slandered in the Thai press as Pridi's henchman allegedly dispatched to Switzerland to harm King Rama IX.[95] Under such bureaucratic pressure and harassment, Supha resigned from the Ministry of Foreign Affairs on his return to Thailand in July. Unfortunately, there was no immediate prospect of going back to his beloved journalism since his former newspaper colleagues were too scared to publish anything written by this lone Pridi man and target of the new government's vendetta. Supha was reduced to selling some of his personal belongings to support his family.

But he did not give up his political fight easily. Although when requested by his former Free Thai colleagues to take part in the Pridi/Free Thai counter-coup attempt in February 1949, he refused on the grounds of personal disapproval of the use of force,[96] he took great interest in the incipient struggle of Thammasat University students against government harassment and discrimination, believing he could help these politically inexperienced youths through non-violent, intellectual means. Hence *Aksornsarn* appeared two months later, originally conceived between November 1947 and January 1948 in a hunting forest in Paris by Supha and Direk Jayanama, then Thai ambassador to Great Britain.[97] Regardless of the commercial risk involved, *Aksornsarn*'s political mission, in Supha's words, was as follows:

I then saw that I ought to perform the duty of casting light on the Thammasat kids' struggle to show them which way led to what, which way was near, a little of the right, the left, the front, and the back, and let them choose their own way. We could not make a choice for them, but we could help illuminate it. This is the character of newspaper. It is our duty to illuminate in the dark, but not to judge. Making a judgement is the duty of the high-minded. But I did think that the light was Marxism.[98]

Therefore, instead of any concrete domestic political analysis and guidelines, *Aksornsarn*'s target readers found only general radical theoretical principles and foreign examples, on the basis of which they were expected to make their own informed comparisons, draw their own practical conclusions, and attempt their own activist application to contemporary Thailand. A good example of this can be found in a series of articles on modern Spanish politics written by Supha in the form of letters to an imaginary friend intriguingly named "Thai-ya" (a dear Thai). In them, he criticized the Spanish Republicans' 1930s "Revolution from Above" or "Revolution by Ballot-Boxes" for failing to "destroy completely, resolutely, and violently the various gangs of the status quo by transferring the power of control over the means of production and economic property to the public's hands *in toto*." As "a revolution without a leading organ with the correct view to unify and organize it," this work of "Amateur Revolutionaries" was sure to wreak havoc on the "New Order" and the people, "no matter in which land on earth it is made."[99] Supha also condemned the brutal, repressive, and autocratic Franco regime, the unprincipled and opportunistic Bourbon monarchy, and the unscrupulous pro-Franco-cum-anti-communist foreign policy of the United States.[100] Only a little imagination is needed to guess the likely contemporary Thai objects of Supha's Spanish-derived comments.

Thereafter, the more violent and volatile the political situation in Thailand became, especially following the bloody suppression of the naval Manhattan Rebellion in June 1951, the Coup Group's Radio Coup in November of the same year, and the concomitant ban on political parties and tightening of press censorship, the more oblique and abstract *Aksornsarn*'s content grew, with Supha's carefully calculated addition of more articles on abstruse philosophical and religious subjects rather than on Marxism.[101] But a prudent and enlightened editorial policy for a radical periodical under authoritarian rule failed to satisfy the urgent need of young and politically aroused student activists for instant, concrete, ready-made analysis of the situation and a guide to direct action in the heat of the moment.[102] Nor did it help *Aksornsarn* retain its leftist editors and writers. Squeezed between the phenomenal growth of the communist-engineered and -staffed mass movement against Thailand's participation in the Korean War between July 1950 and November 1952 on the one hand,[103] and correspondingly increasing repression by the government on the other, *Aksornsarn*'s leftist editorial staff dwindled. Kulap Saipradit left after volume 3, number 3, soon after being elected a vice-chairman of the Peace Committee of Thailand in April 1951; Atsani Phonlajan left after volume 3, number 7 to assume the editorship of the Peace Committee's propaganda organ *Karnmuang;* Sanan Waraphreug left after volume 4, number 1, probably for Peking; and Samak Burawas, having been elected to the working subcommittee of the Peace Committee in April 1951, left after volume 4, number 5. But while his former colleagues were campaigning hard throughout the country to collect people's signatures for anti-government peace petitions, the ever wary and fiercely individualistic Supha, always true to his personal philosophy of "knowing the limits" and "staying in the background," refused even to sign any of them (though hundreds of thousands did) for fear of becoming someone else's "political instrument" and clung forlornly to his beloved *Aksornsarn.*[104] He would grumble four years later: "[In 1952]...I had my hands full with the task of publishing the *Aksornsarn* monthly magazine. Almost all of the friends who had helped me [with the magazine] in the previous years went off to other important work. I was tied up alone."[105]

Deserted first by the right for being too radical and then by the left for being insufficiently militant, *Aksornsarn* became so desolate that its final issue of October 1952, shortly before the crackdown on the Peace Rebellion, was produced by only two remaining staff members-cum-writers, Supha and Thaweep. As if to compensate psychologically for their forsaken isolation amidst popular activism,[106] the editors tried in the last few issues to rekindle the magazine's earlier, more outright militancy by publishing lead articles on Soviet socialism and communist doctrine and by introducing a regular eye-catching English quotation from past and present masters of Marxism-communism in the editorial headlines.

Thus, *Aksornsarn*'s August 1952 issue (volume 4, number 5) flagged "J.V.S."'s quotation on "The World Revolution"[107] and featured Kaptan Samut's (alias Samak Burawas) "Phutthit phachoenna kab khommunit" (Buddhism versus communism), which compared the context, contents, and philosophies of the two doctrines, coming down strongly in favor of communism for its superior intellectual development, practical effectiveness, and social critique. Singling out for attack the emerging anti-communist, religious united front between the Thai Buddhist establishment and other theistic faiths, Samak warned Buddhists to stick to their search for spiritual nirvana, leave worldly politics alone, and not let themselves be exploited by unscrupulous right-wing bourgeois politicians and foreign imperialists. In return, he advised Thai Marxists against groundlessly and facilely attacking Buddhism, as well as deceptively coating their communist propaganda with a veneer of Buddhist terminology, since these violated both the materialist principles and the social scientific character of their own doctrine.[108] The next issue (volume 4, number

6) highlighted "V.I.L."'s definition of "Social Chauvinists"[109] and gave pride of place to Phatthana Rammayasut's (alias Suphat Sukhonthaphirom) translation of an article by Soviet author M.D. Kammari, entitled "Sathana khong pajjekchon nai robob sochalist" (The status of the individual in the socialist system), which concluded all too predictably that "the new socialist individuals" indeed had greater individuality, freedom, happiness, and virtue than their counterparts under the capitalist system.[110] Finally, in the last and probably most militant issue of the magazine (volume 4, number 7), ushered in by "V.I.L."'s definition of a "Social Pacifist,"[111] Supha and Thaweep duologically but persistently held high the banner of their own brand of independent, intellectualistic Marxist socialism in two leading articles with a combined length of eighty pages (of a ninety-eight-page issue): "Nai thi sud sochalist ja tong chana, ya songsai loey" (In the end, socialism will be victorious, do not for a moment doubt it) and "Lok kao rudna pai soo sochalist" (The world is advancing towards socialism), both of which restated with elaborate argument, lengthy extracts, and detailed statistics exactly what their titles said at the outset.[112]

Whereas it can be debated whether the world was really advancing towards socialism as Supha would have it, his defiant manifesto, serving willy-nilly as *Aksornsarn*'s political testament before its closure, must have played a part in advancing his name onto the Santibal's list of communist suspects to be rounded up. In fact, it could have advanced him into prison but for his prudent editorial practice and cautious political bearing, which proved its effectiveness in the face of police interrogation following his arrest in November 1952. One of his interrogators, Santibal Police Lieutenant Colonel Rat Watthanamahat, hearing Supha's self-defense that *Aksornsarn* had never published anything about contemporary Thailand or mentioned anybody in political circles, pondered for ten minutes before replying, much to Supha's amusement, "Well, but each of your letters prises open (*ngae*) the whole system."[113] Eventually, after holding him in custody for fifty-two days, interrogating him three times, and trying futilely four times to recruit him as an anti-communist expert, the police came to the conclusion that Supha was a relatively benign if problematical "lonely communist," dropped the charges, and released him.[114] One year later, Supha was again working as assistant manager at *Thai Mai*, under the ownership of Prasit Kanjanawat and his friendly patron Bunchoo, turning the paper into an outlet for works by younger radical writers such as Issara Amantakul, Jit Poumisak, and Thongbai Thongpao and serializing in its pages his own long historical novel, *Jengghizkhan* (Genghis Khan, January 1955– January 1956), actually a searing dissection of the warlord mentality typical of the Phibun regime.[115]

This looked good and useful as far as Supha's recommended method of struggle against the capitalistic political economic system was concerned—*khian nangseu takhe fad hang* (to write like a tail-flogging crocodile).[116] But was a literary "tail-flogging crocodile" really effective in winning the Thai cultural market for socialist ideas, let alone winning Thailand for the socialist camp? Leaving aside for the moment the rather well-worn populist critique of ivory-tower intellectuals who preferred "interpreting the world" to "changing it" (in Supha's case, publishing rather than taking part in the Royal Palace Rebellion or signing a peace petition), was there not something inherent in the functioning and mechanisms of a capitalist market economy that could not but melt all commodified anti-capitalist ideologies into air?

One need only look more closely and unconventionally at *Aksornsarn* to detect a sweltry antipathy between radical ideology and capitalist business right there on its pages. While Naiphi (Atsani Phonlajan) scorned the traditional evaluation of women by physical appearance rather than working experience in a witty *klon* poem on page 107 of volume 1, number 3, an advertisement for the Lao Kim Nguan Company on page 90 showed a half-clad beauty promoting "Diamond" brand soap.[117] Whereas Intharayut (again Atsani Phonlajan) iconoclastically condemned three celebrated Thai poetic classics—*Ramakian*, *Phra Aphaimani*, and *Khun Chang Khun Phaen*—as corrupt, militaristic, pornographic, royalist, "sakdina" (feudal) "opium of the people" in volume 1, number 11 and number 12, all three of them were advertised as "great and immortal literature" by the semi-official Khuru Sapha Trading Agency on the inner front covers of the very same issues.[118] Likewise, although Thaweepvorn (Thaweep Voradilok) and Intharayut pungently denounced the pseudo-scientific, elitist, and epic nature of traditional Thai historiography in volume 1, number 12, and volume 2, number 6, the inner front covers of both issues advertised a history textbook by Prince Damrongrachanuphap entitled *Sadaeng banyai phongsawadan siam* (Lectures on Siamese chronicles). This very epitome of sakdina historiography was alluded to dismissively by Intharayut forty-six pages later as factually unreliable "records by the Sakdinas' 'Founding Father of Thai History.'"[119] And despite the wholesale critique by Suphat Sukhonthaphirom and Phooyingnoi (Samak Burawas' deliberately anti-elitist *nom de plume*, The Small) of the monopolistic and anarchic global finance and banking systems and their unscrupulous speculation in foreign currencies in volume 2, number 4, and volume 2, number 5, an advertisement for the Asia Trust Company's foreign currency trading services was displayed on page 96 of the former issue and page 86 of the latter.[120] And however vehemently Phooyingnoi blamed female prostitution, beauty contests, ballroom dancing, pornographic art, and other forms of sexual oppression of women on the generically erotomaniac "capitalists and power-holders" in volume 4, number 4, the Chinese-communist-owned Anta Company still publicized on the inner back cover of the same issue the aphrodisiac "Pantocrine" as an excellent remedy for male impotence, wet dreams, and premature ejaculation.[121]

Moreover, this recurrent ideological censure was pursued by certain radical writers with such relentlessness and fanaticism that it sometimes bordered on the folly of "smashing one's own rice pot" (*thub mo khao tuaeng*, a traditional Thai saying). For instance, both an *Aksornsarn* partner and a close relative-cum-business associate of Chinda were druggists and the magazine's most regular commercial advertisers were drugstores.[122] Yet Phooyingnoi nevertheless virulently denounced "mo ya" (druggists) in volume 2, number 6 as opportunistic profiteers who made money by taking advantage of people's medical needs, hoarding medical supplies in time of war, increasing prices in time of peace, and serving wealthy urban customers rather than the rural poor.[123] But his uncompromising denunciation was immediately compromised by its encapsulation in advertisements for four different drugstores within the same magazine covers.[124] This ideology versus business tension appeared consistently in the pages of *Aksornsarn*, for instance, between Phooyingnoi and cosmeticians and between Phooyingnoi and the insurance industry.[125] Probably realizing what an outrageous if exceptional kind of self-defaming publicity they had been paying for, many of these censured companies soon withdrew their advertisements from the poor but principled pages of *Aksornsarn*.

At this point, a brief pause plus a healthy dose of skepticism are appropriate. One may reasonably wonder if too much is not being read into these minor details of advertisement, in other words, if a mountain of significance is not being made of an insignificant molehill. Is it not generally the case, both then and now, in Thailand and elsewhere, that readers of radical periodicals hardly read the commercial advertisements therein, but habitually skip them without a glance in a rush to reach the serious substantial articles? And if so, does that not fundamentally undermine the argument about ideology versus business tension in *Aksornsarn* by depriving it of its *sine qua non* in reality, i.e., that people did read the advertisements?

Well, not really, for underlying this skeptical counter-argument is the assumption that people did and do read and understand the substantial contents of radical periodicals as against their advertisements which, in the case of *Aksornsarn*, might not be true. Testimony against this assumption has been provided by Khamsing Srinawk, a rising independent radical fiction writer and protégé of Kulap in the 1950s, who, as a wide-eyed young student fresh from a distant rural village in the northeastern province of Nakhon Ratchasima, arrived in Bangkok to attend both Thammasat and Chulalongkorn universities in 1949. One of the more exciting things he remembers doing in Bangkok was shopping for progressive books and magazines like *Aksornsarn*, which one of his hometown schoolteachers had subscribed to and lent him. But he confessed that he did not much understand their contents, especially the more difficult and abstruse ones, such as Supha's *Khaepitalist*, nor for that matter did they really count as books to him. Rather, he bought them as impressive "patima" (images), "phra saksit" (talismans), or "sanyalak" (symbols) of progressivism.[126] And there is ample evidence to suggest that Khamsing's was far from being a singular case among *Aksornsarn*'s enthusiastic if muddled audience.[127]

Secondly, in addition to the fact that *Aksornsarn*'s advertisements furnished shorter, splashier, simpler, not to say more enjoyable distractions from the longer and heavier main body of reading, it was also hard to miss them. The chief editor always took great care, as a matter of policy, to give these rare remunerative items considerable prominence by featuring, on or next to the contents page of every issue, an orderly list of advertised products, their patrons, and the page numbers where they could be found. The point, according to Supha, was to make explicit the importance of advertising to the magazine:

> Let's say they pay you 5,000 baht [for an advertisement]. How many copies do you have to sell before you can earn that amount? So, when they pay us money, we must show that their advertisement page is worth something.[128]

Finally, the counter-argument is self-defeating in so far as the stated ideological purpose of *Aksornsarn* was concerned. Let us suppose for the sake of argument that *Aksornsarn*'s readers really paid no attention to the advertisements, what then would ensue? Either the patron companies got smart and withdrew their fruitless ads, or they went on wasting their advertising budgets until their businesses suffered. Either way, the hard-pressed *Aksornsarn* would lose more of its inadequate advertising income and would inch closer to bankruptcy. Consequently, whether read or not, commercial advertisements could not bode well for the magazine's mission of radical enlightenment.

So, perforce, *Aksornsarn* had to live with this heated tension, which continually threatened to melt away either its radical message or its financial lifeline. But what of contemporary Thai radical periodicals that, unlike *Aksornsarn*, had the support of outside political organizations, more solid financial backup, and hence more room for maneuver, like the TCP's

Mahachon?[129] One might reasonably expect them to have avoided the kind of dire necessity, tension, and dilemma that plagued *Aksornsarn*. But, alas, printed evidence suggests otherwise. For example, one regular advertisement on the pages of *Mahachon* was for a *mo doo* (seer) named No. Maijeud or Thongyoo Yoskrit, whose zealously promoted astrological craft went against every scientistic grain of Marxism-communism, dialectical materialism, historical materialism, or what have you. Be that as it may, this astrological superstition appeared alongside scientific socialism on the pages of the leading propaganda organ of the Thai Communist Party. Even more astounding is the fact that *Mahachon* itself made no bones about its opposition to the "utter nonsense" of astrology.[130] Yet the paper published one advertisement for astrological nonsense after another! One begins to wonder whether it was simply (mis)calculated political camouflage or perhaps something larger, deeper, and impersonal at work—the "invisible hand" of the market.

Karnmuang

The *Karnmuang* (Politics) *Weekly* (circa 1944–November 1951) was originally published during the Second World War, its first issue appearing on July 28, 1944.[131] The first period of the paper's publication lasted for six years until it changed hands in early 1951 as a consequence of what appeared to be an editorial coup and business-cum-political take-over by the communist-dominated Peace Movement.[132] Becoming much more radicalized in its second period, the renewed *Karnmuang* soon languished under mounting government pressure and closed in the aftermath of the Radio Coup in November of the same year.[133]

The founder and owner of *Karnmuang* throughout its first period was Khow Tongmong (in the Teochiu dialect) or Prasit Kanjanawat, an ascendant lookjin lawyer.[134] Born to Chai Kanjanawat (alias Meun Suwansiriphong), a wealthy Chinese rice miller and ennobled village headman, and his Thai wife, Somjin, in Bang Khanak Village, Bang Namprieo District, Chachoengsao Province, on June 20, 1915, "Ti Noi Tongmong" (Little Brother Tongmong) was sent by his father to attend the Kuomintang-founded, Teochiu-speaking Chinese Xinmin School in Bangkok, reputedly the best of its kind in the country at the time.[135] After graduation around 1933, he was recruited as a teacher by his alma mater on account of his good knowledge of Chinese and English. Quickly, he earned his Thai secondary education degree and rose to become principal of another leading Chinese school, Huang-hun, later renamed in Thai, Sahakhun Seuksa. Under the sponsorship of the Kuomintang government, Khow Tongmong and ten other Chinese teachers from Thailand were sent to receive further pedagogical training at Jinan University in Shanghai for a year and on a study tour through northeastern China for another three months.

Khow Xiansheng (Teacher Khow)'s promising teaching career was cut short, however, by the wholesale closure of Chinese schools by the nationalist-playing Phibunsongkhram government in 1939/40.[136] Adapting deftly to the changing times, Khow Tongmong enrolled in Thammasat University, got a new job as a translating clerk at the Department of Commercial Registration in the Ministry of Commerce, and changed his unfashionable un-Thai name to an officially favored Thai one, Prasit Kanjanawat. After graduating from Thammasat, Prasit resigned from his government job and set up a private law office called Manukij with a number of Thammasat friends, the more important of them being Phethai Chotnuchit (Thep Chotnuchit's younger brother and Thonburi's mayor and MP in 1949), Bunchoo Rojanasathian (a junior classmate at both Xinmin School and Thammasat University, from which he graduated with a diploma in accountancy, and owner of an accounting office called Banchikij), and Prasert Praphasanobol (master of economics graduate of Thammasat University).

While his law practice and joint ventures with Bunchoo and Chin Sophonphanich at the Asia Trust Company prospered, Prasit had his eye on something else.[137] Partly to indulge his dilettantish literary and journalistic interests, but mainly to create a handy public relations instrument for his personal political ambition, he began to invest his money and engage his close business colleagues in some publishing and printing enterprises. Near the end of World War II, he founded and edited *Karnmuang*, a weekly newspaper; bought a controlling interest in *Thai Mai*, a daily newspaper; owned a shop making woodblocks for use in printing, also called Thai Mai; and was deeply involved in establishing the Rungnakhorn Printing House, of which his friend Bunchoo was co-founder and shareholder.[138] Capitalizing on the regular public exposure he commanded as a newspaper owner and deploying his editorial staff in his election campaigns, Prasit was elected, after three tries, as a pro-government MP for his home province in February 1952. By no means a professional journalist, "Hia Sit" (Elder Brother Sit), as he was affectionately called by his newspaper employees, was a crafty politician who used his papers as stepping-stones on his path to greater political power and higher government position, for example, MP for Chachoengsao (February 1957, December 1957) and deputy minister of cooperatives (August–October 1958).[139]

Prasit was *Karnmuang*'s owner, editor, publisher, and advertiser during the first few years of its publication (circa 1944–1946), with Prasert Praphasanobol serving as assistant editor, and Amphan Thongwanich as manager. From 1947 to mid-1949, Prasit relinquished the editor and publisher-advertiser positions to Phethai Chotnuchit, while Jari Amattayakul, another underling, took over the management from Amphan, who had fallen ill. From mid-1949 until late 1950, when the paper fell into TCP hands, Bunchoo replaced Jari as manager and the latter became assistant editor to Phethai. The range of known ideological variations within *Karnmuang*'s editorial staff included moderate leftist populism (Phethai), radical bourgeois democracy or left-wing Kuomintang (Prasit and Bunchoo), and liberalism (Prasert). And yet, given the fact that all these people were Hia Sit's junior business partners or subordinates, their ideological differences paled beside the patronage of their boss.

Representing itself as an avowedly independent and informative mouthpiece of, by, and for the people, completely free from commercial interests and the mandate or financial influence of any political party or capitalist, *Karnmuang* under Prasit's ownership pursued a generally liberal, critical, left-of-center editorial line.[140] This meant that its pages were open to writers and articles of widely different, even opposing, ideological tendencies, ranging from Marxist-communist (Udom Sisuwan, Atsani Phonlajan, Pleuang Wannasri, Samran Kanlayanamit, "Assanikorn," "Khosmik," "Thatnamdi," "Thipphaya Atchariyakorn," "Watthanachon") and socialist-leftist (M.C. Sakol Wannakon Worawan, Suphat Sukhonthaphirom, Thawin Udon, Jamlong Daoreuang, Kulap Saipradit, Samak Burawas, Leuan Saraphaiwanich, Kamol Janthasorn, "Issarawut," "Phram Noi") to liberal (Khun Prasertsuphamattra, Natthawut Sutthisongkhram, Prasit na Phatthalung, Jinda Yimrewat, Direk Jayanama, Sanya Pholprasit, "Kornsit," "Montri," "Seriniyom," "Wijaranayan") and conservative royalist (Phraya Sriwisanwaja, Yai Sawitchat, "Menoo," "Yothin na Rangtal"). One frequently found pro- and anti-communist articles, or translations of typical Soviet and American Cold War propaganda, published side by side in the same issue.[141]

But judging from its overall content, it is fair to say that *Karnmuang* largely identified itself politically with the moderate left wing of the Pridi group, especially through the special bonds of solidarity most of its editorial staff and contributors felt with Thammasat University, their alma mater and most enduring and influential brainchild of Pridi.[142] This general political stance did not prevent the paper from publishing severe criticism of the widespread blatant corruption and overbearing press censorship of the Pridi and Thawan governments. But it did lead to a typically sympathetic attitude towards Pridi, distinctly little space being allotted to conservative royalist opinion, and a cautiously critical posture towards military rule in general and Field Marshal Phibunsongkhram's anti-Chinese militaristic nationalism in particular. Even after Pridi had been chased out of the country by the November 1947 military

Plate 8-3. Prasit Kanjanawat (1915–1999), banker and owner of *Karnmuang* (photo taken
in the 1990s; photo credit: Matichon Press)

coup, *Karnmuang* continued to publish articles in defense and praise of the
exiled "Senior Statesman," amidst the torrent of vicious slander and abuse with
which the Coup Group and the Prachathipat government were splattering
him.[143] No wonder that soon after the Coup Group seized power in November
1947, *Karnmuang* was classified as an anti-government newspaper, from then
on excluded from the official selections of the Thai press mailed regularly to
Thai embassies and consulates abroad.[144]

Nevertheless, it was not *Karnmuang*'s temperate opposition to the Prachathipat and Phibunsongkhram governments that gave it prominence among the radical press. What did so was the fact that Prasit devoted a good portion of the paper to articles, profiles, and translations about the communist camp, the Soviet Union, and Communist China from 1946 onwards. These included Prasit Kanjanawat's widely read translation of the revised Soviet Constitution of 1947,[145] translations of the Lao Issara and Democratic Republic of Vietnam's Constitutions,[146] profiles of many Soviet, East European, and Chinese communist leaders,[147] expositions of communist doctrine and concepts,[148] an extended scholarly history of the Soviet Union,[149] and many brief reports on aspects of Soviet society, such as its educational system, physical education, the press, workers, scientific development and inventions, and Soviet views on Thailand.[150] The keen interest shown, the largely, though by no means universally, sympathetic undertones, and the extensive and conspicuous nature of the coverage caused not a few readers to question *Karnmuang*'s political motives, necessitating repeated apolitical excuses about the paper's "journalistic duty to provide useful and scarce information."[151] And although *Karnmuang*'s editors and writers expressed conflicting opinions about the feasibility and desirability of communism in Thailand, a controversial issue that pitted Atsani Phonlajan and Issarawut in favor[152] against Natthawut Sutthisongkhram and Yothin na Rangtal against,[153] they were unified in opposition to Prime Minister Phibun's anti-communist policies, callling them "unwise,"[154] "unconstitutional,"[155] "frenzied and provocative,"[156] "indiscriminate,"[157] "pro-western,"[158] "undemocratic,"[159] "superfluous,"[160] "ignorant,"[161] "adventurous,"[162] "futile,"[163] "McCarthyistic,"[164] and "divisive and anti-peace."[165] One inevitable consequence was the sporadic labelling of *Karnmuang* as "a leftist newspaper" and of its owner as "a communist."[166]

Whereas the smear of communism against Prasit was a well-worn and convenient slander thrown in the heat of parliamentary election campaigning, it does point to the curious question of why a rich, successful business lawyer and aspiring politician would waste money printing so many good and informative things about communism.[167] Why, too, would he co-author a book on the Soviet Constitution with a socialist outcast from the Ministry of Foreign Affairs (Suphat Sukhonthaphirom) and a communist columnist of *Mahachon* (Udom Sisuwan)?[168] Up to his death in 1999, His Excellency the former deputy prime minister and president of the Bangkok Bank showed no inclination to discuss this embarrassingly radical journalistic and literary skeleton in his cupboard in any detail. So one must resort to his writings (re)published in the post-war period, especially a hagiography entitled *Chiang kaishek: Pramuk khong jin mai* (Chiang Kaishek: The head of new China, 1947, first published

1939) and the introduction to his translation of the Soviet Constitution entitled "Botnam: Prawat kanpatiwat doi yo khong russia" (Introduction: A brief history of the Russian Revolution, 1948), which contain some illuminating clues to these questions.

In a chapter of his hagiography of Generalissimo Chiang called "35 pi haeng kanplianplaeng kanpokkhrong khong jin" (Thirty-five years of the change of regime in China), Prasit characterized the 1911 overthrow of the Qing dynasty by the Zhongguo Tong Meng Hui (Chinese Revolutionary League) under Sun Yatsen's leadership as "a democratic republican revolution against the absolute monarchy for popular sovereignty" that effected a great transformation in the Chinese system of government rather than a mere traditional change of the imperial dynasty. However, the 1911 Revolution was "unfinished," claimed Prasit, for it failed to abolish the unequal treaties between China and various foreign powers, as well as to annihilate all vestiges of the *ancien regime*. Instead, for the sake of temporary short-term interests, the Chinese Revolutionary League made the monumental mistake of compromising with Yuan Shikai, the last Qing premier and imperial commissioner, who soon betrayed the democratic revolution and thwarted the democratic republic. To put it in a nutshell, the Revolution went wrong not because it was too radical, but because it was not radical, extreme, or resolute enough in dealing with its domestic and external enemies. And this was due to the shortcomings of the Chinese Revolutionary League itself: failure to enlist popular participation, resultant weakness and proneness to compromise, lack of firm political beliefs or ideology, and absence of internal unity. In conclusion, Prasit generalized the following lesson for other revolutions in the making:

> The lesson received which is an important one for revolutions in general is that with neither popular base, nor popular awakening, nor guided popular cooperation and participation, the task of revolution is hard to achieve completely.[169]

But if the Chinese Revolution of 1911 was a warning of how not to make a revolution, what actual revolution did Prasit think showed the way? The answer, according to his historical introduction to the translated Soviet Constitution, was the Russian Revolution of 1917, which, unlike the "unfinished" French, Chinese, and Siamese revolutions of 1789, 1911, and 1932, was completely finished. Not only did it transform the existing system of government, but it also led society to its destined condition in accordance with the ideology of the Revolution itself, namely "the democratic system of government by, for, and of the people."[170]

In their uncompromisingly radical conception of revolution, with their stress on the socio-economic over and above the political, the views that emerged from these writings were remarkably "un-Thai" (à la King Vajiravudh, King Prajadhipok, and Prince Damrongrachanuphap) and Phra Sri Arya-like (à la Pridi Banomyong).[171] They were the views of a radical democrat or, perhaps more aptly, a Kuomintang left-winger on the verge of conversion to, or at least sympathy with, communism. It was precisely this process of ideological conversion and political realignment that was then happening to democratic and nationalist intellectuals throughout China, Southeast Asia, and Thailand as communist-led or -inspired social revolutions and national liberation movements roared through colonial and semi-colonial lands and leftism became for a good while very fashionable.[172] Given the fact that a lot of the best political, trade unionist, journalistic, and literary Thai talent of the period was following this trend, the leftist inclination of *Karnmuang* and the radical posture of its owner must have seemed predictable, possibly even mainstream and normal. Besides, owning a leftist newspaper and translating the Soviet Constitution might have been an expedient and far-sighted thing to do; there was no telling what the rising communist camp and, in particular, millions of armed Chinese communists, might be capable of doing to the thorny dissenting anti-communist minorities in power in their southern neighbors, especially in view of the rapid communist expansionism in Eastern Europe.

It was possible that a similar mixture of radicalism and opportunism might have motivated Bunchoo Rojanasathian's involvement in the radical press and his patronage of certain leftist intellectuals. Apart from *Aksornsarn*, the Bunchoo-associated Rungnakhorn Printing House also printed the CPT's *Sethasarn* (1953–1958) and two lectures on socialism delivered at Thammasat University by M.C. Sakol Wannakon Worawan and Phraya Saraphaiphiphat (alias Leuan Saraphaiwanich) in 1951. Actually, Bunchoo's name appeared as the publisher and advertiser of the latter publication, a fact that would be used by some radicals in the 1970s to credit him retrospectively with socialistic sympathy.[173] In addition to assisting Supha financially, Bunchoo was said to have defended the young Thaweep Voradilok against a charge of egoism by other backbiting leftists, an act of political sympathy that left a lasting impression on Thaweep.[174] As a matter of fact, Bunchoo continued this curious practice of providing for leftists in hard times into the heyday of the radical student movement of the 1970s and 1980s, during which he employed many persecuted or displaced former student activists, radical intellectuals, and ex-communists as personal advisers and assistants or otherwise helped find them jobs.[175] All the while, he closely followed in the footsteps of his senior mentor, Prasit Kanjanawat, dabbling in student activism at the Chinese Xinmin

School,[176] attending Thammasat University, entering the financial profession, joining and managing the Bangkok Bank, and rising in politics from appointed senator (1971) and member of the National Assembly (1972) to elected MP for Chon Buri (1975 and since), minister of finance (1975), and deputy prime minister (1980).

If *Karnmuang* was not much different from contemporary Thai leftist newspapers in the kind of stories it carried, it was distinct in the way it was treated by the Phibunsongkhram government. Marvelously, throughout the period when the paper was under Prasit's ownership, while other leftist papers were severely censored and/or closed down and their owners and editors arrested, jailed, killed, or on the run,[177] the notorious censorship authorities never touched Prasit and *Karnmuang*. This wonderful journalistic feat was achieved not through any magic censorship-proof writing formula, but owed entirely to Prasit's political connections among Coup Group leaders, namely Field Marshal Phin Chunhawan, army commander-in-chief since 1948, and Police General Phao Sriyanond, assistant director of the Police Department since 1948 and director-general in 1951. It so happened that the Khow and Chunhawan families had become close friends during the Second World War, when the Chunhawans, in their flight from Allied air raids on Bangkok, took shelter at the Khows' comfortable residence in Bang Khanak Village.[178] With regard to Phao, it was an open secret in journalistic circles that Prasit was a Phao henchman who put his papers at the service of the police chief when the latter engaged Field Marshal Sarit Thanarat and other political rivals in an intensifying "newspaper war" from 1955 to 1957.[179] Hence Phao's special protection for *Karnmuang* and the unusual tolerance of its leftist deviation as long as its leash was in Prasit's reliable hands and it attacked the right enemies.[180]

This patron-client relationship between Phin-Phao and Prasit should be viewed within the perspective of ongoing multi-million-baht dealings between the expanding Sophonphanich business group and the so-called Soi Rajkhroo faction of the ruling Coup Group, which included Field Marshal Phin, Police General Phao, Major General Chatchai Chunhawan, Major General Praman Adireksan, Major General Siri Siriyothin, Colonel Nai Worakanbancha, Police Colonel Phansak Wisesphakdi, and Adisorn Khowintha.[181] Phao, Siri, Praman, Nai Worakanbancha, and other members of the faction with high-ranking government positions served simultaneously as nominal presidents and board members of the Bangkok Bank, the Asia Trust Company, the Witthasin Insurance Company, and other businesses under the effective control of Chin-Prasit-Bunchoo, providing them with government investment, deposits, subsidies, loans, collateral, protection, promotion, concessions, purchase orders, tax reductions and exemptions, favorable price fixing, import permits, and export quotas in return for payoffs and kickbacks in the form of free or underpriced shares, dividends, unearned salaries, and bonuses. This deeply-rooted, co-prosperous economic practice of the 1950s enabled state power-holding bureaucrats to privatize public resources into their own property with the help of capitalist entrepreneurs whose businesses flourished under their political patronage. Called "bureaucratic capitalism" by latter-day Thai researchers, it created the solid financial base and golden opportunity for the spectacular growth of the Bangkok Bank, the rapid expansion of the Sophonphanich business empire, the steady political rise of Prasit and Bunchoo, and the extraordinary political resiliency and comebacks of the Soi Rajkhroo faction in the 1970s and 1980s; it culminated in the victory of the Soi Rajkhroo faction-based Chat Thai Party in the 1988 general election and the resulting prime ministership of party head Major General (retired) Chatchai Chunhawan.[182]

Hia Sit's political double-dealing did not escape the notice of his papers' leftist employees and contributors, and they reacted indignantly. Some mocked him openly, others simply quit. For example, Atsani Phonlajan, warning his readers of "those who are 'leftists' by mouth but not by feet," once wrote in *Karnmuang*:

> A newspaper normally consists of capital and people with knowledge and ideas. As it is, how can a capitalist newspaper-owner possibly become the voice of the poor in good faith? Even in the case of this paper for which I am writing, I am not yet very sure of that.[183]

He went on to call for "a genuine newspaper of the poor" to be funded and produced by workers and government officials themselves that would lead, first, to the election of reliable representatives of the poor to parliament and, eventually, to the establishment of "the true Religion of Phra Sri Arya in our country so that we will not have to waste our ears anymore on the prevarications of the capitalists who proclaim themselves 'leftists.'" In another instance, Issara Amantakul (alias Abrahim Aman, 1920–1969), a Philippine-educated, anglophone son of a Thai Muslim merchant family, a fiercely independent, brilliant, and versatile leftist journalist-cum-writer and close friend of Atsani, upon learning of his employer's Janus-faced politics and rapport with Police General Phao, became so disgusted that he resigned from *Thai Mai* and went to work for Ari Liwira at the Thai Phanitchayakan Company. Before long, Issara had turned some of that company's many newspapers into best sellers with his unusual editorial talent and innovation.[184]

But under the omnipotent, unholy dominion of Mammon, worlds away from the Religion of Phra Sri Arya, there was not much the *Karnmuang* left could do about Prasit's private ownership and control except grumble or quit. Thus, the uneasy coexistence persisted until the TCP apparently came up with a new idea—to beat the capitalist Prasit at his own game through an editorial and business take-over. There is no clear and direct account of how it was done, but based on available circumstantial evidence, this much can be said: first, the take-over became part of the TCP's plan to launch a mass peace movement against the United States-led and Thai-supported military intervention in Korea; second, it took place sometime between August and December 1950; third, it involved a marked shift to the radical left in the paper's overall language, contents, columns, and contributors beginning partially in volume 6, number 44 (May 27, 1950) and concertedly in volume 7, number 1 (July 29, 1950); fourth, it made the paper into a pivotal printed medium for inciting, mobilizing, launching, directing, and coordinating a nationwide campaign to collect signatures on anti-government peace petitions; and fifth, it resulted in the wholesale replacement of the paper's old owner (Prasit), manager (Bunchoo), editorial staff (Phethai and Jari), and liberal and conservative contributors with new staff from the TCP and its allies.[185]

The first issue of the new *Karnmuang Weekly* was published on January 13, 1951, ostensibly under the ownership of Jaroen Seubsaeng (leftist MP for Pattani), with Jamras Sapthanawin as editor, and Sarit Phrombot as manager. Signalling the paper's turn-about were the change of its printing house and office address from Bunchoo's Rungnakhorn Printing House to one called Pholphaibool, the discontinuation of the sequential numbering of its issues and beginning of a new sequence,[186] and the following statement from its new team of publishers:

> To the readers, subscribers and agents: Due to the fact that *Karnmuang Weekly* newspaper has renewed its publication so as to serve the people more effectively and better than before in accordance with the present conditions and situation, we would like to inform you that our printing house and office is now located at the Pholphaibool Printing House...In case you want to contact us, please use the address of the new office so that together we can achieve the results we hope for.[187]

I say "ostensibly" because actually things were otherwise. Behind the scenes, the new *Karnmuang*'s real owner was not Jaroen but Udom Sisuwan, head of the TCP's press and publication department; its real editor not Jamras but Atsani Phonlajan, the renowned writer-cum-poet and new recruit to the TCP; its real office not at the Pholphaibool Printing House but at a secret safe house of the Party in an alley on Ladya Road in Thonburi; and its real financial, political, and organizational backer not the newly-formed Peace Movement but the older Thai Communist Party.[188] Regular columnists and contributors to the new *Karnmuang* were assembled from most of the old *Karnmuang* left, the *Aksornsarn* left, and the soon-to-be defunct communist *Mahachon*.[189]

In content and style, the new *Karnmuang* was a recognizable, but modified version of *Mahachon* with less (actually minimal) commercial advertisements and a less explicitly communist-partisan manifestation, but sharper focus (on American imperialism, the Korean War, and the Phibun government's pro-American, pro-war, and anti-communist policies), greater dynamism (based on the growing Thai and international peace movement), and a spicier and more sophisticated literary style. Probably modelling itself on *Mahachon*, it carried extensive updated reports on the Thai and international peace movement, leftist domestic and foreign news and comment, activism-orientated analyses of the situation and directives, poems, literary reviews, and glossaries of Marxist-communist terms. The center of the paper's propaganda crusade was, of course, the Thai Peace Movement, for which it served as mouthpiece, triumphantly proclaiming the formation of the Peace Committee of Thailand under the presidency of the paper's owner,[190] enthusiastically launching a new signature campaign for a peace treaty among the five major powers (U.S., U.S.S.R., P.R.C., Great Britain, and France),[191] and publishing lengthy lists of public luminaries who had signed the peace petition.[192]

But while the paper gained enormously in popular support, it lost political protection, now shorn of Phao-Prasit's privileged umbrella and fully exposed to the police searchlight. Furthermore, given the highly sensitive political issues it relentlessly pursued, the stiff opposition to the government it put up, the great potential popular base of the communist movement it revealed, and the militant activism and radical ideology it advocated, it could not but become a prime target for government censorship and suppression. The paper soon received an order (dated March 12, 1951) from its former patron, Police General Phao himself, forbidding the sale, distribution, and giving away of one issue of the paper.[193] This was followed a month later by a police raid on the office, during which 197 copies of *Karnmuang* volume [8], number 15 were confiscated.[194] The situation went from bad to worse until, in the aftermath of the Radio or Silent Coup in November 1951, the paper ceased publication altogether.[195]

For obvious reasons, when the Phibunsongkhram government decided to crack down on the leftist and communist opposition one year later, the ostensible owner, editor, and many writers of the new *Karnmuang* found themselves in jail alongside their colleagues from other opposition newspapers. Among those who were released shortly afterwards, owing to lack of incriminating evidence, were Supha Sirimanond, the ever-cautious chief editor of *Aksornsarn*, and Ari Liwira, the director of Thai Phanitchayakan Company. Although Supha lost *Aksornsarn*, the police soon left him alone. Ari, however, was not so fortunate, for Police General Phao suspected him of being a communist sympathizer and/or Pridi man and was therefore dead set on taking over the Thai Phanitchayakan's giant newspaper chain. When Ari steadfastly rejected Phao's personal offer to buy out his controlling interest in the company and resolutely refused either to make a confession or name names, his fate was sealed. On March 9, 1953, two weeks after his marriage, Ari was gunned down by Phao's police assassins while honeymooning at the Huahin seaside resort.[196] With the death of his straightforward employer, Issara Amantakul lost his pillar at Thai Phanitchayakan Company and soon found himself out of work again.

Without money, protection, or jobs, there was not much choice for radical journalists in reactionary times. So Supha Sirimanond and Issara Amantakul, the two battered veterans of radical journalism from *Aksornsarn* and *Karnmuang*, ended up working (in Issara's case, for the second time) at *Thai Mai* for Hia Sit, now more powerful and affluent than ever as elected MP for Chachoengsao and top executive of the Bangkok Bank. In a matter of weeks, both journalistic wizards helped transform the old languishing daily into the new best-selling *Thai Mai Yuk Mai* (New Thai Mai) with their management skills and editorial expertise and the quality writing of their leftist friends.[197] Be that as it may, it must have seemed to both of them practically impossible publicly to reproduce the modern Marxist-communist religion of Phra Sri Arya without reproducing simultaneously the Mammonish structure and network of power that stood squarely in the way of the coming of Phra Sri Arya.

Perhaps becoming weary of this dilemma and the difficulties plaguing each attempt to reproduce Marxism-communism in the capitalist market under a military authoritarian regime, Supha and later Thaweep finally left journalism for good and went, respectively, into the insurance business and legal practice.[198] And with the advent of Field Marshal Sarit Thanarat's absolutist rule in October 1958, other radical and communist intellectuals who persisted with their ideological mission could do so only in exile, like Pridi Banomyong; underground, like Phayap Angkhasing; in the maquis, like Jaroen Wanngam; or in prison, like Issara Amantakul, now nicknamed "Fidel Castro." The "Cuba" group of radical inmates under his leadership reproduced in Ladyao Penitentiary a miniature "commune" whose members shared food, worked collectively, fought for the rights and welfare of political and criminal prisoners, read Marxist-communist books, wrote or translated leftist scholarship, fiction, and poems, taught languages and subjects of knowledge to one another, composed songs, played music and sports, organized a theater troupe, grew vegetables and flowers, celebrated leftist holidays, and drank liquor, worlds away and free from the omnipotent coercive mechanisms of bourgeois civil society.[199]

9
Conclusion: What Is Left?

There are a number of interesting and useful lessons one can draw from the foregoing story of the first generation of Thai radical Marxist-communist intellectuals. Some of them are theoretical while others have a more practical relevance.

The Ethno-Ideology of Thainess and Its Other

Historically speaking, the official nationalist project of the Thai nation had two salient dimensions. The first one was purportedly racialized or ethnicized, according to which "Thailand unites the Thai blood and race. A people's state, all parts belong to Thais…," as the national anthem goes. This imagined nation of pure Thais had from the beginning been positioned by the Thai royal and subsequent military rulers primarily not against the western colonial powers, nor its colonized and hence pacified neighbors, but against Chinese immigrants and their descendants who, as entrepreneurs and coolies, dominated the modern sector of its economy and urban society since the late nineteenth century.

These so-called "Jews of the Orient," in the menacing words of King Vajiravudh, the founder of Thai royalist official nationalism,[1] or simply "Jeks" in Thai derogatory popular parlance, were in fact the key agents of economic modernization and political modernity in Siam, the pioneers of its modern civil society, so to speak. As such, they constituted the only potent domestic socio-economic force that could effectively challenge state authority, as they did in an organized general strike to protest a capitation tax increase that paralyzed the capital city for several days in 1910. And yet, their collective entrepreneurial skills and labor were too precious to the modernizing efforts of the Thai state for them to be simply killed or expelled. Hence the need to ideologically construct and perpetually invoke their un-Thai ethnicity and status as "settlers" (not native "owners") in Thailand so as to bluff them into accepting a subservient position in a patron-client relationship with Thai state authorities. Thus, in essence, Thai official nationalism was not racism per se but a racializing or ethnicizing discourse aimed at establishing and reproducing unequal power relations between the "Thai" state on the one hand, and "un-Thai" or "never-adequately-Thai" capital and society on the other, on the basis of which state clientelism was practiced and maintained.[2]

The second dimension of the Thai official nationalist project was directly political-ideological and aimed at instilling a conservative and royalist, conformist and submissive pattern of clientelist beliefs and behavior into the populace at large. Thus, for King Vajiravudh, the *sine qua non* for an authentic Thai national lay not so much in one's ability to speak the Thai language as in one's absolute and unconditional "allegiance to the King of Siam."[3] Prince Damrong, foremost court historian, authoritatively characterized the disposition of the Thai nation in a 1927 lecture as comprising "love of national independence, toleration, and power of assimilation."[4] Later, the militaristic government of Field Marshal Plaek Phibunsongkhram, the Thai Führer, simply decreed in a series of *ratthaniyom* (cultural mandates of the state) that "Thailand is a nation of conformists and followers of the leader."[5]

Thus imagined, this nation of sheep would plainly disown and have no place for "black" fellow countrymen, be they liberal dissenters, democratic activists, or socialist parliamentary oppositionists, let alone communist revolutionaries, regardless of actual race or ethnicity. Since it so happened that the first generation of communists in Siam were all Chinese and Vietnamese immigrants and their descendants, they easily fell prey to the othering, alienating strategy of the Thai official nationalist project in a double sense, both ethnically and ideologically. From the viewpoint of the ethno-ideology of Thainess, the *jek* and/or lookjin communists couldn't possibly be Thai.

Once incorporated into Thai as the epitome of un-Thainess, communism became *khommunit*, a potent and deadly signifier in Thai cultural politics whose arbitrary and ever-changing legal and/or political definition was opportunistically applied by the ideological and repressive state apparatuses and political elite to repress all kinds of dissenters and opponents, regardless of their actual ideological persuasion. In the end, *khommunit* in Thailand did not really signify a distinctive, particular ideology; anyone who stood in the way of the Thai official nationalist project was, in effect, a *khommunit*.

And yet, it was precisely through the ethno-ideological othering process of Thai official nationalism, the legal-political exclusion and oppression it sanctioned, the cultural marginalization and subordination it justified, and the human degradation and suffering it exacted, that a sense of camaraderie and fraternity, solidarity and community as fellow Thai countrymen gradually emerged and materializd against the "Thai" state among its countless "un-Thai" victims in prisons, schools, universities, newspaper and magazine offices, mass movements, underground cells, and socialist and communist parties, at Bangkhwang, Ladyao, Xinmin, Assumption, St. Gabriel, Thammasat, Chulalongkorn, *Mahachon*, *Aksornsan*, *Karnmuang*, Sahaachiwa Kammakorn, Peace Movement, Thai-issara, Ongkan Thai Koochat, Sahachip Party, and Communist Party of Thailand. In the face of such an oppressive, exclusive, and discriminatory nation-state, its exact other, an anti-state nation, so to speak, arose as a radical alternative.

That the emergence of Thai radical nationalism among the lookjin communists during the Second World War was ushered in by the parallel radical nationalism of the Chinese immigrants attests to the intimate complicity and inter-national nature of popular, anti-state nationalisms. Translation thus serves much more than merely an informational function since it transposes concepts, values, and beliefs from one national imagination to the formation of another. Given a favorable historic moment when a window of political opportunity swings open, one can see the beauty of comparisons and fall in love with a nation just for the love of another.

Commodifying Marxism and Its Contradictions

The evident crises and failures of pre-existing political systems from the 1930s, be they absolute monarchy, military authoritarianism, or constitutional democracy, had created in post-war Thailand a structure of political feelings, or cultural opportunity structure, uniquely conducive to the propagation of a self-proclaimed radically new and different, alternative political ideology and system which was Marxism-communism. Further, its coincident political liberalization and legalization allowed its cultural products unprecedented opportunity to freely enter the market on a large scale as printed commodities. However, the commodification and marketization of such an anti-market radical discourse under an increasingly authoritarian and anti-communist military regime entailed a set of intractable contradictions and peculiar dilemmas between legality and militancy, business and ideology, community and conflict, and plurality and monopoly, with which Thai radical intellectuals had to live and contend.

Legality versus Militancy

While legality was a *sine qua non* for the market existence of the radical press, militancy in its opposition to the government and ruling class was its selling point. Put simply, people *could* buy radical periodicals openly because they were legalized, but people *did* buy them, from among a host of other publications, because they were distinctly, politically, and ideologically militant. At the same time, the government under attack by the radical press had every reason to seek to narrow or abolish that democratic space by limiting or removing its legal status. This was especially true when an unpopular government was forced upon various discontented segments of population, as was the situation in Thailand after the military coup of 1947. Thus sandwiched, the radical press could find its militant political position willy-nilly egged on by presumably insurgent readers towards the contracting legal boundaries circumscribed by the alarmist government. So much so that at one point, radical publishers would face a fateful marketing dilemma: risk their legal status and sell well or lose their militant appeal and survive police censorship.

One should bear in mind that despite the repeal of the Anti-Communist Act, the Thai military government still had on hand repressive security, censorship, criminal, and libel laws, as well as special constitutional measures such as the declaration of a state of emergency and martial law, to deal with the press whenever it was perceived to be going too far in its opposition to the government, especially during a crisis. And if all legal means, including the restoration of the Anti-Communist Act in 1952, still failed to curb its independent anti-government militancy, there was always the covert use of deadly violence, to which the Thai political police could and increasingly did resort in order to put some of the oppositional press out of circulation, market and otherwise.

Business versus Ideology

The owner and publisher of ideologically "red" publications always ran the risk of going into the "red." Among the usual unfavorable factors to be reckoned with were the business community's ideologically or politically motivated reluctance to place advertisements in radical newspapers and magazines, leftist publishers' missionary zeal to sell papers even at a loss for the sake of ideological propagation, and an attendant lack of entrepreneurship and attention to accounting. Unless a radical paper was securely under the pecuniary patronage of a financially solid political boss or organization, it could not be choosy about the kinds of commercial advertisements it carried, as these were not only indispensable for its continued market survival but also hard to come by.

However, as a specific *Weltanschauung*, Marxism-communism entailed a series of radical, non-conformist socio-economic and cultural ideas, values, and beliefs that went completely against *les affaires bourgeoises* and could not help but show up in articles, essays, and stories the radical press published. On the one hand, these might scare off prospective advertisers. On the other hand, printing writings of an anti-bourgeois and anti-business mentality alongside commercial advertisements for capitalist enterprises could be read simply as moral hypocrisy and ideological corruption. Whether an act of bad business or bad faith, the dilemma of bankruptcy or profanation in a capitalist market could not be avoided.

Community versus Conflict

Marxism-communism, as it was extensively imported into Thailand and prolifically translated into Thai by lookjin communists and Thai leftist intellectuals for the first time after the Second World War, functioned above all as a new, radical, and militant political oppositional discourse which opposition parties, protest groups, and dissident individuals adapted and utilized to comprehend, articulate, and give meaning and purpose, historical direction, and grandeur to their anti-establishment struggles. Chiefly through thousands upon thousands of copies of radical newspapers, magazines, and books, with hundreds of letters among editors, translators, writers, and readers serving as regular channels of communication, and supported by such socializing institutions as private homes and drinking circles, publishing offices and bookstores, universities and temples, political parties and trade unions, hide-outs and prisons, a vague awareness of a new, as yet unsettled, identity and a loose solidarity—an embryonic community consciousness, so to speak—was created out of the common use of a distinct set of Thaified Marxist-communist words in verbal resistance to the government and dominant classes.

These radical signifiers performed several key functions: first, as symbolic unifiers, they unified the communist and leftist intellectuals, dissident individuals, protest groups, and opposition organizations of various socio-economic interests and political convictions into a pluralistic, loosely structured, discursive community based on a common denominator, their shared oppositional discourse; second, as political identifiers, they helped identify their users as "progressive" or "communist" members of this community for both fellow members and the political police; and finally, as linguistic currency, they served as the collective medium with which community members attacked the powers-that-be and through which they communed and conflicted with one another. In short, they were the identity-constitutive discourse of radical intellectuals in post-war Thailand.

But if this Marxism-communism-derived Thaified radical discourse was a major source and vehicle of community within the Thai "progressive" opposition in general, communists and leftists in particular, it also sowed a seed of discord among them. Issues in dispute included which of the canon of

Marxist-communist classics should be translated and in what order; which of their foreign versions was reliable and should be used in the translation; how to translate them, that is, what Thai words (signifiers) should be used as equivalents of the foreign Marxist-communist key terms; whether new words should be coined or old ones adopted; what exactly they meant (signifieds); what things or processes in Thai history and society they referred to (referents); how to interpret and apply them to the analysis of past and contemporary Thailand; and ultimately how to put them into practice or act them out. Trifling though these might seem, they were questions of primary importance for at their crux lay the crucial question of authority.

With great political potential and forceful claims to universal truth and world-historical mission based on the triumphant experiences of certain foreign regimes and movements, Thai radical discourse promised to be a powerful cultural-political instrument of opposition over whose production and circulation different groups of radical intellectuals vied for control. Furthermore, like an alien seed planted in an unfamiliar land beset by ignorant growers, weeds, diseases, and bugs, Thai radical discourse needed protection against vulgarization, (over) intellectualization, degeneration, corruption, and manipulation by unworthy hands. It was a relatively new and alien discourse, imported from foreign countries and translated from foreign languages, which most Thai radical intellectuals in and outside the TCP, let alone the reading public at large, did not initially know very well. Hence the need to focus on the discourse and try to achieve cultural hegemony over its vocabulary, coinage, gloss, exegesis, and usage by persistently fixing its lexical representations, standardizing its conceptual definitions, identifying its perceptual realities, and authorizing its textual interpretations, analytical usages, and practical applications—in short, by policing the use value of the discourse itself as an apparently feasible way to exercise control over it in a free market situation.

But wherever there were discourse-police, there were destined to be discourse-criminals, especially in a situation where more than one such self-proclaimed discourse authority existed. It should be borne in mind that when the Anti-Communist Act was repealed in 1946, the mostly-lookjin TCP was only four years old and had just learned to speak and write Thai, while the Pridi group, more precisely Pridi himself, though well-established politically, widely respected intellectually, and famed for the authorship and advocacy of the country's first radical socialistic economic plan, had since shelved that program, consistently denied allegations of communism, been publicly reticent about radical ideological commitment, and kept his socialist inclination largely within inner circles of like-minded friends and followers. The Thai credentials of Marxist-communist authority and hegemony over Thai radical discourse were thus by no means pre-ordained, but had to be contended for and won again and again in the capitalist marketplace. Hence the serious and ongoing conflict over the political use values of Thai radical discourse, exclusive to fellow community members and their outside ideological opponents, and paid no heed by others who just wanted to "fish" for fashionable and fanciful signifiers in troubled discursive waters with no regard to their radical significance.[6]

Plurality versus Monopoly

But there was a deeper reason for the chronic character of conflict over Thai radical discourse, one that had to do with the nature of the capitalist market itself and particularly with the predicament of commercialized culture within it: any attempt to establish an omnipotent and omnipresent ultimate authority over Thai radical discourse, in other words to make the discourse monolithic, would be constantly baffled as long as it remained at large in the capitalist marketplace. Set loose and allowed by necessity to roam, the more broadly Thai radical discourse spread through market channels and made its influence felt in the form of cultural commodities, the more difficult it was to control its meanings and usages across different literary genres, political contexts, and social groups with their separate, independent structures and norms, interests and demands. Consequently, the more impotent any self-proclaimed discourse authority became. Committed now to the future and to strangers, the discourse assumed autonomous, situational, and multiple avatars of its own, tending relentlessly towards plurality of unauthorized meanings and usages in the "unworthy" hands of "revisionists" and opponents, poets and advertisers, dilettantes and gurus, "fishermen" and rulers. Alas, in the capitalist world of abstract universal exchange-values, where Marxist-communist radical discourse, packaged and sold as cultural commodities, could be exchanged for any and all things, how on earth could one effectively police or fix its desired concrete particular use-values?

Paradoxically, accompanying the tendency of radical discourse towards plurality in the capitalist market was the inverse tendency of Marxist cultural market towards monopoly. Under the constant and growing combined pressure of repressive political regime, unfavorable business conditions, and intra-community estrangement and desertion, the market environment of Marxist cultural commodities would become increasingly adverse to the point where the weaker radical cultural enterprises, those without political protection, financial subsidy, or organizational back-up, would lose more and more ground to their stronger competitors or be jostled out of business altogether. Moreover, depending on the degree of political and discursive conflict involved and the organizational and financial capacity of the adversaries, a spontaneous (or organized) commercial and editorial boycott and even hostile takeover could be launched, resulting in further reduction of competition in the marketplace.

Whether this tendency of the Marxist cultural market towards monopoly would be actually and fully realized was a function of factors such as the relative strengths of existing competitors and the startup risks, costs, and difficulties involved for new ones. The dominant and decisive factor, nonetheless, was government policy toward the radical press and cultural commodities as a whole—all-out government repression and prohibition of them would make the continued smuggling, processing, and distribution of Marxist-communist cultural products underground so difficult, costly, risky, and even fatal that only the most dedicated, best-organized, and best-funded group could survive to carry on the unenviable illicit trade. As, ironically, the Prohibition helped Al Capone gain the monopoly of bootleg alcohol in 1920s Chicago, so did the restoration of the Anti-Communist Act in 1952 and the major crackdowns on leftist press and intellectuals in 1952 and 1958 greatly help the CPT win the monopoly of Marxist-communist cultural products and establish dominant authority over radical discourse in the black market afterwards.

But what good would that monopolistic authority bring, banished as it was to the underground? It could not be exercised directly and openly, nor could it operate indirectly and covertly without some degree of compromise with the powers-that-be, even when an opportunity was found through "the interstices between the power domains" of contending ruling cliques.[7] With Marxist-communist cultural products now banned from the market, the scope of dissemination of radical discourse would be greatly narrowed and its influence much reduced. Besides, what appeal could a fully authorized and strictly regimented radical discourse possibly hold for different groups of people and cultural forms once it was programmed to be impervious to their structures, norms, interests, and demands and to refuse unauthorized adaptation and accommodation to them? In the final analysis, was waxing amidst the conflicting plurality and confusing anarchy of the open market better than waning amidst the orthodox monopoly and monolithic authority of the underground ghetto? Another dilemma to face, another predicament to negotiate.

The Politics of Translation

Situated at the margins of a national language, translation guards the linguistic border and integrity of a nation-state's "body cultural."[8] Where language is standardized and coinages need to be sanctioned by central authorities, as in modern Thailand, the translation of key foreign political and ideological words becomes a highly politicized and fiercely contested borderland in which language border patrol police try to screen newly translated lexical immigrants, discriminating against radical ones and declaring them *lexicon non grata*. Failing that, they retranslate (in some cases pre-translate) them in such a way as to make of them either quarantined and alien permanent non-residents, or emasculated and tamed, harnessed and domesticated, incorporated and de-radicalized, naturalized neuters, while the unauthorized radical translators seek persistently to smuggle in and procreate their illegitimate lexical brainchild.

In this regard, the modern Thai cultural elite was exceptionally conscious of the politics of translation, as evidenced by the following principle of Thai neologism laid down as early as December 1932 by the late Prince Wan, an Oxford-educated member of the royalty, top diplomat, senior cabinet minister, and longest-reigning, most prolific, highest authority of Thai official neologism:

> It is the Thai language that will guarantee the security of the Thai nation. This is because if we favor the use of Thai transliterations of Western words about ideas, we may walk too fast. That is we may imitate other people's ideas directly instead of pre-modifying them to accord with our ideas. But if we use Thai words and hence must coin new ones, we will have to walk deliberately.[9]

Among the key Thai cultural political coinages he invented are *sangkhom* (society), *setthakij* (economy), *nayobai* (policy), *rabob* (system), *raborb* (regime), *phatthana* (development), *patiwat* (revolution), *patiroop* (reform), *wiwat* (evolution), *kammachip* (proletariat), *kradumphi* (bourgeoisie), *mualchon* (masses), *sangkhomniyom* (socialism), *ongkan* (organization), *sahaphap* (union), *watthanatham* (culture), *wiphak* (critique), *judyeun* (standpoint), *pratya* (philosophy), *atthaniyom* (realism), and *jintaniyom* (romanticism). Thai radicals and communists simply could not open their mouths without echoing some of the Prince's neologisms! Following are examples of the politics behind some official Thai coinages:

Revolution. Prince Wan's coinage for it in Thai was *patiwat*, literally "turning or rolling back," with the conservative connotation of "restoration," instead of denoting the radical break with the past or the progressive and qualitative change of affairs of the English original.

Communism. Although Prince Wan did tentatively coin a couple of Thai words for it as early as 1934, i.e., *latthi niyom mualchon* and *sapsatharananiyom* (literally massism and pan-publicism), the transliterated *khommunit* became universally adopted in both official and popular usages, beginning around 1932 and continuing until today.[10] Sulak Sivaraksa, a conservative royalist intellectual and noted cultural critic, has suggested that the reason for this might be to maintain the alien sound and appearance of the word and the idea, to deny it a legitimate place in the Thai language, and to keep it forever as the un-Thai Other at the lexical gate, so to speak. Radical leftists' subsequent feeble attempts to coin a new Thai word for it, such as Naiphi's *latthi sahachip* (literally unionism), failed to catch on.

Democracy. The present Thai equivalent is *prachathipatai.* Curiously enough, this coinage of King Rama VI (as early as 1912) initially meant "republic," i.e., a government with no king. The shift in its meaning from "republic" to "democracy" followed from a compromise between the People's Party and the monarchy in the anti-absolutist revolution of 1932 when a constitutional monarchy was chosen in place of a republic, thus allowing the characterization of the present Thai political system as *rabob prachathipatai an mi phramahakasat song pen pramuk* or (keeping the original meaning of *prachathipatai* in mind) "republic with the King as the head of state," an oxymoron made possible by the successful taming or metathesis of a foreign-derived radical signifier.

Historically speaking, Thai radicals and communists were at a disadvantage in the politics of translating foreign Marxist-communist words into Thai. From the 1920s to the mid-1940s, while the ruling elite, state ideologues, and intelligence officials were busy translating and coining words for the purposes of surveillance and repression, as well as economic policy debate, the first-generation Chinese and Vietnamese communists were still largely speaking their own languages, organizing and mobilizing their respective immigrant communities, and directing their political concerns and activities towards their homelands as good long-distance *huaqiao* and *Viet kieu* nationalists.

It was only after the Second World War that a new generation of radicals and communists, consisting of both Thai-literate *jeks* (or lookjins) and native Thais, saw the necessity and had the interest and language proficiency to begin their own translation and coinage of Marxist-communist words in earnest.[11] But by then, the anti-communists had already occupied the strategic commanding heights in the discursive field. Here are some examples of Thai radical and communist attempts at retranslating Marxist-communist words:

Aphiwat. Dissatisfied with the conservative connotation of *patiwat,* Pridi Banomyong coined the word *aphiwat,* literally "super-evolution."

Phaessaya. In place of Prince Wan's rather neutral-sounding and low-key *kradumphi,* Atsani Phonlajan, alias Naiphi, retranslated the bourgeoisie as *phaessaya,* a Sanskrit-derived Thai word with the wonderful double meaning of "merchant class" and "prostitute or bitch."

Kammakorn. A pioneering group of ethnic Thai labor union activists and organizers in the 1920s deliberately called their organization and newspaper "Kammakorn," a word with a residual meaning of slavery and cruel punishment, as the Thai equivalent of the English "worker." The authorities obviously did not like its negative connotation and have been waging a protracted war against the word ever since. For example, the official dictionary of the Ministry of Public Instruction published in 1927, and that of the Royal Institute issued in 1950, added an unusual note of caution to the entry to explain that *kammakorn* was not a slave, as in the English "laborer (laboring class)."[12] In 1956, Police Director General Phao Sriyanond bargained with delegates of the radical labor union movement for a change in the Thai rendering of May Day from *wan kammakorn* to *wan raengngan* (Labor Day) as a pre-condition for allowing public celebration on that day.[13] More than 30 years later, Prime Minister General Prem Tinsulanond (1980–1988) pleaded with labor leaders at the Government House for the same nominal change!

Rhyming Marxism

Yet no matter who did the translation or what kind of hidden political agenda he or she originally had in mind, once translated, these Thaified or naturalized Marxist-communist words had their own indigenous ways of filtering from the political margins through the thick of Thai culture to the center. One such route was poetry, more simply rhyming, whose centrality to Thai traditional culture was confirmed by two chief representatives of modern Thai poets, one a royalist and the other a communist, in these respective testimonies:

Thailand Is a Nation of Rhymers. Siamese Thais are rhymers by habit. There are plenty of poets from the highest to the lowest classes. Some of them are scholars but many more are illiterates. The scholars who become poets may do so because of their literacy as well as disposition. But the illiterates do so purely on account of their disposition. If we are to publish a collection of all the verses composed by these illiterate rhymers in a year, it will take up a great many volumes...If one is to estimate what percentage of the population of this country are rhymers, the figure should not be less than that of any other country in the world. We love rhyming so much that we versify not only in our own traditional genres, but also in those of other languages. And once we get hold of them, we do not follow their original version but modify them to suit our ears by adding rhymes, thus making them much more difficult...(No.Mo.So., alias Prince Phitthayalongkorn).[14]

Thai people are rhymers by habit. The sweet-sounding saying of rhymes is almost a commonplace but its content is another matter (Intharayut, alias Atsani Phonlajan).[15]

The translated Marxist-communist words were perfectly admissible and convenient candidates for inclusion in Thai poetry for the simple reason that the translations were much easier to rhyme with other Thai words than were their original foreign equivalents. For example, according to the only existing Thai rhyming dictionary known to me, only fifteen Thai words rhyme with "socialism" together with other -isms, whereas 294 rhyme with its Thai translation, *sangkhomniyom*.[16]

A particular quality of Thai poetry makes it an ideal literary genre conducive to an expanded reproduction of Marxist-communist signifiers. This is its capacity to say the same thing over and over again lengthily, verbosely, gracefully, powerfully, rhythmically, and rhymingly, making it easy to remember and recite or sing. Volumes of beautiful Thai poems have been composed just to say "Oh, my dear, how much I love you! Do you love me?" or "How great the Lord Buddha is!" in a hundred different ways.[17]

Moreover, the practice of composing poetry to convey political ideas had begun in Siam in the late nineteenth and early twentieth century. Under the impact of western culture and education, many royal, aristocratic, and even commoner poets had transformed the traditional style and function of Thai poetry from long narratives to short "vehicles of thought," be they liberal, democratic, royalist, or nationalist. In this regard, Thai radical and communist poets were simply following in their footsteps by turning Thai poetry into a vehicle of Marxist-communist thought.

In the decade following the Second World War, scores of translated Marxist-communist signifiers majestically reigned and melodiously rhymed with fellow Thai words in Thai radical and communist poems. More often than not, they were printed in bold letters or under inverted commas, clearly visible and distinguishable from non-radical words in the same line, as if to mark them off as verbal icons or emblems of the poems' radicalism. In some cases, reference was given to inform the readers of the source (usually a translated article or essay) from which the original idea of a poem was derived,[18] or the original English equivalent of a translated radical word was provided in a footnote to the poem.[19] In one instance, a translator-poet added two Thai words to his translation of a radical English poem that did not appear in the original, namely *kaona* (progressive) and *sajjatham* (truth). It must have been absolutely clear to him that these two radical signifiers rightfully belonged there.

Thus hundreds of Thai radical poems were composed and published, and consequently thousands of Marxist-communist signifiers were literally reproduced and displayed on the pages of radical periodicals and books in easily noticeable and memorable forms, owing to their printing style and fluent rhyming and alliteration. Many lines and stanzas of these poems have since been reprinted innumerable times in periodicals and collections, turned into political songs or slogans, written on big posters during labor strikes and mass rallies, and softly or silently recited and sung in serene solitude or extreme danger. In this manner Thai poetry helped preserve and pass on the Marxism-communism of the radical signifiers.

And yet, rhyming Marxism did come at a price. For eventually, the Thai radical poets came up against the dialectical tension inherent in any such attempt, a tension between the theoretical logic of Marxism-communism and the complex regulations of Thai poetry. The various types of Thai poetry, whether *khloong*, *chand*, *kab*, *klon*, or *rai*, are well known for their highly formalistic and strictly regulated character called *chanthalak*, or prosody-characteristics. Their composition must adhere to a series of complicated patterns, regulations, and requirements governing the number of syllables, tone, rhythm, internal rhyming (within a line), and external rhyming (between lines and stanzas), which follow a logic totally different from and incompatible with Marxist-communist theory.

Consequently, rhymed and Thaified Marxism-communism couldn't possibly maintain its pristine theoretical integrity and meaning across languages and cultures, contexts and media, reproducers and audiences. Especially when undergoing the further processes of mechanical and electronic reproduction and commodification in an open capitalist cultural market, it became hopelessly open and subject to adulteration, profanation, de-contextualization, interpretation, negotiation, revision, re-signification, re-functionalization, and de- and re-radicalization *ad infinitum* over which no single authority could have absolute or monopolistic control.

It was as if, once imported or smuggled across linguistic boundaries, stripped of their original foreign script and sound, made to incarnate Thai ones, thrown into a new semantic field, and then shoved into various Thai verse genres, those poor alien Marxist words ran into a virtual mine-field of immensely complex rhyming, syllabic, accentual, rhythmic, and tonal rules and regulations that followed a totally disparate logic. Crashing into these cultural obstacles head-on, they disintegrated on impact into free-floating radical signifiers, multiple confusing signifieds, substituted referents, and incongruous practice, each going their own separate, mind-boggling, centrifugal way. The cultural political task of recollecting, reintegrating, reinterpreting, and redeeming these fragments is left for later generations of Thai radicals to carry out.

What Is Left?

Amid the ruins of Thai and world communism upon the arrival of the new globalized millennium, one wonders if anything is left of the now defeated and disgraced, Marxism-communism-inspired, modern Thai radical culture that is still of value to, and hence worthy of redemption by, the millions of disadvantaged and dispossessed victims of Thai and global capitalist development, those whose unprofitable skills, obsolete ways of life, and delicate natural environment are being crushed by the wheel of progress, steered, as always, by shortsightedly avaricious captains of finance and industry.

Perhaps, just as one encounters in the former Soviet Union residual mechanisms of power created by the long-established combination of official communism and Russian national culture, now being borrowed and reconditioned by western capital in its search for profit at the expense of the Soviet peoples, one can argue that there still exist in Thailand the residual nuts and bolts of cultural resistance that had been tempered and moulded by the long, frictional combination of communism and Thai culture. And that as long as the modern ravages of dictatorship and capitalism are still visited upon the Thais, there will be enough new radicals to reassemble them into powerful cultural weapons in the fight for their own and humanity's survival and dignity.

Notes

Chapter 2

1 *Nangseu krab bangkhomthul khong kromphra nakhornsawanworaphinit*
   [Report to His Majesty from Kromphra Nakhornsawanworaphinit] (439/
   125116, January 6, 1930), quoted in Suwadee Charoenphong, "Bot thi 5:
   Patikiriya khong ratthabal phrabatsomdej phrapokklaojaoyoohua to
   kankhleuanwai thang khwamkhid sangkhomniyom khommunit (Pho.So.
   2468–2475)" [Chapter 5: The reaction of King Prajadhipok's government
   to the communist-socialist ideological movement, B.E. 2468–2475],
   *Kanmeuang-kanpokkhrong thai samai mai: Ruam nganwijai thang
   prawattisat lae ratthasat* [Modern Thai politics and government: A
   collection of research in history and political science], ed. Chai-anan
   Samudavanija and Suwadee Charoenphong (Bangkok: Chulalongkorn
   University, 1979), 318.

2 For more detailed arguments, see Benedict R. O'G. Anderson, "Studies
   of the Thai State: The State of Thai Studies," in *The Study of Thailand:
   Analysis of Knowledge, Approaches, and Prospects in Anthropology, Art
   History, Economics, History and Political Science*, ed. Eliezer B. Ayal
   (Athens, Ohio: Center for International Studies, Ohio University, 1979),
   193–247.

3 See Saneh Chamarik, *Kanmeuang kab kanseuksa khong thai* [Thai
   politics and education] (Bangkok: Development of Education-Related
   Social Sciences Project, Office of the National Education Committee,
   Office of the Prime Minister, 1983), 22, 38–57, 89–90; and Seksan
   Prasertkul, "The Transformation of the Thai State and Economic Change
   (1855–1945)" (Ph.D. diss., Cornell University, 1989), 431–40.

4 The growing significance of translation was signalled by the monthly
   Lakwitthaya (Knowledge stealing), whose publishers, one member of the
   royalty and two nobles, declared: "Stories published in this newspaper
   will be mostly translated or 'stolen' from other languages. Therefore,
   Lakwitthaya will be an interpreter of foreign news and various frivolous
   or serious stories rather than an original author." See Homhual Cheunjit,

chapter 2 of *Kanplae: Achip soo puangchon* [Translation: Career for the
people] (Bangkok: United Productions Publisher, 1984); Laortong
Amarinratana, "Kansong nakrian pai seuksato tangprathet tangtae
Pho.So. 2411–2475" [The sending of students abroad from 1868–1932]
(master's thesis, Chulalongkorn University, 1979), 21–33; and Sukanya
Tirawanich, *Prawat kannangseuphim nai prathet thai phaitai rabob
somboonnayasitthiraj (Pho.So. 2325–2475)* [A history of journalism in
Thailand under absolute monarchy (B.E. 2325–2475)] (Bangkok: Thai
Watana Panich, 1977), 8–9, 102.

5 See Supha Sirimanond, interview by Napaporn Ativanichayapong on
the development of political economy thought in Thailand, Bangkok,
September 4, 1985; and Chinda Sirimanond, *Anusorn nai supha
sirimanond* [In memory of Mr. Supha Sirimanond] (Cremation Volume
of Supha Sirimanond, Somnaswarawihan Temple, Bangkok, June 25,
1986), 11–43.

6 This observation was made in a general account of the beginning of
communism in Siam by a veteran member of the Communist Party of
Thailand in a party publication. See Phinyo Rojjana, "Kanphoeyphrae
sajjatham latthi marx nai prathet thai" [The dissemination of Marxist truth
in Thailand], *Mahachon-Thaiphijan* 1, no. 1 (March 1983): 45.

7 M.C. Akatdamkoeng Raphiphat, *Lakhorn haeng chiwit* [The circus of
life] (Bangkok: Prae Pittaya, 1960), 259–60, 263–64, 532.

8 Benjamin A. Batson, *The End of the Absolute Monarchy in Siam* (New
York: Oxford University Press, 1986), 79–83, 168, 181 n. 14.

9 Quoted in Ukris Patthamanan, "Khana ratsadorn kab kanplianplaeng
sangkhom thai dan kanthahan" [The People's Party and the transformation
of the military in Thai society], in Chaiwat Bunnag et al., "Khana ratsadorn
nai prawattisat thai" [The People's Party in Thai history] (papers presented
in the seminar, "The People's Party in Thai History," Krirk College, May
9–10, 1985, mimeograph), 9.

10 See Laortong, "Kansong," 213–14, 285–87.

11 See James T. Kloppenberg, *Uncertain Victory: Social Democracy and
Progressivism in European and American Thought, 1870–1920* (New
York: Oxford University Press, 1986), 199–224.

12 A democratic nationalist and radical socialist, Pridi (1900–1983) went
into exile in the aftermath of the right-wing, conservative-royalist military
coup of 1947. He lived in Communist China for the next two decades and
then in Paris, where he stayed until his widely mourned death.

13 See David K. Wyatt, *Thailand: A Short History* (New Haven: Yale
University Press, 1984), 238; Suthachai Yimprasert, "Kankhleuanwai

thang kanmeuang thi totan ratthabal samai jomphol plaek phibunsongkhram (Pho.So. 2491–2500)" [Political movement against Field Marshal Pibulsonggram's regime, 1948–1957] (master's thesis, Chulalongkorn University, 1989), 221, 231–32; and Thipphawan Jeamteerasakul, chapter 4 of *Pathomthas thang kanmeuang khong pridi banomyong* [Pridi Banomyong's early political thought] (Bangkok: Aksornsarn Press, 1988).

14 Anderson, "Studies," 220–23. Estimated figures are from G. William Skinner, *Chinese Society in Thailand: An Analytical History* (Ithaca, New York: Cornell University Press, 1957), 183; and Le Manh Trinh, "In Canton and Thailand," in *Days with Ho Chi Minh* (Hanoi: Foreign Languages Publishing House, 1962), 115.

15 Skinner, *Chinese Society*, 155–59; Le, "In Canton," 115.

16 Batson, *The End*, 166–67, 169, 170. Huynh Kim Khanh, *Vietnamese Communism, 1925–1945* (Ithaca: Cornell University Press, 1986), 173; Phinyo, "Kanphoeyphrae," 45; Suwadee, "Patikiriya," 297; Thongchai Phuengkanthai, "Latthi khommunit lae nayobai totan khong ratthabal thai Pho.So. 2468–2500" [Communism in Thailand and government policy against communism B.E. 2468–2500] (master's thesis, Chulalongkorn University, 1978), 71–72, 75–76, 85, 88, 109, 139.

17 The Chinese Communist Party (CCP) was founded in 1921 and entered into an anti-imperialist, anti-warlord alliance with the Kuomintang in 1923, while the Viet Nam Thanh Nien Kach Menh Hoi (Vietnamese Revolutionary Youth League) or Thanh Nien (Youth) for short, was set up by Nguyen Ai Quoc and his comrades in Canton, China in 1925.

18 See Batson, *The End*, 167, 168, 181 n.19; Jean Lacouture, *Ho Chi Minh: A Political Biography*, trans. Peter Wiles (New York: Vintage Books, 1968), 51–52, 56–57; and Helen Jarvis, "Tan Malaka: Revolutionary or Renegade?" *Bulletin of Concerned Asian Scholars* 19, no. 1 (1987): 47–49.

19 The earliest reported was *Qiaosheng* or *Quesheng Bao* (1922–1926), published by Tham Jinsam or Tham Jansam, a Dutch colonial subject of Chinese descent who was expelled for anti-British, anti-Japanese, pro-Bolshevik, and pro-republic propagation in May 1926. Tham's enterprise was taken over by Tae Sae-id and Heng Powsoi, Chinese communists affiliated with the local Kuomintang branch, who issued the pro-communist *Lisae Bao* until a year later, when both Tae and Heng were purged by the Kuomintang for being communists and Tae was arrested and expelled for life by the Siamese authorities. Often related to these and other leftist newspapers were libraries and *shubaoshe* (book and

newspaper clubs), such as Liqing Shubaoshe and Zhonghua Zhenxing Shubaoshe. See Eiji Murashima, *Kanmeuang jinsiam: kan khleuanwai thang kanmeuang khong chao jin phonethale nai prathet thai kho.so. 1924–1941* [Sino-Siamese politics: The overseas Chinese political movement in Thailand, A.D. 1924–1941], trans. Eiji Murashima and Worasak Mahatthanobol (Bangkok: Chinese Studies Center, Institute of Asian Studies, Chulalongkorn University, 1996), 75–78; Narong Phuangphis, "Khwamkhleuanwai thang kanmeuang khong khon jin nai prathet thai nai rajsamai phrabatsomdej phrapokklaojaoyoohua" [Political movements of the Chinese in Thailand in the reign of King Prajadhipok], *Warasan Thammasat* 1, no. 3 (1972): 4; Skinner, *Chinese Society*, 235–36; Thongchai, "Latthi khommunit," 63–73; Yanyong Jariyaphas, "Prawat nangseuphim jin nai prathet thai" [A history of Chinese newspapers in Thailand], trans. Suthi Techawiriyathawisin, in *Bannanukrom nangseuphim lae warasan phasa jin nai prathet thai* [Bibliography of Chinese newspapers and magazines in Thailand] (Bangkok: National Library, Department of Fine Arts, 1976), 4–6.

20 Murashima, *Kanmeuang jinsiam*, 3–11. Called "Nammeng Shianghuai" (The Second Branch), as against the local Kuomintang "Main Branch," it was allegedly controlled by Tang Sae-ngow and Jiam Chaohung, while the Main Branch was headed by Seow Hootseng Sibunreuang, the top local Chinese community leader and business and newspaper tycoon whose legal status was as a British subject.

21 Apart from the purge of communists from the Kuomintang organization, the breakdown also led to an acrimonious war of words between *Lisae Bao*, the Second Branch's mouthpiece, and *Huasiam Shinpo*, its Main Branch counterpart. See Murashima, *Kanmeuang jinsiam*, 9–11.

It was also in the year 1927/28 that Chinese immigration into Siam reached its peak at approximately 154,600. Most likely caused by Chiang Kaishek's white terror in Kwangtung, this extraordinarily large number of immigrants must have had more than its usual share of communists. See Skinner, Chinese Society, 173–74; and Thongchai, "Latthi khommunit," 136–39.

22 Christopher E. Goscha, *Thailand and the Southeast Asian Networks of the Vietnamese Revolution, 1885–1954* (Surrey: Curzon Press, 1999), 76. See a contemporary account by Le Manh Trinh in Le, "In Canton," 115–20; and also a statement made by a captured Vietnamese communist named Hong Chin Quoc quoted in Thongchai, "Latthi khommunit," 77–79.

23 Thongchai, "Latthi khommunit," 63–70, 77–79; Le, "In Canton," 115–29, which includes a lively account of how Ho Chi Minh advised and trained a green cadre.

24 J.H. Brimmell, *Communism in South East Asia: A Political Analysis* (New York: Oxford University Press, 1959), 93–94.

25 Somsak Jeamteerasakul, "The Communist Movement in Thailand" (Ph.D. diss., Monash University, 1993), 54–56.

26 See Batson, *The End*, 168; Narong, "Khwamkhleuanwai," 7; Suwadee, "Patikiriya," 351–52; Thongchai, "Latthi khommunit," 92, 99, 103, 124–25; Somsak, "The Communist Movement," 57.

27 Somsak, "The Communist Movement," 58–59; Murashima, *Kanmeuang jinsiam*, 80–90.

28 Goscha, *Thailand and the Southeast Asian Networks*, 82.

29 This reconstruction is based on the following sources: Goscha, *Thailand and the Southeast Asian Networks*, 76–83; Brimmell, *Communism*, 94; Lacouture, *Ho Chi Minh*, 56–58; Le, "In Canton," 130; Phin Bua-on, interview by Somsak Jeamteerasakul on his life and the history of the Thai communist movement, Bangkok, July 31, 1985; Phinyo, "Kanphoeyphrae," 45; Suthachai, "Kankhleuanwai," 229. A Japanese researcher by the name of Furuta Moto-o also gives the same information regarding the founding of the CPS in a 1991 study, as cited in Murashima, *Kanmeuang jinsiam*, 90, 147 n. 28.

   Noting that no mention was made, in contemporary Vietnamese memoirs, of any meeting between Nguyen Ai Quoc and Siamese (i.e., ethnic Thai) communists, as against Vietnamese and Chinese ones, in preparation for the founding of the Communist Party of Siam, Goscha comments that this is "probably because there were none" (80).

30 Cited in Batson, *The End*, 165.

31 King Vajiravudh, *Jodmaihet raiwan khong phrabatsomdej phramongkutklao jaoyoohua R.S. 131* [Diary of King Vajiravudh, 1912 A.D.] (Bangkok: Duang Kamol Press, 1981), 1–46.

   These diary entries and the subsequent "Uttarakuru" essay were written before the Russian Revolution of 1917, hence the radical bête noire in them was "socialism," which the King related in his discussion to broad egalitarian values, social reform, and republican politics, especially the oft-mentioned Chinese Revolution of 1911. After 1917, "Bolshevik" became the broad designation covering the government's opponents of all political persuasions, from Kuomintang to communists and anarchists. A move towards a more rigorous official ideological classification commenced only in 1927 when the government was faced with real Sino-Vietnamese communists and wanted to separate them from mere nationalists for special discriminatory punishment. On that particular occasion, however, the government settled for a revision of existing anti-subversion laws without specifying the communists so as to cast a legal net wide enough to catch all its opponents. It was not until April 1933 that the first explicitly labeled Anti-Communist Act was passed under the new constitutional regime as part of an attempted counter-revolution by the royalist-controlled government against the left wing of the People's Party. From then on, while the official definition of communism varied according to changing political circumstances, "communism" stuck as the standard radical threat perceived by the Thai state, with the exception of a short period after the war. See Batson, The End, 166, 169, 173, 175–76, 184 n. 37; Suwadee, "Patikiriya," 314, 320–23, 326–30, 343–44; Thongchai, "Latthi khommunit," 80–83, 128–33, 143–47.

32 See King Vajiravudh, Jodmaihet, 1–3; Banjob Banruji, Phra sri arya ma laew? [Has Phra Sri Arya Come?] (Bangkok: Sukhaphapjai Press, 1986), 147–50; Phra Rajworamuni (Prayut Payutto), comp., Photjananukrom phutthasas chabab pramualsap [A lexical dictionary of Buddhism] (Bangkok: Mahachulalongkorn Royal College, 1984), 290; Samak Burawas, Witthayasat mai lae phrasriarya [New sciences and Phra Sri Arya] (Bangkok: Prae Pittaya Press, 1970), 2–3; and Joseph Campbell, The Masks of God: Oriental Mythology (New York: Penguin Books, 1987), 281.

33 As a prince, Vajiravudh was educated in England at Sandhurst and Oxford from 1893 to 1902, during which time he mingled and conversed with European royalty, including Queen Victoria. His stay there coincided with a period of considerable influence for the socialist views of the Fabian Society, founded in 1884; one could assume the King's misrepresentation of and attack on socialism had its origin in a Fabian frame of reference. See Walter F. Vella, Chaiyo! King Vajiravudh and the Development of Thai Nationalism (Honolulu: The University Press of Hawaii, 1978), 2–3; and Kloppenberg, Uncertain Victory, 202–205.

34 Apart from King Vajiravudh, Supha Sirimanond counted among the keen practitioners of "phasa sontaphai" Luang Wijitwathakan, M.R. Kukrit Pramoj, and the columnists of Mahachon weekly newspaper, a propagandistic organ of the Thai Communist Party in the 1940s and early 1950s. See "Lakhorn haeng chiwit khong supha sirimanond" [Supha Sirimanond's circus of life], Thanon Nangseu 1, no. 4 (September 1983): 17.

35 King Vajiravudh, Uttarakuru: An Asiatic Wonderland (Bangkok: Mahamakud Royal College, 1965).

     That the King chose to write his first published anti-socialist essay in English was typical of the haughty, British-educated Anglophilia of the

Siamese elite. Living and ruling thousands of miles from Britain, culturally speaking they inhabited a world peopled by English characters, opponents, and references. So they developed a taste for writing in English or "slipping" long English passages into their Thai writings. The startling thing is that decades later, some Thai radical intellectuals adopted the same practice, this time using English Marxist concepts.

In a preface written by Prince Dhani, it is unclear whether the first Thai translation of "Uttarakuru" was published. The manuscript and copies of this translation were all lost and a new, abridged, flavorless, and flawed translation by the Prince was published with the English original in the 1965 edition. It is also significant that, retrospectively, the Prince considered the target of attack in this essay to be "communism" rather than "socialism."

36 Some similar features between the Hindu Uttarakuru and the Buddhist Era of Phra Sri Arya Mettraya indicate a certain degree of borrowing or perhaps even derivation. See King Vajiravudh, *Uttarakuru*, 1, 5–17, 19–20; and Sathiankoses (Phraya Anumanrajthon), *Lao reuang nai traiphoom* [Telling the story in Traiphoom] (Bangkok: Klang Vidhaya Publishing House, 1959), 17–20, 92–129.

37 King Vajiravudh, *Uttarakuru*, 16–17, 20–21. George Bernard Shaw (1856–1950) was, of course, the world-famous English playwright and Fabian socialist of the time. James Keir Hardie (1856–1915) was a legendary British militant socialist politician who, in 1893, founded the Independent Labour Party, the forerunner of the present Labour Party, and was also a leading figure in the Second International.

38 Kang Youwei (1858–1927) could at best be described as a monarchist reformist-cum-utopian idealist. His inclusion in the King's essay was based on his utopian ideal of "Datong" as contained in his *Datongshu* (Book of the great community or great unity), written in 1902. More importantly, it served the author's polemical purposes to have an unadulterated utopian like Kang Youwei labeled as "socialist" alongside the less dreamy figures.

Sun Yatsen's (1866–1925) socialist credentials were more complex and debatable than Kang's, though it was obviously Sun's republicanism rather than socialism that made him a target of the King's attack. Better known as the "father of the Chinese Republic," he has been described by several recent studies as the father of Chinese socialism as well.

See Arif Dirlik, "Socialism and Capitalism in Chinese Socialist Thinking: The Origins," Studies in Comparative Communism 21, no. 2 (Summer 1988): 131–52; Jonathan D. Spence, The Gate of Heavenly

Peace: The Chinese and Their Revolution, 1895–1980 (New York: Penguin Books, 1983), 64–73.

39 King Vajiravudh, *Uttarakuru*, 5, 8, 11, 14–15, 16, 19–20.

40 Thaemsook Numnond, *Yangtoek run raek: Kabot R.S. 130* [The first Young Turks: The 1912 conspiracy] (Bangkok: Reuangsin Press, 1979), 88–89, 170–72.

41 Skinner, *Chinese Society*, 156–57.

42 Quoted in Laortong, "Kansong," 212–13. Words in italics appeared as transliterations in the Thai original.

43 Skinner, *Chinese Society*, 162–65.

44 The leaders of the Tongmenghui in Siam had been publishing a Thai newspaper entitled *Jinno-Siam Warasap* since 1907. Although candid, highly independent, and critical in its opinions at times, the newspaper cautiously made it clear that Chinese republican politics was aimed at the Manchu Emperor, not the Siamese King, and tried to promote good relations between the Thai and the Chinese in Siam. According to several studies of the newspapers of that period, it never advocated socialism. All the same, the 1912 conspirators were very excited and inspired indeed by the Chinese Revolution of 1911. See Skinner, *Chinese Society*, 156–57; Sukanya, *Prawat*, 82–84; Wyatt, *Thailand*, 226; Yanyong, "Prawat nangseuphim jin," 6–14.

45 King Vajiravudh, *Uttarakuru*, 11.

46 Sukanya, *Prawat*, 84; Phornphirom Iamtham, *Botbat thang kanmeuang khong nangseuphim thai tangtae plianplaeng kanpokkhrong Pho.So. 2475 theung sinsud songkhramlok khrang thi song* [The political roles of Thai newspapers from the change of regime in B.E. 2475 until the end of World War II] (Bangkok: Khrongkan Tamra Sangkhomsat Lae Manussat, Social Science Association of Thailand, 1977), 11–12.

47 King Vajiravudh, *Jodmaihet*, 44–46.

48 This is of course a pun on Craig J. Reynolds' apt remark on Jit Poumisak's *Chomna sakdina thai* (The real face of Thai feudalism). See Craig J. Reynolds, *Thai Radical Discourse: The Real Face of Thai Feudalism Today* (Ithaca: Southeast Asia Program, Cornell University, 1987), 173.

49 Both terms would be excitingly and energetically revived and revamped by such prominent radical intellectuals as Pridi Banomyong, Atsani Phonlajan, Samak Burawas, and Thaweep Voradilok in the decade after the war. As recently as the early 1980s, Thianchai Wongchaisuwan, a well-known leftist critic of the Communist Party of Thailand, chose as his pen name "Yuk Sriariya" (Era of Sri Arya), which he derived from a poem by Thaweep Voradilok.

50 Suwadee, "Patikiriya," 336–41; Thongchai, "Latthi khommunit," 60–63, 68–72, 79–84, 130–34.

51 Batson, *The End*, 161 n. 80, 169; Suwadee, "Patikiriya," 314, 327–28; Thongchai, "Latthi khommunit," 143–44; and Pridi Banomyong, *Pridi banomyong kab sangkhom thai: Ruam khokhian khong pridi banomyong* [Pridi Banomyong and Thai society: Collected writings of Pridi Banomyong] (Bangkok: Thammasat University Press and the Pridi Banomyong Kab Sangkhom Thai Project, 1983), 275–320.

52 Batson, *The End*, 145, 167–68; Suwadee, "Patikiriya," 299–310; Thongchai, "Latthi khommunit," 63–84.

53 Suwadee, "Patikiriya," 348; Takashi Shiraishi, "The Military in Thailand, Burma and Indonesia," in *Asian Political Institutionalization*, ed. Robert A. Scalapino et al. (Berkeley, California: Institute of East Asian Studies, University of California, 1986).

54 See, for example, Batson, *The End*, 145, 167–68, 180 n. 11–12, 181 n. 13; Suwadee, "Patikiriya," 299, 310–13.

55 In 1924, as part of the Kuomintang-CCP deal, the Kuomintang Party's branches in Southeast Asia were reorganized into Leninist organizations, with anti-imperialist politics and Sun Yatsen's "Three People's Principles" ideology! A bizarre political hybrid bred by Michael Borodin, a Soviet advisor to the Kuomintang. See Brimmell, *Communism*, 90–91; Thongchai, "Latthi khommunit," 71.

56 Brimmell, *Communism*, 92–93; Thongchai, "Latthi khommunit," 63–73, 89–90, 104, 108.

57 Thongchai, "Latthi khommunit," 77–78.

58 Brimmell, *Communism*, 93–94; Lacouture, *Ho Chi Minh*, 51.

59 See the Thai translation of a Chinese document of the South Seas Communist Party, captured in February 1930 entitled "Khao khana tong roo latthi khommunit" [To join the Party one must know communism] in a section called "Samakhom kanmeuang ni kheu samakhom khong phuak khommunit" [This political party is the Communist Party], quoted in Thongchai, "Latthi khommunit," 92–104, 109. Emphasis added.

60 Tom Bottomore et al., eds., *A Dictionary of Marxist Thought* (Cambridge, Massachusetts: Harvard University Press, 1983), 237; and Witold S. Sworakowski, ed., *World Communism: A Handbook 1918–1965* (Stanford, California: Hoover Institution Press, 1973), 84–87; Brimmell, *Communism*, 93–96.

In the Far East, the Comintern's line during the Third Period stressed the priority of the urban revolutionary movement of the proletariat and renounced any collaboration with the authorities and non-communist leaders. See Lyman P. Van Slyke, chapter 3 of Enemies and Friends: The United Front in Chinese Communist History (Stanford, California: Stanford University Press, 1967).

61 Batson, *The End*, 173–77; Suwadee, "Patikiriya," 301, 309, 320–23, 343–44; Thongchai, "Latthi khommunit," 70–72, 79–84, 89–91, 104–15, 128–29, 132–33; Murashima, *Kanmeuang jinsiam*, 80, 82, 86.

62 This was part of a self-criticism made by the Siamese Communist Youth Local Committee in a letter to its Malaysian counterparts in 1933, quoted in Thongchai, "Latthi khommunit," 124–25. Almost all the communist literature seized by the Siamese authority in this period was in Chinese or Vietnamese (in that order of quantity). Very little was in Thai, and there were only two reported cases of communist leaflets in English. See Batson, *The End*, 167, 170, 243, 270 n. 52; and Suwadee, "Patikiriya," 305, 309.

63 Somsak, "The Communist Movement," 70–1; Suwadee, "Patikiriya," 301.

64 Goscha, *Thailand and the Southeast Asian Networks*, 88–9; and Murashima, *Kanmeuang jinsiam*, 101–102. Fifty-five of the 325 CPS members were Vietnamese and the rest were Chinese. However, while based on the same primary source and giving mostly identical information, the two books cited here differ in detail on the dialect-group composition of the CPS's Chinese membership. Goscha identifies 20 of them as Cantonese and the rest as Hainanese, but Murashima claims that only 10 of them were Teochius and the rest Hainanese.

65 Quoted in Goscha, *Thailand and the Southeast Asian Networks*, 89. With reference to the journal, see Murashima, *Kanmeuang jinsiam*, 102, 107.

66 Murashima, *Kanmeuang jinsiam*, 83–90, 101, 103–108; Goscha, *Thailand and the Southeast Asian Networks*, 91; Suwadee, "Patikiriya," 346–47.

67 The account of the Vietnamese group in this passage is derived from Somsak, "The Communist Movement," 70–74; Goscha, *Thailand and the Southeast Asian Networks*, 88–91; and Murashima, *Kanmeuang jinsiam*, 108–17.

68 See Phin, interview, July 31, 1985; Goscha, *Thailand and the Southeast Asian Networks*, 89, 105 n. 100; Murashima, *Kanmeuang jinsiam*, 101–102; and Somsak, "The Communist Movement," 76. At its founding in April 1930, the CPS reportedly had forty-one Vietnamese members, while there were then only 265 Vietnamese communists inside Vietnam itself. By 1932, the number had increased to fifty-five, with more than 1,000 sympathizers in the Northeast, nearly all of whom were ethnic Vietnamese.

69 Brimmell, *Communism*, 94–95, 114; Somsak, "The Communist Movement," 83.

70 Goscha, *Thailand and the Southeast Asian Networks*, 90–91; Murashima, *Kanmeuang jinsiam*, 115–17; Somsak, "The Communist Movement," 73–74; Thongchai, "Latthi khommunit," 170; Brimmell, *Communism*, 115. This little-known incident, largely kept from the public at the time by the Ministry of Interior for fear of causing panic, was perhaps the first real violent clash of the communists with the authorities in modern Siamese history. Sixty or so young Vietnamese arrested in this incident would eventually wind up as political prisoners in Area 6, Bangkhwang Penitentiary. See Chapter 3.

71 Goscha, *Thailand and the Southeast Asian Networks*, 79, 91, 94; Murashima, *Kanmeuang jinsiam*, 117–18; Somsak, "The Communist Movement," 74–75.

72 Suthachai, "Kankhleuanwai," 229; Somsak, "The Communist Movement," 79–81; and Sornsak Ngamkhajornkulkij, *Khabuankan serithai kab khwamkhadyaeng thang kanmeuang phainai prathet thai rawang Pho.So. 2481–2492* [The Free Thai Movement and political conflict in Thailand during B.E. 2481–2492] (Bangkok: Sathaban Asia Seuksa, Chulalongkorn University, 1989), 38.

73 Phin, interview, July 31, 1985; Phinyo, "Kanphoeyphrae," 45; Murashima, *Kanmeuang jinsiam*, 119.

74 Phin, interview, July 31, 1985.

75 This is evident from recurrent reports of arrests of communist teachers and of radical student activities in Chinese schools from various parts of the country from the late 1920s throughout the 1930s. See Murashima, *Kanmeuang jinsiam*, 11, 83–89.

76 Somsak, "The Communist Movement," 77–79.

77 Phinyo, "Kanphoeyphrae," 45.

78 Among the prominent members of this group, Somsak lists Wiroj Amphai, Si Anothai, Wirat Angkhathaworn, Song Nopphakhun, Damri Reuangsutham, Udom Sisuwan, Sak Suphakasem, and Nith Phongdapphet. See Somsak, "The Communist Movement," 78–79.

79 Skinner, *Chinese Society*, 165; Thongchai, "Latthi khommunit," 127–30.

80 Suwadee, "Patikiriya," 326.

81 The following account of this case is based on Suwadee, "Patikiriya," 315, 318, 332, 349; Thongchai, "Latthi khommunit," 115–19, 121; and Murashima, *Kanmeuang jinsiam*, 80–82.

82 According to Phin, who worked closely with Piatoe in the CPT during the late 1950s, Piatoe's father was pure Chinese while his mother, named

Neuang, was a Thai-Khamu who had lived originally in Sukhothai. Phin, interview, July 31, 1985.

83 Quoted in Suwadee, "Patikiriya," 315; and Thongchai, "Latthi khommunit," 119.

84 Skinner, *Chinese Society*, 26, 244–45.

85 Prince Damrongrachanuphap, "Laksana kanpokkhrong prathet siam tae boran" [The character of the administration of ancient Siam] (Cremation Volume of Mr. Dao Buphawes, Rasbamrung Temple, Chon Buri, December 1, 1968), 5–8.

86 Vella, *Chaiyo*, xiii.

87 Asvabahu (King Vajiravudh), "Khwam pen chat doi thaejing" [Real nationhood], in *Pakinnakakhadi* [Miscellanies] (Bangkok: Klang Vidhaya Publishing House, 1975), 241–47.

88 By contrast, the Communist Party of Malaya, the CPS's elder twin-sister, so to speak, had persistently failed throughout the pre-war years to achieve any indigenization of its movement and remained an exclusively ethnic Chinese party. One of the key elements in this failure was, of course, the relative absence of a Malaysian equivalent of the Siamese lookjin communists. This seemed to result largely from the different nature of the Chinese community and education in Malaya in the 1930s.

    In 1931, the Chinese community of Malaya that served as the CPM's mass base had a local-born minority of only 32 percent, whereas the corr-esponding figure of lookjins in Siam was 54 percent. Moreover, Chinese education in Malaya was larger, better, freer, and more segregated from other ethnic groups than that in Siam. In the latter, since 1919 but especially after 1932/33, Chinese schools were subject to increasingly strict government regulation which required all alien teachers to pass a Thai language examination and mandated a maximum of weekly hours for the teaching of Chinese and a minimum for the teaching of Thai. The upshot was the closing of many Chinese schools and the replacement of China-born teachers with lookjin and Thai teachers in most of the rest. Perforce, in Siam, the lookjins in general, and the lookjin communists in particular, had a far greater chance to learn Thai and make Thai friends than their Malaysian counterparts, owing to the Siamese government's compulsory Thaification of Chinese education. See Brimmell, Communism, 90–94, 148–49; and Skinner, Chinese Society, 227–34.

89 Thongchai, "Latthi khommunit," 119.

Chapter 3

1 Mr. Qing and Mr. Long, alien Chinese teachers in Thailand during World War II, were among eleven Thai and Chinese dissident community leaders, teachers, and journalists arrested on January 17, 1942, and charged with belonging to Thai-issara (Independent Thai), a communist-organized, underground, anti-Japanese resistance movement of mostly Chinese and lookjins. After the Japanese invasion of Thailand and alliance with the Phibunsongkhram government in December 1941, the Thai-issara movement briefly became prominent, before being supp-ressed by the government and later incorporated into a more inclusive, communist-led, anti-Japanese umbrella organization. See Skinner, *Chinese Society*, 265; Sungsidh Piriyarangsan, *Prawat kantosoo khong kammakorn thai* [A history of Thai workers' struggle] (Bangkok: Social Research Institute, Chulalongkorn University, 1986), 151–52, 160–61; Somsak, "The Communist Movement," 129–30; Eiji Murashima, "Samphanthamit thai-yipun kab chaojin nai prathet thai samai songkhram lok khrang thi song" [The Thai-Japanese alliance and overseas Chinese in Thailand], Eiji Murashima and Nakharin Mektrairat, trans., in *Yipun-thai-usakhane* [Japan-Thailand-Southeast Asia], ed. Charnvit Kasetsiri and Hayao Fukui (Bangkok: Thammasat-Kyoto Core University Program and the Foundation for the Promotion of Social Sciences and Humanities Textbooks Project, 1998), 135–36.

   The complaint of Qing and Long, the spelling of whose translation I have deliberately altered to capture their Teochiu accent, was made in jail and quoted by a fellow inmate in Phayap Rojjanawiphat, Yuk thamil [Evil age] (Bangkok: Anthai Press, 1989), 103.

2 "Blue" symbolizing the monarchy, and "green" the army.

3 Skinner, *Chinese Society*, 244–53, 261–72.

4 Skinner, *Chinese Society*, 91–98, 117–18, 300–306. The exceptions to this general ethno-occupational pattern were Chinese plantations and agricultural laborers specializing in producing a variety of commercial crops, especially sugar, in the Southeast, Lower, and Southwest of Siam during the nineteenth century. Ibid., 110–11.

5 Krit Sombatsiri, *Jek sakdina* [Feudalized Chinese] (Bangkok: Kaeoprakai Press, 1986), 48 passim.

6 Sukanya, chapters 5 and 6 in *Prawat*; and Thaemsook, *Yangtoek*, 61–91.

7 Named after its leader Prince Bowaradej, who had been minister of war under the absolute monarchy from 1928 to 1931, the rebellion began on October 11, 1933. Its declared aims were the overthrow of the allegedly

communist People's Party's government, the restoration of certain political prerogatives to the constitutional monarch, and the depoliticization of the civil and military bureaucracy. After four days of fierce fighting on the outskirts of Bangkok, the rebels retreated along the northeastern railway and most eventually surrendered, while their leaders were either killed or escaped abroad.

8 Somphop Jantharaprapha et al., *Prawat kanrajthan 200 pi* [200 years' history of the penitentiary] (Bangkok: Department of Penitentiary, Ministry of Interior, 1982), 372–82.

9 Phimphawal Sethaputra, *Chiwaprawat kanthamphotjananukrom angklis-thai thai-angklis khong so sethaputra* [So Sethaputra and the making of his English-Thai, Thai-English dictionary: A biography] (Bangkok: Phimphawal Sethaputra, 1971), 166–69; and Phayap, *Yuk thamil*, 62–63.

10 M.R. Nimitmongkhol Nawarat, "Chiwit haeng kankabot song khrang" [The victim of the two political purges], in *Meuangnimit lae chiwit haeng kankabot song khrang* [The sight of future Siam and The victim of the two political purges] (Bangkok: Aksornsamphan Press, 1970), 390.

11 Nimitmongkhol "Chiwit," 327, 352–56; Leuan Saraphaiwanich (Captain Phraya Saraphaiphiphat), *Fan rai khong khaphajao* [My nightmare] (Bangkok: Bannakhan Press, 1959), 255–61; Phimphawal, *Chiwaprawat so*, 205.

12 Leuan, *Fan rai*, 92; Phayap, *Yuk thamil*, 63.

13 Leuan gave slightly varying numbers of the Bowaradej defendants and convicts in Bangkhwang Penitentiary in *Fan rai*, 38, 92, 179–80. The numbers used here are from Sornsak, *Khabuankan serithai*, 33–34. An extensive but still incomplete list of 154 Bowaradej prisoners is given in Chaiwat Yonpiam, *Fan rai khong meuang thai* [Thailand's nightmare] (Bangkok: Chaophraya Press, 1985), 118–21.

14 Leuan, *Fan rai*, 179–80.

15 The Kabot Naisib was a plot by NCOs in several army battalions to assassinate senior army officers, take command of the battalions, and hold top military leaders hostage. The rebels argued that there was not yet genuine democracy in Siam as proven by the existence of military officers and hence inequality. Their plot discovered in August 1935, fifteen NCOs were tried and the rebel leader was sentenced to death. See Thamrongsak Phechleotanan, "Botnam" [Introduction], in Phayap, *Yuk thamil*, [15]–[16]; Prasert, *Ratthasapha*, 210; Phimphawal, *Chiwaprawat so*, 233.

16 Phimphawal, *Chiwaprawat so*, 201–208 *ff*.

17 Phayap, *Yuk thamil*, 63, 65–66, 76, 89, 95–97, 102–103, 109.

18 The Bangkhwang communists of this period (approximately 1930–
    1946, when the Anti-Communist Law was repealed) left no known
    account of their experience in prison. By contrast, their non-communist
    political inmates published several memoirs, e.g., the memoirs of Leuan
    Saraphaiwanich, Nimitmongkhol Nawarat, and Phayap Rojjanawiphat,
    as well as the biography of So Sethaputra written by his widow.
    Reflected as they were through antithetical ideological lens, they can
    in no way substitute for the communists' own account of their activities
    and ideas, especially in terms of closeness and details. And yet they help
    paint a broad picture of the environment and atmosphere in which the
    communists lived and of the things the communists did and thought
    there. At their best, these accounts provide insights that could be gained
    only from the critical distance of a sympathetic observer. In any case,
    they are the only available data on which the following reconstruction
    of the Bangkhwang communists is based.

19 Leuan, *Fan rai*, 34–36, 125–27, 155–56; Phayap, *Yuk thamil*, 63;
    Phimphawal, *Chiwaprawat so*, 170; Nimitmongkhol, "Chiwit," 330–33,
    336–37, 441.

20 Leuan, *Fan rai*, 100–102, 149–58, 180, 185, 302; Phimphawal,
    Chiwaprawat so, 180.

21 See Leuan, *Fan rai*, 153–54; Phimphawal, *Chiwaprawat so*, 168–69.

22 Leuan, *Fan rai*, 153–54, 180–81, 301.

23 Leuan, *Fan rai*, 155–56; Narong, "Khwamkhleuanwai," 8; Suwadee,
    "Patikiriya," 302, 332, 337, 346–47; Murashima, *Kanmeuang jinsiam*,
    87–89.

24 Leuan, *Fan rai*, 156, 188–91.

25 Leuan, *Fan rai*, 180–81. He remained unnamed by Leuan in the prison
    memoirs for reasons of political expediency.

26 Leuan, *Fan rai*, 155, 157–58.

27 Leuan, *Fan rai*, 154–58, 180–82, 195–96. These imprisoned radical
    Vietnamese youths were supposedly convicts of the 1936 armed uprising
    in Khon Kaen discussed in Chapter 2.

28 Leuan, *Fan rai*, 184.

29 Leuan, *Fan rai*, 303.

30 Leuan, *Fan rai*, 192–96, 301–303.

31 There exists no evidence of such a conversion, though it was perfectly
    possible and therefore imaginable. In his unfinished best-known
    progressive political novel, *Lae pai khangna* (Looking forward), Kulap
    Saipradit had the only substantial working-class character, Taen, whose
    class represented the hope for Siamese democracy, be converted in jail

from petty thief to radical worker by two "worker-comrade" inmates and, in particular, by a "female-comrade" visitor sometime between 1932 and 1939. See Sriburapha (Kulap Saipradit), *Lae pai khangna: Phak majchimwai* [Looking forward: The middle age] (Bangkok: Dokya Press, 1988), 199–218.

32 The title "True Blue" (Namngoen Thae) comes from the name of a staunchly royalist, anti-People's Party weekly newspaper produced in 1934 in Area 6, Bangkhwang, by a group of Bowaradej writers and intellectuals therein, including Leuan, So, and Nimitmongkhol, and circulated among the politicos in jail and among their friends and relatives outside. It was also the name of an English song composed in prison by Prince Sithiporn Kridakara, another Bowaradej prisoner. Leuan, *Fan rai*, 261–63; Nimitmongkhol, "Chiwit," 324–30, 333, 348, 363–64; Phimphawal, *Chiwaprawat so*, 180–81.

33 Leuan, *Fan rai*, 181–84.

34 See, for example, Lo.So. (Leuan Saraphaiwanich), "Kamnoed khong samakhom kammakorn" [The origin of trade unions], *Karnmuang* 2, no. 7 (March 22, 1946): 3–4, 21–22; and his public lecture to an audience of Thammasat University students in 1951, reprinted as Captain Phraya Saraphaiphiphat (Leuan Saraphaiwanich), "Udomkhati khong sangkhomniyom" [The ideal of socialism], in M.C. Sakol Wannakon Worawan et al., *Khamprakas momchao sakol wannakon worawan nak sangkhomniyom khong meuang thai* [Manifesto of M.C. Sakol Wannakon Worawan, a socialist of Thailand] (Bangkok: Chesthaburus Press, [n.d.]), 30–50.

35 Nimitmongkhol, "Chiwit," 353–55, 371, 381–83, 388–89; Phimphawal, *Chiwaprawat so*, 182–83; M.R. Nimitmongkhol Nawarat, "Meuangnimit" [The sight of future Siam], in *Meuangnimit lae chiwit haeng kankabot song khrang* [The sight of future Siam and The victim of the two political purges] (Bangkok: Aksornsamphan Press, 1970), 102–103, 147–48, 154, 163–66, 176, 182, 184–85, 202, 214–29.

36 Leuan, *Fan rai*, 301–303.

37 Phichit Dijai, interview by the author on his life and political activities, Bangkok, May 15, 1989.

38 Leuan, *Fan rai*, 96–97, 133–34, 159, 164–71, 185–86, 192–93, 221–24, 227–38, 243–64, 266, 269–71, 287–88, 292–93; Phayap, *Yuk thamil*, 97; Phimphawal, *Chiwaprawat so*, 198–204; Nimitmongkhol, "Chiwit," 343–47, 356–57.

39 Major Khun Jamnongphoomiwet's letter to the director general of the

Penitentiary Department dated March 5, 1937, quoted in Leuan, *Fan rai*, 236–37.

40 Phimphawal, *Chiwaprawat so*, 200–201.

41 Leuan, *Fan rai*, 255, 260–61; Nimitmongkhol, "Chiwit," 327; Phayap, *Yuk thamil*, 98.

42 Leuan, *Fan rai*, 173. Judging from the contemporary development of the western Trotskyist movement, this event could only have happened between 1936, when a Geneva conference of European and American Trotskyists first resolved to call a founding congress of the Fourth International, and 1939, when Leuan left Bangkhwang. Sworakowski, *World Communism*, 132.

43 Prasert, *Ratthasapha*, 557.

44 Pho. Meuangchomphoo (Udom Sisuwan), *Soo samoraphoom phoophan [phrom phak phanuak] pai meuang hang* [To the Phoophan battlefront with an appendix: To the Hang Town] (Bangkok: Matichon Press, 1987), 120.

45 Vajiravudh, *Pakinnakakhadi*, 79–94.

46 Leuan, *Fan rai*, 156; Phin, interview, July 31, 1985; Suthachai, "Kankhleuanwai," 228–29; Pho. Meuangchomphoo, *Soo samoraphoom*, 21, 46–49, 51–52, 132–33, 135, 141; and Udom Sisuwan, interview by Craig J. Reynolds on communism and literature in Thailand, Bangkok, January 19, 1984; *Mahachon* 139 (July 11, 1948).

There is no extant record of the date of Piatoe's release from prison. This rough estimate is based on the fact that several of his co-convicts in the same case were reportedly set free and expelled from Thailand in July 1938. Ngo Diji was released and expelled in March 1939. See Murashima, Kanmeuang jinsiam, 82, 89.

47 Murashima, *Kanmeuang jinsiam*, 100–104, 107; Thongchai, "Latthi khommunit," 155–56; Batson, *The End*, 243, 270 n. 52; Goscha, *Thailand and the Southeast Asian Networks*, 88.

In contrast with the communist leaflets in absolute monarchical times, which were predominantly in Chinese, most of those issued after the 1932 Revolution were in Thai. While overcoming this linguistic barrier in their propaganda did represent a big step forward for the Siamese communists, it was only the beginning of the Thaification of their movement, especially with regard to its ethnic composition and internal culture.

48 Somsak, "The Communist Movement," 63–67, 71; and Murashima, *Kanmeuang jinsiam*, 84–86. Both studies refer to and summarize a seized Siamese communist programmatic document in Chinese dated March 20, 1930, entitled "The Draft Statement Analyzing the Government and

Economy of Siam and the Procedures of the Party," which had reached that political conclusion before the 1932 Revolution.

49 Thongchai, "Latthi khommunit," 191 n. 2; Phornphirom, *Botbat*, 157; Pridi, *Pridi banomyong*, 272; and Somsak, "The Communist Movement," 98–101. According to Somsak, Sanguan's hope for the pamphlet was unlikely to be realized due to its exclusively British subject-matter and particularly poor quality of translation.

One published version of the CPT's official history claimed that the party (i.e., the then Communist Party of Siam) was involved in the publication of both 24 Mithuna and Sajjang, along with the hitherto unheard-of Muanchon Raisapda (Mass weekly). Phinyo, "Kanphoeyphrae," 45. However, this claim is disputed in a recent study based on Chinese communist sources. See Murashima, Kanmeuang jinsiam, 152 n. 69.

50 Coming to office upon the promulgation of the "permanent" Constitution on December 10, 1932, this coalition government comprised ten leading members of the People's Party plus outsiders of equal number, a delicate power-sharing arrangement between the People's Party and the conservative aristocracy. Prime Minister Phraya Manopakorn had been a senior government official under the old regime and was mistaken by Pridi for a "progressive" outsider who happened to be close to King Prajadhipok. He was thus nominated by Pridi himself and chosen by the People's Party to chair the People's Committee and head the first constitutional government, much to Pridi's later disillusionment and regret. See Vichitvong na Pombhejara, *Pridi Banomyong and the Making of Thailand's Modern History* (Bangkok: [n.p.], [n.d.]), 65, 68; Pridi, *Pridi banomyong*, 360–61.

51 For a comprehensive intellectual and cultural political background, incisive critical analysis, and wide-ranging political appraisal of Pridi's Economic Plan, see Somsak, chapter 2 of "The Communist Movement."

52 Pridi, *Pridi banomyong*, 169–72. Probably among the people Pridi had in mind when penning these words was the author of *Uttarakuru!*

53 The texts of Pridi's Economic Plan and related legislative drafts were reprinted in Pridi, *Pridi banomyong*, 167–259. Detailed studies of his plan can be found in Pierre Fistié, *Sous-développement et utopie au Siam: Le programme de réformes présenté en 1933 par Pridi Phanomyong*, Matériaux pour l'étude de l'extrême-orient moderne et contemporain, Travaux 5 (Paris: Mouton and Maison des Sciences de l'Homme, 1969); and Thipphawan, chapter 4 in *Pathomthas*.

54 The main factors that determined these opposite uses of the Sri Arya myth

by the two cultural politicians were their different linguistic means and presumed specific audience. King Vajiravudh wrote in English for an audience with a presumably scientific, realistic mindset, while Pridi wrote in Thai for an audience with a religious, imaginative one.

55 Pridi, *Pridi banomyong*, 241–42. "Thoilang khaokhlong" would enter the Thai radical lexicon after World War II as a euphemism for "reactionary politics."

56 King Prajadhipok, "Phrabaromrajwinijchai khong phrabatsomdej phrapokklaojaoyoohua rabsanong phrabaromrajongkan doi phraya manopakornnitithada nayokratthamontri" [King Prajadhipok's consideration with Prime Minister Manopakorn responsible to the royal command], in Pridi, *Pridi banomyong*, 183, 232, 256–57.

57 Pridi, *Pridi banomyong*, 176–77, 180–85, 189–91, 197, 202–206, 209–12, 215, 218–25, 230–32, 235–37, 239, 243, 248, 251–53, 255–57.

58 Pridi, *Pridi banomyong*, 176, 184–87, 201, 205, 213–16, 220, 234, 241, 243, 251–52.

59 Pridi, *Pridi banomyong*, 256.

60 Pridi, *Pridi banomyong*, 255.

61 Pridi, *Pridi banomyong*, 177.

62 Pridi, *Pridi banomyong*, 214. The word "Thai," apart from denoting the ethnic majority in Siam, also means "freedom" and "independence." Therefore, King Prajadhipok's clever contrast of "Thai" versus "Thas" was designed to create not only nice alliteration, but a political contrast of their meanings. One should remember at this point, however, the earlier official nationalist definition of Thainess according to King Prajadhipok's predecessor, King Vajiravudh, as essentially and precisely a *thas* or slavish loyalty and submission to the King!

63 Pridi, *Pridi banomyong*, 243.

64 Viewed from this perspective, So Sethaputra's *Pho.So. 2481*, the novel of communist dystopia in Siam referred to above, was probably a fictional offshoot of King Prajadhipok's *Samud pokkhao*. That So had also served as Luang Mahasitthiwohan, the King's close and fiercely loyal journalistic and personal aide, before the 1932 Revolution lends more weight to the association. Phimphawal, *Chiwaprawat so*, 108–32, 153–56.

65 Thongchai, "Latthi khommunit," 174–94.

66 Sawai Sutthiphithak, *Dr. pridi banomyong* [Dr. Pridi Banomyong] (Bangkok: [n.p.], 1983), 260–71.

67 According to the British Legation to Siam; see Thongchai, "Latthi khommunit," 192.

68 "Phrarajbanyat waduai khommunit phutthasakkaraj 2476" [The Royal Act on Communism, B.E. 2476], *Rajkijjanubeksa* [Royal Thai government gazette] 50 (April 2, 1933): 11.

69 Thanin Kraivichien, *Kanchai kodmai pongkan khommunit* [The application of anti-communist laws] (Bangkok: Security Center, Ministry of Defense, 1974), 230, 246.

70 See Prasert Sapsunthorn's comment quoted in Suphot Dantrakul, *Prasert sapsunthorn, adit kammakanklang phak khommunit haeng prathet thai; Khrai? Ma jak nai? Lae khid yangrai?* [Prasert Sapsunthorn, former Central Committee member of the Communist Party of Thailand; Who? Whence? and How does he think?] (Bangkok: [n.p.], 1981), 27–28.

71 Prasert, *Ratthasapha*, 67–74; Thongchai, "Latthi khommunit," 195–201; Vichitvong, *Pridi*, 83–86.

72 Thongchai, "Latthi khommunit," 195–96, 201–205.

73 Pridi, *Pridi banomyong*, 275–330.

74 Prajadhipok, "Phrabaromrajwinijchai," 221. Thawat Riddhidej (1894–1950) was a veteran journalist and labor organizer since the 1920s. He co-founded and led a group of democratic and pro-worker intellectuals called *Khana kammakorn* (Workers' Party) in 1922 and owned and edited two affiliated newspapers, the weekly *Nangseuphim Kammakorn* (The Worker, 1923–1924) and *Nangseuphim Pakkathai* (The Thai Pen, 1925–1927). Following a widespread practice among political newspapers at the time, *Kammakorn*'s official editor was a foreign subject named "S. Maki" (probably a British subject of Indian ethnicity) in order to avoid Siamese jurisdiction by virtue of colonial extraterritoriality. Thawat and his Workers' Party colleagues led the tramway workers to support the People's Party enthusiastically in both the 1932 Revolution and the military campaign against the Bowaradej Rebellion in October 1933. Together, they founded the Tramway Workers Union of Siam, with Thawat as secretary. Sungsidh, *Prawat*, 124–36.

75 This exciting battle ended rather anti-climactically in December with Thawat taken by Prince Wan Waithayakon to Songkhla to beg the King's pardon in person. Batson, *The End*, 246, 271 n. 67; Leuan, *Fan rai*, 2–9; Prasert, *Ratthasapha*, 102–103.

76 Batson, *The End*, 249–53; Prasert, *Ratthasapha*, 165–69, 174–81, 189. For a critical reading of the King's abdication as an overused, backfiring, political ploy, see Somsak, "The Communist Movement," 122–25.

77 "Phrarajbanyat waduai khommunit kaekhai phoemtoem phutthasakkaraj 2478" [The Amendment to the Royal Act on Communism, B.E. 2478], in Thongchai, "Latthi khommunit," 168–69, 209, 491–92.

78 A contrast with Burma is instructive. Had the British not dethroned the Konbaung dynasty, and had it survived to reap the full benefits of capitalist economic change and provide the entrepreneurial class with a respectable, Burman face, capitalism might not have been so readily identified with colonialism as an alien enemy of the nation, while socialism might not have been so naturally associated with Burmese nationalism after independence. See my "Independent Siam and Colonial Burma: A Comparative Historical Perspective," in *Asian Review 1993*, ed. Suwanna Satha-Anand (Bangkok: Institute of Asian Studies, Chulalongkorn University, 1994), 1–62.

79 Murashima, *Kanmeuang jinsiam*, 104–108.

80 Thongchai, "Latthi khommunit," 155. According to Phin Bua-on, who would become a CPT Politbureau member in the 1960s, the major factor accounting for the Siamese communists' typical and long-lasting disparagement of united-front work was the residual founding influence of the extreme leftist "Wang Ming-Li Lisan Line" (Phin, interview, July 31, 1985). Originating from the Executive Committee of the Comintern in July 1929, the anti-united-front "United Front from Below" line was followed by the CCP under Wang Ming's leadership from 1930 to 1935. Almost identical in substance with the strategy and tactics of Li Lisan who headed the CCP from 1928 to 1930, it stressed the priority of the urban revolutionary movement of the proletariat and renounced any collaboration with the authorities and non-communist leaders. See Van Slyke, chapter 3 of *Enemies and Friends*.

81 Apart from fear of communist unrest, the new government was anxious to assure King Prajadhipok and the foreign powers that it was not pro-communist, especially during the initial period when the situation was still fluid. Once its power was consolidated, however, its early pliancy vis-a-vis the King would all but vanish. Prasert, *Ratthasapha*, 78; Thongchai, "Latthi khommunit," 164, 201.

82 Thongchai, "Latthi khommunit," 64.

83 See the minutes of the National Assembly meeting of March 10, 1934, reprinted in Pridi, *Pridi banomyong*, 321–30, especially a speech made by Fak na Songkhla on 322, 326.

84 The Phibunsongkhram government's purported policy of "economic nationalism" discriminated against Chinese economic interests selectively and was not always strictly enforced. Thus, Skinner's account (*Chinese Society*, 261–64) should be balanced against recent research which shows that the government's arbitrary, practical interpretation of "Thai" and "Chinese" resulted in People's Party government officials and certain big

Chinese capitalist families together owning, managing, and profiting from many large, state-promoted, monopolistic trading and insurance companies and commercial banks. In fact, it could hardly be otherwise in view of the objective historical default of both an independent, organized counter-vailing social force outside the state bureaucracy and a local native bourgeoisie, a default partly inherited from the *ancien regime* and partly of the new regime's own making. Thus, the subjective democratic and nationalist thrust of People's Party's policy principles could not but end up in a bureaucratic authoritarian polity and bureaucratic capitalist economy. See Sungsidh Piriyarangsan, *Thunniyom khunnang thai (Pho.So. 2475–2503)* [Thai bureaucratic capitalism (B.E. 2475–2503)] (Bangkok: Chulalongkorn University Social Research Institute, 1983), 76–171; and Akira Suehiro, chapter 4 of *Capital Accumulation in Thailand, 1855–1985* (Tokyo: The Centre for East Asian Cultural Studies, 1989).

85 Following the Sian Incident in December 1936 and the Japanese attack at the Marco Polo Bridge in July 1937, the Kuomintang and CCP declared a truce and formed an anti-Japanese united front in August/September 1937 (Van Slyke, chapters 5 and 6 of *Enemies and Friends*). The Siamese branches of the two parties initially followed suit but suspended cooperation even before Japanese troops landed (Skinner, *Chinese Society*, 265, 277). Apart from patriotic motivation, increasing Japanese business competition in Thailand lent a dimension of personal economic interest to the issue.

86 Skinner, *Chinese Society*, 263, 264–72.

87 David A. Wilson, "Thailand and Marxism," in *Marxism in Southeast Asia: A Study of Four Countries* (Stanford, California: Stanford University Press, 1965), 92.

88 Vichitvong, *Pridi*, 82–83.

89 Batson, *The End*, 87.

90 Skinner, *Chinese Society*, 229–30; Sawai, *Dr. pridi*, 117.

91 See Pridi Banomyong, *Ma vie mouvementée et mes 21 ans d'exil en Chine Populaire* (Paris: Varap, 1974), 89.

92 Goscha, *Thailand and the Southeast Asian Networks*, 88–89, 108 n. 134. Hoang Van Hoan reported to his superiors in Hong Kong in 1935 that "there were not that many [CPS] comrades who were truly Siamese" (89). However, the above-cited information, which appears in the memoirs of an unnamed contemporary Vietnamese communist in Siam, should be contrasted with Murashima's claim, citing contemporary Thai and Chinese newspaper sources, that two Thais were CPS Central Committee members. See Murashima, *Kanmeuang jinsiam*, 114–15.

93 Stephen Uhalley, *A History of the Chinese Communist Party* (Stanford, California: Hoover Institution Press, 1988), 36–37.

94 Thongchai, "Latthi khommunit," 165–66.

95 Van Slyke, chapter 4 of *Enemies and Friends*; and Murashima, *Kanmeuang jinsiam*, 41, 118. My following account of the SOCCP is based on the meticulous and exhaustive research on the pre-WWII political activities of the Kuomintang and CCP organizations in Siam in Eiji Murashima's *Kanmeuang jinsiam*, especially Chapter 2, Section 2: "The Kang Lian Anti-Japanese Movement for National Salvation," 118–43.

Be that as it may, it is a pity that this data-rich work suffers from a persistent under- and mis-conceptualization, in particular Murashima's narrowly-conceived political categorization of the pre-war Chinese in Siam into three groups: 1) those who became Thai and complied with the Thai government's policy; 2) those who remained Chinese and continued to be engaged in China-oriented politics; and 3) those who complied with the Thai government's policy, observed Thai law, were ready to enter into a relationship with Japan for economic self-interest, and yet, still secretly and voluntarily engaged in politics as Chinese (185, 213). This blinkered vision leaves no room for the lookjin communists, i.e., those who considered themselves Thai but were engaged in Thai politics as a radical anti-government force, thus refusing either to comply with the Thai government's policy or to observe Thai law. This leads to a paradoxical feature of his research, namely, that it is empirically cognizant of, but conceptually blind to, the lookjin communists as a group. More importantly, it thereby completely misses the crucial political development associated with the lookjin communists at that crucial juncture—how they turned from being anti-Japanese Chinese nationalists into anti-Japanese Thai nationalists upon the Japanese occupation of Thailand. In other words, its author fails to understand and notice the translation of one nationalism to another that was then taking place among the objects of his research.

96 Murashima, *Kanmeuang jinsiam*, 42–43, 96–99, 119–21, 124–25, 127–28, 131.

97 Murashima, *Kanmeuang jinsiam*, 125–27.

98 Murashima, *Kanmeuang jinsiam*, 128–29, 132–37.

99 Murashima, *Kanmeuang jinsiam*, 126, 129–30, 141–42.

100 Murashima, *Kanmeuang jinsiam*, 43, 121, 130–31, 136, 142.

101 Murashima, *Kanmeuang jinsiam*, 94, 97.

102 Murashima, *Kanmeuang jinsiam*, 94, 122–24, 132, 156–7 n. 108; Somsak, "The Communist Movement," 136.

103 My reconstruction of the lookjin communists' pre-war activities leading
     up to the founding of the Thai Communist Party is based mainly on: 1)
     Sungsidh, *Prawat* (1986), a pioneering and thorough, if at times
     unpolished, research on the early history of the labor movement in Siam,
     which contains a series of extremely instructive profiles of eleven Thai
     labor leaders of different political persuasions from the 1920s through
     the 1950s; 2) Damri Reuangsutham and Jaroon Lasa, *Khabuankan*
     kammakorn nai prathet thai kab kantosoo khleuanwai lae phatthanakan
     khong raengngan [Workers' movement in Thailand and the struggle,
     activities and development of labor] (Bangkok: Santitham Press, 1986).
     The book's main author was Jaroon Lasa, who had been a radical leader
     of the railwaymen's union in the mid-1950s. The text was then "revised"
     by Damri Reuangsutham, who was a top communist labor leader from
     the Second World War until the late 1940s; 3) Kanya Lilalai, "Prawat
     kantosoo khong kammakorn thai" [A history of Thai workers' struggle]
     (Party-commissioned study based on CPT publications, 1980); and 4)
     interviews given by Phin Bua-on and Udom Sisuwan, both of whom were
     members of the CPT's Politburo during its Third Congress period.

104 Sungsidh, *Prawat*, 150–51. It is remarkable that the life of one of Kulap's
     main characters in *Lae pai khangna* followed more or less the same path
     as that of Si and his radical colleagues. A devout Christian and brilliant
     lookjin-lookyuan (Thai-born Vietnamese) from a poor urban family
     whose father was a Chinese watchmaker and mother a Thai national of
     Vietnamese descent, "Seng" studied in an upper class Thai school called
     Thewesrangsaris (actually modeled on the Thepsirin School, where
     Kulap had been educated in his youth) and suffered from the traditional
     anti-Chinese and pro-aristocratic bias of its teaching staff. However,
     unlike Si, poverty and his father's untimely death forced him to drop out
     of school and earn his living as a foreign news translator for a Thai
     newspaper called *Prachamati* (again modeled on the real *Prachachat*, of
     which Kulap was the first editor). See Sriburapha (Kulap Saipradit),
     chapters 9, 10, and 12 of *Lae pai khangna: Phak pathomwai* [Looking
     forward: The tender age], Khrongkan anurak wannakam kao lae hayak
     [Old and rare literature conservation project], no. 36, ed. Chuai
     Phulphoem (Bangkok: Dokya Press, 1988); and Sriburapha, chapter 6 of
     Lae pai khangna: Phak majchimwai.

105 The number of manufacturing laborers in Thailand was 110,322 in
     1937; 195,875 in 1947; and 212,500 in 1954. Virginia Thompson,
     Labor Problems in Southeast Asia, cited in Somkiat Wanthana,
     "Wiwatthanakan chonchan raengngan thai: Khaokhrong prawatsat

raengngan khrob rob songroi pi" [The evolution of the Thai laboring
class: An outline of labor history in two hundred years], Thammasat
University Academic Paper no. 23 (presented in the seminar Song
satawas rattanakosin: Khwamplianplaeng khong sangkhom thai
[Rattanakosin bicentennial: The changes of Thai society], February 3–
5, 1982, mimeographed), 41.

According to one estimate, in 1940, 75 percent of workers in Thailand
were Chinese. See Bevars D. Mabry, The Development of Labor
Institutions in Thailand (Ithaca, New York: Department of Asian Studies,
Cornell University, 1979), 36. The proportion of non-Chinese workers
in the industrial labor force might have increased somewhat owing to the
Phibunsongkhram government's attempt to Thaify it since 1939 (Skinner,
Chinese Society, 264). This was another instance of Phibunsongkhram's
inadvertent contributions to the Thaification of the lookjin communists.

106 By the late 1930s, Japan had replaced Great Britain as Thailand's largest
trading partner, accounting for approximately a quarter of her foreign
trade (Somkiat, "Wiwatthanakan," 35–36). These increasingly close
economic links with Japan, coupled with her strategic location as the
gateway to British Malaya and Burma, made Thailand an obvious outpost
of Japanese military expansion. See Pridi Banomyong, "Prawat pramot
lae botkhwam bangreuang khong nai pridi banomyong" [Pramot's profile
and selected articles of Pridi Banomyong], in Anusorn nai pramot
pheungsunthorn, nakaphiwat, serithai, naisanammuai wethirajdamnoen
khonraek [In memory of Mr. Pramot Pheungsunthorn, a revolutionary, a
Free Thai, and the first director of the Rajdamnoen Boxing Stadium]
(Bangkok: Bunphring T. Suwan, 1982), 18.

107 Sungsidh, Prawat, 151, 160.

108 The account in this part is based on Prasert, Ratthasapha, 359–61, 377–
88; Pridi, "Prawat pramot," 10–30, which contains extracts from the
minutes of the key cabinet meetings on December 8–9, 1941; Vichitvong,
Pridi, 159–78; Wyatt, Thailand, 256–58; and especially Murashima,
"Samphanthamit thai-yipun," 115.

Based on extensive and meticulous research into Japanese and Thai
military intelligence, archival sources, contemporary Thai, Chinese and
Japanese press, personal memoirs, and interviews of surviving historical
figures, Murashima's cited article presents a richly-detailed, highly-
nuanced, and complex narrative of the tripartite relationships, double
dealings, and double-crossings among the Phibunsongkhram government, the Japanese imperial government and occupation authorities, and
the Chinese community in Thailand. The only major player left out of

the picture is Pridi and the domestic Free Thai Movement, which, in turn, receive full and uncompromisingly critical treatment and interpretation in Somsak, chapter 3 of "The Communist Movement": "The Thai Communist Party and the Seri Thai," especially 137–59. Hence, Murashima's article and Somsak's dissertation should be read complementarily.

109 Murashima, "Samphanthamit thai-yipun," 116.

110 Pridi, "Prawat pramot," 13–16, 24; Murashima, "Samphanthamit thai-yipun," 116.

111 Murashima, "Samphanthamit thai-yipun," 117–18, 120, 122–23, 139–40, 189 n. 13.

112 Murashima, "Samphanthamit thai-yipun," 188 n. 10.

113 Pridi, "Prawat pramot," 17–18; Vichitvong, *Pridi*, 158–59. Another noteworthy point in the cabinet debates on the Japanese invasion is that, as far as Phibun was concerned, the "Thai nation" was essentially the armed part of it. Pridi, "Prawat pramot," 15–16; Vichitvong, *Pridi*, 169 *ff.* Also see Sornsak, *Khabuankan serithai*, 35–40.

114 Pridi, "Prawat pramot," 52–54, 60; Prasert, *Ratthasapha*, 383–88; Vichitvong, *Pridi*, 180–82.

115 See perceptive discussions on this point in Sornsak, chapter 3 of *Khabuankan serithai*; and Nigel J. Brailey, *Thailand and the Fall of Singapore: A Frustrated Asian Revolution* (Boulder: Westview Press, 1986), 67–98.

116 Somsak, "The Communist Movement," 139–43.

117 Murashima, "Samphanthamit thai-yipun," 156–73, especially 166–68. Phibun ordered the commander of his Kongthap Phayap (Northern Army) to secretly contact the Kuomintang troops across the border in China to negotiate a cessation of hostilities and formulate a plan to drive Japanese troops out of Thailand.

118 Remarkably, much the same sentiments in almost exactly the same words were expressed by Kulap in a novel and Pridi in a memoir. Sriburapha, *Lae pai khangna: Phak majchimwai*, 245–52; Pridi, "Prawat pramot," 47.

119 Murashima, "Samphanthamit thai-yipun," 117, 119–20.

120 Murashima, "Samphanthamit thai-yipun," 127, 133–34, 139, 147–55, 176–78, passim. The Japanese military asked the Joint Thai-Japanese Committee to pass on such demands to the local Chinese Trade Association on four different occasions (March and June 1943 and April and May 1944). Altogether, 32,800 laborers were solicited. Initially, the Thai authorities refused to cooperate, but very soon yielded to Japanese demands and helped mediate and broker the deal with the Chinese Trade

Association, while consistently diverting the brunt of the demands from the Thai population to the Chinese. Though free and well-paid wage labor in principle, some of those recruited were indeed forced or even held to ransom. The job itself was far away and reportedly onerous, as publicized by the Chinese press. Eventually, 26,546 workers were delivered to the Japanese. However, of that number, only about 17,300 actually reached the destination and did the work. The rest simply took an advance and disappeared or fled during the journey.

121 Murashima, "Samphanthamit thai-yipun," 126–39, 154–55, 183–84, 192 n. 40. The reference is, of course, to Lu Xin's famous short story, "Diary of a Mad Man."

122 Murashima, "Samphanthamit thai-yipun," 139, 148–49, 153–55.

123 They were the Ban Pong Incident on December 18, 1942, in which Thai police and railway workers fought Japanese sentries, resulting in six Japanese deaths, in the central province of Ratchaburi; and the Ranong Incident on July 30, 1944, in which Japanese troops stormed and seized the provincial administrative center, police station, and army barracks in the province of Ranong near the Burmese border, due to a prevailing mistrustful atmosphere and the misinformation that fighting had broken out in Bangkok between the two sides. Nineteen Thai soldiers, police, and civilians were killed. See Murashima, "Samphanthamit thai-yipun," 173–74, 194 n. 62.

124 Somsak, "The Communist Movement," 129–30, 140–42.

125 Murashima, "Samphanthamit thai-yipun," 142–43.

126 Murashima, "Samphanthamit thai-yipun," 143, 145–47.

127 Murashima, "Samphanthamit thai-yipun," 156–73.

128 Somsak, "The Communist Movement," 145–46. Among the top leaders were Police Director General Major General Adul Aduldejjaras, Head of Military Police Rear Admiral Luang Sangworn Suwannachip, Defense Minister and Acting Commander-in-Chief of the Armed Forces Luang Sinat Yotharak, and Commander of the First Army Circle Luang Wirawatyothin.

129 Pridi, "Prawat pramot," 46–66. This hard-hitting interpretation of the nature of the domestic Free Thai Movement is derived from and based on Somsak, "The Communist Movement," 146–56. Though developed separately, my understanding of Pridi concurs in essence with Somsak's.

130 The Japanese occupation of Indochina began in September 1940 and was completed in July 1941. Huynh, *Vietnamese Communism*, 238–40.

131 Somsak tries fruitlessly to probe the problematical relationship between the overseas Chinese communists and their lookjin comrades in the

organizational and ethnic dimensions (i.e., SOCCP versus TCP, Chinese versus Thai), while Murashima's opinion that the activities of the Thai Communist Party still formed part of the Chinese political movement in Thailand is precisely beside the point. See Somsak, "The Communist Movement in Thailand," 135–36; and Murashima, "Samphanthamit thai-yipun," 182–83.

132 I owe the conception in this part to a thought-provoking conversation with Dr Caroline Hau of the Center for Southeast Asian Studies, Kyoto University. Its inspiration comes from a book of essays on nationalism and Southeast Asia by Benedict Anderson under that title.

133 The data concerning the establishment of the TCP come from the following sources: Phin, interview, July 31, 1985; Udom, interview, January 19, 1984; Udom Sisuwan, interview by Craig J. Reynolds on communism and literature in Thailand, Bangkok, December 27, 1983; Suthachai, "Kankhleuanwai," 229–30; Murashima, *Kanmeuang jinsiam*, 94–95, 156–57 n. 108.

134 Murashima, *Kanmeuang jinsiam*, 122–23, 156–57 n. 108; Murashima, "Samphanthamit thai-yipun," 181–83; Somsak, "The Communist Movement," 136.

135 Phin, interview, July 31, 1985. Whereas Phin gives 1950 as the year of the dissolution of the CCP-TB's Chinese Department, some recent Chinese communist memorial publications have specified the year as 1953. See Murashima, *Kanmeuang jinsiam*, 75, 144 n. 2.

136 *Mahachon* 139 (July 11, 1948); Murashima,"Samphanthamit thai-yipun," 182–83.

137 Udom, interview, January 19, 1984.

138 Suthachai, "Kankhleuanwai," 234. The earlier (TCP) and later (CPT) names are used here alternately, depending on the temporal context.

139 Kanya Lilalai, Personal file of documents of the Communist Party of Thailand and the Voice of the People of Thailand, 1981.

140 Quoted in Murashima, "Samphanthamit thai-yipun," 182–83.

141 For a participant's account of the TCP-led anti-Japanese movement in the South of Thailand, see Cholthira Sattayawatthana, "Wanakhadi chud 'Phlik adit: Kankhleuanwai khong sattri thai nakpatiwat run bukboek'" ['Digging up the past: The activities of Thai female revolutionary pioneers' Junglelogue series], *Samakkhi Soorob* 1, no. 5 (July–August 1977): 59–68.

At the end of the unfinished novel Lae pai khangna, Kulap, who with ten other dissidents in late January 1942 was arrested on the Thai-issara rebellion charge but released about three months later, told of the anti-

Japanese activities of an underground party of patriots called Thai-issara in December 1941 and January 1942, which included distributing clandestine leaflets and sending anonymous letters to the public strongly attacking the government for dragging the country into the dangerous quagmire of war in alliance with Japan. In response, the government accused the Thai-issara of being "communist." In the novel's last episode, a group of policemen were arresting Seng and searching his home on a Thai-issara-related charge. The fact that of all the characters in this story, it is a Christian lookjin-yuan (Thai-born Sino-Vietnamese) who is the first to act out the role of a Thai patriot tells its own tale about the official nationalism and racialized opportunism of the Phibun regime.

Sriburapha, Lae pai khangna: Phak majchimwai, 252–53; Witthayakorn Chiangkul, Seuksa botbat lae khwamkhid Sriburapha [A study of the role and thought of Sriburapha] (Bangkok: Community for Development Research Project and Phleuk Press, 1989), 44; David Smyth, "Introduction: Kulap Saipradit (Siburapha): His Life and Times," in Siburapha (Kulap Saipradit), Behind the Painting and Other Stories, trans. David Smyth (New York: Oxford University Press, 1990), 15.

142 Sungsidh, *Prawat*, 152–53, 160–61, 174, 191–92, 233; Kanya, "Prawat," 23–25.

143 The Communist Party generally used the first name in its publications while Damri's account and Sungsidh's study used the second. See an official history of the Party broadcast by the Voice of the People of Thailand radio station on December 9, 1977, and reprinted as "VOPT Recounts CPT History Covering 1942–1977," *Foreign Broadcast Information Service Daily Report, Asia & Pacific* 4, no. 241 (December 15, 1977): J-7; Kanya, "Prawat," 24–25, 30; Damri and Jaroon, *Khabuankan*, 36–37; Sungsidh, *Prawat*, 160–61.

144 Sungsidh, *Prawat*, 152; Damri and Jaroon, *Khabuankan*, 37; "VOPT Recounts CPT History," J-7; Somsak, "The Communist Movement," 132; Murashima, "Samphanthamit thai-yipun," 143.

145 Phin, interview, July 31, 1985; Pho. Meuangchomphoo, *Soo samoraphoom*, 101.

146 Phin, interview, July 31, 1985; Pho. Meuangchomphoo, *Soo samoraphoom*, 23, 25; Supha Sirimanond, interview by Craig J. Reynolds on his life and the Thai left, Bangkok, October 28, 1979.

147 Sornsak, *Khabuankan serithai*, 2, 12–13, 19–22; Supha Sirimanond, *Jodmai jak bannathikan* [Letters from the editor] (Bangkok: Supha Sirimanond Foundation, 1988), 77–79.

148 Kanya, "Prawat," 25; Udom, interview, January 19, 1984.

149 Cholthira, "Wanakhadi," 63.

150 The Japanese military, which by that time had grown mistrustful of Phibun, told him to comply with the constitutional political process. See Murashima, "Samphanthamit thai-yipun," 173; Prasert, *Ratthasapha*, 435–39; Vichitvong, *Pridi*, 200–205.

151 Vichitvong, *Pridi*, 227–55.

152 The issue of the communists' actual role in, and relative contribution to, the Thai resistance movement against the Japanese has long been a bone of contention between the CPT and Pridi, each side trying to inflate their own and depreciate the other's role for political reasons. See, for example, "VOPT Recounts CPT History," J7; and Pridi, "Prawat pramot," 66–67.

It is indisputable that, in terms of Allied recognition of the Thai resistance movement, the Free Thai Movement under Pridi was of central importance, not the communists or their many anti-Japanese resistance organizations, united fronts, and underground newspapers. However, the Chinese and lookjin communists, variously organized as the SOCCP, Kang Lian, Thai-issara, and TCP, were indeed engaged in anti-Japanese activities earlier, more continually, and probably more seriously and devotedly than the Free Thai Movement. And they did gain politically from their movement, especially among industrial workers and Chinese, who were mostly outside the Free Thai Movement's constituency of police, military, civil servants, school teachers, writers, journalists, university students, Thai students in the United States and Great Britain, Isan MPs, and peasants in some rural areas. See Sornsak, Khabuankan serithai, 12–13, 19–22; and Somsak, chapter 3 of "The Communist Movement," especially 156–61.

153 M.C. Sakol Wannakon served as advisor to both the Bangkok Labor Union and the Central Labor Union, thus helping to defend, legitimize, and further the communist-led labor movement with his royal prestige. Sungsidh, *Prawat*, 162, 216–17; *Mahachon* 137 (June 27, 1948); and his speech on May Day 1948 published in "Kankhleuanwai khong kammakorn mai chai khommunit" [The workers' movement is not communist], *Mahachon* 138 (July 4, 1948).

154 Damri and Jaroon, *Khabuankan*, 41–44; Kanya, "Prawat," 31–32; Sungsidh, *Prawat*, 163–64; Skinner, *Chinese Society*, 323. Also see profiles of Thai labor leaders of that generation who were greatly influenced by the communists, such as Bunsong Wijarana, Wisit Sriphatthra, and Jamnong Noothong in Sungsidh, *Prawat*, 178–96, 231–38.

To help distinguish the many communist labor organizations from one another (a mess which seemed to confuse even the meticulous Skinner), it may be useful to give here the barest outline of their organizational metamorphosis in chronological order: 1) Samakhom Songkhrao Kammakorn (Workers' Welfare Associations), 1942; 2) Sahasamakhom Kammakorn Krungthep (Bangkok Workers' United Association) or Sahabal Kammakorn Krungthep (Bangkok Workers' Union), 1945; 3) Samakhom Kammakorn Songkhrao Krungthep (Bangkok Workers' Welfare Association), 1945/46; 4) Samakhom Sahaachiwa Kammakorn Nakhorn Krungthep (Bangkok Labor Union), 1946; 5) Ongkan Sahaachiwa Kammakorn Haeng Prathet Thai (Central Labor Union), 1947.

155 *Mahachon* 87 (May 11, 1947); Damri and Jaroon, *Khabuankan*, 40–41; Phin, interview, July 31, 1985; Skinner, *Chinese Society*, 287, 323; Sungsidh, *Prawat*, 154.

156 The drama of the complex political maneuvers leading to the eventual abrogation of the Anti-Communist Act in October 1946, involving the Soviet Union, American officials, the TCP, the Pridi Group, Isan MPs of the Sahachip Party, Prasert Sapsunthorn, and M.R. Kukrit Pramoj, was told in more detail in Suphot, *Prasert*, 27–46; Sornsak, *Khabuankan serithai*, 230–31; Reynolds, *Thai Radical Discourse*, 25; *Karnmuang* 2, no. 32 (September 13, 1946): 4–5; and United States, American Embassy, Bangkok, "The Sahacheep Party: A Chronology," Enclosure no. 2 in "Fortnightly Summary of Political Events in Siam for the Period July 16–July 31, 1947," NADD, Washington, D.C., 1, 3, 4.

157 Suphot Dantrakul, a faithful lifelong leftist follower of Pridi, claimed in a recent interview that originally Pridi and M.C. Sakol Wannakon Worawan planned to have Prasert Sapsunthorn and Thianthai Aphichatbut arrange for a European-type parliamentary communist party separate from the TCP to contest an election. However, the plan was aborted by the military seizure of power in November 1947. Quoted in Suthachai, "Kankhleuanwai," 222.

158 Prasert, *Ratthasapha*, 557; United States Embassy, "The Sahacheep Party," 4.

159 The figures appeared originally in the December 7, 1946, issue of *Bangkok Post*, an English daily newspaper in Thailand, and were quoted by Virginia Thompson and Richard Adloff in *The Left Wing in Southeast Asia*, published under the auspices of the Institute of Pacific Relations (New York: William Sloane, 1950), 61.

160 Even today, one can (over)hear complaints, in private and public, about the inability of, say, the rector of Thammasat University, the managing director of Bangkok Bank, or the Speaker of parliament to speak Thai clearly. Amazing is the ludicrous extent to which some lookjin elite are

willing to go to confirm their Thainess. For example, a leading Chinese business tycoon was alleged to have had his Chinese-sounding name, Wan Sanseu, changed expediently to the Thai-sounding Van Chanseu once elected Speaker of parliament. True or not, the allegation obviously upset him. So much so that, whenever the opportunity arose, he reiterated his correct Thai name and explained its meaning to the Thai public in the following manner: "Van" = kind, "Chan" = steep, "Seu" = honest; therefore "Van Chanseu" = the kind of people with a high degree of honesty, QED! See Bunchai Jaiyen, *Ruai baeb jaosua neung* [Rich-tycoon style, volume 1] (Bangkok: Bunchai Press, 1990), 78.

161 Phin, interview, July 31, 1985.

Chapter 4

1 Intharayut (Atsani Phonlajan), "Kawitaphutthi" [Poetic enlightenment], *Aksornsarn* 1, no. 7 (October 1949): 88. The quotation is in English in the original.

2 From one of his letters to Supha Sirimanond, editor of the well-known and erudite Marxist monthly *Aksornsarn*, dated September 25, 1949, published in Aurasom Sutthisakhorn, *Nakfan khonkla or. udakorn* [Bold dreamer: Or. Udakorn] (Bangkok: Dokya Press, 1989), 153–54.

3 Reynolds, *Thai Radical Discourse*, 25.

4 Marshall Berman has masterfully shown that Marx and Engels' famous dictum on capitalist modernity, "All that is solid melts into air, all that is holy is profaned...," is true of communism as well. See his perceptive and brilliant arguments on modernity and modernism from which the underlying idea of this part of my book is gained in Marshall Berman, *All That Is Solid Melts into Air: The Experience of Modernity* (New York: Simon and Schuster, 1982), 118–20.

5 Thailand, Office of the National Education Commission, Office of the Prime Minister, *Sathiti prachakorn phoo mai roo nangseu khong prathet thai Pho.So. 2490–2513* [Statistics of the illiterate population of Thailand, B.E. 2490–2513] (Bangkok: Office of the National Education Commission, Office of the Prime Minister, 1977), 2.

The estimated total Thai population in 1947/48 was between 17.89 and 18 million. Prachoom Chomchai, "Thailand," chapter 4 of The Economic Development of East and Southeast Asia, ed. Shinichi Ichimura (Honolulu: The University Press of Hawaii, 1975), 144; Karnmuang 5, no. 1 (July 28, 1948).

6 There are no data on the cultural or sociological background of the approximately 1.52 million people who were literate, but had no formal education.

7 See Phaithoon Sinlarat, *Rabob kanseuksa thai nai rob sam thossawas (Pho.So. 2490–2520): Kanseuksa pheua sanongtob lae pentua khong tuaeng* [The Thai educational system in three decades (B.E. 2490–2520): Education for responsiveness and autonomy] (Bangkok: Chulalongkorn University, 1983), 14; Aurasom, *Nakfan khonkla*, 57–58; Phin, interview, July 31, 1985; Phichit, interview, May 15, 1989; and Kanlaya Phichaikul, interview by the author on her life and lookjin communist circles, Rayong, March 26, 1989.

8 They were Chulalongkorn University, Thammasat University, the Fine Arts University, Kasetsart University, the Medical Science University, the College of Education, and the Technical College. Charnvit Kasetsiri et al., part 2 of *Raingan kanwijai reuang prawat mahawitthayalai thammasat* [Research report on the history of Thammasat University] (Bangkok: Thai Khadi Research Institute, Thammasat University, 1989), 77–78.

9 The figures are taken from Constance M. Wilson, *Thailand: A Handbook of Historical Statistics* (Boston: G.K.Hall, 1983), 72; and Charnvit et al., part 2 of *Prawat thammasat*, 48.

10 Some examples of the reading lives of radical university students in this period can be found in the following: for Chulalongkorn students, see Mit Ruamrob (Prawut Srimantra), "Chiwaprawat bangton khong jit poumisak" [Some episodes from Jit Poumisak's biography], *Aksornsatphijan* (Special Double Issue on Jit Poumisak) 3, no. 11–12 (April–May 1976): 23–44; for Fine Arts University students, see Siriusa Phonlajan (Cholthira Sattayawatthana), "Ajan jit poumisak kab chaosinlapakorn" [Lecturer Jit Poumisak and Fine Arts University's people], *Aksornsatphijan* (Special Double Issue on Jit Poumisak) 3, no. 11–12 (April–May 1976): 5–22; and for Thammasat students, see Charnvit et al., part 2 of *Prawat thammasat*, 78–93; Phin Bua-on, interview by Craig J. Reynolds on his life and the Thai communist movement, Bangkok, August 31, 1984; Phin, interview, July 31, 1985; and Chan Kaeochoosai, interview by the author on post-war Thai politics and the radical press, Bangkok, February 5, 1989. Suffice it to point out that it was in the personal collection donated to his alma mater of the late Ophas Jayanama, a Thammasat alumnus of that period and later career diplomat, that I randomly found an unexpected number of rare radical publications of the 1950s.

11 Samak Burawas, the radical philosopher and member of the prestigious Royal Institute. See *Anusorn nai ngan phrarajthan phloeng sop phanek samak burawas* [Cremation volume of Colonel Samak Burawas], The Army Crematorium, Wat Sommanaswihan, Bangkok, 15 November 1975, [2], [10]; Supha, interview by Napaporn Ativanichayapong on the development of Marxist political economy in Thailand, Bangkok, September 4, 1985; and especially Supha, *Jodmai*, passim. The selection of assorted letters from readers of the radical *Aksornsarn* contained in this book shows that a large number of them were indeed graduates of domestic and foreign universities.

12 Udom Udakan. See Aurasom, *Nakfan khonkla*, 114–21; Supha, *Jodmai*, 7–8, 14–15, 26–28.

13 Thailand, Department of Secondary Education, Ministry of Education, *Sathiti kanseuksa rob yi sib paed pi* [Statistics of education in twenty-eight years] (Bangkok: Department of Secondary Education, Ministry of Education, 1960), 2–3.

14 For example, at the Phranakhorn Witthayalai School and among Laotian teachers from the Northeast. See Phichit, interview, May 15, 1989.

15 For example, Teacher Phoo Chaichan, the leader of the renowned "Khoosod (subdistrict) Communist Unit," whose reading of radical literature led him and many of his family members and friends, in turn, to the communist weekly *Mahachon*, the TCP, Bangkhwang Penitentiary, and eventually Ladyao Prison. See Phichit, interview, May 15, 1989; Wiwat Catithammanit, "Kabot santiphap" [Peace rebellion] (master's thesis, Chulalongkorn University, 1989), 168, 180–81, 185–86; and Thongbai Thongpao, *Khommunit ladyao* [Communists of Ladyao Prison] (Bangkok: Khonnum Press, 1974), 42–43.

16 Where radical publications were regularly sent by mail from Bangkok through a front ally to communist cadres working among local peasants. See Phichit, interview, May 15, 1989.

17 At the Udomwitthaya School, where a group of four radical teachers were regular readers. See Phichit, interview, May 15, 1989.

18 At the Buayai District School, where a teacher lent issues of *Aksornsarn* and Supha Sirimanond's *Khaepitalist* (Capitalism) to a young student named Khamsing Srinawk, who would later become the finest short-story writer of his generation. See Khamsing Srinawk, interview by the author on his life, writings, and radical literature, Nonthaburi, April 12, 1989.

19 Phichit, interview, May 15, 1989; Kanlaya, interview, March 26, 1989; Sungsidh, *Prawat*, 155.

20 Phin, interview, August 31, 1984; Phin, interview, July 31, 1985; Rungwit Suwanaphichon, *Sriburapha sri haeng wannakam thai* [Sriburapha, the glory of Thai literature] (Bangkok: Pasiko Press, 1979), 181; Thongchai, "Latthi khommunit," 265.

21 See "VOPT Recounts CPT History," J-9. Some extracts from Tho.Ko.Cho.'s statute appeared in Police Major General Banleu Reuangtrakul, *Khoomeu kansobsuan khadi aya ton thi neung* [A handbook of criminal investigation, pt. 1] (Bangkok: Police Department, 1962), 152–54.

22 See the testimony of Phramaha Dilok Suwannarat (Thammathatto Bhikkhu), vice-chairman of the Peace Committee of Thailand and a key prosecution witness in the criminal trial of the Peace Rebels, in Thailand, Criminal Court, Ministry of Justice, Criminal Court Proceedings of the Cases No. Black 158, 168, 202/2496, November 1953; and Wiwat, "Kabot santiphap," 180.

23 Wiwat, "Kabot santiphap," 166; and Pho. Meuangchomphoo, *Soo samoraphoom*, 12–13.

24 See Phichit, interview, May 15, 1989; Chinda, *Anusorn*, 51–54; *Mahachon* 135 (June 13, 1948); *Karnmuang* 5, no. 18 (November 27, 1948) and 6, no. 48 (June 24, 1950); Supha, *Jodmai*, 105, 118; Phaisal Malaphan (Sawai Malayavej), *Bantheuk nakthos kanmeuang* [Memoirs of a political prisoner] (Bangkok: Santitham Press, 1985), 163–67.

25 These figures are calculated from data given in Thailand, National Statistical Office, Office of the Prime Minister, *Samud sathiti raipi prathet thai* [Thailand's yearbook of statistics] (Bangkok: National Bureau of Statistics, Prime Minister's Office, [n.d.]), 64.

26 Sungsidh related the case of a communist Muslim labor organizer with merely four years of primary education named Jamnong Noothong, who in the heyday of the radical labor movement after the war used to read radical newspapers and magazines aloud to fellow rice-mill workers during their breaks. Sungsidh, *Prawat*, 234–35.

27 Chai-anan Samudavanija, *Kanmeuang-kanplianplaeng thang kanmeuang thai (Pho.So. 1893–2475)* [Politics and political change in Thailand, B.E. 1893–2475] (Bangkok: Social Science Association of Thailand, 1975), 72–73; and Prajadhipok, "Phrabaromrajwinijchai," 183, 203.

It should be noted that the Phibunsongkhram government had attempted to resume formal diplomatic relations with the Soviet Union as early as March 12, 1941, when the Thai envoy to Berlin concluded an agreement on diplomatic, commercial, and consular relations with the Soviet foreign minister in Moscow. But before the two countries could exchange envoys, their relations were cut short by the Nazi invasion of the Soviet Union in June and the outbreak of the Pacific War in December of the same year. Thongchai, "Latthi khommunit," 220.

28 Reynolds, *Thai Radical Discourse*, 25. The negotiation between the Thai government's representative, Prince Wan Waithayakon, and the Soviet permanent delegate to the United Nations Security Council, Andrei Gromyko, took place in New York. Yielding to Gromyko's argument that the Thai Anti-Communist Act violated the Universal Declaration of Human Rights, Prince Wan undertook in writing on behalf of the Thai government to repeal the law. Thongchai, "Latthi Khommunit," 222; Prince Narathipphongpraphan (M.C. Wan Waithayakon Worawan), "Prasobkan nai kanrabrajkan nai saharat america" [My experience while serving in the United States], in *Chumnum phraniphon khong sassatrajan pholtri phrajaoworawongthoe krommeun narathipphongpraphan* [Selected writings of Professor, Major General, Prince Narathipphongpraphan], ed. Songwit Kaeosri (Bangkok: Bangkok Bank, 1979), 226–28.

29 This is based on a random survey of movie advertisements and reviews in radical newspapers from 1947 to 1950. See *Mahachon* 72 (January 26, 1947); 77 (March 2, 1947); 93 (June 22, 1947); 103 (August 31, 1947); 134 (June 6, 1948); 135 (June 13, 1948); and 151 (October 3, 1948); *Karnmuang* 6, no. 44 (May 27, 1950): 16; Pho. Meuangchomphoo, *Soo samoraphoom*, 25; Thaweep Voradilok, interview by Craig J. Reynolds on Jit Poumisak and contemporary radical literature and politics, Bangkok, September 27, 1979.

30 Issarawut, trans., "Krungthep nai saita chaorussian" [Bangkok in the Russian view], *Karnmuang* 6, no. 44 (May 27, 1950): 16. Reflecting the Soviet reporter's own wayward cult of Stalin rather than any genuine enthusiasm on the Thai audience's part, this "observation" should of course be taken with more than the usual drop of fish sauce.

31 They covered, for example, who was who in the Soviet and East European leadership, the progress and achievements of Soviet culture, sciences, and technology, and the historical development and present socio-economic and political conditions of the Soviet Union. Even a translation of the 1947 Soviet Constitution was duly published. See various issues of *Karnmuang* 2–6 (1946–1950).

32 *Karnmuang* 2, no. 34 (September 27, 1946); 3, no. 17 (April 18, 1947); 5, no. 43 (May 21, 1949).

33 Skinner, 183, 206, 322–45; *Karnmuang* 6, no. 12 (October 15, 1949): 4–5. "Double Tenth" was designated the national day of Republican China

to commemorate the Wuchang Uprising against the Manchu Imperial Dynasty on October 10, 1911.

34 The Thai and Chinese communists themselves claimed as much. See Liu Shaoqi's statement quoted in Roland Lew, "Maoism, Stalinism and the Chinese Revolution," in *The Stalinist Legacy: Its Impact on Twentieth-Century World Politics*, ed. Tariq Ali (Middlesex: Penguin Books, 1984), 309–310: and the TCP's commendation and suggestion in "Prathet meuangkheun keung meuangkheun" [Colonial and semi-colonial countries], *Mahachon* 86 (May 4, 1947); "Chaichana an yingyai khong kongthap plodaek prachachon jin" [The great victory of the Chinese People's Liberation Army], *Mahachon* 123 (March 21, 1948).

35 Jonathan D. Spence, chapter 18 of *The Search for Modern China* (New York: W.W. Norton, 1990). News about the Chinese civil war was a regular item in the contemporary Thai press. With the growing intensity of the fighting towards the end of 1948, more space and features were devoted to the story and a new magazine devoted primarily to Chinese news was published under the title of *Maitrisarn* (Friendship) in 1949. See, for example, *Mahachon* (January 1947–December 1948); *Karnmuang* 5–6 (July 1948–July 1950).

36 Thongchai, "Latthi khommunit," 273.

37 Skinner, *Chinese Society*, 323–24.

38 Thaweep Voradilok, interview by the author on radical literature and the Thammasat University student movement, Bangkok, December 27, 1988; Thaweep Voradilok, "Supha sirimanond pheua khwampenloet khong nangseuphim thai" [Supha Sirimanond for the excellence of Thai newspapers], *Photjanalai supha sirimanond* [Eulogies to Supha Sirimanond] (Bangkok: Songphorn Woraphithaksanond, 1986), 34. Thaweep mentioned in particular an article with extensive quotations from foreign communist documents and leaders such as Lenin and Kim Il Sung, entitled "Songkhram klangmeuang nai jin pajjuban kheu saphan patiwat sangkhomniyom" (The present civil war in China is the bridge to socialist revolution), which left a deep impression on him and his Thammasat friends. It was written by a Thammasat student-cum-TCP-member named Sanao Phanichjaroen and published in *Aksornsarn* 1, no. 3 (June 1949): 42–61.

39 Entitled "Teun laew! Teun laew!" (Awaken! awaken!) and "Dae thong won thai" (For free golden…[?]), they were originally published in *Siam Samai* 149 (March 26, 1950) and 169 (August 26, 1950). Both were quoted in Suchira Guptarak, "Wikhrao bot roikrong khong naiphi" [An

analysis of Nai Phee's poetical works] (master's thesis, Srinakharinwirot University, 1983), 441–44.

40 *Karnmuang* 2, no. 28 (August 16, 1946). There is no information on whether the Reverend actually went on this peace mission. Most likely not. It should be mentioned, however, that Phrakhroo Naphisi was neither the first nor the last Thai monk to try to do this. For data concerning the similar, aborted attempt of his predecessors and the successful ones of his successors, with alas fateful consequences, see Pho. Meuangchomphoo, *Soo samoraphoom*, 12–13; Sakdina Chatkul na Ayudhya, "Narin phasit: Khonkhwanglok" [Narin Phasit: A heretic], *Jodmaikhao Sangkhomsat* 10, no. 4 (May–July 1988): 24–26.

41 United States, Office of Strategic Services, "Appendix C: Political Warfare Executive, Plan of Political Warfare against Japan, Appreciation of Siam, Siamese Personalities," June 1945, NADD, Washington, D.C., 3.

42 United States, American Embassy, Bangkok, "Fortnightly Summary of Political Events in Siam for the Period March 16–March 31, 1947," NADD, Washington, D.C., 1.

43 Pridi, *Ma vie*, 85–115; Sawai, *Dr. pridi*, 770–838; Thongchai, "Latthi khommunit," 344–52.

44 Suthachai, "Kankhleuanwai," 276; Thongbai, *Khommunit ladyao*, 487. The three merchants who traveled were Yuk Jiaraphan, Iam Jaroensuk, and Krasae Mahaphol.

45 Somboon Woraphong, *Bon senthang nangseuphim* [On the journalistic road] (Bangkok: Pheuanchiwit Press,1984), 93; Suchat Phoomborirak, "Chiwit sriburapha nai satharanarat prachachon jin" [Sriburapha's life in the People's Republic of China], *Ongkorn Wannakam* 12 (July 15–August 14, 1982): 4; Udom Sisuwan, "Pai chom ho sadaeng phap sil thi moscow" [Visiting a Moscow art gallery], *Saithan* 6 (October 1958): 28–38.

46 An unfinished travelogue of Kulap entitled "Pai sahaphap soviet" (To the Soviet Union, 1958) and an exotic political novel of Suwat entitled *Phirab daeng* (Red pigeon, 1958). See Kulap Saipradit, *Pai sahaphap soviet* [To the Soviet Union] (Bangkok: Suphapburus Press, 1951); Thongbai, *Khommunit ladyao*, 309, 312; "Chumthang sinlapa wannakhadi" [Artistic and literary junction], *Saithan* 6 (October 1958): 98; "Mittraphap rawang prachachon thai-jin jong jaroen" [Long live the friendship between the Thai and Chinese peoples!] *Pituphoom* 2, no. 70 (August 12, 1957): 12–14, 47.

47 Suwat Voradilok, who headed the troupe, was locked up by police upon his return. "Mittraphap rawang prachachon thai-jin jong jaroen" [Long live the friendship between the Thai and Chinese peoples!] *Pituphoom* 2, no. 70 (August 12, 1957): 12–14, 47.

48 "Santi-Vina," produced by Hanuman Pictures. Sil Phithakchon (Jit Poumisak), "Sapda phapphayon haeng asia" [The Asian Film Week], *Pituphoom* 2, no. 78 (October 7, 1957): 29.

49 "Song phinong" was produced by Assawin Pictures. "Chumthang sinlapa wannakhadi" [Artistic and literary junction], *Saithan* 6 (October 1958): 99.

50 "Ratthabal plian nayobai laeo reu?" [Has the government changed its policy?], *Pituphoom* 2, no. 56 (May 6, 1957): 3.

51 Upon their return, they were arrested by police. See *Pituphoom* 2, no. 56 (May 6, 1957): 2–3; Sungsidh, *Prawat*, 42–43; Thongchai, "Latthi khommunit," 374 n. 2.

52 Upon their arrival in Bangkok, Suwit was arrested. See *Pituphoom* 2, no. 69 (August 5, 1957): 11; Siriusa, "Ajan jit," 13–14.

53 See Pho. Meuangchomphoo, *Soo samoraphoom*, 12–13.

54 Suthachai, "Kankhleuanwai," 269.

55 Brailey, *Thailand*, 197; "Kansadaeng khong khana sinlapin soviet" [The performance of the Soviet troupe], *Pituphoom* 2, no. 56 (May 6, 1957): 16.

56 Chiab Amphunan (Chiab Chaisong), "Bantheuk reuang khaphajao mai dai khai chat" [I did not sell the nation: A memoir], *Thai Nikorn* [98] (September 3, 1979): 15; No. Praphasathit (Nongphot Praphasathit), *Kao pi nai pakking* [Nine years in Peking] (Bangkok: Prae Pittaya Press, 1966); Phin, interview, August 31, 1984; Pho. Meuangchomphoo, *Soo samoraphoom*, 137–38.

57 David Joel Steinberg, ed., *In Search of Southeast Asia: A Modern History* (Honolulu: University of Hawaii Press, 1987), 356–62; T. E. Vadney, *The World since 1945* (New York: Penguin Books, 1987), 148–63.

58 Steinberg, ed., *In Search of Southeast Asia*, 383–84.

59 Ben Kiernan, *How Pol Pot Came to Power: A History of Communism in Kampuchea, 1930–1975* (London: Verso, 1985), 52–105.

60 Steinberg, ed., *In Search of Southeast Asia*, 394–97.

61 Steinberg, ed., *In Search of Southeast Asia*, 407.

62 Steinberg, ed., *In Search of Southeast Asia*, 418–24; Vadney, *The World since 1945*, 374–78.

63 Benedict J. Kerkvliet, *The Huk Rebellion: A Study of Peasant Revolt in the Philippines* (Berkeley: University of the California Press, 1982).

64 Charles F. Keyes, *Thailand: Buddhist Kingdom as Modern Nation-State* (Bangkok: Editions Duang Kamol, 1989), 15–22, 126, 134–35.

65 Steinberg, ed., *In Search of Southeast Asia*, 383–84; Kiernan, *How Pol Pot*, 41–42, 52–55, 58–59.

66 Brailey, *Thailand*, 123; Kiernan, *How Pol Pot*, 52.

67 Kiernan, *How Pol Pot*, 53.

68 Chiab Amphunan (Chiab Chaisong), *Mahawitthayalai khong khapajao* [My university] (Bangkok: Ruamsan Press, 1958), 561–64; Kiernan, *How Pol Pot*, 52–55, 58, 60; Sornsak, *Khabuankan serithai*, 231–32; Pho. Meuangchomphoo, *Soo samoraphoom*, 130.
69 Brailey, *Thailand*, 121–23; Kiernan, *How Pol Pot*, 52; Sornsak, *Khabuankan serithai*, 232–33; *Mahachon* 105 (September 14, 1947).
70 *Mahachon* 105 (September 14, 1947). The rally, in which "Thai, Chinese, Vietnamese and Indonesian workers" were reported to have participated, took place in Bangkok on September 6 and 7, 1947.

A survey of an incomplete set of the TCP's weekly Mahachon, published during 1947 and 1948, shows that it carried over thirty news items, articles, and features on the nationalist and communist movements in every Southeast Asian country. Similar publicity and coverage of the same subjects were common in Karnmuang after the Party gained covert control over that paper in 1951.
71 Phichit, interview, May 15, 1989. This hitherto-unheard-of international military aim of Tho.Ko.Cho. was identified by Phichit Dijai, who was closely involved in organizing it in Isan from its early stage. Notably, the statute of the Tho.Ko.Cho. specified that one of the organization's six tasks was:

To contact people's organizations abroad that fight for independence and national freedom and oppose the invasion of American Imperialism, especially in the nearby neighbors of Thailand. (Quoted in Banleu, *Khoomeu kansobsuan*, 154.)
72 That is, they seemed to have gone to fight a war of national liberation in another country out of a sense of ethnic identity and solidarity with the nationalist cause of the indigenous population there, rather than any kind of class identity and solidarity with the revolutionary cause of the working class in the Marxist-communist sense. It was perhaps the same kind of imagination that motivated Piatoe or Phayap Angkhasing, along with some Sino-Thai youths, to go to China to fight with the Chinese communists against the Japanese invaders after his release from jail during the Second World War. Udom, interview, January 19, 1984.
73 Udom Sisuwan told of a Kuomintang-trained, mostly Thai fighting force of the Lao Issara which eventually joined the communist Neo Lao Hak Xat (Laotian Patriotic Front) (Pho. Meuangchomphoo, *Soo samoraphoom*, 131). In another instance, four hundred Thais led by a suspected communist who had fled the country after the November 1947 coup joined combined Lao-Vietnamese insurgent units in Siemreap and Battambang in Cambodia later that year. Kiernan, *How Pol Pot*, 57.

74 Brailey, *Thailand*, 119, 121; Kiernan, *How Pol Pot*, 42, 53–54, 58–60; Phichit, interview, May 15, 1989; Pho. Meuangchomphoo, *Soo samoraphoom*, 13, 129–31.

75 *Mahachon* 134 (June 6, 1948); Brailey, *Thailand*, 173–74; Wiwat, "Kabot santiphap," 91–92.

76 Thongchai, "Latthi khommunit," 382.

77 Thongchai, "Latthi khommunit," 269, 281–82, 295–98, 303.

78 Thongchai, "Latthi khommunit," 323–24, 326–30, 333–34, 382, 383.

79 Thongchai, "Latthi khommunit," 322, 382. The Taiwan government took the initiative in anti-communist cooperation with the Phibun government in January 1952. From 1954 to 1956, the Thai Special Branch Police and the Taiwan authorities jointly operated a clandestine Sino-Thai anti-communist intelligence exchange radio broadcasting unit in both countries by order of Police General Phao Sriyanond, director general of the Police Department. In typically corrupt Thai bureaucratic style, the unit was cunningly turned by its police operators into a lucrative international business communications service until its final shut-down due to press exposés and criticisms. Chit Wiphasthawat, *Phao saraphap (Burus lek haeng asia)* [Phao confesses (The Iron Man of Asia)] (Bangkok: "Thainoi" and Prae Pittaya Press, 1960), 270–72.

80 Noteworthy Philippine contributions to Thai anti-communist efforts included: President Quirino's proposal of July 1949 for an anti-communist "Pacific Pact" (which would also include Taiwan and South Korea); a secret-urgent airmail report to the Thai foreign minister from Luang Phattharawathi, then Thai envoy in Manila, entitled "Kanseuksa seubsuan kiaokab kanronnarong totan lae pongkan khommunit" [The study of and investigation into anti-communist campaign], of June 19, 1950, which suggested an emphasis on freedom and private property in Thai anti-communist propaganda since the two were favorite themes in the Philippines; and Benigno Aquino, Sr.'s article, "50 Traders Plot Asian Red Strategy in Bangkok," *The Manila Times*, May 20, 1952. While Quirino's proposal was coolly received by Phibun, the Thai envoy's report was hotly applied by the Publicity Department. In addition, the Philippine government helped train Thai police experts on communism, for example, Police Colonel Chai Suwannasorn, who attended a three-month course on communism in the Philippines. See Brailey, *Thailand*, 173; Chiab, *Mahawitthayalai*, 524 *ff.*; Thongbai, *Khommunit ladyao*, 265 n. 1; Thongchai, "Latthi khommunit," 280, 324–26, 381–86.

81 *Mahachon* 129 (May 2, 1948); "Panha si jangwad phaktai" [The problem of the four southern provinces], *Mahachon* 130 (May 9, 1948);

Mahachon 147 (September 5, 1948); Seriniyom, "Ja prab khommunit pheua khrai?" [For whom is the suppression of communists?], *Karnmuang* 5, no. 19 (December 4, 1948): 2; Wyatt, *Thailand*, 268; and Brailey, *Thailand*, 172–73, according to whom, "Britain agreed to supply military aid to equip eight Thai army battalions, and make available to the Thai her jungle warfare training facilities in Malaya."

82 Saifa (Atsani Phonlajan), "Pheua santiphap, Pour la paix, For Peace," *Karnmuang* 6, no. 46 (June 10, 1950): 17.

83 See an interview given by Colonel M.L. Khab Kunchorn, secretary of the Prime Minister's Office, on March 16, 1950, in *Karnmuang* 6, no. 40 (April 29, 1950): 17.

84 Wiwat, "Kabot santiphap," 91–92.

85 Brailey, *Thailand*, 173. Needless to say, these restrictions brought in their wake severe chaos, hardship, and dislocation. In addition, many Vietnamese were arrested and deported to Vietnam for dubious and unwarranted charges such as displaying a picture of Ho Chi Minh. See several letters expressing grievances against the Thai government from some Vietnamese published in *Karnmuang* [8], no. 2 (January 20, 1951): 4; [8], no. 3 (January 27, 1951): 4, 22; and [8], no. 18 (May 19, 1951): 4, 9, 25.

86 Goscha, *Thailand and the Southeast Asian Networks*, 326–28; Wiwat, "Kabot santiphap," 91–92. This led subsequently to the exchange of anti-communist intelligence and information between the Thai government and its Vietnamese counterpart, for example, the Vietnamese foreign secretary's report on methods of communist aggression in Europe and Asia was sent to Prime Minister Phibun in August 1950. Thongchai, "Latthi khommunit," 269 n. 1, 281–82.

87 Saifa (Atsani Phonlajan), "Pheua santiphap, Pour la paix, For Peace," *Karnmuang* 6, no. 44 (May 27, 1950): 18; "Kansaeksaeng indojin ja nam prathet thai pai soo mahantaphai" [Intervention in Indochina will lead Thailand to disaster], *Karnmuang* [8], no. 2 (January 20, 1951): 3, 20.

88 Wiwat, "Kabot santiphap," 93–94. Thailand was proudly the first Asian state to respond to the U.N.'s call to arms in Korea.

89 Chaired by Prince Wan Waithayakon Worawan (the foreign minister and royal pundit who had chaired the parliamentary's special commission to investigate Pridi in 1933/34), this Committee's members were Air Chief Marshal Feun Ronnaphakas Ritthakhani (air force commander-in-chief and minister of communications), Admiral Luang Yutthasatkosol (naval commander-in-chief and minister of co-operatives), Police General Phao Sriyanond (police director general and deputy minister of the interior),

General Sarit Thanarat (deputy army commander-in-chief and deputy minister of defence), General Dej Dejpradiyut (deputy minister of the interior), Lieutenant General Prayoon Phamornmontri (deputy minister of finance), and Major General M.L. Khab Kunchorn (director general of the Public Relations Department). See Thongchai, "Latthi khommunit," 384.

90 Brailey, *Thailand*, 169 *ff.*

91 "Kongtek" is the Teochiu word for a Chinese Buddhist funeral ceremony in which fake banknotes and all kinds of fanciful merchandise made of paper are burnt as sacrifices to the dead. The baht notes issued by the Thai Ministry of Finance during the war were so called by the public because of the poor quality of the paper. Prasert, *Ratthasapha*, 426; Phraya Sriwisarnwaja, "Kanphim thonnabat" [The printing of banknotes], *Karnmuang* 2, no. 35 (October 4, 1946): 21.

92 During the four-year period of Thailand's direct involvement in the Second World War (1942–1945), government budget deficits rose steadily and totaled over 512 million baht. Prasert, *Ratthasapha*, 389, 417, 430, 458.

93 Between 1941 and 1945, Thailand loaned Japan more than 1.2 billion baht. Thak Chaloemtiarana, *Thailand: The Politics of Despotic Paternalism* (Bangkok: Social Science Association of Thailand and the Thai Khadi Research Institute, Thammasat University, 1979), 18.

At the end of the war, provisions for the remaining one hundred thousand plus Japanese soldiers pushed the inflationary spiral even higher. United States, American Legation, Bangkok, "The Political Situation in Siam," November 21, 1945, NADD, Washington, D.C., 4.

94 The war had greatly reduced Thailand's capacity for production and much physical capital (e.g., productive equipment, bridges, transport facilities, power generation capacity) was destroyed. Restrictions placed on the country's major exports (rice, rubber, tin, teak) by the Anglo-Siamese Treaty of 1946 and the resultant low foreign exchange earnings further delayed its replacement. The problem was tragically reflected in a train derailment in Kanchanaburi on February 1, 1947, which took the life of M.L. Kri Dejchatwong, minister of communications. See Prachoom, "Thailand," 129, 131–34; Thanet Aphornsuvan, "The United States and the Coming of the Coup of 1947 in Siam," *Journal of the Siam Society* 75 (1987): 201, 212–13 n. 57; and Prasert, *Ratthasapha*, 565–66.

95 Such basic necessities as cloth, matches, soap, etc. had been in short supply since the war. See Prachoom, "Thailand," 130–31, 134; Thanet, "United States," 201; Phimphawal, *Chiwaprawat so*, 232–34; Fongjan Thaleya (Wimol Phonlajan), "Phak tam: Khwamngam khong chiwit"

[Appendix: The beauty of life], Wimol Phonlajan, comp. *Ramleuk theung naiphi jak pa lom: Chuang chiwit lae phonngan thi pheung poed phoey pen khrang raek* [Auntie Lom's remembrance of Naiphi: Episodes in his life and some of his writings revealed for the first time], ed. Chuai Phulphoem (Bangkok: Dokya Press, 1990), 80; United States, American Legation, Bangkok, "Fortnightly Summary of Political Events in Siam for the Period July 15–July 30, 1946," NADD, Washington, D.C., 4.

96 These included the prices of rice, pork, and rent. See Prasit na Phatthalung, "Khwamonlaweng nai thuk wanni" [The present turmoil], *Karnmuang* 2, no. 7 (March 22, 1946): 2, 17–18; "Siangthok jak prachachon" [People's voices], *Karnmuang* 3, no. 5 (January 24, 1947): 5–6; "Siangthok jak prachachon" [People's voices], *Karnmuang* 3, no. 19 (May 2, 1947); Thongchai, "Latthi khommunit," 245 n. 1.

97 Prachaniyom, "Jodmai poed phaneuk" [Open letter], *Karnmuang* 2, no. 13 (May 3, 1946): 5, 11, 17–18.

98 Prasit, "Khwamonlaweng," *Karnmuang* 2, no. 7 (March 22, 1946): 2, 17–18.

99 United States, American Legation, Bangkok, "The Political Situation in Siam," 4.

100 The annual growth rate of the Thai population from 1937 to 1947 was about 2 percent, while growth of rice output in the same period fluctuated between negative 1.37 and 1.4 percent, though it jumped to 18.5 percent in the final year. Prachoom, "Thailand," 131, 144.

101 This was the case when big floods destroyed 34.2 percent of planted areas in 1942 and 24.9 percent in 1945. Rice output also declined in 1949 and 1950 for unspecified reasons. Wiwat, "Kabot santiphap," 56; Prachoom, "Thailand," 130–131.

102 The rice delivery was part of the price Thailand paid to buy herself out of the state of war with Great Britain and India, according to the Anglo-Siamese Treaty concluded in January 1946. See Thak, *Thailand*, 16 n. 39.

103 The Anglo-Siamese Treaty of 1946 prohibited unauthorized exports of rice, tin, rubber, and teak to ensure adequate supplies of these key products for the British (Thanet, "United States," 212–13 n. 57). But given that the world price for Thai rice was many times the domestic price, there was no lack of smugglers, who supplied the hungry world in connivance with underpaid government officials. (In 1946, the domestic price of rice was thirty pounds sterling/long ton. The fixed price of rice delivered to the British was twelve pounds, fourteen shillings/long ton in May, raised to twenty pounds/long ton in December. The price of rice

in neighboring Malaya ranged from 200 to 500 pounds/ton.) According to one informed estimate, smuggled rice in 1946 and 1947 at least equaled or even exceeded official deliveries to the British under the rice agreement. Prachoom, "Thailand," 132; Thak, *Thailand*, 16 n. 39, 17.

104 Consumer prices rose from 1.33–1.66 baht/bin (twenty liters) in 1941 to 10–12 baht under Japanese occupation, to 19–20 baht in early 1946, to 28–31 baht in 1947. Prasit, "Khwam onlaweng," *Karnmuang* 2, no. 7 (March 22, 1946), 2, 17–18; Thongchai, "Latthi khommunit," 245 n. 1.

105 Chiab, *Mahawitthayalai*, 519–524; *Karnmuang* 2, no. 31 (September 6, 1946): 5–6.

106 *Karnmuang* 2, no. 31 (September 6, 1946): 5–6; Nai Saduak, "Jodmai poed phaneuk" [Open letter], *Karnmuang* 3, no. 3 (January 10, 1947): 7–8.

107 *Karnmuang* 2, no. 41 (November 15, 1946): 7; Thak, *Thailand*, 18. The second time this happened was in the early 1970s, not long before the mass uprising of October 1973. See David Morell and Chai-anan Samudavanija, *Political Conflict in Thailand: Reform, Reaction, Revolution* (Cambridge, Massachusetts: Oelgeschlager, Gunn and Hain, 1982), 146.

108 Thak, *Thailand*, 20–21.

109 Thailand, Department of Fine Arts, Ministry of Education, *Prawat nakkhian thai lem neung* [Profiles of Thai writers, vol.1] (Bangkok: Department of Fine Arts, Ministry of Education, 1981), 116–17; United States, American Embassy, Bangkok, "The Free Thais: A Chronology," August 27, 1947, NADD, Washington, D.C., 4, 6.

110 United States, American Legation, Bangkok, "The Political Situation in Siam," 3.

111 Quoted in Thak, *Thailand*, 20 n. 54.

112 See Prachaniyom, "Jodmai poed phaneuk" [Open letter], *Karnmuang* 2, no. 13 (May 3, 1946): 5, 11, 17–18; Mahothorn, "Riview kanseuksa" [Review of education], *Karnmuang* 3, no. 1 (January 1, 1947): 13–14. It was during these needy days that Atsani Phonlajan, then a third-grade government prosecutor in the provinces of Saraburi and Ayutthaya, earning 700 baht per month, had to sell his brand-new graduation ceremonial gown and allow his wife to engage in small trade and handicraft to support their new-born daughter. He became less troubled financially only with the extra income he got from his radical writings. Fongjan, "Khwamngam khong chiwit," 84–88, 90.

113 Natthawut Sutthisongkhram, "Latthi prachathan" [Popular justice], *Karnmuang* 3, no. 17 (April 18, 1947): 3–4, 20. A similar opinion was expressed by Kenneth Landon, American political adviser to the U.S.

legation in Bangkok, who referred to "the development of corruption throughout the nation among all classes of people." See United States, American Legation, Bangkok, "The Political Situation in Siam," 3.

114 Thanet, "United States," 198–99. Otherwise known as "Thai bureaucratic capitalism," it was meticulously researched in Sungsidh, chapter 3 and 4 of *Thunniyom khunnang*.

115 According to Landon's report, "The revolutionary [People's Party] leaders almost without exception have engaged in large scale graft and theft and have made themselves wealthy according to local standards. The lower officials tended to copy the examples of their superiors. Corruption is so usual that it is referred to as a commonplace thing." United States, American Legation, Bangkok, "The Political Situation in Siam," 3.

116 Montri, "Khwamwadphawa thang kanmeuang" [Political alarm], *Karnmuang* 3, no. 13 (March 21, 1947): 2, 8. That would be equivalent to roughly 60.45 million dollars or fifteen million pounds sterling. The rate of foreign currency exchange in 1946 was 40 baht per pound sterling and 9.925 baht per dollar. It changed to 35 baht per pound and 12.50 baht per dollar in 1949. Prachoom, "Thailand," 135, 137.

117 In the decade that followed, the United States would spend 6.13 times that amount in dollars (7.72 times in baht) to buy an anti-communist foreign and domestic policy from the Phibunsongkhram government in the form of lavish military aid ($222 million) and economic aid ($149 million). Wyatt, *Thailand*, 272.

118 Prasit, "Khwam onlaweng," *Karnmuang* 2, no. 7 (March 22, 1946): 2, 17–18. Also see Phetai Chotnuchit, "Rob pi haeng thurayuk" [The year of calamity], *Karnmuang* 3, no. 1 (January 1, 1947): 6; and Wijaranayan, "Moonthan khong khorrupchan" [The roots of corruption], *Karnmuang* 3, no. 11 (March 7, 1947): 3–4, 26.

Chapter 5

1 *The Politician and Other Stories*, trans. Domnern Garden (Singapore: Oxford University Press, 1973), 2.

2 "Uttarakuru thaweep [The land of Uttarakuru]," *Karnmuang* 5, no. 4 (August 21, 1948): 14.

3 Inflation declined, while the output and export of major export commodities climbed. The trade and current account balances changed from negative to positive, and gold and foreign exchange reserves grew. The manufacturing sector was expanding and transportation networks

were being repaired with western help. Thanet, "United States," 206; Prachoom, "Thailand," 129–36, 137–38.

4 See Anderson, "Studies," 225–26; and Thak's study of the Sarit regime in his *Thailand: The Politics of Despotic Paternalism.*

5 This is both an elaboration and slight variation of Thak's precise characterization of this period, in which, according to Thak, force became the "common currency" in Thai politics and constitutionalism declined as a source of political legitimacy. Thak, *Thailand*, 57.

6 See the detailed account and superb analysis of this intricate political process in Sornsak, chapter 4 of *Khabuankan serithai.*

7 See Benedict Anderson's "black comedy" article on Thai political murder, "Murder and Progress in Modern Siam," *New Left Review* 181 (May–June 1990): 33–48. The relevant discussion is on page 36.

8 *Karnmuang* 5, no. 22 (December 25, 1948): 1.

9 Prasert, *Ratthasapha*, 381–82, 464–65; Pridi Banomyong, *Chiwaprawat yo khong nai pridi banomyong (Jon theung 24 karakadakhom 2525)* [A short biography of Mr. Pridi Banomyong up to July 24, 1982] (Bangkok: Khrongkan Pridi Banomyong Kab Sangkhom Thai, 1983), 27–49; Pridi, "Prawat pramot," 46–77; Vichitvong, *Pridi*, 177–224; United States Department of State, Division of Southwest Pacific Affairs, "Annex D: Thailand, Controls during and after Liberation"; "Annex E: Thai Resistance"; "Annex F: Thai Declaration of War against Japan," June 7, 1945, NADD, Washington, D.C.

　　The figure of eight thousand results from Sornsak's impressively meticulous critique of previous exaggerated counts of the Free Thai force and his own conservative reasonable re-count. By way of comparison, in 1945, the Thai Army numbered 32,082 from the NCO rank upwards. Sornsak, Khabuankan serithai, 9–13, 255.

10 These Free Thai displays were mostly intended for Allied consumption to attest to the Movement's anti-Japanese efforts and war readiness. Prasert, *Ratthasapha*, 478; Sornsak, *Khabuankan serithai*, 258–59; United States, American Embassy, Bangkok, "The Free Thais: A Chronology," 1.

11 Prasert, *Ratthasapha*, 478–80; United States, American Embassy, Bangkok, "The Free Thais: A Chronology," 1, 5–8.

12 Founded after the war by different groups of Pridi's followers, both the liberal Naeo Ratthathammanoon (Constitutional Front) Party and the social democratic Sahachip (Unionist) Party supported the leadership of Pridi. The Naeo Ratthathammanoon Party was composed mainly of People's Party's old guard and Thammasat liberals, while the Sahachip Party backbone was the Isan MPs and a few socialist intellectuals.

Together, they won the 1946 general elections and by-elections and formed a series of loose coalition governments under Prime Minister Pridi and Thawan from 1946 to 1947. However, due to both policy and personal differences, the conflict between and within the two ruling coalition parties became progressively open and so serious that the coalition and the two parties themselves were often on the verge of breaking apart. Although the Naeo Ratthathammanoon Party was more notorious for corruption, the Sahachip Party had its fair share of scandals, being accused by the opposition of using the government-owned sugar factory at Lampang as the party's financial reserve. See United States, American Legation, Bangkok, "Appendix: Brief Guide to Political Parties in Siam," [n.d.], NADD, Washington, D.C., 7; United States, American Embassy, Bangkok, "The Sahacheep Party: A Chronology," passim.

13 These people were Thongin Phooriphat, Tiang Sirikhan, Jamlong Daoreuang, Thongpleo Chonlaphoom, Thawin Udon, Tai Panikabut, Thawi Tawethikul, Rear Admiral Luang Sangwornyutthakij, Luang Bannakornkowit, and Louis Banomyong (Pridi's brother). The banks were the Bank of Asia and Bank of Ayudhya. After the 1947 coup, their accounts were briefly frozen by the Coup Group. Prasert, *Ratthasapha*, 514; United States, American Embassy, Bangkok, "The Free Thais: A Chronology," 1–3; United States, American Embassy, Bangkok, "Outline of Events: Coup D' Etat November 9, 1947," [n.d.], NADD, Washington, D.C., V, VII.

14 United States Department of State, "Annex E: Thai Resistance," 2–5.

15 Chiab, *Mahawitthayalai*, 561–64.

16 United States, American Embassy, Bangkok, "Fortnightly Summary of Political Events in Siam for the Period August 1–August 15, 1947," August 27, 1947, NADD, Washington, D.C., 2.

17 The University was also designated as the emergency meeting place of the Thawan cabinet in case of coup d'état. Chiab, *Mahawitthayalai*, 548; United States, American Embassy, Bangkok, "The Free Thais: A Chronology," 7.

18 The commander of military police at the time was Rear Admiral Sangwornyutthakij (Sangworn Suwannachip), a top Free Thai leader in the navy, who was concurrently director general of police and customs as well. United States, American Embassy, Bangkok, "The Free Thais: A Chronology," 8.

19 The keeper of Free Thai weapons there was Police Captain Chiab Chaisong, a former Free Thai who was also known as the Free Thai "Clandestine Arsenal." Chiab, *Mahawitthayalai*, 537–38.

20 Such as Tiang Sirikhan, Thongin Phooriphat, Thong Kanthatham, and Chan Bunnag. See Chiab, *Mahawitthayalai*, 561–64; Sornsak, *Khabuankan serithai*, 259–60; Suthachai, "Kankhleuanwai," 94–95, 140; United States, American Embassy, Bangkok, "Coup D' Etat November 9, 1947," II, VII, XIII.

21 Pridi also tried to explain why the Free Thai Movement had not yet been disbanded nor its weapons catalogued and collected, but his arguments were winding, circular, and unconvincing. Sornsak, *Khabuankan serithai*, 244–46.

22 United States, American Embassy, Bangkok, "The Free Thais: A Chronology," 8.

23 United States, American Embassy, Bangkok, "Coup D' Etat November 9, 1947," II, VII, VIII, X, XII; Chan, interview, February 5, 1989; Prathip Saisen, *Kabot wangluang kab sathana khong pridi banomyong* [The Royal Palace Rebellion and Pridi Banomyong's status] (Bangkok: Aksornsarn Press and Santiprachatham Institute, 1989), 62–127; Sornsak, *Khabuankan serithai*, 290–324.

24 The term "civilian Free Thai governments" here means those Pridi-controlled, Free Thai-dominated, civilian governments that came to power during the little over three-year period from July 24, 1944 (when Prime Minister Field Marshal Phibunsongkhram resigned from office due to Free Thai-maneuvered defeats of two government-sponsored bills in the National Assembly) to November 8, 1947 (when the army Coup Group, led nominally by Phibun, seized power). It thus includes the first Khuang Aphaiwong government (August 1, 1944–August 17, 1945), the Thawi Bunyaket government (August 31–September 17, 1945), the M.R. Seni Pramoj government (September 17, 1945–January 31, 1946), the Pridi Banomyong government (March 24–August 21, 1946), and the Thawan Thamrongnawasawat government (August 23, 1946–November 8, 1947), and excludes the short-lived, anti-Pridi, anti-Free Thai, civilian Prachathipat government of Prime Minister Khuang Aphaiwong (January 31–March 18, 1946).

25 Rangsan Thanapornpun, *Krabuankan kamnod nayobai setthakij nai prathet thai: Botwikhrao choeng prawattisat setthakij kanmeuang Pho.So. 2475–2530* [The process of economic policy formation in Thailand: A historical analysis of political economy, B.E. 2475–2530] (Bangkok: Social Science Association of Thailand, 1989), 60, 63, 66; Saneh Chamarik, *Kanmeuang thai kab phatthanakan ratthathammanoon* [Thai politics and constitutional development], Phatthanakan sitthi manussayachon nai prathet thai [Development of human rights in thailand] Research Series

(Bangkok: Thai Khadi Research Institute, Thammasat University, and the
Social Sciences and Humanities Textbooks Project Foundation, 1986),
212–13; Sornsak, *Khabuankan serithai*, 254; Thak, *Thailand*, 27.

26 *Karnmuang* 2, no. 13 (May 3, 1946): 15.

27 Sornsak, *Khabuankan serithai*, 259.

28 Quoted in Sornsak, *Khabuankan serithai*, 254–56.

29 There were some vague echoes of it in the Pridi-Thawan governments'
   stated military policy that the armed forces belonged exclusively to the
   nation, that military administration and regulations would be adjusted in
   accord with the democratic system of government, and that military
   affairs would be adapted to the status and living conditions of the country.
   Prasert, *Ratthasapha*, 440, 471–72, 476–78, 507, 537, 552, 571–72.
   Government expenses went from 1.16 billion baht in 1946 to 0.96 billion
   baht the following year. Prasert, *Ratthasapha*, 491, 565.

30 Suthachai, "Kankhleuanwai," 55.

31 Thirteen hundred discharged junior army officers were retrained and
   reemployed in the Customs, Police, Co-operative, Penitentiary, and
   Revenue Departments and in the Food Organization. United States,
   American Embassy, Bangkok, "The Free Thais: A Chronology," August
   27, 1947, 3–6.

32 Suthachai, "Kankhleuanwai," 56–57; Thak, *Thailand*, 24–27. See a letter
   of complaint about the miserable, demoralized, undisciplined, and
   lawless life in an army unit in Phi, "Jodmai poed phaneuk" [Open letter],
   Karnmuang 2, no. 7 (March 22, 1946): 5–6, 19–20.

33 Suthachai, "Kankhleuanwai," 57.

34 Thao Phanta, "Siangthok jak prachachon" [People's voices], *Karnmuang*
   2, no. 35 (October 4, 1946): 18. See a similar comment by an army
   general quoted in Thak, *Thailand*, 28.

35 Sornsak, *Khabuankan serithai*, 164–66, 256, 261; United States,
   American Legation, Bangkok, "Fortnightly Summary of Political Events
   in Siam for the Period July 15–July 30, 1946," 6.

36 Sornsak, *Khabuankan serithai*, 255–58; Suthachai, "Kankhleuanwai,"
   57–58; Thak, *Thailand*, 27–28; "Siangthok jak prachachon" [People's
   voices], *Karnmuang* 3, no. 5 (January 24, 1947): 5–6.

37 Quoted in Suthachai, "Kankhleuanwai," 58.

38 Quoted in Suthachai, "Kankhleuanwai," 82–83.

39 Quoted in Sornsak, *Khabuankan serithai*, 255–56, 264–65; and Thak,
   Thailand, 28. I have slightly altered Thak's translation.

40 The Prachathipat (Democrat) Party was the main opposition party of the
   post-war decade. Founded in early 1946, it was a heterogeneous group

of royalty, disgruntled members of the People's Party, old-time aristocrats, ex-political prisoners, conservative MPs, and some bourgeoisie and radicals, united initially by their common opposition to the Pridi/Free Thai/People's Party regime. Basically representing Bangkok upper class interests, the party was staunchly anti-communist. It had a conservative royalist leadership and a platform favoring a monarchy-dominated constitutional regime (purportedly *à la* Britain) and a *laissez-faire* economy. It managed to rule briefly twice, from January 31 to March 18, 1946, and from November 10, 1947, to April 8, 1948. Thereafter, it became the main parliamentary opposition to Phibun's military regime. Sornsak, *Khabuankan serithai*, 207–54; Suthachai, "Kankhleuanwai," 183–97; United States, American Legation, Bangkok, "Appendix: Brief Guide to Political Parties in Siam," 8.

41 Among those alleged or proven to have been involved in these anti-Pridi, anti-Free Thai smear campaigns were royal leaders of the British Section of the Free Thai Movement; Prince Phanuphanyukhol (royalist and anti-communist); Khuang Aphaiwong, M.R. Seni Pramoj, M.R. Kukrit Pramoj, Dr. Chote Khumphan, Liang Chaiyakal, Daeng Wongsuwan, Thongpan Wongsanga, and Prayoon Aphaiwong (all of the Prachathipat Party); Colonel Phraya Wichitsorasat and his second and fourth wives (Prachathipat-paid agitators); M.C. Chaloemsrijantharathat Jantharathat (senior senator); M.R. Nophakaeo Nawarat, Damri Patthamasiri, and Yodtham Bunbandal (pro-Prachathipat newspaper editors); Lieutenant General Phin Chunhawan and Lieutenant General Kat Katsongkhram (Coup Group); Yanyong Bunnag; Lieutenant General Prayoon Phamornmontri and Colonel Nitas Chiraprabati (Phibun group); Samai Reuangkrai (pro-Phibun newspaper editor); and Major Arkadej Bijayendrayothin (U.S.-educated, pro-American, anti-communist, republican army officer). Chiab, *Mahawitthayalai*, 473, 482–86; Prasert, *Ratthasapha*, 550; Pridi, *Chiwaprawat*, 71–94; Sornsak, *Khabuankan serithai*, 241–54, 284–89, 293–96; Suthachai, "Kankhleuanwai," 93–96; *Karnmuang* 2, no. 11 (April 19, 1946): 16–17; *Karnmuang* 2, no. 27 (August 9, 1946): 8, 18; "Siangthok jak prachachon" [People's voices], *Karnmuang* 3, no. 11 (March 7, 1947): 24; Seriniyom, "Khwamphanphuan nai wongkanmeuang" [Turmoil in the political cirlces], *Karnmuang* 3, no. 42 (October 11, 1947): 2; Thid Rung, "Reuang na anat" [Pitiful story], *Karnmuang* 5, no. 13 (October 23, 1947): 1; United States, American Legation, Bangkok, Letter dated 16 September 1945 from Major Arkadej Bijayendrayothin, enclosure in "The Political Situation in Siam," 1–3; United States, American Legation, Bangkok,

"Fortnightly Summary of Political Events in Siam for the Period July 31–
August 15, 1946," August 19, 1946, NADD, Washington, D.C., 2–3;
United States, American Embassy, Bangkok, "The Free Thais: A
Chronology," 6; United States, American Embassy, Bangkok, "Phya
Wichit Case: A Special Chronology," October 15–October 27, 1947,
NADD, Washington, D.C.; United States, American Embassy, Bangkok,
"Fortnightly Summary of Political Events in Siam for the Period
November 1–November 15, 1947," NADD, Washington, D.C., 5, 9;
United States, American Embassy, Bangkok, "Airgram A-357, August
18, 1949," August 31, 1949, NADD, Washington, D.C.; United States
Department of State, Office of Far Eastern Affairs, Division of Southeast
Asian Affairs, Memorandum of Conversation, "Siam," November 12,
1948, NADD, Washington, D.C.

42 Suthachai, "Kankhleuanwai," 60–61, 82–83; Sornsak, *Khabuankan
serithai*, 265.

43 Sornsak, *Khabuankan serithai*, 261.

44 Sornsak, *Khabuankan serithai*, 259.

45 In the words of Lieutenant Colonel Krit Punnakan, who, together with
one of his subordinates, Army Captain Chatchai Chunhawan, joined the
Coup Group. Sornsak, *Khabuankan serithai*, 265. See some accounts of
similar cases of army officers-turned-rebels in Sornsak, *Khabuankan
serithai*, 261, 263–66; Suthachai, "Kankhleuanwai," 66–76; Thak,
Thailand, 32–34.

46 Reportedly, Prime Minister Thawan's reputation was so bad that one
night, while riding a pedicab, he was cursed by its driver. "Siangthok jak
prachachon" [People's voices], *Karnmuang* 3, no. 3 (January 10, 1947):
5–6.

47 Badly upset by the harsh criticisms leveled at him, Prime Minister
Thawan complained sullenly: "Better be a dog than a prime minister
because, while a stray dog is not cursed by anyone, a prime minister is
cursed day and night." Having said that, he did not forget to warn those
prime minister-bashing newspapers to be careful or they might be closed
down. "Siangthok jak prachachon" [People's voices], *Karnmuang* 3, no.
13 (March 21, 1947): 7–8.

48 United States, American Embassy, Bangkok, "The Sahacheep Party: A
Chronology," passim; *Karnmuang* 3, no. 23 (May 31, 1947), 1; *Karnmuang*
3, no. 25 (June 14, 1947): 3; *Karnmuang* 3, no. 45 (November 1, 1947): 1, 2.

49 Reportedly, army commander-in-chief General Luang Adul Aduldejjaras
stated in a special cabinet meeting on July 3, 1947: "If the [Thawan]
government still behaves so badly, in case of a revolution or a coup right

now, I don't think I will suppress it for I don't want to let Thai soldiers or Thai people kill one another." Quoted in Sornsak, *Khabuankan serithai*, 229; and Thongchai, "Latthi khommunit," 248.

50 Attending the same meeting, navy commander-in-chief Admiral Sindh Kamolnawin was said to have concurred with Luang Adul. Sornsak, *Khabuankan serithai*, 229.

51 Both the commander-in-chief of the air force and his deputy cooperated with the Coup Group by barring provincial troops from coming to the aid of the Thawan government. Suthachai, "Kankhleuanwai," 77.

52 In response to the personal request of Police Captain Chiab of the Special Branch for permission to arrest the coup conspirators, Rear Admiral Luang Sangworn Suwannachip, the police chief and military police commander, said:

Why the arrest? They have even asked me to join in but I want to remain neutral. Just let them do it, we will not obstruct them...Mr. Chiab, you at the Special Branch already know well that people do not like the Luang Thamrong government, don't you? The press often curse its mother...Since the people already hate this worthless government, it isn't right for us to continue supporting it in office. You at the Special Branch must know inside out how much it "sengli." Better let it go. We have nothing to do with it because we are regular bureaucrats...I have already given a standing order that in case of seizure of power, the police...[and] military police are to stay put in their stations and barracks.

Quoted in Chiab, *Mahawitthayalai*, 557–60.

53 All of them except the air force commander-in-chief ultimately did try, belatedly and halfheartedly, to resist the Coup Group. But as Rear Admiral Luang Sangworn stated, "What are you going to fight [the coup] for? For the return of those hoe-spade-banknote-cloth-and-rice eaters to become masters over the people's heads again?" United States, American Embassy, Bangkok, "Coup D' Etat November 9, 1947," I; Chiab, *Mahawitthayalai*, 552–61; Sornsak, *Khabuankan serithai*, 229; Suthachai, "Kankhleuanwai," 76–80.

54 One could not miss the cynicism of Phibun's overnight flying of "a blue flag of convenience"; of all the marvelous qualities that had been known of this wartime Thai "Leader," devotion to the throne was not one. It was under his first premiership that the anti-People's Party, royalist opposition was ruthlessly crushed, the royalty in general treated much more sternly in political, legal, financial, and symbolic terms, and a personality cult built up around himself, above and beyond the monarchy.

Even such a senior member of the Chakri dynasty as Prince Rangsit, son of King Rama V, brother of King Rama VI and VII, and uncle of King Rama VIII, had been unprecedentedly and disgracefully deprived of his royal rank and status and imprisoned on trumped-up charges. Phayap, *Yuk thamil*, 20–22, 34–35, 54–55, 95–96, 101; Sornsak, *Khabuankan serithai*, 41–63.

55 Vadney, *The World since 1945*, 64; United States, American Embassy, Bangkok, "Fortnightly Summary of Political Events in Siam for the Period March 16–March 31, 1947," passim.

The prosecution of Phibun and his associates on war crimes charges was aimed primarily at wrecking Phibun's political reputation, influence, and career once and for all rather than at his legal punishment. Therefore, when the highest Thai court stopped the prosecution in April 1946 on the grounds that the War Crimes Act was retroactive and hence un-constitutional, the case was not pursued further. Sornsak, Khabuankan serithai, 257–58; Prasert, Ratthasapha, 513.

56 This graffiti made the headlines of the opposition newspaper *Seriphap* and was quoted in "Siangthok jak prachachon" [People's voices], *Karnmuang* 3, no. 5 (January 24, 1947): 5–6.

57 Sornsak, *Khabuankan serithai*, 262–64; United States, American Embassy, Bangkok, "Fortnightly Summary of Political Events in Siam for the Period March 16–March 31, 1947," passim; *Karnmuang* 3, no. 45 (November 1, 1947): 1.

58 Pho. Meuangchomphoo, *Soo samoraphoom*, 102; Sornsak, *Khabuankan serithai*, 269–70; United States, American Embassy, Bangkok, "Coup D' Etat November 9, 1947," II–III.

Actually, Phibun could well have become a member of the privy council after the 1947 coup but for the fact that Prince Rangsit, fully rehabilitated by Pridi since 1944 and then serving as regent to King Rama IX, absolutely refused to sit in the same council with his former captor. Prasert, Ratthasapha, 443–45; United States, American Embassy, Bangkok, "Fortnightly Summary of Political Events in Siam for the Period November 1–November 15, 1947," 7.

59 United States, American Embassy, Bangkok, "Fortnightly Summary of Political Events in Siam for the Period November 1–November 15, 1947," 6–10.

60 Only Police Colonel Banjongsak Chippensuk, a bold, honest, frank, and conscientious ex-Free Thai police officer, then commander of the Special Branch Police and a personal foe of Police Major General Phao Sriyanond, stuck his neck out by volunteering eight hundred policemen for resistance

at Premier Khuang's command, but to no avail. For his anti-Phao audacity on this and other occasions, he later paid with his life. Chit, *Phao saraphap*, 303–34; Sornsak, *Khabuankan serithai*, 270–77, 304, 312, 316; Suthachai, "Kankhleuanwai," 99–103; Thak, *Thailand*, 37–41, 85–86.

61 The two best general accounts of Thai politics in these two periods are Thak, part 1 of *Thailand*; and Suthachai, "Kankhleuanwai." However, the "triumvirate" portrayal of the latter period has been significantly supplemented and partially superseded by the more nuanced and complete picture of six different players, including the communist movement, involved in the complex and intricate political conflict of the time given by Somsak Jeamteerasakul in "The Communist Movement," 17–22.

62 Chan, interview, February 5, 1989; Sornsak, *Khabuankan serithai*, 298–99, 301–302; Suthachai, "Kankhleuanwai," 149, 156.

63 Naiphi's poems of this period were partly compiled and reprinted with some lexical and contextual exegeses in Naiphi (Atsani Phonlajan), *Kaapklon naiphi* [Naiphi's poems] (Bangkok: Aksornwatthana Press, 1958); Naiphi (Atsani Phonlajan), "Khloong-chand khong 'naiphi'" [Naiphi's *khloong* and *chand*], *Ramleuk* 17–76; and Suchira, chapter 4 and appendix of "Wikhrao roikrong naiphi."

For Thaweepvorn's poems, see his recently published anthology: Thaweepvorn (Thaweep Voradilok), *Jong pen athit meua uthai: Ruam kawiniphon nai rob si thossawas* [Be the sun at dawn: Collected poems of four decades] (Bangkok: Anthai Press, 1989), 61; and Thaweep, interview, December 27, 1988.

64 It is not clear how the Phahon government (1933–1938) should be classified. As head of the army faction of the People's Party, Prime Minister Phahon himself was generally regarded with favor as a sincerely democratic military leader (dubbed "Jaopho Haeng Rabob Prachathipatai" or Godfather of Democracy by one commentator) and a selfless and honest "Elder Statesman" with no personal political ambition. Natthawut Sutthisongkhram, "Pholek phraya phahonphonphayuhasena: Chesthaburus awuso phoo sathapana rabob prachathipatai khong thai" [General Phraya Phahonphonphayuhasena: Elder statesman who founded Thai democracy], *Karnmuang* 3, no. 9 (February 21, 1947): 7–8, 10. Judging from its political record, his government could be considered a mildly authoritarian constitutional regime.

65 Montri, "Phadejkan rob thi song" [Second round of dictatorship], *Karnmuang* 5, no. 5 (August 28, 1948): 2; Seriniyom, "Adit lae pajjuban" [Past and present], *Karnmuang* 5, no. 15 (November 6, 1948): 2.

66 This took place at Sanam Luang, a large open ground in the middle of
    Bangkok and regular site of political demonstrations, during an anti-Phibun
    rally organized by the Sahachip Party and a group of TCP-affiliated
    Thammasat students on April 7, 1947. Phibun was portrayed in full army
    uniform, holding an officer baton and trampling on a pile of soldiers' skulls
    with his military boots. Kittisak, *Prachathipatai*, 38–39.
67 Peter Sally, "Phibun kab tojo" [Phibun and Tojo], *Karnmuang* 5, no. 19
    (December 4, 1948): 3, 13–15.
68 "Nayok khon mai" [The new prime minister], *Karnmuang* 3, no. 19 (May
    2, 1947): 2.
69 The author was Samak Burawas, an Anglo-educated philosopher-
    scientist, member of the Royal Institute, one-time politician, and
    Marxist-to-be, who also declared himself an "anti-nationalist" and (rather
    imprudently) dared any future dictator not to forget him. See Samak
    Burawas, "Mahaamnaj—chat thai" [Thai nation—a great power],
    Karnmuang 3, no. 19 (May 2, 1947): 3–4, 20.
70 Saifa (Atsani Phonlajan), "Thahan kab kanmeuang" [The military and
    politics], *Karnmuang* 4, no. 16 (April 17, 1948): 4, 14; Raelek, "Thahan
    kab kanmeuang" [The military and politics], *Karnmuang* 5, no. 20
    (December 11, 1948): 6, 14.
71 Intharayut (Atsani Phonlajan), "Thaksinottaraphakhi" [The south-north
    or rightist-leftist parties], *Karnmuang* 2, no. 13 (May 3, 1946): 12–14,
    20–22.
72 These and other democratic improvements in the 1946 Constitution
    resulted from a consensus reached by all anti-Phibun political groups and
    parties (except the TCP) in the preparatory process. However, there was
    a major disagreement on the scope of constitutional power to be assigned
    to the Senate. The Pridi/Free Thai group wanted it expanded while the
    Prachathipat Party wanted it restricted. The final outcome inclined
    towards the Pridi/Free Thai position, with the Senate empowered to
    control the administration of the country in principle and cast a vote of
    confidence or censure in favor of or against the incoming government.
    Saneh, *Kanmeuang thai*, 212–13; Sornsak, *Khabuankan serithai*, 213–
    20; Thak Chaloemtiarana, ed., *Thai Politics: Extracts and Documents,
    1932–1957* (Bangkok: The Social Science Association of Thailand,
    1978), 96–108, 504–23.
73 Quoted in Sornsak, *Khabuankan serithai*, 220–22.
74 "Sapha kab ratthathammanoon mai" [The parliament and the new
    constitution], *Karnmuang* 2, no. 4 (March 1, 1946): 2, 18; "Siangthok jak
    prachachon" [People's voices], *Karnmuang* 3, no. 15 (April 4, 1947): 23–

25; Prasit na Phatthalung, "Khwamyungyak khong meuang thai" [Thailand's chaos], *Karnmuang* 3, no. 15 (April 4, 1947): 7–8.

75 Yai Sawitchat, "Khwamhayana khong chat" [National disaster], *Karnmuang* 3, no. 17 (April 18, 1947): 2, 27.

76 Khuang Aphaiwong or Luang Kowitaphaiwong, a former senior civilian member of the People's Party and later head of the Prachathipat Party, fell out with Pridi over the latter's refusal to support his bid for premiership in 1946. Reportedly, Khuang had already changed his mind about the 1932 Revolution in 1938 when, during his official visit to Britain, the former King Prajadhipok granted him an audience and invited him to dinner. Thereafter, Khuang often muttered to his close friends and relatives: "We have been wrong and ought to give the power back to His Majesty." However, what should be borne in mind when reading this statement is that the "His Majesty" whom Khuang was referring to might not be King Prajadhipok, who had long since abdicated, but the teenaged King Ananda. Suthachai, "Kankhleuanwai," 186–87.

77 Based on the comments of M.R. Seni Pramoj, Prince Dhani, and Louis Girivat. The more imaginative ones belong to Seni, quoted in Sornsak, *Khabuankan serithai*, 117–18; Suthachai, "Kankhleuanwai," 188.

78 Sornsak, *Khabuankan serithai*, 112–20; Suthachai, "Kankhleuanwai," 184–85. The late King's British-based relatives were alleged by Major Arkadej Bijayendrayothin to have gone so far as to actually plan and campaign for a British-backed royalist coup and a restoration-type regime. Nonetheless, this information has not been confirmed by any other primary source. United States, American Legation, Bangkok, Letter dated 16 September 1945 from Major Arkadej Bijayendrayothin, 1–3.

79 Sornsak, *Khabuankan serithai*, 117–18, 200, 219–20; Suthachai, "Kankhleuanwai," 184–85, 188–89.

80 Quoted in Suthachai, "Kankhleuanwai," 188–89.

81 See, for example, a letter from Lieutenant Colonel M.C. Suphasawatwongsanit Sawatdiwat (the late King Rama VII's brother-in-law and head of the British Section of the Free Thai Movement) to Pridi Banomyong dated April 10, 1947, in which he deplored the disgraceful hardship of King Bhumibol and solicited the Thawan government through Pridi for more royal stipend, intelligence information, a renovated and comfortable palace, and a higher royal rank for the King's elder sister. Published in Sawai, *Dr. pridi*, 910–26.

82 The key link between the Coup Group and the Prachathipat Party was Leuan Phongsophon, Prachathipat MP for Nakhon Ratchasima and long-time acquaintance of Lieutenant General Phin Chunhawan. For this

crucial service, he was "rewarded" with a ministerial post by Phin. Apart from Leuan, the civilian wing of the Coup Group included Nai Worakanbancha (alias Bunkoed Sutantanon, a wealthy British-educated businessman, former page of King Vajiravudh, former elected MP for Chiang Rai, Colonel Phao Sriyanond's employer, the Coup Group's financier, and the head of its civilian wing) and Khemchat Bunyaratphan (former MP for Roi Et).

Chiab, Mahawitthayalai, 28–34; Sornsak, Khabuankan serithai, 271–76; Suthachai, "Kankhleuanwai," 71, 83–92; United States, American Embassy, Bangkok, "Fortnightly Summary of Political Events in Siam for the Period November 1–November 15, 1947," 5–7; United States, American Embassy, Bangkok, "Coup D' État November 9, 1947," III ff.

83 According to Group Commander Luang Kat Katsongkhram, the "Under Waterjar Constitution," so-called because it had been hidden under a red waterjar in his house to foil discovery, was gradually drafted by himself in consultation with Phraya Ladphlithamprakhal (alias Wong Ladphli, director general of the Supreme Court), Colonel Suwan Phenjan (commander of the Judge Advocate General Department), and Khemchat Bunyaratphan (former MP). A parliament-elected constituent assembly drafted the 1949 Constitution; its forty members consisted of twenty-two Prachathipat members, a dozen or so pro-Prachathipat old-time aristocrats, a handful of independent outsiders, and only a single Coup Group member. Suthachai, "Kankhleuanwai," 88, 189–91; Thak, *Thailand*, 34.

84 Thak, ed., *Thai Politics*, 524–41. The royalist nature of the 1947 Provisional Constitution reflected the Coup Group and Phibun's tactical compromise with the conservative Prachathipat Party rather than any genuine loyalty to the throne on their part, as their later behavior would clearly prove. Suthachai, "Kankhleuanwai," 83, 88–89; Thak, *Thailand*, 36.

85 The tally of the parliamentary vote in favor of the 1949 Constitution was eighty-four to three in the Senate, and forty-one to twenty-seven in the lower house. Suthachai, "Kankhleuanwai," 189–91, 194.

86 Thak, ed., *Thai Politics*, 822–84.

87 Deposed Prime Minister Thawan Thamrongnawasawat attacked it as being undemocratic and a "fall-back into the canal" (reactionary) since it created "many kings and many categories of MPs" and gave absolute power to the king, while Sanguan Tularak, then Siamese ambassador to the Republic of China, criticized it as effecting a change in principle from "the approval of the House of Representatives" to "the permission of the king." Quoted in Suthachai, "Kankhleuanwai," 143.

88 For instance, by Liang Chaiyakal, MP for Ubon Ratchathani and head of the pro-Phibun Prachachon Party (Suthachai, "Kankhleuanwai," 194), by the liberal press ("Amnaj kao kab amnaj mai" [Old versus new powers], *Karnmuang* 5, no. 26 [January 22, 1949]: 2, 19), and by the communists (At na Phrakhanong [Udom Sisuwan], "Ya phoe bok sala" [Don't say farewell yet], *Karnmuang* 5, no. 11 [October 9, 1948]: 4, 12).

89 By such Sahaphak members as Suwich Phanthuset (former MP), Feun Suphansan (Prachachon MP for Ayutthaya), and First Lieutenant Jongkol Krairoek (Sahaphak MP for Phitsanulok). Suthachai, "Kankhleuanwai," 192–94. And see Kornsit, "Wan ratthathammanoon" [The constitutional day], *Karnmuang* 5, no. 20 (December 11, 1948): 3, 15.

90 Pridi, *Pridi banomyong*, 382–83; Sornsak, *Khabuankan serithai*, 218–19.

91 Quoted in Suthachai, "Kankhleuanwai," 194, which actually should read: "We had better bar the royalty from playing politics and soldiering" (Article 11) and "Let's get rid of the Senate nuisance!" (Article 65).

92 While the total membership of the House of Representatives went up from ninety-nine in early 1949 to one hundred and twenty in June of the same year in accordance with the new constitution, the Prachathipat Party's seats in the House went down from forty-one or so in January 1949 to thirty-five in November 1950 and to twenty-eight in mid-1951. Prasert, *Ratthasapha*, 599–601, 644; Suthachai, "Kankhleuanwai," 194–95.

93 Among these one hundred senators were twelve royals and seventy-eight aristocrats (one Chaophraya, fifty-three Phraya's, fifteen Phra's, and nine Luang's), making this Senate a political bastion of conservative royalism. Prasert, *Ratthasapha*, 585–87; Suthachai, "Kankhleuanwai," 90–91.

94 Suthachai, "Kankhleuanwai," 194–97; Thak, *Thailand*, 58–64.

95 And also Pridi's second-best choice after the 1946 Constitution. He opted for it to replace the 1949 one in his abortive coup attempt in February 1949. Prasert, *Ratthasapha*, 704–24; Suthachai, "Kankhleuanwai," 152, 199–205; Thak, *Thailand*, 64–75.

96 Which provided for the "full liberty of...public meeting, association, formation of political parties..." The 1946 Constitution itself was abrogated by the Coup Group in November 1947. Thak, ed., *Thai Politics*, 506.

97 Which guaranteed the same liberty as in Article 14 of the 1946 Constitution but stated it in greater detail. The 1949 Constitution was abrogated by the reincarnated Coup Group in November 1951. Thak, ed., *Thai Politics*, 829.

98 This was the first such legislation in Thai history. It was abolished, together with the right to political assembly, by the Revolutionary Group

under Field Marshal Sarit Thanarat in October 1958. Thak, ed., *Thai Politics*, 880–84; Prasert, *Ratthasapha*, 804–805, 924.

99 Again, this was the first of its kind in Thailand, providing for the right of workers to set up trade unions. It was also abolished by Field Marshal Sarit after the 1958 coup. Kanya, "Prawat," 43–48.

100 The Thammasat Student Committee lasted until 1958. The Sarit Government replaced it the following year with a university administration-controlled "Club Committee" consisting of appointed lecturers and students. Charnvit et al., part 2 of *Prawat thammasat*, 50–55, and chapter 5 of part 3 of *Prawat thammasat*.

101 United States, American Legation, Bangkok, "Fortnightly Summary of Political Events in Siam for the Period July 15–July 30, 1946," 3–4.

102 For example, in an anti-imperialist rally at Sanam Luang on November 11, 1956, where allegedly Kuomintang-organized thugs attacked people; in a by-election rally of the opposition Sahaphoom Party in Samut Sakhon province in July 1957, where Sahaphoom members were attacked by a hoodlum and a local government official; and in a rally against a leftist student committee by rightwing students at Thammasat University on November 8, 1957. "Kannongleuad thi sanam luang" [Bloodshed at Sanam Luang], *Pituphoom* 1, no. 32 (November 19, 1956): 16–19; Kulap Saipradit, *Adit thi pen botrian* [Lessons from the past] (Bangkok: Saengthian Group, 1979), 68–75; Charnvit et al., part 2 of *Prawat thammasat*, 107–109.

103 For example, between supporters and opponents of Field Marshal Phibun in the anti-Phibun rally organized by the Sahachip Party and the communist-affiliated Student Group of Thailand at Sanam Luang on April 7, 1947; and between leftist and rightist students in a Thammasat Unity Day festival on November 5, 1957. Kittisak, *Prachathipatai*, 38–42; Charnvit et al., part 2 of *Prawat thammasat*, 102–104.

104 For example, in one of the weekly so-called Hyde Park public rallies at Sanam Luang in 1955 where an anti-police speaker was almost killed by a police sergeant. Kittisak, *Prachathipatai*, 56–57.

The Hyde Park public rallies were one of several "democratizing" pet measures initiated by Prime Minister Phibun after his return from a trip around the world from April 14 to June 22, 1955. Impressed by the exemplary free public speeches in London's Hyde Park, he promoted the same kind of democratic exercise at Sanam Luang in central Bangkok. The subsequently called Hyde Park forum at Sanam Luang every Saturday soon became extremely popular with the public both in and outside the capital as a channel for venting anti-government sentiments, slanders, and ridicule, which the Phibun group, the Phao group, the Prachathipat Party, and the communists all tried to manipulate. While the Hyde Park forum itself lasted only from August 1955 until February 1956, when its growing militancy caused the alarmed army and government to shut it down, its twenty or so regular speakers coalesced to form the populist Khabuankan Hyde Park (Hyde Park Movement) Party afterwards. Kittisak, Prachathipatai, 35–93; Suthachai, "Kankhleuanwai," 261, 269–71; Phin, interview, July 31, 1985.

105 For example, between rickshaw drivers and police in a protest rally by the former against anti-rickshaw traffic regulations on Jaroenkrung Road in 1949; and between marchers and mounted policemen in a protest march for democratic reform led by the Hyde Park group on Rajdamnoen Avenue on December 10, 1955. Damri and Jaroon, *Khabuankan*, 65–68; Suthachai, "Kankhleuanwai," 270.

106 Which happened at a police-staged Hyde Park rally to "launder" Police General Phao Sriyanond's alleged bloody linen in public at Sanam Luang on January 7, 1956, after something was thrown at the platform and someone shouted "grenade! grenade!" Kittisak, *Prachathipatai*, 72–91.

107 In an election rally for Thangai Suwannathat, an MP candidate of the opposition Prachathipat Party, in Thonburi on August 4, 1946. *Karnmuang* 2, no. 27 (August 9, 1946): 7–8.

108 *Karnmuang* 3, no. 45 (November 1, 1947): 1; Sornsak, *Khabuankan serithai*, 276; and Suthachai, "Kankhleuanwai," 102.

109 Kittisak, *Prachathipatai*, 37, 43–46.

110 Charnvit et al., part 2 of *Prawat thammasat*, 95–97; Mit, "Chiwaprawat jit," 38.

111 Suthachai, "Kankhleuanwai," 304. No wonder many people had an odd sense of *déja vu* on Wednesday, October 6th, nineteen years later.

112 Based on "VOPT Recounts CPT History," J-8–J-12.

113 The Bangkok Labor Union was founded on December 18, 1946, and at its peak had fifty-one affiliated labor organizations and thirty thousand members. The Central Labor Union, a well-staged culmination of the TCP's labor organizational drive, was founded on April 25–28 of the following year, with twenty-three affiliated local labor organizations and an alleged membership of 60,000 to 75,000 throughout the country. Damri and Jaroon, *Khabuankan*, 39–45; Kanya, "Prawat," 30–32; Sungsidh, *Prawat*, 153–54, 162–65.

The Student Group of Thailand was a TCP front organization of mostly radical Thammasat students. Mahachon 83 (April 13, 1947).

The Thai Youth Organization was probably a forerunner of the TCP-affiliated People's Democratic Youth League of Thailand; it was headed by Ruam Wongphan, a Thammasat student. Mahachon 104 (September 7, 1947).

114 Largely formed and staffed by the TCP in April 1951, the Committee was chaired by Jaroen Seubsaeng, an MP for Pattani province, and included Thammathatto Bhikkhu (alias Phra Maha Dilok Suwannarat, progressive monk from Mahathat Temple) as vice-chairman, So. Chotephan (alias Corporal Roeng Mekphaiboon, TCP member) as secretary, Phethai Chotnuchit (ex-*Karnmuang* editor and MP for Thonburi), Samak Burawas (radical philosopher, scientist, and writer), and Kulap Saipradit (famous radical novelist and journalist). See *Karnmuang* [8], no. 16 (May 5, 1951): 3–4, 12, 16, 21–22, 25–28; Wiwat, "Kabot santiphap," 156–64.

115 Charnvit et al., part 2 of *Prawat thammasat*, 50–55, 57; Phin, interview, July 31, 1985.

116 Sungsidh, *Prawat*, 175–76.

117 Damri and Jaroon, *Khabuankan*, 136–53; Sungsidh, *Prawat*, 229–38.

118 "Phak naeoruam sangkhomniyom thalaengkan khadkhan kansomrob seato" [The Socialist United Front parties' statement against a SEATO military exercise], *Pituphoom* 1, no. 29 (October 29, 1956): 15, 43–44; "Phak klum sangkhomniyom tang naeoruam" [The socialist parties' bloc forms a united front], *Pituphoom* 2, no. 41 (January 21, 1957): 13.

119 Wilson, "Thailand," 95, 314–15 n. 116; "Prakas krasuang mahadthai reuang kanjodthabian phak kanmeuang setthakorn" [The proclamation of the Ministry of Interior on the registration of the Economist Party], *Rajkijjanubeksa* [Royal Thai government gazette] 72, no. 86 (November 8, 1955): 2689–96.

120 Wilson, "Thailand," 96, 315 n. 117; Suthachai, "Kankhleuanwai," 274.

121 Sungsidh, Prawat, 176–96; Wilson, "Thailand," 97, 315 n. 118; "Prakas krasuang mahadthai reuang kanjodthabian phak kanmeuang sangkhomniyom" [The proclamation of the Ministry of Interior on the registration of the Socialist Party], *Rajkijjanubeksa* [Royal Thai government gazette] 73, no. 25 (March 27, 1956): 1036–45.

122 Kittisak, *Prachathipatai*, 35–93; Phin, interview, July 31, 1985; Suthachai, "Kankhleuanwai," 261, 269–71; Wilson, "Thailand," 96–97; "Prakas krasuang mahadthai reuang kanjodthabian phak kanmeuang khabuankan hyde park" [The proclamation of the Ministry of Interior on the registration of the Hyde Park Movement Party], *Rajkijjanubeksa* [Royal Thai government gazette] 73, no. 30 (April 3, 1956): 1101–1106; "Prakas krasuang mahadthai reuang kanplianplaeng huana phak khabuankan hyde

park" [The proclamation of the Ministry of Interior on the change of the head of the Hyde Park Movement Party], *Rajkijjanubeksa* [Royal Thai government gazette] 73, no. 74 (September 18, 1956): 2658.

123 Chiab, "Bantheuk," 14–16; "Prakas krasuang mahadthai reuang kanjodthabian phak kanmeuang sri arya mettraya" [The proclamation of the Ministry of Interior on the registration of the Sri Arya Mettraya Party], *Rajkijjanubeksa* [Royal Thai government gazette] 74, no. 8 (January 22, 1957): 217–23.

124 Damri and Jaroon, *Khabuankan*, 130–34; Sungsidh, *Prawat*, 198–210; Wilson, "Thailand," 97–98, 314 n. 111; "Prakas krasuang mahadthai reuang kanjodthabian phak kanmeuang kammakorn" [The proclamation of the Ministry of Interior on the registration of the Worker Party], *Rajkijjanubeksa* [Royal Thai government gazette] 72, no. 86 (November 8, 1955): 2685–88.

125 Charnvit et al., part 2 of *Prawat thammasat*, 101; Wilson, "Thailand," 96.

126 Charnvit et al., part 2 of *Prawat thammasat*, 70–78, 94–112.

127 The main argument in this passage is derived from Antonio Gramsci's theory of intellectuals and education in Antonio Gramsci, *Selections from the Prison Notebooks of Antonio Gramsci*, ed. and trans., Quintin Hoare and Geoffrey Nowell Smith (New York: International Publishers, 1983), 3–43.

128 Phaithoon, *Rabob kanseuksa*, 3–31.

129 See relevant discussion of the dialectics of ideological subjection in Göran Therborn, *What Does the Ruling Class Do When It Rules?* (London: New Left Books, 1978).

130 Amnuaichai Patiphatphaophong, "Botbat khong nakseuksa to rabob prachathipatai" [The role of university students towards democracy], Editorial Board of the Journal of Political Economy, *Ha sib pi bon senthang prachathipatai Pho.So. 2475–2525* [Fifty years on the path of democracy, B.E. 2475–2525] (Bangkok: Social Research Institute, Chulalongkorn University, 1983), 57–58, 360–61, 371; Isaac Deutscher, "Marxism and the New Left," *Marxism in Our Time*, ed. Tamara Deutscher (Berkeley, California: The Ramparts Press, 1971), 71–73.

131 The account in this part is based on the path-breaking and meticulously researched history of Thammasat University by Charnvit et al., part 2 of *Prawat thammasat*.

132 Charnvit et al., part 2 of *Prawat thammasat*, 63, 78–93. Many Thammasat student activists had developed a close relationship with, or even worked as journalists for, various radical newspapers and magazines (e.g., Sanao Phanichjaroen, Thaweep Voradilok, and Ari Imsombat), thus making their connection with politics and the radical press even more direct and immediate.

133 Phin, interview, August 31, 1984.

134 See especially Mit, "Chiwaprawat jit"; Siriusa, "Ajan jit"; Charnvit et al.,
     part 2 of *Prawat thammasat*, 75–78, 107–108; Reynolds, *Thai Radical
     Discourse*, 29–32, 35.

135 Intharayut (Atsani Phonlajan), "Phak phanuak: Bantheuk khong
     'intharayut' kiaokab run khong issara amantakul" [Appendix:
     "Intharayut"'s memoir on Issara Amantakul's generation], in Sathian
     Janthimathorn, *Saithan wannakam pheua chiwit khong thai* [The current
     of Thai literature for life's sake] (Bangkok: Chaophraya Press, 1982),
     221–25; "Lakhorn haeng chiwit khong supha sirimanond" [Supha
     Sirimanond's circus of life], *Thanon Nangseu* 1, no. 4 (September, 1983):
     26; Sriburapha, *Lae pai khangna: Phak majchimwai*, 107; Yos
     Watcharasathian, *Kulap saipradit: Sriburapha thi khaphajao roojak*
     [Kulap Saipradit: the Sriburapha I knew] (Bangkok: Arts and Sciences
     Press, 1982), 33.

136 Uayporn Milindankura, chapters 3 through 5 of "Laksana khampraphan
     roikrong khong thai tangtae Pho.So. 2475 – 2501" [The characteristics
     of Thai poetical works from 1932–1958 A.D.] (master's thesis,
     Chulalongkorn University, 1976).

137 Reynolds, *Thai Radical Discourse*, 9–13, 149–61; Somkiat Wanthana,
     "'Sangkhom thai' nai manophap khong si nakkhid thai samai mai" ["Thai
     Society" in the conception of four modern Thai thinkers], *Jodmaikhao
     Sangkhomsat* 10, no. 4 (May–July 1988): 91–111.

138 Napaporn, chapters 1 and 2 of *Phatthanakan*.

139 Wijaranayan, "Ayudhya yos lom laeo?" [Has Ayudhya already fallen?],
     Karnmuang 3, no. 13 (March 21, 1947): 3–4, 25–27; Supha Sirimanond,
     interview by Craig J. Reynolds on his life and Jit Poumisak, Bangkok,
     October 17, 1979.

140 Trisilp Bunkhajorn, chapter 2 of *Phatthanakan seuksa khonkhwa lae wijai
     wannakhadi thai* [The development of Thai literary studies and research]
     (Bangkok: the Faculty of Arts, Chulalongkorn University, 1987).

141 From 1947 to 1957, Samak published twelve books and scores of articles
     on various branches of the natural sciences, Buddhism, Western
     philosophy, and intellectual history. *Anusorn Samak*, [17]–[25].

142 Sathian, *Saithan*, 247–334; Trisilp Bunkhajorn, chapter 4 of *Nawaniyai
     kab sangkhom thai (2475–2500)* [Novels and Thai society (B.E. 2475–
     2500)] (Bangkok: Sangsan Press, 1980).

143 Or. Udakorn (Udom Udakorn), *Teuk gross: Ruam reuangek* [Gross
     building: Collected best stories], ed. Suwit Wongwira (Bangkok: Anthai
     Press, 1988), 83–102.

144 The initial plight of Udom's main character closely resembles that of a real Pridi/Free Thai Thammasat M.E. graduate named Suphat Sukhonthaphirom. (For more details, see chapter 6.) Suphat Sukhonthaphirom, interview by Napaporn Ativanichayapong on Thai radical political economic thought in the 1950s, Bangkok, September 7, 1985.

145 "VOPT Recounts CPT History," J-9.

146 Several victims of police political murder were falsely accused of being "communists" by Phao's henchmen before being summarily executed. Chit, *Phao saraphap*, 250–63, 349.

        Phao's "Knights" were middle-ranking police officers—usually from the rank of captain to colonel—who did all kinds of illegal, dirty, and cruel jobs for Phao, including murder and drug smuggling. Phao symbolically rewarded each of them with a diamond ring, so they were sometimes referred to as "diamond-ringed knights."

147 See Table 5-2.

148 See Naiphi (Atsani Phonlajan), "Naiphi kheu khrai?" [Who is Naiphi?], *Siam Nikorn* (December 28, 1946); Intharayut (Atsani Phonlajan), "Kho mai na seuksa thang kanpraphan" [What should not be studied about literary composition], *Aksornsarn* 1, no. 5 (August 1949), 70–71; Naiphi (Atsani Phonlajan), "A Specter Is Haunting Siam? [*sic*]," *Siam Samai* 122 (September 18, 1949); Naiphi (Atsani Phonlajan), "A Specter's Confession [*sic*]," *Siam Samai* 141 (January 27, 1950); Phraya Sajjaphirom (Sruang Sriphen), *Thewakamnoed: Khao khwampenma khong puang thep thewada thanglai phromduai aphinihan khwamsaksit* [Theogenesis: The story of all gods and angels with their might and miracles] (Bangkok: Sermwitbannakhan, 1968), 1–28; Thaweep, interview, December 27, 1988; Chaiwat Satha-anand, "Thewawitthaya haeng wathakam: Tham khwamkhaojai amnaj haeng wathakam duai 'Narai Sib Pang'" [Theology of discourse: Understanding the power of discourse through "The ten incarnations of Vishnu"] (paper presented at the annual meeting of the Historical Association of Thailand, Chulalongkorn University, February 1990, mimeograph).

149 Sri-Intharayut (Atsani Phonlajan), "Uttarakuru thaweep" [The land of Uttarakuru], *Karnmuang* 5, no. 4 (August 21, 1948): 3, 11–14.

150 King Vajiravudh, *Uttarakuru*, 1–21.

151 Sri-Intharayut (Atsani Phonlajan), "Uttarakuru thaweep" [The land of Uttarakuru], *Karnmuang* 5, no. 4 (August 21, 1948): 3.

152 Ibid., 14.

153 Set's lecture was replete with economic neologisms and contained such outlandish (to rural ears) English terms and names as "production,"

"Stuart Mill," "Physiocrats," "wage fund," "Walker," and of course "Karl Marx." Or. Udakorn, *Teuk gross*, 83–87.

Chapter 6

1 Headline news, page 1 of the TCP's official weekly newspaper *Mahachon* 140 (July 18, 1948).
2 Quoted in *Siam Nikorn* 17 (January 19, 1952): 8. This is an extract from Phibun's testimony in the criminal trial of the defeated Manhattan Rebellion defendants in June–July 1951. Under the leadership of Lieutenant Commander Manas Jarupha and Group Commander Anond Puntharikapha, the Khana Koochat (National Liberation Party) audaciously abducted Prime Minister Phibun on the dredger *Manhattan* to force the resignation of the Coup Group government, only to discover that Phibun's lieutenants in the army and air force cared much more about the prime ministership than the dispensable prime minister. They proceeded to bomb the battleship *Sriayudhya*, where Phibun was being detained, to a wreck. In the fifty hours of fighting, sixty-nine soldiers and policemen and 118 civilians were killed, 431 wounded, and fifteen million baht worth of property destroyed, including two ships. To the dismay of many people on both sides, the prime minister miraculously survived. See a detailed account of the rebellion in Niyom, *Thahanreua kabot*.
3 Napaporn, *Phatthanakan*, 7.
 Professor J.F. Hutcheson was an English barrister-at-law who earned his doctorate in law from France. Having worked as a legal adviser to the Siamese Ministry of Justice prior to 1932, he accepted Pridi's invitation to become a lecturer in economic doctrines at Thammasat University in 1934 and, two years later, served as director of the University Student Settlement (student housing project). Said to be "a socialist" who helped advise Supha Sirimanond on his study of Marx's Capital, Hutcheson was dismissed from his teaching position and detained by the Phibunsongkhram government as an "enemy national" during World War II. He never resumed his teaching job and reportedly left Thailand for Britain after the war. Charnvit et al., part 1 of Prawat thammasat, 46; Sakkasem Hutakhom, "Tia hut" [Papa Hut], ed. Charnvit Kasetsiri, Thammasat ha sib pi [50 years of Thammasat] (Bangkok: Thammasat University, 1984), 350–63; Supha, interview, September 4, 1985.
 Dr. Thawi Tawethikul was Professor Hutcheson's teaching assistant and interpreter at Thammasat University in 1934. He later earned a

doctorate in law in France, worked as a diplomat, a pro-Pridi/Free Thai government minister, and private businessman. After taking part in the defeated Royal Palace Rebellion led by Pridi in February 1949, he was summarily shot dead by police. See J.F. Hutcheson and Thawi Tawethikul, Latthi setthakij [Economic doctrines] (Bangkok: Thammasat University Press, 1980), [4]–[6].

Dr. Uphai Phinthuyothin (1907–1991), an early supporter of Pridi Banomyong and the People's Party, earned his doctorate in law and economics from the Université de Grenoble in 1934. He lectured part-time on economic doctrines at Thammasat University for both undergraduate and graduate students from 1936 to 1951 when, due to his political association with Pridi and the Free Thai Movement, he was pressured into resigning by the Phibunsongkhram government. Uphai Phinthuyothin, interview by Suphaphorn Jaralphat, Nakharin Mektrairat, Sunthari Asawai, and Suvimol Roongcharoen on the history of Thammasat University, Bangkok, March 7, 1983.

4 See Hutcheson and Thawi, *Latthi setthakij*; Uphai, interview, March 7, 1983. Uphai said he divided his undergraduate course curriculum into two parts: non-socialist economic doctrines (first year) and socialist economic doctrines (second year). His two-volume textbooks were likewise organized.

5 In Dr. Uphai's assessment, the majority of his students, who numbered several thousand each year, failed to understand the economic doctrines he taught. This was especially true of those who resided in the provinces and had to rely almost exclusively on textbooks without the benefit of his lectures. The fifty to sixty students who fully comprehended his teachings were mostly Bangkokians who attended his lectures and question-answer sessions regularly. Uphai, interview, March 7, 1983.

6 Kulap's first writing on Marxism, it showed that his interest in the doctrine predated his study in Australia (1947–1949). The translation was published after his return from Australia as "Thrissadi song prakan khong karl marx: Latthi sochalist lae latthi collectivist" [Karl Marx's two-part theory: Socialism and collectivism], *Aksornsarn* 1, no. 7 (October 1949): 57–65; and "Kho sanoe lae nayobai khong sochalist collectivist" [The socialist-collectivist proposals and policies], *Aksornsarn* 1, no. 9 (December 1949): 62–69.

7 Passing over his strong Thai accent, one heard: "De chacun selon ses capacités, à chacun selon son travail!" and "De chacun selon ses capacités, à chacun selon ses besoins!" Suphat, interview, September 7, 1985.

8 See, for instance, one of Udom Udakan's letters to Supha Sirimanond in
   Supha, *Jodmai*, 26; Wijaranayan, "Nehru," *Karnmuang* 3, no. 20 (May
   9, 1947): 9–12, 22–23; and Prasan (Udom Sisuwan), "Khai panha"
   [Answering the questions], *Pituphoom* 2, no. 69 (August 5, 1957): 33.

9 According to one of Charnvit Bannakhan's regular advertisements
   published in the TCP's *Mahachon*, the bookshop offered for retail or
   subscription the periodicals *New Times* and *Soviet Literature* in English,
   French, and Chinese editions. *Mahachon* 110 (October 19, 1947).

10 Supha, interview, September 4, 1985; Thaweep, interview, December 27,
   1988; Thaweep Voradilok, panel discussion on "Soviet Russian Literature"
   at Thammasat University, December 16, 1988; and Thaweep, "Supha," 35,
   45–46.

11 See, for example, a May Day book sale advertisement of Hua Chiao Book
   Store published in *Aksornsarn* 4, no. 2 (May 1952): 6. These interesting
   advertisements can be found in various issues of *Mahachon*, *Karnmuang
   Weekly*, *Aksornsarn*, *Pituphoom (La Patrie) Weekly*, and *Saithan Monthly
   Magazine*. For Nibondh, see Thaweep, "Supha," 35, 45–46.

12 Since the late 1940s, Nibondh has been patronized by a small group of
   leading, independent (i.e., non-TCP), English-reading-and-translating,
   radical intellectuals whose members include the late Supha Sirimanond,
   Sakchai Bamrungphong, and Thaweep Voradilok. For them, Nibondh
   became the main domestic placenta of alternative foreign leftist intellectual
   and informative nourishment under the subsequent censorship regime of
   military dictatorship in the 1960s and 1970s, providing them with such
   publications as the British *New Statesman*, Lenin's collected works,
   various Verso books, and other Marxist classics and contemporary
   writings. As a result, upon his death in 1986, Supha left behind the best
   and largest private collection of English-language Marxist books in
   Thailand, totaling over four thousand volumes, in the custody of the
   Faculty of Economics, Chulalongkorn University. Still, in an interview
   given not long before his death, Supha claimed that his own formidable
   collection of Marxist classics was "less complete" than that of Thaweep.
   Supha, interview, September 4, 1985; Thaweep, interview, December 27,
   1988; Thaweep, "Supha," 35, 45–46.

13 Some of its imported items, e.g., a white-covered, four-volume *Selected
   Works of Mao Tse-tung*, found its way into the private library of the young
   University of Fine Arts lecturer in English Jit Poumisak, who would
   become the most popular radical poet and Marxist historian in modern
   Thailand. Siriusa, "Ajan jit," 12.

14 Thailand, Department of Commercial Registration, Ministry of Commerce, "Dazhong Wenhua Company Limited" Registration Profile File no.1024. It should be noted that the company was generally known to the Thai public by the name "Ta Jong Un Fa," following its own dialectal Thai transliteration.

15 Skinner, *Chinese Society*, 251–52; Yanyong, "Prawat nangseuphim jin," 76.

16 The statute is contained in a booklet printed by the TCP-affiliated Uthai Printing House. A copy of it is kept in "Dazhong Wenhua Company Limited Registration" Profile File no.1024.

It is probable that one of the company's seven original founders and subsequently its managing director, Ngow Jekyim, might be Liao A-ngow (Ngow Sengchin or Ngo Diji), the veteran communist leader who taught Chinese to many Thai royalists in Bangkhwang Penitentiary before the Second World War. Liao A-ngow's profile is given in Chapter 3. My conjecture about Ngow Jekyim's identity is based on the affinity between his name and those of Liao A-ngow, despite different dialectal pronunciations, and on the account of Liao A-ngow's business activities after his release from Bangkhwang. See "Dazhong Wenhua Company Limited," Registration Profile File no.1024; and Leuan, Fan rai, 156.

17 Skinner, *Chinese Society*, 324, 332–33; and see, for instance, the detailed statement of the company's annual expenditures during the year 1950, included in "Dazhong Wenhua Company Limited," Registration Profile File no.1024.

18 Thaweep, discussion on "Soviet Russian Literature"; Wiwat, "Kabot santiphap," 184. Examples of Dazhong Wenhua's interesting book advertisements can be found in *Mahachon* 110 (October 19, 1947); *Karnmuang* [8], no. 7 (February 24, 1951); *Aksornsarn* 3, no. 1–12 (April 1951–March 1952). However, this kind of financial support was not substantial. According to the company's own accounts, its sales department paid only 3,480 baht for advertising expenses in 1950. "Dazhong Wenhua Company Limited," Registration Profile File no.1024.

19 It was Dazhong Wenhua that linked Supha Sirimanond, the editor of *Aksornsarn*, with Sanan Waraphreug, who would be the magazine's key translator from Chinese. Chinda Sirimanond, interview by the author and Wiwat Catithammanit on Supha Sirimanond and *Aksornsarn* weekly magazine, Bangkok, September 27, 1988. Dazhong Wenhua also arranged a clandestine trip to China for many Pridi followers and TCP cadres. See No. Praphasathit, *Kao pi*, 3, 31–32. According to a police charge, Lim Ha (or Lim Huk) and Khoo Song (or Khoo Kiang), the second editor and

the second manager of *Chuanmin Pao*, respectively, also acted as the PRC's travel agents. Wiwat, "Kabot santiphap," 184–85.

20 "Dazhong Wenhua Company Limited," Registration Profile File no.1024.

21 Yanyong, "Prawat nangseuphim jin," 79; *Karnmuang* 6, no. 11 (October 8, 1949): 4; *Siam Nikorn* 15 (February 1, 1951): 1.

22 The newspaper offices were searched by police five times from June 1948 to December 1952, resulting in the arrests of over sixty members of *Chuanmin Pao* editorial, typesetting, printing, and distribution staff and the confiscation of many materials. See Skinner, *Chinese Society*, 324–25, 336; Wiwat, "Kabot santiphap," 166.

On police surveillance, Thaweep Voradilok delightedly tells of being given a friendly warning by a Dazhong Wenhua salesclerk while browsing there that "someone" was tailing him. Unperturbed, Thaweep replied that actually that "someone" was not tailing him but watching the bookshop. Thaweep, discussion on "Soviet Russian Literature."

23 The letter, no. 54/2494, dated July 30, 1951, from Police Lieutenant Srichat Jindalath of Section 3, Division 5 of the Special Branch Police, asking for the information is kept in "Dazhong Wenhua Company Limited," Registration Profile File no.1024.

24 See *Aksornsarn* 4, no. 2 (May 1952); Banleu, *Khoomeu kansobsuan*, 71–72.

25 Skinner, *Chinese Society*, 336; Wiwat, "Kabot santiphap," 166.

26 Thaweep, discussion on "Soviet Russian Literature." Bangkok Witthayakhan's advertisements appeared in *Aksornsarn* 3, no. 5–10 (August 1951–January 1952).

27 Bangkok Witthayakhan, together with its affiliate, the Sahabannakorn Press, published literary criticism, essays, and translations of Soviet novels by Banjong Banjoedsil (Udom Sisuwan), Naiphi (Atsani Phonlajan), and Seni Saowaphong (Sakchai Bamrungphong), among others. In an interview, Udom himself testified to the link between the publication of these books and the TCP, although he misnamed the publishing house as Krungthep Bannakhan. Udom, interview, January 19, 1984.

28 Thongchai, "Latthi khommunit," 396–97, 410–14.

29 The discussion in the following passage is based partly on book advertisements and commentaries published in various issues of *Pituphoom* and *Saithan* during 1957 and 1958.

30 Thaweep, discussion on "Soviet Russian Literature."

31 Phin, interview, August 31, 1984; Phin, interview, July 31, 1985; Udom, interview, January 19, 1984; Sawai Malayavej, interview by the author on his profile and the Thai communist movement, Bangkok, April 22, 1989.

32 See the regular advertisements of English radical books by Aksornwatthana in *Pituphoom* and *Sethasarn* in 1957 and 1958.

It should be noted that there was no late 1950s counterpart to the defunct Dazhong Wenhua on the part of the Chinese communists, whose party organization in Thailand had reportedly been disbanded since 1953 and whose ranks were, in any case, decimated by repeated police roundups from 1952 to 1954. Murashima, Kanmeuang jinsiam, 75; Skinner, Chinese Society, 335, 337; Thongchai, "Latthi khommunit," 337–43.

33 The union leader responsible for this library was a CPT cadre named Si Anothai, head of the BLU and CLU Education Departments. See Chapter 3 and *Mahachon* 97 (July 20, 1947).

34 Sungsidh, *Prawat*, 234–35; Kanlaya, interview, March 26, 1989.

35 For example, Thaweep, interview, December 27, 1988.

36 My judgement is inferred from the publication dates as well as the acquisition and borrowing records of these books. As records kept by the library are incomplete and date back only to 1960, the result is inconclusive.

37 "Beuanglang khon kheu khwamkhid beuanglang jit kheu khwamjing" [Behind the man is the thought, Behind Jit is reality], *Thanon Nangseu* 3, no. 11 (May 1986): 21.

38 Supha, interview, September 4, 1985; Seni Saowaphong (Sakchai Bamrungphong), "Yiap yurop kab supha sirimanond" [Roaming Europe with Supha Sirimanond], in *Photjanalai supha sirimanond* [Eulogies to Supha Sirimanond] (Bangkok: Songphorn Woraphithaksanond, 1986), 52–53; Murashima, *Kanmeuang jinsiam*, 44, 68 n. 112.

39 "Lakhorn," 26.

40 It was Supha who gave a copy of Stalin's *Dialectical and Historical Materialism* to Samak, a disgruntled, middle-ranking government official and brilliant British-educated scientist and philosopher, and persuaded him to translate it. *Aksornsarn* 2, no. 8–11 (November 1950–February 1951). He also introduced Thaweep, then a rising poet and Thammasat student activist, to the world of foreign radical literature and the Nibondh Bookshop. Supha, interview, September 4, 1985; Thaweep, "Supha," 32–35, 45–46.

41 Thaweep, "Supha," 34.

42 "Phookhian khong rao nai chabab ni" [Our writers in this issue], *Aksornsarn* 1, no. 1 (April 1949): 6; Witthayakorn, *Seuksa Sriburapha*, 48–51. This brief but politically tumultuous and intellectually significant episode in Kulap's life, with unexpectedly wide and serious

repercussions for Thai-Australian relations, has been fully researched by Scot Barmé, making extensive use of Australian archival, newspaper and testimonial sources, in his *Kulap in Oz: A Thai View of Australian Life and Society in the Late 1940s* (Clayton, Victoria: Monash Asia Institute, Monash University, 1995). See especially his "Introduction."

43 Barmé, "Introduction," xxxv–xxxvii. In a letter dated April 14, 1982, Davies, described by Barmé as "a noted intellectual on the Australian Left," related that his weekly tutorial session with Kulap usually lasted "for two hours" each "for some 15–18 months." He portrayed Kulap as "highly intelligent, sensitive and imaginative," and added that, "No doubt we would both have described ourselves as socialists."

44 Barmé, "Introduction," xxxvii–xl, xlii–xliv; and Smyth, "Introduction," 35–36 n. 23.

45 Cited in Barmé, "Introduction," xlv, see also xxxiii–xxxiv, xxxvii–xxxviii, xl, xliv, xlix, lvi–lvii, lix.

46 Barmé, "Introduction," xxxix, xlviii, lix, lxiii.

47 Barmé observes that the Department of Immigration had no reason, "except perhaps…an ingrained racism," to consider Kulap a communist. Barmé, "Introduction," xliv.

48 Barmé, *Kulap in Oz*, 51–62; Supha, interview, September 4, 1985. Kulap's translation, entitled *Pratya khong latthi marxism* [The philosophy of Marxism], was serialized in *Aksornsarn* 2, no. 3, 5, 6, 8, 10; and 3, no. 3 (June 1950–June 1951). Since then, it has been reissued in book form many times.

49 Smyth, "Introduction," 19.

50 The Beards' history of the U.S. was "reproduced" by Supha in a review essay. See Jittin Thammachat (Supha Sirimanond), "Nakprawattisat american phoopranam ratthathammanoon" [The American historians who denounced the constitution], *Aksornsarn* 1, no. 6 (September 1949), 64–75.

51 Siriusa, "Ajan jit," 7–11, 13–14; Sil Phithakchon (Jit Poumisak), "Dae jed nakseuksa thai phoo waek man 'dollar' pai soo krung moscow" [For 7 Thai students who part the 'dollar' curtain to Moscow], *Pituphoom* 2, no. 70 (August 12, 1957), 30, 41–44.

52 The People's Republic of China was out of the picture for it was not recognized by Thailand until 1975.

53 Thompson and Adloff, *The Left Wing*, 72; *Mahachon* 123 (March 21, 1948).

54 Thompson and Adloff, *The Left Wing*, 73–75; Thongchai, "Latthi khommunit," 281–82, 303, 324–26.

55 The scandal had to do with the Khuang government's new policy to send

only pro-government newspapers to Thai embassies and consulates abroad. The government's own political classification divided the press into three major groups: pro-government press—*Prachathipatai, Nakhornsan, Kiattisak, Sri Krung, Seriphap*, and *Liberty*; anti-government press—*Prachakorn, Siam Nikorn, Siang Thai, Chat Thai, Suwannaphoom, Phim Thai, Karnmuang*, and *Bangkok Post*; and "vacillating" press—*Suphapburus, Ekkaraj, Tawan, Thai Mai*, etc. *Karnmuang* 3, no. 51 (December 13, 1947): 1. Interestingly, the TCP's *Mahachon* did not appear in the list. *Karnmuang* later published an open letter of complaint from Suphat about his arbitrary dismissal from the Ministry of Foreign Affairs. See Suphat Sukhonthaphirom, "Seri thai rong kho khwamyuttitham" [A Free Thai pleads for justice], *Karnmuang* 4, no. 7 (February 14, 1948): 6.

56 Suphat, interview, September 7, 1985.

57 Suphat, interview, September 7, 1985. According to the flexible working arrangements, Suphat had to hand in translations and accept new assignments only twice a week.

58 These articles appeared in *Karnmuang, Aksornsarn*, and *Thammajak* under his own name or the pen name "Phatthana Rammayasut." See, for example, "Sathiaraphap khong dollar kamlang pen thi songsai" [The stability of dollar currency is doubtful], *Aksornsarn* 2, no. 1 (April 1950): 19–22; "Setthakij khong lok yungyak phrao baibun america" [World economy is in turmoil due to American aid], *Aksornsarn* 2, no. 2 (May 1950): 20–29; "Rabob kanngoen lae rabob kanthanakhan khong soviet" [The Soviet financial and banking systems], *Aksornsarn* 2, no. 3 (June 1950), 17–23; and 2, no. 4 (July 1950): 12–16; "Kanpatiroop setthakij lae kanngoen nai poland" [The economic and financial reform in Poland], *Aksornsarn* 3, no. 3 (June 1951): 17–23; "Sathana khong pajjekchon nai rabob sochalist" [The status of the individual in the socialist system], *Aksornsarn* 4, no. 6 (September 1952): 16–83.

59 Thompson and Adloff, *The Left Wing*, 74–75; Thongchai, "Latthi khommunit," 258, 281–82, 301, 303–305, 307–308, 320–21, 324–26, 330–31.

60 *Siam Nikorn* 15 (March 5, 1951): 1, 10.

61 A source of much confusion for later students of Thai politics of the 1950s, there were three separate clandestine political organizations using "koochat" (national liberation) in their titles, each trying to overthrow the Phibun government in its own way: 1) Ongkan Thai Koochat or Tho.Ko.Cho. (Thai National Liberation Organization), 1949–1961, a CPT-led peasant organization, by popular insurgency; 2)

Khana Koochat (National Liberation Party), 1950–1951, a small group
of conspiratorial naval officers, by coup; and 3) Khabuankan Koochat
(National Liberation Movement), 1951–1952, a small group of pro-
Pridi leftist journalists and dissident military officers, by coup and
popular uprising.

62 This account of the Khabuankan Koochat is based on Suthachai,
"Kankhleuanwai," 241–44; Wiwat, "Kabot santiphap," 137–38, 181–84,
226–35.

63 Wiwat, "Kabot santiphap," 229–230.

64 Ibid., 231.

65 Ibid., 181, 234.

66 Ibid., 138, 180–81, 227–29, 232–33; Thailand, Criminal Court,
Ministry of Justice, "The Testimony of Phramaha Dilok Suwannarat
(Thammathatto Bhikkhu)," Criminal Court Proceedings of the Cases
No. Black 158, 168, 202/2496, November 1953.

67 Apart from actively organizing and co-ordinating the Peace Movement
and the TCP-affiliated Ongkan Thai Koochat, Pan, along with Suphat,
co-authored the political program *Prachathipatai phaen mai* (New
Democracy), which was used as an internal political study document by
both "koochat" organizations.

68 Suthachai, "Kankhleuanwai," 240; Reynolds, *Thai Radical Discourse*,
28. I say "misinformed" advisedly, for "a young Thai air force officer who
had been stationed in London," mentioned by western intelligence, could
be none other than Squadron Leader Phrangphej Bunyaratphan, then
receiving additional aviation training there. The so-called "Soviet agents"
must have meant Suphat and his friends. Wiwat, "Kabot santiphap," 234.

69 Quoted in Thanin, *Kanchai kodmai*, 239–41. Also see Phao's similar
statement to the press (quoted in Suthachai, "Kankhleuanwai," 246),
statements issued by the government on both occasions (quoted in
Thongchai, "Latthi khommunit," 317, 414), and the prosecution's charges
in the Criminal Cases No. Black 158, 168, 202/2496 (summarized in
Wiwat, "Kabot santiphap," 175–89).

70 Suphat, interview, September 7, 1985.

71 Wiwat, "Kabot santiphap," 165–68, 178.

72 With so many writer-journalists among them, the Peace Rebellion
inmates produced not a few prison memoirs, on some of which I have
based my account: 1) Phaisal Malaphan (Sawai Malayavej), *Bantheuk
nakthos kanmeuang* [Memoir of a political prisoner] (Bangkok:
Santitham Press, 1985); 2) Pheuan ruam khuk 2495–2500 lae
Sahathammik (Fellow inmates B.E. 2495–2500 and laymen), *Ramleuk*

theung kulap saipradit [Remembering Kulap Saipradit] (Bangkok: Santitham Press, 1985); and 3) Jareuk Chomphoophol (Chat Bunyasirichai), "Bantheuk jak bangkhwang" [Bangkhwang memoir], in *Beuangraek prachathipatai: Bantheuk khwamsongjam khong phoo yoo nai hetkan samai Pho.So. 2475–2500* [The early days of democracy: Memoirs of participants in the events during B.E. 2475–2500] (Bangkok: The News Reporters Association of Thailand, 1973).

73 Suphat, interview, September 7, 1985; Sawai, interview, April 22, 1989.

74 This article was later published as Phatthana Rammayasut (Suphat Sukhonthaphirom), "Phikhrao reuang chonchan khong sangkhom thai pajjuban" [Class analysis of present Thai society], in the celebrated, historic *Nitisat Rab Satawas Mai* [Journal of law: The new century issue] 7, no. 4 (1957): 248–56.

75 Phaisal, *Bantheuk*, 87–88; Rungwit, *Sriburapha*, 108–109.

76 Sawai, interview, April 22, 1989.

77 Phaisal, *Bantheuk*, 146–51; Suthachai, "Kankhleuanwai," 245; Wiwat, "Kabot santiphap," 185.

78 Quoted in Thongchai, "Latthi khommunit," 414.

79 Quoted in Thongchai, "Latthi khommunit," 332–33.

80 Suphat, interview, September 7, 1985.

81 During the 1950s, internal security, surveillance, and suppression of communists was the main responsibility of the Santibal Police. It was not until the 1960s under the Sarit and Thanom regime that the military became heavily involved in these matters, especially after the outbreak of the communist rural insurgency in 1965. Buncha Suma, "Kankhleuanwai khong phuak khommunit kab nayobai pongkan lae prabpram khong ratthabal (Pho.So. 2500–2523)" [The communist movement and the preventive and suppressive policies of the Thai government, 1957–1980] (master's thesis, Chulalongkorn University, 1985), 96–114.

82 Chiab, *Mahawitthayalai*, 460–61.

83 Chiab, *Mahawitthayalai*, 471, 550; Chit, *Phao saraphap*, 308; Sornsak, *Khabuankan seri thai*, 138; Suthachai, "Kankhleuanwai," 97.

84 Chiab, *Mahawitthayalai*, 41–54, 465–524; Sungsidh, *Prawat*, passim. See details below.

85 Chit, *Phao saraphap*, 346–58; Reynolds, *Thai Radical Discourse*, 185; Supha, interview, September 4, 1985; Thaweep, discussion on "Soviet Russian Literature"; Thongbai, *Khommunit ladyao*, 265 n. 1.

86 Phaisal, *Bantheuk*, 146–60; Suthachai, "Kankhleuanwai," 245; Sawai, interview, April 22, 1989; Thaweep, "Supha," 42; and Wiwat, "Kabot santiphap," 163.

87 For example, Associated Press, *Times* (London), *Washington Post, Trud, Scotsman*, World Government Association, *Gazette de Lausanne, Journal de Génève, La Libre Belgique, Manila Bulletin, Manila Times, The Philippines Herald, L'Humanité, Pravda, Komsomol Pravda*, Radio Moscow, Radio Peking, etc. See Suthachai, "Kankhleuanwai," 240; Thongchai, chapters 4 and 5 of "Latthi khommunit," passim; Thompson and Adloff, *The Left Wing*, 74.

88 Some of them were so fantastic that the more sensible Thai officials could not bring themselves to believe them. See Thongchai, "Latthi khommunit," 323–34, 383–84.

89 See Chapter 2 of this book and the succinct analysis of Thai anti-communist discourse by Craig J. Reynolds, *Thai Radical Discourse*, 27–29. A typical restatement of this bias can be found in Thongchai, "Latthi khommunit," 449–51.

90 The two prominent exceptions were Prasert Sapsunthorn and Pan Kaeomat.

91 Major exceptions were the Sahachip-Isan politicians, whose "provincial" background many Bangkok political leaders found objectionable. Thak, *Thailand*, 11 n. 23.

92 Cited in *Siam Nikorn* 15 (January 17, 1951): 1, 8.

93 Thak, *Thailand*, 64; *Siam Nikorn* 15 (February 3, 1951): 1, 8; *Siam Nikorn* 15 (February 14, 1951): 1, 8; *Siam Nikorn* 15 (February 27, 1951); 1, 8; and Jaralrat, "Meua ratthamontri thai thook ha pen khommunit" [When a Thai minister is accused of being a communist], *Siam Nikorn* 15 (March 5, 1951): 4–6.

94 Thailand, Criminal Court, Ministry of Justice, "The Statement of the Defense Lawyers," Criminal Court Proceedings of the Cases No. Black 158, 168, 202/2496, February 1955, 10.

95 Cited in Suthachai, "Kankhleuanwai," 215. The incident was so called because Bangkok was then widely inundated with heavy rains.

96 Thongchai, chapters 4 and 5 of "Latthi khommunit," passim.

97 From the official translation of "Phrarajbanyat pongkan kankratham an pen khommunit phutthasakkaraj 2495" [The Anti-Communist Activities Act, B.E. 2495], *Rajkijjanubeksa* [Royal Thai government gazette] 69, no. 18 (November 13, 1952).

98 Thanin, *Kanchai kodmai*, 250–51.

99 Thanin, *Kanchai kodmai*, 252–53; Wiwat, "Kabot santiphap," 168.

100 Chai-anan and Phirasak, *Khomoon*, 62–65; Kulap, *Adit*, 291–336; Thak, *Thailand*, 32, 69–71, 89–90, 150–51.

101 Chit, *Phao saraphap*, 205–303. The "communist" charge was not an

indispensable component of their formula for political killings. For example, although their plot to plant communist documents on Phorn Malithong, a fearless opposition MP for Samut Sakhon, was foiled by their own spy's betrayal, Police Colonel Annop and his gang murdered both men anyway, on March 24, 1954. Chit, *Phao saraphap*, 335–88.

102 *Mahachon* 140 (July 18, 1948): 1. *Mahachon*'s allegation that Mr. Bullwit's communist books were "fake or unauthorized" should be taken as a symptom of anti-imperialist ideological paranoia rather than as the result of any conclusive investigation on the TCP's part.

103 This account is based mainly on the pioneering research on Jit Poumisak done by Craig J. Reynolds in *Thai Radical Discourse*, 32 as well as some other Thai sources.

The American Embassy did not seem to be aware of a previous, possibly the first, complete Thai translation of The Communist Manifesto, entitled Kamnodkan khommunit, published in early 1947. Its independent translator and publisher was a young, arrogant, pipe-smoking journalist and Thammasat student named Sanao Phanichjaroen, who soon joined the Thai Communist Party. Pho. Meuangchomphoo, Soo Samoraphoom, 43, 107.

104 Jit Poumisak, *Khwamfaifan saen ngam: Ruam ngankawiniphon chudsomboon 2489–2509* [Beautiful dream: A complete anthology of Jit Poumisak's poetry, B.E. 2489–2509], ed. Meuang Boyang (Bangkok: Dokya Press, 1981), 47–80; Meuang Boyang, *Botphleng haeng rungarun: Waduai chiwaprawat nai waiyao khong jit poumisak* [The song of dawn: On Jit Poumisak's early life] (Bangkok: Tonkla Book Club, 1980), 105–107, 141–43, 201–209.

105 Meuang, *Botphleng*, 48, 191–92, 210–12; Reynolds, *Thai Radical Discourse*, 2–23.

106 Meuang, *Botphleng*, 17–65, 213–14; Mit, "Chiwaprawat jit," 23–25; Siriusa, "Ajan jit," 11–12.

107 The lengthy caption of the article tells its own tale: "The Philosophy of Buddhism Improves Social Conditions by Focusing on Moral Defilements; Dialectical Materialism Improves Social Conditions by Focusing on Society Itself, and it does this by Revolution, not by Siddhartha's Reformism. The Philosophy of Dialectical Materialism and Siddhartha's Philosophy are thus in Serious Disagreement." From Nakhorn That (Jit Poumisak), "Phi tong leuang" [The spirits of the yellow leaves], trans. Craig J. Reynolds, Echols Collection, Kroch Library, Cornell University, June 2, 1980 (mimeograph), 1.

108 Mit, "Chiwaprawat jit," 25–28; Jit, *Khwamfaifan*, 84–89; Reynolds, *Thai Radical Discourse*, 30–31.

109 Mit, "Chiwaprawat jit," 26–29; Reynolds, *Thai Radical Discourse*, 30–31.

110 Reynolds, *Thai Radical Discourse*, 31–32.

111 Except between the end of 1952 and mid-1955 when anti-communist censorship was in full swing.

112 My research on this issue is built on Reynolds' observation in *Thai Radical Discourse*, 27.

These eighty-one orders were published in a chronological but scattered manner in Rajkijjanubeksa [Royal Thai government gazette] 67–74 (1950–1957). The volume numbers of the Gazette in which they appear and their dates of publication are as follows: 67 (June 27, 1950); 68 (February 7, February 27, and April 3, 1951); 69 (February 19, July 2, July 15, September 23, October 7, and November 11, 1952); 70 (January 13, 1953); 71 (January 12, January 26, February 9, May 18, August 31, November 9, and November 16, 1954); 72 (January 18, April 12, April 26, May 24, May 31, and June 14, 1955); 73 (February 21, March 20, March 27, April 24, May 22, July 17, August 14, August 28, September 1, September 11, December 4, and December 25, 1956); 74 (February 5, February 26, March 9, March 19, March 26, March 29, April 9, April 16, May 28, July 9, August 6, October 29, November 5, November 12, and December 24, 1957).

The total number of items listed in the orders was 254, but three of them (two in English and one in Chinese) were entered twice in the very same orders, a revealing indicator of the quality of Santibal censorship.

113 *Rajkijjanubeksa* [Royal Thai government gazette] 69 (July 2,1952); and 73 (December 25, 1956).

114 *Rajkijjanubeksa* [Royal Thai government gazette] 69 (July 2 and December 7, 1952).

115 *Rajkijjanubeksa* [Royal Thai government gazette] 71 (January 26 and May 18, 1954); 72 (April 26 and May 31, 1955); 73 (August 28 and December 25, 1956).

My conclusion does not imply that Pratya prayuk was the only Thai radical publication forbidden during the post-war decade; there were other kinds of censorship measures than outright banning taken by the Phibun government against the radical press, such as censorship of news reports before publication, confiscation of individual issues of a radical newspaper or periodical, closure of publications altogether, arrest or murder of its owner, editor and staff, etc. The Chuanmin Pao, Mahachon,

Karnmuang, and Aksornsarn had all undergone these measures at one time or another.

116 Reynolds, *Thai Radical Discourse*, 27.

117 Major General M.L. Khab Kunchorn (royalist politician, then secretary of the Prime Minister's Office and later director general of the Public Relations Department), Luang Saranupraphan (veteran journalist and story-writer who composed the words of the Thai National Anthem, then director general of the Publicity Department), Sang Phatnothai (key leader of the government-organized right-wing labor movement), and Chai Wirojsiri (husband of a younger sister of Phibun's wife and Sang's colleague in the labor movement).

118 "Phra anti khommunit" [Anti-communist monks], *Karnmuang* [8], no. 2 (January 20, 1951): 25–27; "Ai kruak khon thi song" [The second liar], *Karnmuang* [8], no. 6 (February 17, 1951): 28; "Chai sam sassana pen khreuangmeu totan khommunit" [Using the 3 religions as anti-communist instruments], *Karnmuang* [8], no. 14 (April 21, 1951): 20; Damri and Jaroon, *Khabuankan*, 60–64, 126–30, 152–53; Kanya, "Prawat," 34–37; Sungsidh, *Prawat*, 197–230; Wiwat, "Kabot santiphap," 172.

119 See, for instance, "Kankratham thi na khaina" [Shameful acts], *Karnmuang* [8], no. 6 (February 17, 1951): 3, 27–28; "Sannibat seriphan ok 'mahachon' plom ik" [League of Free Assemblies issues fake *Mahachon* again], *Karnmuang* [8], no. 6 (February 17, 1951): 7, 22; "Nangseu pok daeng" [A red-covered book], *Karnmuang* [8], no. 18 (May 19, 1951): 9.

120 The year witnessed in succession the growing estrangement of strategic political forces from the Phibun government, culminating in its overthrow by the army in September. For details, see Suthachai, "Kankhleuanwai," 285–304.

121 *Nitisat Rab Satawas Mai* [Journal of law: The new century issue] 7, no. 4 (1957); Reynolds, *Thai Radical Discourse*, 34–35. Professor Reynolds has kindly made available to me his records of the two interviews on which my account is based, i.e., Prawut Srimantra, interview by Craig J. Reynolds on Jit Poumisak and the Thai left, Bangkok, December 18, 1983; and Thaweep Voradilok, interview by Craig J. Reynolds on Jit Poumisak and contemporary radical literature and politics, Bangkok, January 13, 1984.

122 Which reads:
   Section 5: Whoever incites, advises, encourages, conducts a propaganda...with an intent to carry on Communist activities...shall be punished with imprisonment from five to ten years.

Section 9: Whoever assists any Communist organization or member of a Communist organization...by giving financial or other assistance shall be punished with imprisonment from five to ten years.

From the official translation of "Phrarajbanyat pongkan kankratham an pen khommunit phutthasakkaraj 2495" [The Anti-Communist Activities Act, B.E. 2495], Rajkijjanubeksa [Royal Thai government gazette] 69, no. 18 (November 13, 1952).

123 *Nitisat Rab Satawas Mai* [Journal of law: The new century issue] 7, no. 4 (1957) was later banned by the Sarit government and has since become a rare item, very much sought after by collectors of radical publications. A photocopy of the journal has generously been made available to me by Mrs. Phatcharaphorn Ngamthipwatthana.

The five contributions by Jit Poumisak in the 1957 issue are a poem by Khwannara (Jit Poumisak), "Kanthambun pheua tuakoo doo chobkol" [Making merit for "myself" looks strange], 9; a poem by Srinakhorn (Jit Poumisak), "Sang sawan kheun thi nai lok duai meu" [Build heaven on earth with our hands], 15–16; Somsamai Srisootphan (Jit Poumisak), "Chomna khong sakdina thai nai pajjuban" [The real face of Thai feudalism today], 356–491; a march called "March yaowachon thai" [The Thai youth march], 525; and a march called "March anti jakkaphadniyom" [The anti-imperialist march], 527. The contribution by Suphat is Phatthana Rammayasut (Suphat Sukhonthaphirom), "Phikhrao reuang chonchan khong sangkhom thai pajjuban" [Class analysis of present Thai society], 248–256.

Jit's "Feudalism" essay has been translated into English by Craig J. Reynolds in his Thai Radical Discourse, 43–148.

124 Suphat, interview, September 7, 1985.

125 Mit, "Chiwaprawat jit," 34–39. In an interview, Supha said that Jit "led a demonstration of students" during this period which later brought about his arrest. (Supha Sirimanond, interview by Craig J. Reynolds on his life and the Thai left, Bangkok, September 16, 1979.) The incident he referred to may have been the demonstration of Chulalongkorn and other university students against the Phibun government's "dirty" general election on March 2, 1957, in which, according to Pawina Sajjaphan, Jit's fellow student at Chulalongkorn and later CPT leader, Jit was so moved by the massive student march that he called it "the Thai May Fourth Movement."

126 Suthachai, "Kankhleuanwai," 299. Examples of the CPT's tactical support for Sarit can be found in *Pituphoom* 2, no. 48 (March 11, 1957): 3, 32; and 2, no. 49 (March 18, 1957): 11.

127 Two best general accounts of Sarit's rise to power at this critical juncture
    are Thak, *Thailand*, 117–52; and Suthachai, "Kankhleuanwai," 285–306.
    On the CPT and leftists' "divided heart" between Phibun and Sarit, the
    fatal decision of most of them to throw in their lot with Sarit, and the
    negative lesson they regretfully drew afterwards, see Damri and Jaroon,
    Khabuankan, 171–75; Phin, interview, July 31, 1985; Pho.
    Meuangchomphoo, Soo Samoraphoom, 14; Thaweep, "Naknangseuphim,"
    18–21; Dae thanong satthathip [For Thanong Satthathip], published on the
    occasion of the one hundredth day after Thanong Satthathip's death,
    Amphoe Pakthongchai, Nakhon Ratchasima, May 27, 1973, 19 ff.
128 Chit, *Phao saraphap*, passim; Kulap, *Adit*, 250 *ff.*; Kulap, *Pai sahaphap
    soviet*, 1–12.
129 See Somphob et al., *Prawat*, 403–408; Thongbai, *Khommunit ladyao*.
130 Mit, "Chiwaprawat jit," 40–42.

Chapter 7

1 Supha, interview, September 4, 1985.
2 An optimistic estimation of the number of Thais who could read western-
  language radical publications in the post-war period would be 10,000 in
  a country of eighteen million, if all students and graduates of Thai and
  foreign universities constitute our basic figure (see Table 4-1). In the case
  of Chinese radical publications, no data is available, though my guess is
  that their readership would have numbered no less than 10,000.
3 Both motives were at work, for example, in the cases of Supha
  Sirimanond and Atsani Phonlajan. Supha, interview, September 4, 1985;
  Fongjan, "Khwamngam khong chiwit," 90.
4 See Phin, interview, August 31, 1984 and July 31, 1985; Napaporn,
  Phatthanakan, 17–20; Napaporn Ativanichayapong, "The Development
  of Political Economy Thought in Thailand, 1932–1982" (master's
  thesis, Thammasat University, 1986), 53–55; Phornphirom Iamtham,
  "Phatthanakan khong 'khabuankan sangkhomniyom' nai prathet thai
  lang songkhram lok khrang thi song theung Pho.So.2526" [The
  development of the "socialist movement" in Thailand after the Second
  World War until B.E. 2526], *Journal of Political Economy* 5, no. 1–2
  (October 1985–March 1986): 110–14.
      For the argument that this binary categorization of the Thai left turns
  easily into a false dichotomy that underestimates or denies the key
  historical role of the Thai communist movement, see Somsak, "The

Academic Exclusion of Thai Communism," introduction to "The Communist Movement." Arguing passionately, polemically, and meticulously, Somsak devotes almost his whole dissertation to proving that "since the late 1940s there has been only one real force on the Left [in Thailand]: Communism and the Communist Party" (9, 43). Though persuaded by him of the possible political bias, substantive vacuity, and analytical misapplication frequently associated with the hitherto use or abuse of the group dichotomy, I still find myself sincerely convinced that it accurately reflects the objective relationship among the Thai left in the post-war decade and that it is analytically useful as a strictly heuristic tool rather than a fetishized reality. I only hope that my particular application of it here is reasonable, carefully circumscribed, and flexible enough to meet any objection.

5　Ngiew and Shan are northern hill-tribe minorities of Thailand.

6　There are two exceptions to my general characterization of the educational background of this group, as far as I can ascertain: Sak Suphakasem and Sujin Akharasamit, graduates of Chulalongkorn University and Thammasat University, respectively. Pho. Meuangchomphoo, *Soo Samoraphoom*, 23–25.

7　Members of this group who remained in Thailand were either imprisoned or silenced by the Phibun government, while those who joined Pridi in exile, like Sanguan Tularak and Suri Thongwanich, one by one fell out with their "ajan" (master) over personal, theoretical, and tactical matters until finally only Police Captain Chiab Chaisong stuck fast beside him. A particularly sore point with Pridi was that not a few of his disenchanted disciples were won over by the CPT, which by the late 1950s had become his chief rival for leadership of the Thai leftist movement, as well as for Chinese political favor and material aid. Chiab, "Bantheuk," 13–15; No. Praphasathit, *Kao pi*, 308–309, 312–15, 319–20, 322–23, 348–50, 452–56, 487–89, 494–95; Wiwat, "Kabot santiphap," 198, 212.

8　Prasan (Udom Sisuwan), "Khai panha" [Answering the questions], *Pituphoom* 2, no. 40 (January 14, 1957): 30–32.

9　Sornsak, *Khabuankan serithai*, 302, 455–56; No. Praphasathit, *Kao pi*, 299–301.

10　No. Praphasathit, *Kao pi*, 216–24, 292–94, 310, 359, 566–69; Chiab, "Bantheuk," 11–13.

11　Thongchai, "Latthi khommunit," 344–45, 349–52.

12　No. Praphasathit, *Kao pi*, 348–50.

13　Ibid., 487–89.

14　Ibid., 232–44, 566; Chiab, "Bantheuk," 13–14.

15 The inexperience was reflected in the often inept, petty, and superficial way its members conducted study and "criticism-and-self-criticism" sessions in China. See a participant's account in No. Praphasathit, *Kao pi*, 308–309, 312–68.

16 See an example in "VOPT [Voice of the People of Thailand] Recounts CPT History," J-8–J-12. The only major intra-Party conflict of the post-war decade mentioned in the document involves the so-called "erroneous theory" of the "revisionist" "renegade" Prasert Sapsunthorn against the rural peasant armed struggle. Ibid., J-11.

17 Pho. Meuangchomphoo, *Soo Samoraphoom*, 43–44, 107.

18 Phin, interview, July 31, 1985.

19 Ibid.

20 Ibid.

21 "Kham hai samphas khong khoesok phak khommunit haeng prathet thai kiaokab phreuttikan khong nai prasert sapsunthorn thi thorayos to kanpatiwat lae thorayos to prachachon" [Interview of the spokesman of the Communist Party of Thailand about Mr. Prasert Sapsunthorn's traitorous behavior against the revolution and the people], VOPT radio broadcast, Kunming, July 27, 1968; "VOPT Recounts CPT History," J-11; Phin, interview, July 31, 1985; Pho. Meuangchomphoo, *Soo Samoraphoom*, 45.

22 Pho. Meuangchomphoo, *Soo Samoraphoom*, 45.

23 Sanao Thamsathian (Sanao Phanichjaroen), "Kanyaek thangdoen rawang tito kab klum prachathipatai prachachon kheu kanphookpom songkhram lok khrang mai" [The parting of the ways between Tito and the People's Democracy group of countries is a source of a new world war], *Aksornsarn* 1, no. 9 (December 1949): 33–43; Supha, interview, September 4, 1985; Pho. Meuangchomphoo, *Soo Samoraphoom*, 43–44.

24 Pho. Meuangchomphoo, *Soo Samoraphoom*, 44–45; Phin, interview, July 31, 1985.

25 Charnvit et al., part 2 of *Prawat thammasat*, 71–75, 95–96.

26 Pho. Meuangchomphoo, *Soo Samoraphoom*, 13–14; Suthachai, "Kankhleuanwai," 269.

27 See Damri and Jaroon, *Khabuankan*, 171–75; Phin, interview, July 31, 1985; Somsak, "The Communist Movement," 18–21, 36–38.

28 Pho. Meuangchomphoo, *Soo Samoraphoom*, passim; Phin, interview, July 31, 1985.

According to Phin Bua-on, a Thammasat student leader in the 1950s who rose to membership in the CPT Politbureau in the mid-1960s before being captured by the authorities in 1967 and denounced as a "renegade" and "fake Marxist" by the VOPT in 1975, there were two unofficial "prohibitions" within the CPT, the "violation" of which would scar a member's political career and fortune for life: "1) don't get arrested; 2) don't make a united front with the upper class."

29 Pridi Banomyong, "Khana ratsadorn kab kanaphiwat prachathipatai 24 mithunayon" [The People's Party and the June 24 democratic revolution] in Pridi, *Pridi banomyong*, 333–62; contrast with "VOPT Marks Anniversary of End of Absolute Monarchy," *Foreign Broadcast Information Service, Daily Report: Asia & Pacific* 4, no. 128 (July 2, 1975): J9–J11.

30 Phin, interview, July 31, 1985.

31 While the CPT staunchly advocated a militant pro-socialist foreign policy, Pridi as well as Suphat of the Khabuankan Koochat and Chiab of the Sri Arya Mettraya Party preferred a more cautious neutralist position. See Wiwat, "Kabot santiphap," 138, 232–33; Chiab, "Bantheuk," 15–16.

32 Chiab, "Bantheuk," 14–15.

33 Suphat, interview, September 7, 1985. The term "second-hand" refers to the fact that most CPT members whom Suphat knew personally seemed to have read Marxism-communism only in secondary abridged sources.

34 "Lakhorn," 17, 26; Supha, interview, September 4, 1985; Thaweep, "Supha," 43.

35 Thaweep, "Supha," passim.

36 The allegation was based on Khamsing's long friendship and association with a few Americans in Thailand, which automatically made him a prime "CIA agent" suspect in the xenophobic atmosphere of the Party's intensifying anti-U.S. imperialism campaign of the late 1950s. Kulap's inclusion of Khamsing, a literary protégé of his and a close friend of his family, thus greatly worried the CPT, which feared Khamsing would write negatively about China on his return. After several failed attempts, the Party managed to convince Kulap, still angered and disappointed by the groundless allegation, not to take Khamsing with him. Sawai, interview, April 22, 1989; Khamsing, interview, April 12, 1989.

37 Phin, interview, July 31, 1985; Suphot, *Prasert*, 31–48.

38 Damri and Jaroon, *Khabuankan*, 42–45.

39 Pho. Meuangchomphoo, *Soo samoraphoom*, 8; Udom, interview, January 19, 1984; Wiwat, "Kabot santiphap," 158–59, 161, 163–64, 198, 201–204.

40 Prasit Kanjanawat, *Khosangket jak ratthathammanoon soviet* [Comments on the Soviet constitution] and Suphat Sukhonthaphirom and Udom Sisuwan, *Ratthathammanoon thi pen prachathipatai thisud nai lok* [The

most democratic constitution in the world], *Mahachon* 148 (September 12, 1948).

41 The following were published under the pen-names "Seni Saowaphong" and "Krasnai Porachat": *Jed phaendin* [Seven lands], 1951; *Wara sudthai khong sevastopol* [The last days of Sevastopol], 1951; *Sinlapa lae wannakhadi* [Art and literature], 1952; *Atthaniyom kab jintaniyom* [Realism and romanticism], 1952; and *Khwamrak khong wanlaya* [Wanlaya's love], 1952. See Udom, interview, January 19, 1984.

42 They were the Dazhong Wenhua Bookshop (alias Hua Chiao Book Store), the Anta Company, the Fa Daen Thai Company (or Hua-Luo-Tai Company; the Thai name means "Thai Sky" while the Chinese can be either a transliteration of the Thai or an acronym for *Huaqiao-Eluo-Taiguo*, "Overseas Chinese-Russia-Thailand"), and the Bangkok Witthayakhan Bookshop. The first three were secretly owned and operated by the CCP-TB and the last was linked with the TCP; these firms were in the import-export and book-selling business to finance the two parties' activities and propagate Marxism-communism. Banleu, *Khoomeu kansobsuan*, 71–72. My survey shows that their ads together comprised about 11.5 percent of the advertisements published in all forty-three issues of *Aksornsarn*. Supha, *Jodmai*, 107–109; Sawai, interview, April 22, 1989; Chinda Sirimanond, "Bantheuk jak kong jadkan" [Notice from the management] *Aksornsarn* 3, no. 9 (December 1951): 2.

43 See various issues of *Aksornsarn* (1949–1952); "Lakhorn," 14–15, 23; Supha, interview, September 4, 1985; Wiwat, "Kabot santiphap," 182–83.

44 More specifically: Marxist-communist ideology, Stalinist orthodoxies, the analysis of Thailand as a semi-colonial semi-feudal society, the need for a national democratic revolution, and the overthrow of the Phibun regime. Supha, interview, September 4, 1985; Napaporn, chapter 2 of *Phatthanakan*.

45 Udom, interview, January 19, 1984.

46 Supha, interview, September 4, 1985.

47 No. Praphasathit, *Kao pi*, 487–89.

48 Sawai, interview, April 22, 1989.

49 Such as Prasert Sapsunthorn's renowned and popular *Chiwathas* [Life conception], first serialized in *Mahachon* in late 1948 and later published many times in book form; Udom Sisuwan's *Chiwit kab khwamfaifan* [Life and aspirations] and *San dae nid* [Letters to Nid], both published by the Pituphoom Publishing House in 1957; Samak Burawas' *Setthiwitthaya* [Plutology], serialized in *Aksornsarn* 2 under the pen-name "Phooyingnoi" [The Small] in 1950; and Leuchai Rangsan's *Bon*

senthang rak [On the path of love], published by the Aksornwatthana Publishing House in 1958.

This "self-help" category of Thai radical books, with its intimate subject-matter of personal conduct, viewpoints, romance, and idealism, its friendly conversational style (except Samak's caustic satire Setthiwitthaya) and its mildly preachy tone, was far more enjoyable and accessible to young readers in their first encounter with Marxism-communism than, say, theoretical texts, and thus deserves a detailed analysis in its own right.

50 Such as Jaroen Wanngam's *Phai hed phai sang* [Who makes, who builds?], written in Laotian specifically for peasants in the rural Northeast of Thailand. Pho. Meuangchomphoo, *Soo samoraphoom*, 25. A Thai version was published anonymously as *Khrai sang khrai tham?* (Bangkok: Chomrom Daorung, 1975).

Another well-known example is a seven-chapter standard textbook for new recruits to the CPT's armed force (the People's Liberation Army of Thailand) called Panha kanpatiwat prathet thai [The problem of the revolution of Thailand] or Patiwat jed bot [Seven-chaptered revolution] in popular abbreviation.

Chapter 8

1 *Mahachon* 143 (August 8, 1948).

2 "Mahachon" was widely used to denote 1) "the public," in Thai political and legal writings during the 1920s and 1930s, such as in the terms "kodmai mahachon" (public law) and "mahachonrat" (republic). Its meaning shifted to 2) "the people," in the late 1930s, even though some earlier usages in the 1920s had also suggested that meaning. During the Second World War, due to Prime Minister Phibunsongkhram's repeated and manipulative invocation of "mahachon" in his nationalist rhetoric, a group of anti-Phibun and anti-Japanese liberal journalists found the word so repugnant that they defiantly named their weekly newspaper "Ekkachon" (1941), meaning "the private" or "the individual," the precise antonym of "mahachon." It was probably "mahachon" in the sense of "people" which the Siamese communists intended when they began to publish the *Mahachon* weekly newspaper. However, in the 1950s, "mahachon" would be used more and more by Thai radical intellectuals in the sense of 3) "the masses," rather than in the first two senses, whose popular Thai signifiers became "satharanachon" (the public) and "prachachon" (the people).

From Intharayut (Atsani Phonlajan), "Phak phanuak: Bantheuk khong 'intharayut' kiaokab jamkad phlangkoon lae nangseu ekkachon" [Appendix: "Intharayut"'s memoir on Jamkad Phlangkoon and the Ekkachon newspaper], Sathian, Saithan, 230; Reynolds, *Thai Radical Discourse*, 25, 174.

3 According to a Japanese researcher, some early issues of *Mahachon* (beginning in late 1944) are available at the National Archives of Thailand. (Murashima, *Kanmeuang jinsiam*, 162 n. 154.) The Echols Collections at Kroch Library, Cornell University, contains a microfilmed reproduction of an incomplete set of *Mahachon* from January 1947 to December 1948, the original copy of which is at the United States Library of Congress in Washington, D.C. Another collection of *Mahachon* (1945 to 1948) was located at the so-called Nuai Uppakorn (Equipment Unit) library in the CPT's Voice of the People of Thailand radio station in China. (Kanya Lilalai, interview by the author on the Voice of the People of Thailand radio station, Bangkok, January 27, 1989.) I have also heard from a communist journalistic cadre of one other "complete" collection being kept secretly in a safe house in Bangkok in the 1970s. Regrettably, it was completely disposed of as a precaution upon the bloody military coup of October 6, 1976.

4 According to *Mahachon*'s own account; see *Mahachon* 100 (August 10, 1947).

5 Pho. Meuangchomphoo, *Soo Samoraphoom*, 23–24, 34–35; Phin, interview, July 31, 1985.

6 Pho. Meuangchomphoo, *Soo Samoraphoom*, 34–35.

7 These are *Mahachon* 72–163 (1947–1948); Phin, interview, July, 31, 1985; Pho. Meuangchomphoo, *Soo Samoraphoom*, 23–25, 34–35; Udom, interview, January 19, 1984; and Suphot, *Prasert*, 8, 48–49.

8 From the TCP pamphlet published in 1945/46, "Phak khommunit thai ja tham arai nai pajjuban" [What will the Thai Communist Party do now?]. No longer available, the document was discussed and cited in Prapanta Virasakdi's (Phayap Angkhasing) reply to MP Khlai Laongmani's question about TCP policy in *Mahachon* 73 (February 2, 1947); also Wilson, "Thailand," 92–93; and Thompson and Adloff, *The Left Wing*, 61–63.

9 "VOPT Recounts CPT History," J-8.

10 This kind of rhetoric showed up most frequently in general statements about the Party's ultimate program and in expositions and analyses of communist theory and concepts as applied to Thailand. See, for example, Prapanta Virasakdi's reply to Nationalist Party MP Pramual Kulmat's

question about the TCP's program in *Mahachon* 75 (February 16, 1947); and a theoretical column, "Phak khommunit kheu arai?" [What is the Communist Party?], *Mahachon* 83 (April 13, 1947).

11 On trade unionism, see news reports on the communist labor movement and trade unions in *Mahachon* 74, 85, 86, 87 (February 9, April 27, May 4, and May 11, 1947). On parliamentary politics, see Prapanta Virasakdi's statements and interviews in *Mahachon* 73, 78, 85, 91 (February 2, March 9, April 27, and June 8, 1947).

12 On the Soviet Union, see "Prathet thi damnoen tam latthi sangkhomniyom—sahaphap soviet—mi saphap pen yangrai?" [How are the conditions in a country that follows socialism—the Soviet Union?], *Mahachon* 84 (April 20, 1947); and the special issue, *Mahachon* 113, published on November 9, 1947, to commemorate the Russian Revolution. The constant theme on the Chinese Communist Revolution was that given the similar conditions in China and Southeast Asian countries, the CCP's correct and victorious strategy and tactics had to be profoundly and minutely studied as a very relevant example. "Prathet meuangkheun keung meuangkheun" [Colonial and semi-colonial countries], *Mahachon* 86 (May 4, 1947); "Chaichana an yingyai khong kongthap plodaek prachachon jin" [The great victory of the Chinese People's Liberation Army], *Mahachon* 123 (March 21, 1948).

13 See, for example, Prapanta Virasakdi (TCP spokesman Phayap Angkhasing) interview, "Thammai rao jeung yang khong deuadron yoo?" [Why are we still suffering?], *Mahachon* 78 (March 9, 1947); Prapanta Virasakdi (Phayap Angkhasing) interview, "Hetdai phak khommunit jeung sanabsanun ratthabal?" [Why does the Communist Party support the government?], *Mahachon* 91 (June 8, 1947); and the anti-Phibunsongkhram editorials, articles, and news reports in *Mahachon* 80, 81, 83 (March 23 and 30 and April 13, 1947). For data concerning Phibun's Thammathipat Party and his opportunistic exploitation of anti-communist and royalist politics in the Party's policies, see Thanet, "United States," 191, 200–201.

14 Damri and Jaroon, *Khabuankan*, 37–38, 54–58; Sungsidh, *Prawat*, 181–84, 234. Reportedly, during 1946 and 1947, there were 173 strikes in the whole country, twenty-eight of which were of major importance. Skinner, *Chinese Society*, 287. One CPT source claims that from May 1946 to April 1947, in Bangkok alone, there were ninety-four strikes involving more than twenty thousand workers. Kanya, "Prawat," 29.

15 This demonstration was held in the name of the Party itself. "VOPT Recounts CPT History," J-8; Pan Kaeomat, "Phak khommunit haeng

prathet thai nai sam sib pi thi phom roojak" [My 30-year acquaintance with the Communist Party of Thailand], *Samakkhi Soorob* 2, no. 1 (January 1978): 6.

16 The 1946 and 1947 May Day celebrations were held, respectively, by the Bangkok Workers' Welfare Association together with the Samakhom Traijak (Tricycle Association, an organization of pedicab drivers) and the Central Labor Union. The other big workers' rally was held by the Bangkok Labor Union to celebrate its inauguration on January 1, 1947. Damri and Jaroon, *Khabuankan*, 40–44; United States, American Embassy, Bangkok, "The Sahacheep Party: A Chronology," 3, 5, 8.

17 Speakers at the rally included Thianthai Aphichatbut, Prasert Sapsunthorn, Wiroj Amphai, and Police Second Lieutenant Vas Sunthornjamorn (legal adviser and activist in several communist labor unions). United States, American Embassy, Bangkok, "The Sahacheep Party: A Chronology," 4.

18 Jointly organized by the Sahachip Party and Klum Nakseuksa Haeng Prathet Thai (Student Group of Thailand, one of several TCP youth front organizations), the anti-Phibun rally was addressed by Sanao Phanichjaroen (then a Thammasat student and journalist at *Suwannaphoom* newspaper) and Corporal Roeng Mekphaiboon (NCO in the army's anti-aircraft unit). United States, American Embassy, Bangkok, "The Sahacheep Party: A Chronology," 7; *Mahachon* 83 (April 13, 1947); Kittisak, *Prachathipatai*, 38–42; Sornsak, *Khabuankan serithai*, 262. All except one of the above-mentioned rallies took place at Sanam Luang, a large open ground strategically located in the middle of Bangkok and symbolically surrounded by Thammasat University, the old Royal Palace, the Srirattanasassadaram Temple, and the Ministry of Defense.

19 The proposed coalition government was to include the TCP, the two pro-Pridi parties, and some "new-thinking" Prachathipats. Prapanta, interview, *Mahachon* 78 (March 9, 1947); *Mahachon* 85 (April 27, 1947).

20 *Mahachon* 91 (June 8, 1947).

21 Damri and Jaroon, *Khabuankan*, 45–47; United States, American Embassy, Bangkok, "The Sahacheep Party: A Chronology," 10, 11.

22 Pan, "Phak khommunit," 7; Kanya, "Prawat," 30.

23 For example, see *Mahachon* 87 (May 11, 1947) and 86 (May 4, 1947); Damri and Jaroon, *Khabuankan*, 40–45. M.C. Sakol Wannakon, the so-called "Socialist Prince," was also adviser to the government Labor Committee responsible for studying local labor problems, which was

chaired by the minister of interior under the Pridi government. United States, American Legation, Bangkok, "Fortnightly Summary of Political Events in Siam for the Period July 31–August 15, 1946," 5.

24 Thanet, "United States," 196.

25 Chiab, *Mahawitthayalai*, 465–524.

26 The anti-aircraft guns were harmless to those on the ground. Pho. Meuangchomphoo, *Soo samoraphoom*, 102.

27 Cited in Thak, *Thailand*, 31–32.

28 *Mahachon* 127 (April 18, 1948) and 137 (June 27, 1948); Saifa (Atsani Phonlajan), "Kanprab khommunit nai prathet thai" [The suppression of communists in Thailand], *Karnmuang* 5, no. 1 (July 28, 1948): 6, 18–19.

29 *Mahachon* 142 (August 1, 1948) and 155 (October 31, 1948); *Karnmuang* 5, no. 11 (October 9, 1948): 1; Thongchai, "Latthi khommunit," 387; and Thanin, *Kanchai kodmai*, 237.

30 See Wiwat, "Kabot santiphap," 172; "Ai kruak khon thi song" [The second liar], *Karnmuang* [8], no. 6 (February 17, 1951): 28.

31 *Mahachon* 141 (July 25, 1948); "Kankratham thi na khaina" [Shameful acts], *Karnmuang* [8], no. 6 (February 17, 1951): 3, 27–28; "Sannibat seriphan ok 'mahachon' plom ik" [League of Free Assemblies issues fake *Mahachon* again], *Karnmuang* [8], no. 6 (February 17, 1951): 7, 22; Prapanta Virasakdi (Phayap Angkhasing), "Jodmai jak khosok phak khommunit thai" [Letter from the Thai Communist Party's spokesman], *Karnmuang* [8], no. 6 (February 17, 1951): 7, 22; Wiroj Amphai, "Jodmai jak jaokhong no.so.pho. 'mahachon'" [Letter from the owner of *Mahachon*], *Karnmuang* [8], no. 6 (February 17, 1951): 22; "R.M.T. thep chotnuchit wa mahachon chabab thi laew plom" [Minister Thep Chotnuchit says the last issue of *Mahachon* is fake], *Karnmuang* [8], no. 7 (February 24, 1951): 9; "Nangseu pok daeng" [Red-covered book], *Karnmuang* [8], no. 18 (May 19, 1951): 9; Thongchai, "Latthi khommunit," 384–87; Wiwat, "Kabot santiphap," 172.

32 See Chapter 5, n. 113.

33 Though becoming much smaller and less influential due to government intimidation, both communist unions continued to function under the leadership of Sun Kijjamnong up to 1952. *Mahachon* 136 (June 20, 1948); *Karnmuang* 6, no. 50 (July 8, 1950): 9; *Karnmuang* [8], no. 16 (May 5, 1951): 10; Damri and Jaroon, *Khabuankan*, 58–60; Kanya, "Prawat," 37–38; Skinner, *Chinese Society*, 322–35; Sungsidh, *Prawat*, 175–77, 215–17.

34 Damri and Jaroon, *Khabuankan*, 60–64, 126–30, 152–53; Kanya, "Prawat," 34–37; Sungsidh, *Prawat*, 197–230.

35 Thongchai, "Latthi khommunit," 390–92, 398, 410.

36 The minister of education of the first post-coup Prachathipat government was none other than Leuan Saraphaiwanich, resulting in a bizarre situation in which two formerly friendly Bangkhwang inmates (see chapter 3) found themselves again on opposite sides of the political arena, one as cabinet minister, the other as Communist Party spokesman. Prasert, *Ratthasapha*, 584; Thongchai, "Latthi khommunit," 255–57, 278–79.

37 Khana kammakan borihan phak khommunit thai (Executive Committee of the Thai Communist Party), "Thalaengkan phak khommunit thai waduai sathanakan lae naeonayobai nai pajjuban" [The TCP's statement about the present situation and Party policies], *Mahachon* 115 (January 25, 1948).

38 See *Mahachon* 119 (February 22, 1948) through 131 (May 16, 1948).

39 *Mahachon* 127 (April 18, 1948).

40 *Mahachon* 140 (July 18, 1948).

41 *Mahachon* 153 (October 17, 1948).

42 *Mahachon* 156 (November 7, 1948).

43 For example, Aram Sawaschai, "Khaphajao kho khan" [I oppose], *Mahachon* 127 (April 18, 1948); "Phoey withi thamlai khommunit thai, ja pid samakhom sahaachiwa, lenngan phak khommunit" [Methods to destroy Thai communists exposed, Bangkok Labor Union to be closed down, Communist Party set upon], *Mahachon* 136 (June 20, 1948); "Kanprab khommunit" [The suppression of communists], *Mahachon* 138 (July 4, 1948).

44 *Mahachon* 162 (December 19, 1948).

45 Suvimol Roongcharoen, "Botbat khong naknangseuphim nai kanmeuang thai rawang Pho.So. 2490–2501" [Roles of journalists in Thai politics, 1947–1958 A.D.] (master's thesis, Chulalongkorn University, 1983), 142–44; *Karnmuang* 5, no. 46 (June 11, 1949): 4.

46 Thongchai, "Latthi khommunit," 280.

47 Suvimol, "Botbat," 144–45.

48 The original order was published in *Rajkijjanubeksa* [Royal Thai government gazette] 67, no. 40, Special Edition (July 21, 1950): 1. The repeal appeared in *Rajkijjanubeksa* [Royal Thai government gazette] 73, no. 50 (June 26, 1956): 1765–66.

49 Suthachai, "Kankhleuanwai," 232; Suvimol, "Botbat," 145–48.

50 Pho. Meuangchomphoo, *Soo samoraphoom*, 23.

51 Sornsak, *Khabuankan serithai*, 316–24; Suvimol, "Botbat," 141–51; Somboon, *Bon senthang*, 85, 91–92.

52 U.S. military and economic assistance began to pour in following a succession of Thai-American agreements, prompted by Phibun's

decision in July 1950 to send Thai troops to fight alongside United Nations forces in Korea. Brailey, *Thailand*, 169–89; and *Karnmuang* [8], no. 6 (February 17, 1951): 7.

53 See a perceptive observation on the characteristics of post-war Thai mainstream politics in Wiwat, "Kabot santiphap," 142.

54 Thongchai, "Latthi khommunit," 259–60.

55 Phichit Dijai, interview by the author on his life and political activities, Bangkok, April 23, 1989. A May 1951 issue of *Mahachon* was referred to in Wilson, "Thailand," 346. But according to another source, *Mahachon* lasted until the government's general crackdown on the leftist opposition in November 1952. However, there are neither evidence nor other sources to confirm this information. See Thaweep, interview, December 27, 1988.

56 Pho. Meuangchomphoo, *Soo samoraphoom*, 6–7; Udom Sisuwan, interview, December 27, 1983; Sathian, *Saithan*, 316–18.

57 Thaweep, interview, December 27, 1988.

58 "Sannibat seriphan ok 'mahachon' plom ik" [League of Free Assemblies issues fake *Mahachon* again], *Karnmuang* [8], no. 6 (February 17, 1951): 7, 22; Wiroj Amphai, "Jodmai jak jaokhong no.so.pho. 'mahachon'" [Letter from the owner of *Mahachon*], *Karnmuang* [8], no. 6 (February 17, 1951): 22; "R.M.T. thep chotnuchit wa mahachon chabab thi laew plom" [Minister Thep Chotnuchit says the last issue of *Mahachon* is fake], *Karnmuang* [8], no. 7 (February 24, 1951): 9.

59 Although the said meaning of the term "aksornsarn" was explicitly specified by Supha Sirimanond himself, it is not strictly in line with traditional Thai grammar. Its right meaning should be "written instructions," according to Atsani's funny and erudite protest written as a *klon* poem. See Naiphi (Atsani Phonlajan), "Khwamchokcham khong naiphi" [Naiphi's hurt], *Aksornsarn* 1, no. 1 (April 1949): 69.

A complete set of Aksornsarn is jealously guarded at the misnamed Krathom Pakpao (Puffer Cottage), the late Supha's house, in Bangkok. The collection of Aksornsarn at the National Library of Thailand is in tatters, with pages cut or torn away, presumably by irresponsible leftist readers in the 1970s. Delightfully, the Echols Collection at Kroch Library in Cornell University has an almost complete set of the magazine, with only a single issue missing (volume 1, number 2). According to Craig J. Reynolds, another fairly complete set of Aksornsarn is to be found in the Library of Congress in Washington, D.C.

60 During the course of which Supha coughed up a lot of blood and was treated successively by three doctors. Chinda, *Anusorn*, 51–59.

61 Chinda, *Anusorn*, 52.

62 "Lakhorn," 15.

63 This average approximation is calculated on the basis of all works published in the forty-three issues of *Aksornsarn* according to the above-mentioned rates of contributors' fees. Apparently, this category of expenses fluctuated widely from more than 5,000 baht for the initial issues to 1,000–2,000 baht for the final ones.

64 Supha Sirimanond, "San jak aksornsarn" [Message from *Aksornsarn*], *Aksornsarn* 1, no. 4 (July 1949): 2–3.

65 Khana kammakan hanghunsuan jamkad aksornsarn [The Board of *Aksornsarn* Limited Partnership], "San jak aksornsarn" [Message from *Aksornsarn*], *Aksornsarn* 2, no. 1 (April 1950): 2–3.

66 The length declined from 150 pages (volume 1, numbers 1–3) to 128 (volume 1, numbers 4–12) to finally 100 for the remaining issues.

67 Supha, *Jodmai*, 16–18. Chinda Sirimanond, "Bantheuk jak kong jadkan" [Notice from the management], *Aksornsarn* 2, no. 2 (May 1950): 2; Thaweep, "Supha," 38.

68 Khana kammakan ongkan aksornsarn [The Board of *Aksornsarn* Organization], "San jak aksornsarn" [Message from *Aksornsarn*], *Aksornsarn* 2, no. 10 (January 1951): 2–3; Chinda Sirimanond, "San jak aksornsarn" [Message from *Aksornsarn*], *Aksornsarn* 2, no. 11 (February 1951): 2–3.

69 Chinda, *Anusorn*, 51–61.

70 Supha Sirimanond, *Khaepitalist: khambanyai waduai kamnoed, khrongsang, khwamsongyoo lae kod haeng khwamkhleuanwai khong yuk khaepitalist* [Capitalism: Lectures on the origins, structure, existence, and laws of motion of the age of capitalism] (Bangkok: Chulalongkorn University Social Research Institute Publications, 1986), (25)–(26).

71 Supha Sirimanond, "San jak bannathikan" [Editorial], *Aksornsarn* 1, no. 1 (April 1949): 2; Supha, *Jodmai*, 33–34, 35–36; Reynolds, *Thai Radical Discourse*, 25.

When asked by the author to give a broad comparison between Mahachon and Aksornsarn, Chan Kaeochoosai, a former Thammasat University student leader in the 1950s and avid reader of both publications, came up with the following very perceptive analogies. In terms of scholarly rigor and theoretical sophistication, said Chan, Aksornsarn could be compared to Buddhadasa Bhikkhu (a nationally recognized and highly respected Thai Buddhist philosopher-monk), and Mahachon to Panyanantha Bhikkhu (a clever and popular preacher) though not quite to Phra Phayom Kalyano (a best-selling and demotically entertaining simplifier of Buddhism). Chan, interview, February 5, 1989.

72 This editorial policy statement was printed on page 6, following the contents page, of every issue of *Aksornsarn*.

73 Supha, interview, September 4, 1985. However, by the third year of *Aksornsarn*'s publication, Supha had given up much of his original objective to rectify the thought of his ignorant, slavish, anti-communist "antiquated readers," considering it "unachievable at present." Supha, *Jodmai*, 105–106.

74 Colonel Watthana Phayakkhanithi, "Songkhram klangmeuang nai jin mai chai songkhram udomkhati?" [The civil war in China is not an ideological war], *Aksornsarn* 1, no. 1 (April 1949): 30–33. Sanao Thamsathian (Sanao Phanichjaroen), "Songkhram klangmeuang nai jin pajjuban kheu saphan patiwat sangkhomniyom" [The present civil war in China is the bridge to socialist revolution], *Aksornsarn* 1, no. 3 (June 1949): 42–61. Kulish Indusakh (Atsani Phonlajan), "Sampai hati" [To have the heart to do], *Aksornsarn* 1, no. 3 (June 1949): 108–119. The title is in Malay.

75 So. Sattaya (Colonel Sanong Thamangraksat), "Beuanglang khophiphat rawang yugoslavia kab soviet kheu panha reuang rat macedonia an pen praduj awut song khom" [Behind the Yugoslav-Soviet dispute: The Macedonian Republic, a two-edged weapon], *Aksornsarn* 1, no. 9 (December 1949): 22–33. Sanao, "Kanyaek," *Aksornsarn* 1, no. 9 (December 1949): 33–43.

76 So. Sattaya (Colonel Sanong Thamangraksat), "Prachathipatai prachachon khong yugoslavia kwadlang naithun modsin thang thang thi khamen kab sahaphapsoviet" [Yugoslav people's democracy gets rid of all capitalists despite its discord with the Soviet Union], *Aksornsarn* 2, no. 1 (April 1950): 13–19.

77 Intharayut (Atsani Phonlajan), "Kho mai na seuksa thang kanpraphan" [What should be unlearned about literary composition], *Aksornsarn* 1, no. 5 (August 1949): 64–77; *Aksornsarn* 1, no. 6 (September 1949): 54–63; *Aksornsarn* 1, no. 7 (October 1949): 78–88.

78 Intharayut (Atsani Phonlajan), "Ramayana kheu arai? lae ramakian nan chanai? than thanglai oey" [What is Ramayana? And how is Ramakian, good sirs?], *Aksornsarn* 1, no. 12 (March 1950): 66.

79 Intharayut (Atsani Phonlajan), "Botassajan pen laksana kanpraphan khong chonchan thi theukthak ton pen sommut thewada" [Erotic verse is characteristic of the literary composition of the class which proclaims itself demigod], *Aksornsarn* 2, no. 2 (May 1950): 60–62.

80 Chinda, interview, September 27, 1988.

81 Supha, *Jodmai*, 32–33.

82 Supha Sirimanond, "San jak aksornsarn" [Message from *Aksornsarn*], *Aksornsarn* 2, no. 9 (December 1950): 2–3.

83 Supha, *Jodmai*, 106.

84 Seni, "Yiap yurop," 50.

85 Supha, interview, September 4, 1985. The translation in question was serialized as So. Sattaya (Colonel Sanong Thamangraksat), trans., "Kolwithi khong khommunit tam thassana amerikan" [The tactics of communism in the American view], *Aksornsarn* 1, no. 4–8 (July–November 1949). According to Supha, he obtained a copy of the congressional report indirectly from Lieutenant General Luang Katsongkhram, a colorful Coup Group leader and then deputy army commander, through Sawaeng Senanarong, a friendly army officer at the Ministry of Defense. Its publication in *Aksornsarn* was said to have greatly displeased Udom Sisuwan in particular.

86 "Lakhorn," 27. Samak's translation was serialized as J.V. Stalin, "Latthi sasanniyom baeb dialektik lae sasanniyom thang prawattisat" [Dialectical and historical materialism], trans. Kaptan Samut (Samak Burawas), *Aksornsarn* 2, no. 8–11 (November 1950–February 1951).

87 According to Thaweep, three backbiting "comrades" at *Karnmuang* (then under TCP control) had made Supha's special summer lectures on Marx's *Capital* at Thammasat University in February and March 1951 the object of malicious gossip at the Rungnakhorn Printing House. As it turned out, an employee there who knew Supha overheard them and related the content of their gossip to him. Deeply hurt, he made a caustic retort in the preface to the first edition of his lectures by alluding dismissively to a rhetorical and self-proclaimed "public opinion" that distorted the facts and betrayed the common people. See Thaweep, "Supha," 43–44; Supha, *Khaepitalist*, (16).

88 See the oblique debate on this issue between Udom Sisuwan and Samak Burawas in Or. Pho. (Udom Sisuwan), "Phak phanuak waduai sap lae khwammai thang marxist" [Appendix on Marxist terminology and meanings], *Aksornsarn* 3, no. 3 (June 1951): 97–100; Kaptan Samut (Samak Burawas), "Kanplae kham nai pratya" [The translation of philosophical terms], *Aksornsarn* 3, no. 6 (September 1951): 16–31; Thaweep, interview, December 27, 1988.

89 After three decades of glaring omission during which Supha and *Aksornsarn*'s outstanding contribution to the diffusion and advancement of Marxist-communist theory in Thailand had never even been mentioned in the Party's literature, the CPT finally recognized the

man and his magazine in passing in a recent underground party publication. Phinyo, "Kanphoeyphrae," 45–46. As for Supha and his *Aksornsarn* colleagues, their discussions of the CPT usually contained clear negative connotations and personal contempt, though never wholesale political condemnation or personal malice. See, for example, Supha, interview, September 4, 1985; Suphat, interview, September 7, 1985; Thaweep, interview, December 27, 1988.

90 Supha, interview, September 4, 1985.

91 This account of Supha's life is compiled from the following sources: Supha, interview, September 16, 1979; Supha, interview, October 17, 1979; Chinda, *Anusorn*, 41–49; "Lakhorn," 9–27; Thammakiat Kanari, "Supha sirimanond nakwicha nangseuphim namkhang haeng thalesai nai wan thi kheun soo mahannop" [Supha Sirimanond, scholar of journalism, desert dew on the day it returns to the sea], in *Photjanalai supha sirimanond* [Eulogies to Supha Sirimanond] (Bangkok: Songphorn Woraphithaksanond, 1986), 88–89.

92 This piece of information comes from a letter from Pleuang Wannasri to Supha, reprinted in Supha, *Jodmai*, 89.

93 Lasting for sixty days, the censorship committee was finally dissolved by the new Thawan government. Its notoriety can be gauged from the fact that even a newspaper usually sympathetic to Pridi attacked it as "more terrible than a witch." Thao Phanta, "Siangthok jak prachachon" [People's voices], *Karnmuang* 2, no. 32 (September 13, 1946): 5.

Commenting on this uneasy experience, Supha later said: "As a journalist, it was a sure thing I would get scolded for being a censorship committee member. But since Ajan [a respectful Thai word for "master," here referring to Pridi] told me to, I did it.despite the scolding." Quoted in "Lakhorn," 21.

94 Among these was the later quite influential socialist journalist, Utthorn Phonlakul (Chinda, *Anusorn*, 44, 47). In fact, there was even a likelihood that Supha had a hand in literally cutting out some parts of Atsani's political poems published during that brief period in *Siam Nikorn*. Suchira, "Wikhrao roikrong naiphi," 30–32; Thao Phanta, "Siangthok jak prachachon" [People's voices], *Karnmuang* 2, no. 33 (September 20, 1946): 6, 11, 18.

95 See, in this regard, similar rumors against Pridi reported by John Coast in *Some Aspects of Siamese Politics* (1953), quoted in Wyatt, *Thailand*, 264.

96 Though he said he gave "moral support" to his colleagues' effort. Quoted in Sornsak, *Khabuankan serithai*, 302.

97 Supha, interview, October 17, 1979.

98 Supha, interview, September 4, 1985.
99 Supha Sirimanond, "Yiap yurop: Nai sapen ratsadorn pen tae phiang trayang khong aphichon" [Roaming Europe: In Spain, the people are merely the aristocrats' rubber stamp], *Aksornsarn* 2, no. 9 (December 1950): 28–65; and "Yiap yurop: An leh kanmeuang chat tawantok dai nai korani sapen" [Roaming Europe: The western nations' political intrigue could be read in the Spanish case], *Aksornsarn* 2, no. 10 (January 1951): 17–53.
100 Supha Sirimanond, "Yiap yurop: Kanfadkan khong foong majingjok bon hua samanchon" [Roaming Europe: The dogfight among the pack of foxes on the common people's heads], *Aksornsarn* 2, no. 11 (February 1951): 18–56. Supha Sirimanond, "Yiap yurop: Deung franco khao soo sangkhom yurop ja thamlai yurop eng" [Roaming Europe: To draw Franco into the European Community will destroy Europe itself], *Aksornsarn* 2, no. 12 (March 1951): 26–66.
101 Thaweep, interview, December 27, 1988.
102 Phin, interview, July 31, 1985; Napaporn, *Phatthanakan*, 20; and Napaporn, "The Development," 54.
103 The movement was spearheaded by Khana Kammakan Santiphap Haeng Prathet Thai (The Peace Committee of Thailand), which was set up and coordinated by the TCP in April 1951. Wiwat, "Kabot santiphap," 162–64.
104 Supha, interview, September 16, 1979; Supha, interview, October 28, 1979. The CPT asserted that some 150,000 signatures were collected in the first round of the campaign in late 1950 and another 170,000 in the second round in early 1951. "VOPT Recounts CPT History," J-10.
105 Supha Sirimanond,"Prawat jing khong ah q kab mahachon chaothai" [The true story of Ah Q and the Thai people], in *Wannasan samneuk: Khwamsamneuk nai itthiphol seusan khong nangseu, lem song* [Literary consciousness: The consciousness of the communicative influence of books, vol. 2] (Bangkok: Supha Sirimanond Foundation, 1986), 305.
106 In a spectacular but imprudent show of force, on August 25, 1952, the Peace Committee of Thailand convened about two hundred peace-activist delegates from all over the country, ranging from workers, peasants, students, teachers, and monks to journalists, writers, and politicians, at the Suriyanond Hotel on Rajdamnoen Avenue in the middle of Bangkok, ostensibly to prepare for the coming Asian and Pacific Peace Conference in Peking. In October, in the aftermath of drought followed by floods in the Northeast, the Peace Committee, together with six daily newspapers, also organized a well-publicized and widely popular relief campaign for local residents there, collecting and donating many clothes and 60,000

baht from people in Bangkok. On account of these two events, the Phibun government became greatly alarmed at the unexpected strength and broad popular base of the leftist opposition.

See Wiwat, "Kabot santiphap," 215–19; Thailand, Criminal Court, Ministry of Justice, "The Testimony of Phramaha Dilok Suwannarat (Thammathatto Bhikkhu)," Criminal Court Proceedings of the Cases No. Black 158, 168, 202/2496, November 1953.

107 Which reads:

The World Revolution is not our creation. We only showed how to lead it and make a success of it in the interests of the great majority of humanity. We shall continue to do our duty...

Cited in Yeoman Pakpao (Supha Sirimanond), "Rob rabiang aksornsarn" [Around Aksornsarn's veranda], Aksornsarn 4, no. 5 (August 1952): 2.

108 Kaptan Samut (Samak Burawas), "Phutthit phachoenna kab khommunit" [Buddhism versus communism], Aksornsarn 4, no. 5 (August 1952): 10–45.

109 Which reads:

Social Chauvinists? Socialists in word and Chauvinists in action, people who are in favor of national defense in an imperialist war.

Cited in Yeoman Pakpao (Supha Sirimanond), "Rob rabiang aksornsarn" [Around Aksornsarn's veranda], Aksornsarn 4, no. 6 (September 1952): 2.

110 Phatthana, trans., "Sathana khong pajjekchon nai robob sochalist" [The status of the individual in the socialist system], Aksornsarn 4, no. 6 (September 1952): 16–83.

111 Which reads:

A social pacifist is a socialist in words and a bourgeois pacifist in deeds: bourgeois pacifists dream of an everlasting peace without the overthrow of the yoke and domination of capital.

Cited in Yeoman Pakpao (Supha Sirimanond), "Rob rabiang aksornsarn" [Around Aksornsarn's veranda], Aksornsarn 4, no. 7 (October 1952): 2.

112 "Nai thi sud sochalist ja tong chana, ya songsai loey" [In the end, socialism will be victorious, do not for a moment doubt it], Aksornsarn 4, no. 7 (October 1952): 7–15; Supha Sirimanond, "Lok kao rudna pai soo sochalist" [The world is advancing towards socialism], Aksornsarn 4, no. 7 (October 1952): 16–86.

113 Supha, interview, September 4, 1985.

114 Supha, interview, September 4, 1985; Supha, interview, September 16, 1979; Thaweep, "Supha," 42. The other two interrogations of Supha were conducted by Police Colonel Banleu Reuangtrakul and Police Second Lieutenant Ari Karibut.

115 Reynolds, *Thai Radical Discourse*, 32–33; Supha Sirimanond, *Jengghizkhan: Nawaniyai ing prawattisat* [Genghis Khan: A historical novel] (Bangkok: Supha Sirimanond Foundation, 1988), especially the introduction by Thaweep Voradilok and the author's preface and epilogue on pages 9–32 and 849–51.

116 Actually, "tail-flogging crocodile" is a well-known ferocious tactic in the repertoire of traditional Thai kickboxing. It involves a quick turn-around of the body followed by an unexpected rearward kick at the opponent. Supha's application of the term here signifies an oblique literary attack on the powers-that-be under conditions of press censorship, his personal favorite trick of the opposition journalistic trade. Supha, interview, September 4, 1985; "Lakhorn," 17.

117 Naiphi (Atsani Phonlajan), "Doo thi nai" [Where to look], *Aksornsarn* 1, no. 3 (June 1949): 107; Lao Kim Nguan, "Saboo tra phej" [Diamond brand soap], *Aksornsarn* 1, no. 3 (June 1949): 90.

118 Intharayut (Atsani Phonlajan), "Wannakhadi kao kao" [Old literature], *Aksornsarn* 1, no. 11 (February 1950): 84–88; Intharayut, "Ramayana kheu arai?," *Aksornsarn* 1, no. 12 (March 1950): 66–70; Khuru Sapha, "Kammanit thang chud rakha 6 baht" [6 baht for a set of kammanit], *Aksornsarn* 1, no. 11 (February 1950) and 1, no. 12 (March 1950): inner front cover.

119 Thaweepvorn (Thaweep Voradilok), "Prawattisat yoo thi nai?" [Where is history?], *Aksornsarn* 1, no. 12 (March 1950): 121; Intharayut (Atsani Phonlajan), "Khokangkha 3 prakan nai wannakhadi khong siam" [Three riddles in Siamese literature], *Aksornsarn* 2, no. 6 (September 1950): 45–50; Khuru Sapha, "Kammanit thang chud rakha 6 baht" [6 baht for a set of kammanit], *Aksornsarn* 1, no. 12 (March 1950) and 2, no. 6 (September 1950): inner front cover.

120 Suphat, "Rabob kanngoen," [The financial system], *Aksornsarn* 2, no. 4 (July 1950): 12–16; Phooyingnoi (Samak Burawas), "Setthiwitthaya ton thi song" [Plutology, part 2], *Aksornsarn* 2, no. 5 (August 1950): 55–56; Asia Trust, "Seu lae khai ngoentra tang prathet" [Foreign currency trading], *Aksornsarn* 2, no. 4 (July 1950): 96; and 2, no. 5 (August 1950): 86.

Formed in 1949 with a registered capital of ten million baht, the Asia Trust Company was in the 1950s the key financial base and launching pad of a lookjin financial wizard and business strategist named Chin Sophonphanich and would propel him and the Bangkok Bank, whose management he took over in 1952, to the topmost position in the Thai banking industry in the 1960s. Mainly involved in the highly lucrative business of immigrant remittances to China and foreign currency trading, the company had an average annual income of 2.8 million baht and an average annual profit of .94 million baht from 1950 to 1957. Chin's successful career was partly attributed to his partnership with two leading lookjin businessmen whose respective expertise was ideally complementary to his: Prasit Kanjanawat (lawyer) and Bunchoo Rojanasathian (accountant).

See "Prasit kanjanawat phoosang tamnan kanmeuang-thurakij" [Prasit Kanjanawat, creator of a political-business legend], Phoonam Thurakij 3, no. 26 (February 1989): 17–18; Phanni Bualek, Wikhrao naithun thanakan phanich khong thai Pho.So. 2475–2516 [An analysis of Thai commercial banking capitalists, B.E. 2475–2516], Khrongkan nangseulem sathaban wijaisangkhom chulalongkorn mahawitthayalai [Chulalongkorn University Social Research Institute Book Publications Project], ed. Kanoksak Kaewthep (Bangkok: Sangsan Publishing House, 1986), 78–88, 110–27.

121 Phooyingnoi (Samak Burawas), "Jit manus ni sai ngai thae yang theung" [The human mind is easy to fathom], *Aksornsarn* 4, no. 4 (July 1952): 24; Anta, "Pantocrine," *Aksornsarn* 4, no. 4 (July 1952): inner back cover.

122 Uthai Sakhornwasi, a minor partner of the magazine, owned a Bangkok drugstore called Tra Nokyoong (Peacock Brand). Chinda had another relative who owned the drugstore Bangkok Osot. Both drugstores published advertisements regularly in *Aksornsarn*. See Chinda, *Anusorn*, 43; Chinda Sirimanond," Bantheuk jak kong jadkan" [Notice from the management], *Aksornsarn* 2, no. 3 (June 1950): 2.

123 Phooyingnoi (Samak Burawas), "Setthiwitthaya ton thi sam" [Plutology, part 3], *Aksornsarn* 2, no. 6 (September 1950): 77–78.

124 Tra Nokyoong, "Ya raksa rok prajam khrobkhrua" [Household medicines], *Aksornsarn* 2, no. 6 (September 1950): outer back cover; Sakol Pharmacy, "Atarsol," ibid., 22; Tra Ngoo, "Lexington F.G.," ibid., 56; Bangkok Osot, "Ya thai jinda" [Thai jinda medicine], ibid., inner back cover.

125 Phooyingnoi compared cosmeticians and jewelers to drug dealers, tobacconists, and liquor-sellers as so many "opium merchants who intoxicate the people." See Phooyingnoi, "Setthiwitthaya ton thi song," *Aksornsarn* 2, no. 5 (August 1950): 57; Srikanchang Company, "Max Factor Hollywood: What a Wonderful New Lipstick!" *Aksornsarn* 1, no. 1 (April 1949): 106; Nightingale-Olympics Company, "Kila, sam-ang, dontri" [Sports, cosmetics, music], *Aksornsarn* 1, no. 3 (June 1949): inner back cover; 1, no. 5 (August 1949): 104; 1, no. 6 (September 1949): inner

back cover; 1, no. 7 (October 1949): inner back cover; 1, no. 8 (November 1949): inner back cover.

Phooyingnoi berated insurance brokers as "mo ngoen" (moneygrubbers) who got rich through devious and effortless means. See Phooyingnoi, "Setthiwitthaya ton thi sam," Aksornsarn 2, no. 6 (September 1950): 75–76; Akhane Insurance Company, "Prakan anakhot khong look noi pheua kanseuksa" [Insure your small child's future education], Aksornsarn 1, no. 12 (March 1950): 18; 2, no. 1 (April 1950): 20; 2, no. 2 (May 1950): 22; 2, no. 3 (June 1950): 88; 2, no. 4 (July 1950): 98.

126 Khamsing, interview, April 12, 1989.

127 Supha, *Jodmai*, 18–19, 29–30, 32, 42–44, 47–52, 57–69, 77–79, 82–83, 100–104, 107–110, 113–17.

128 Cited in "Lakhorn," 20.

129 For example, various radical trade unions were reported to have made a contribution of three thousand baht to *Mahachon* in February 1948. *Mahachon*, 119 (February 22, 1948).

130 Khun Dong (Udom Sisuwan), "Nai rob sapda" [The week in review], *Mahachon* 139 (July 11, 1948).

131 "Dae than phooan" [For the readers], *Karnmuang* 3, no. 31 (July 28, 1947): 1, 20. This issue was subtitled: "The Third Anniversary Issue." Since volume 1 of *Karnmuang* has not been found, the beginning year of its publication is inconclusively gauged from this evidence.

In transliterating the Thai name of this weekly newspaper as Karnmuang, I follow the paper's own version. Otherwise, the same Thai word is transliterated as "kanmeuang" in this book.

132 An extensive but incomplete collection of *Karnmuang* during its first period (circa 1944 to 1950), covering volumes 2–7, is kept on microfilm at the Central Library, Academic Resources Institute, Chulalongkorn University (reels 1014, 1015, and 1016). The second period (1951) cannot be found in Thailand. Fortunately, an incomplete collection of it (identified in this thesis as volume [8]) is available in the Echols Collection, Kroch Library, Cornell University.

133 Wiwat, "Kabot santiphap," 215.

134 The following profile of Prasit is based on "Prasit kanjanawat," *Phoonam Thurakij* 3, no. 26 (February 1989): 15–64.

135 Skinner, *Chinese Society*, 159, 169. The name of the school was transliterated as "Hsin-min" by Skinner.

136 Skinner, *Chinese Society*, 267, 269.

137 Concerning Chin Sophonphanich and the Asia Trust Company, see the earlier discussion in this chapter. This so-called "Thanarachan"

(Plutomonarch) of Thailand also had a Chinese alias, "Chen Bichen" in
Mandarin or "Tang Piakching" in the Teochiu dialect, the name "bi-chen"
meaning "assisting the subjects." However, in Bangkok business circles,
he was widely called "Naihang Piak," a Thai term meaning Proprietor
Piak. It is by this latter name that I first heard of him in my boyhood from
one of his reputedly innumerable distant admirers, enviers, and debtors,
namely Tae Ngeksong, my eventually bankrupt father.

138 Thailand, Department of Commercial Registration, Ministry of Commerce,
"Rungnakhorn Company Limited," Registration Profile File no. 2349.

139 And later, one hastens to add, member of the Bangkok Bank's board of
directors (May 1968), senator (July 1968), deputy director of the economic,
fiscal, and industrial division of the ruling military Revolutionary Group
under Field Marshal Thanom Kittikachorn (November 1971), deputy
minister of the economy (November 1971), minister of commerce
(December 1972), MP for Chachoengsao (January 1975, April 1976),
president of the House of Representatives and the National Assembly
(February 1975), vice president of the Bangkok Bank (January 1976),
deputy minister of justice (April 1976), deputy prime minister (October 5,
1976), senator (April 1979), and president of the Bangkok Bank (since
August 1984).

140 See examples of *Karnmuang*'s editorial policy statements during the first
period in Prasit Kanjanawat and Prasert Praphasanobol, "Jodmai theung
khun srisarakorn athibadi krom sanphasamit" [An open letter to Khun
Srisarakorn, director-general of the Excise Duties Department],
Karnmuang 2, no. 1 (February 8, 1946): 7; "Nangseuphim thai thuk wan
ni" [Thai newspapers today], *Karnmuang* 3, no. 20 (May 9, 1947): 3–4;
Khana nangseuphim karnmuang [*Karnmuang* Newspaper Board],
Karnmuang 4, no. 1 (January 3, 1948): 1; *Karnmuang* 5, no. 21
(December 18, 1948): 2.

141 For instance, Samran Kanlayanamit, "Watthanatham thang kaiyaphap nai
sahaphap soviet" [Physical culture in the Soviet Union], *Karnmuang* 5, no.
3 (August 14, 1948): 4, 13; versus "Latthi khommunit nai malayoo"
[Communism in Malaya], ibid., 3 *ff*, 13. Or Samran Kanlayanamit,
"Kannangseuphim lae kanphimjamnai nai sahaphap soviet" [Journalism and
commercial publication in the Soviet Union], *Karnmuang* 5, no. 4 (August
21, 1948): 3, 12; versus Kornsit, "Phaenkan yaek lok khong stalin" [Stalin's
plan for world division], ibid., 8–9. Or Seriniyom, "Ja prab khommunit
pheua khrai?" [For whose sake is the suppression of communism?],
Karnmuang 5, no. 19 (December 4, 1948): 2; versus Amateur, "Russia yang
mai rob" [Russia does not go to war yet], ibid., 8, 9, 15.

142 These common Thammasat background and bonds among *Karnmuang*'s editorial staff and writers have been perceptively raised by Wiwat Catithammanit in his well-researched dissertation "Kabot santiphap," 159. They were dramatically expressed in a barrage of articles criticizing the Phibun government's discriminatory measures against Thammasat University as well as supporting and advising Thammasat students' protests against them. These were written by *Karnmuang* columnists of various ideological persuasions: Tham Niyom, "Anakhot khong mahawitthayalai thammasat" [The future of Thammasat University], *Karnmuang* 4, no. 3 (January 17, 1948): 4, 13–14; Seriniyom, "Thammasat phoorabkhrao" [Thammasat, the scapegoat], *Karnmuang* 5, no. 2 (August 7, 1948): 2; Saifa (Atsani Phonlajan), "Phooprasatkan mahawitthayalai wicha thammasat lae kanmeuang" [The chancellor of the University of Moral and Political Sciences], ibid., 8, 11; Witthawas Phawaphootanon, "Kanmeuang thi bibkhan kanseuksa" [Political pressure on education], *Karnmuang* 5, no. 3 (August 14, 1948): 3; "Nakseuksa 200 khon ja krid leuad to na jomphol" [200 students will slash their wrists in front of the Field Marshal], *Karnmuang* 5, no. 7 (September 11, 1948): 1; Saifa (Atsani Phonlajan), "Kankhleuanwai khong nakseuksa" [The student movement], *Karnmuang* 5, no. 11 (October 9, 1948): 3, 11; Watthanachon, "Khokhid jak kantosoo khong nakseuksa" [Thoughts on the students' struggle], *Karnmuang* 6, no. 48 (June 24, 1950): 5, 14; Watthanachon, "Sitthi thang kanmeuang lae seriphap nai kankhleuanwai khong nakseuksa" [Students' political rights and freedom of activism], *Karnmuang* 6, no. 49 (July 1, 1950): 11, 13–14; Watthanachon, "Jong chai khwamrunraeng hai thook thang" [Use violence in the right way], *Karnmuang* 6, no. 52 (July 22, 1950): 9, 13–15; Watthanachon, "Luang wijitwathakan phoopen wassakanphram" [Luang Wijitwathakan, a fifth columnist], *Karnmuang* 7, no. 5 (August 26, 1950): 10–11, 20.

         However, what really held these people together as well as finally broke them apart was, I would argue, the personal patronage of Prasit Kanjanawat.

143 See, for instance, X.O.3., "Beuanglang kanlonghon khong ratthaburus awuso" [Behind the disappearance of the Senior Statesman], *Karnmuang* 3, no. 49 (November 29, 1947): 5, 17, 19; a translation of Pridi's speech in English broadcast from Singapore in *Karnmuang* 3, no. 50 (December 6, 1947): 5–6; Chanathikorn and X.O.3., "Meua ratthaburus awuso doenthang rob lok" [When the Senior Statesman travelled around the world], *Karnmuang* 4, no. 11 (March 13, 1948) and following issues; Sri-

Intharayut (Atsani Phonlajan), "Kam khong khrai?" [Whose karma?], *Karnmuang* 5, no. 5 (August 28, 1948): 3, 13–14; Ko. Kho. na Boyang, "Phap prathab jai" [Impression], *Karnmuang* 5, no. 6 (September 4, 1948): 3, 12–13; Thid Rung, "Reuang na anat" [Tragic story], *Karnmuang* 5, no. 13 (October 23, 1948): 1.

144 *Karnmuang* 3, no. 51 (December 13, 1947): 1.

145 Prasit Kanjanawat, trans., "Ratthathammanoon haeng sahaphap satharanarat sochiallist soviet" [The Constitution of the Union of Soviet Socialist Republics], *Karnmuang* 4, no. 17–29 (April 24–July 17, 1948). The text of the translation was introduced by the translator's own radical, sympathetic, historical essay entitled "Botnam: Prawat kanpatiwat doi yo khong russia" [Introduction: A brief history of the Russian Revolution], *Karnmuang* 4, no. 17 (April 24, 1948): 7, 10, 14, and followed by an analytical commentary written by Suphat Sukhonthaphirom (who also helped check Prasit's Chinese-Thai translation against the English version), entitled "Botsarup: Ratthathammanoon sahaphap satharanarat sochiallist soviet" [Conclusion: The Constitution of the Union of Soviet Socialist Republics], *Karnmuang* 4, no. 29 (July 17, 1948): 7, 13, 15. The three pieces of writing and another commentary by Udom Sisuwan, then TCP head of party press and publication, were later compiled and published by a TCP-affiliated publisher, thus providing printed evidence of the future tycoon's youthful flirtation with communism.

Notably, when Phin Bua-on, a future member of the CPT's Politbureau, was asked to name off the top of his head important reading in his youth, Prasit's translation of the Soviet Constitution stood out in his list of works mostly written by communist authors. Phin, interview, August 31, 1984.

146 Dao Isan, trans., "Ratthathammanoon prathet lao" [The Constitution of Laos], *Karnmuang* 3, no. 36 (August 30, 1947), and following issues; Wirachphan, trans., "Ratthathammanoon haeng satharanarat prachathipatai vietnam" [The Constitution of the Democratic Republic of Vietnam], *Karnmuang* 5, no. 42 (May 14, 1949) and following issues.

147 For example, "Khrai pen khrai nai russia" [Who is who in Russia], *Karnmuang* 3, no. 17 (April 18, 1947): 11–12, 21–23.

148 Kamol Janthasorn, "Chon kammachip" [The proletariat], *Karnmuang* 4, no. 9 (February 28, 1948): 5, 11; Natthawut Sutthisongkhram, "Lok haeng khommunit" [The world of communism], *Karnmuang* 4, no. 20 (May 15, 1948): 8–10, 13–15.

149 Serm Reuangsawas, "Sahaphap satharanarat sochialist soviet" [The Union of Soviet Socialist Republics], *Karnmuang* 5, no. 41 (May 7, 1949)

and following issues. Said to be a product of many years of research by a Thai student from abroad, this story was serialized in *Karnmuang* for six months before it came to an end.

150 Issarawut, trans., "Krungthep" [Bangkok], *Karnmuang* 6, no. 44 (May 27, 1950): 16.

151 Prasit Kanjanawat, "Sonthana kab than" [Conversation with you], *Karnmuang* 2, no. 34 (September 27, 1946): 19; "Khrai pen khrai nai russia," *Karnmuang* 3, no. 17 (April 18, 1947): 11; Phethai Chotnuchit, "Sonthana kab than" [Conversation with you], *Karnmuang* 5, no. 43 (May 21, 1949): 2.

152 Sri-Intharayut, "Uttarakuru thaweep," *Karnmuang* 5, no. 4 (August 21, 1948): 3, 11–14; Issarawut, "Sassana phrasrian kab latthi khommunit" [The religion of Phra Sri Arya and communism], *Karnmuang* 6, no. 24 (January 7, 1950): 10–11.

153 Natthawut Sutthisongkhram, "Prathet thai kab khommunit" [Thailand and communism], *Karnmuang* 4, no. 21 (May 22, 1948): 8–11, 13; Natthawut Sutthisongkhram, "Lang neua chob lang ya" [There's no accounting for taste], *Karnmuang* 6, no. 22 (December 24, 1949): 5, 15–16; Yothin na Rangtal, "Meua klab songkhla" [Back to Songkhla], *Karnmuang* 5, no. 41–48 (May 7–June 25, 1949).

154 Prasit Kanjanawat, "Meuang thai ja pai thang nai" [Which way will Thailand go], *Karnmuang* 5, no. 1 (July 28, 1948): 2.

155 Saifa, "Kanprab khommunit" [The suppression of communists], *Karnmuang* 5, no. 1 (July 28, 1948): 6, 18–19.

156 Thid Rung, "Withi nai ja di kwa" [Which method is better], *Karnmuang* 5, no. 12 (October 16, 1948): 2.

157 The political cartoon on the front page of *Karnmuang* 5, no. 12 (October 16, 1948), which depicts a policeman inspecting three tiny suit-wearing "communist" suspects with a magnifying glass.

158 Seriniyom, "Ja prab khommunit pheua khrai?" [For whose sake is the suppression of communism?], *Karnmuang* 5, no. 19 (December 4, 1948): 2.

159 Phethai Chotnuchit, "Withi pongkan khommunit" [The anti-communist method], *Karnmuang* 5, no. 23 (January 1, 1949): 5, 14.

160 Temi, "Khommunit kab khon thai" [Communism and the Thai people], *Karnmuang* 5, no. 28 (February 5, 1949): 3, 19.

161 Suphat Sukhonthaphirom, "Naeotan khommunit" [The anti-communist front], *Karnmuang* 6, no. 1 (July 30, 1949): 10, 17.

162 "Thathi thi ok ja lodphon" [A rather adventurous posture], *Karnmuang* 6, no. 10 (October 1, 1949): 2.

163 Kamol Janthasorn, "Phai khommunit" [The communist peril], *Karnmuang* 6, no. 13 (October 22, 1949): 2.

164 Kulap Saipradit, "Nakkanmeuang khirok nai america" [Sick politicians in America], *Karnmuang* 6, no. 47 (June 18, 1950): 3, 8, 16.

165 Thatnamdi, "Withi kantosoo pheua santiphap khong prachachon chaolok" [The world people's method of struggle for peace], *Karnmuang* 6, no. 48 (June 24, 1950): 3, 16–18.

166 "Prasit kanjanawat," *Phoonam Thurakij* 3, no. 26 (February 1989): 24; Phethai, "Sonthana," *Karnmuang* 5, no. 43 (May 21, 1949): 2.

167 Although *Karnmuang* did not appear to have a large deficit like *Aksornsarn*, it was no big earner and it often ran into financial difficulties. "Nangseuphim thai thuk wan ni" [Thai newspapers today], *Karnmuang* 3, no. 20 (May 9, 1947): 3–4; *Karnmuang* 3, no. 36 (August 30, 1947): 2; Khana Nangseuphim Karnmuang, *Karnmuang* 4, no. 1 (January 3, 1948): 1; "Thuang ni agent tang jangwat" [Calling on provincial agents to pay debts], *Karnmuang* 5, no. 18 (November 27, 1948); "Thuang ni agent tang jangwat," *Karnmuang* 6, no. 48 (June 24, 1950).

168 See an advertisement for this book in *Mahachon* 148 (September 12, 1948).

169 Prasit Kanjanawat, "35 pi haeng kanplianplaeng kanpokkhrong khong jin: Tad ton jak nangseu *Chiang kaishek: Pramuk khong jin mai*" [35 years of the change of regime in China: An excerpt from *Chiang Kaishek: The head of New China*], *Karnmuang* 2, no. 36 (October 11, 1946): 12–14, 19–21.

170 Prasit, "Botnam: Prawat kanpatiwat," *Karnmuang* 4, no. 17 (April 24, 1948): 7, 10, 14.

171 Vajiravudh, *Jodmaihet*, 1–46; Prajadhipok, "Phrabaromrajwinijchai," 214, 255–56; Damrongrachanuphap, "Laksana kanpokkhrong," 5–8; Pridi, *Pridi banomyong*, 173–74, 241–42.

172 Van Slyke, chapter 9 of *Enemies and Friends*; Steinberg, ed., *In Search of Southeast Asia*, 349–54.

173 Publisher's preface to Sakol Wannakon et al., *Khamprakas*.

174 Thaweep, interview, December 27, 1988.

175 Among those leftists whom Bunchoo helped were Witthayakorn Chiangkul and Samai Aphaphirom.

176 Thaweep, interview, December 27, 1988.

177 Suvimol, "Botbat," 139–51.

178 One of the first things Major General Chatchai Chunhawan did after taking the Prime Minister's office for the first time in mid-1988 was to pay a widely publicized visit to Prasit's mansion at Bang Khanak Village,

where the two old men reminisced fondly about their youthful wartime days together.

179 Prasit's connection with Phao was attested to by Supha Sirimanond and Nara Phreutthinan, both of whom used to work for Prasit at *Thai Mai*. Mongkol Poonpermsuksombat, "Wikhrao reuangsan khong Issara amantakul" [An analytical study of Isara Amantakool's short stories] (master's thesis, Srinakharinwirot University, 1981), 40–41; Supha, interview, October 28, 1979.

   During the "newspaper war" of 1955–1957, the political divisions among the more important political press were roughly as follows: Pro-Phibun–Sathiaraphap; pro-Phao–2500, Chao, Phao Thai, Thai Seri, and Thai Mai; pro-Sarit–San Seri and Thai Raiwan; conservative royalist— Siam Rat and Prachathipatai; and leftist-communist–Pituphoom. See Suthachai, "Kankhleuanwai," 280–81; Thaweep Voradilok, "Naknangseuphim kab thoraraj" [Journalists and tyrants], Matichon 9 (January 9, 1986): 18–21; Pho. Meuangchomphoo, Soo Samoraphoom, 14; Sungsidh, Thunniyom, 297–98; Supha, interview, September 4, 1985.

180 The same principle applied to Field Marshal Sarit's protection for *San Seri* and its leftist editor, Thanong Satthathip. See Thaweep, "Naknangseuphim," 18–21.

181 The faction derived its name from an alley in Bangkok where the residences of the Chunhawan, Adireksan, and Siriyothin families were located close together. Members of this faction were also related to one another by marriage.

182 See two magnificent and meticulous complementary works on this subject by members of the Marxian Political Economy Group at Chulalongkorn University: Sungsidh, chapter 4 of *Thunniyom*, especially 118–21, 184–88, 194–200; and Phanni, *Wikhrao naithun*, 108–27.

183 Intharayut (Atsani Phonlajan), "Siang khong khon mai mi siang" [The voice of the voiceless], *Karnmuang* 2, no. 39 (November 1, 1946): 3–4, 19, 21–22.

184 Mongkol, "Wikhrao reuangsan," 30–41. For more details of Issara's early career struggles and team of talented young self-made journalists, see Intharayut, "Phak phanuak: Bantheuk khong 'intharayut' kiaokab run khong issara amantakul," 221–25.

185 Wiwat, "Kabot santiphap," 122, 159; and *Karnmuang* 6, 7 and [8].

186 See n. 132 above.

187 "Thalaengkan khong khana nangseuphim karnmuang raisapda theung than phooan, samachik lae agent" [A statement of the publishers of the

Karnmuang Weekly newspaper to the readers, subscribers and agents],
Karnmuang [8], no. 3 (January 27, 1951): 28.

188 Pho. Meuangchomphoo, *Soo Samoraphoom*, 6–8.

189 Apart from Atsani (whose pen-names in the new *Karnmuang* were
"Intharayut," "Sri-Intharayut," "Naiphi," "Kulish Indusakh," and "Malini
Sunthorntham") and Udom (alias "Pho. Meuangchomphoo"), they
included Kulap Saipradit, Samak Burawas (alias "Kaptan Samut"), Issara
Amantakul (alias "XYZ"), "Watthanachon," Pleuang Wannasri, Thaweep
Voradilok (alias "Thaweepvorn"), Prakhin Chumsai na Ayudhya (alias
"Ujcheni"), Doctor Prasit Tantiwej (alias "Or.So. Mekphoot"), and
occasionally even Prapanta Virasakdi (alias Phayap Angkhasing or
Piatoe, the TCP spokesman) and Wiroj Amphai (*Mahachon*'s owner).
See Malini Sunthorntham (Atsani Phonlajan), "Than phoaan thi rak"
[Dear readers], *Karnmuang* [8], no. 2 (January 20, 1951): 14–16.

190 "Thalaengkan lae san khong khana kammakan santiphap haeng prathet
thai" [Statement and letter from the Peace Committee of Thailand],
Karnmuang [8], no. 16 (May 5, 1951): 12, 21; "Khana kammakan
santiphap: Thongchai haeng santi khong prachachon thai" [The Peace
Committee: The victory banner of peace of the Thai people], ibid., 3, 16,
26; "Kanchumnum santiphap khrang raek nai prathet thai" [First peace
rally in Thailand], ibid., 28, 27; "Jodmai jak prachachon" [Letters from
the people], ibid., 4, 25.

191 The whole issue of *Karnmuang* [8], no. 20 (June 2, 1951) was devoted to
the launch of this campaign, with statements and articles by the Peace
Committee of Thailand (special pages Ko.-Kho.), Jaroen Seubsaeng (5,
27), Kulap Saipradit (6, 22, 27), Atsani Phonlajan (9, 20), Pleuang
Wannasri (special page Kho.), Issara Amantakul (special page Kho.), and
So. Chotephan alias Corporal Roeng Mekphaiboon (special page Ngo.).

192 See, for instance, "Chumnum santichon nai sapda thi kao khong
kanronnarong santiphap" [The rally of peaceniks in the ninth week of the
peace campaign], *Karnmuang* [8], no. 1 (January 13, 1951): 11, 21; Santi,
"Sarup kanlongnam santiphap nai rob 7 sapda" [Progress report on the
signature campaign for peace in 7 weeks], ibid., 12–13, 20; "Khao phood
yangrai meua longnam santiphap" [What did they say when they signed
the peace petition], ibid., 13, 20; "Kanronnarong pheua santiphap" [The
campaign for peace], *Karnmuang* [8], no. 2 (January 20, 1951): 13, 16,
23; "Khrai bang thi longnam riakrong hai mahaamnaj thang ha tham
katika sanya santiphap" [Who signed the petition calling upon the five
major powers to make a peace treaty], *Karnmuang* [8], no. 21 (June 9,

1951): 5, 23, 24; "Khwamsamrej khong kanlongnam nai sapda raek" [The success of the signature campaign in the first week], *Karnmuang* [8], no. 22 (June 16, 1951): 5, 24, 26.

193 "Jodmai jak prachachon" [Letters from the people], *Karnmuang* [8], no. 13 (April 14, 1951): 23.

194 Jamras Sapthanawin, "Jak bannathikan" [From the editor], *Karnmuang* [8], no. 20 (June 2, 1951): 21.

195 According to Jamras Sapthanawin, then nominal editor of *Karnmuang*, cited in Wiwat, "Kabot santiphap," 215.

196 Salao Lekharuji, "Khadi khatakam ari liwira phoo amnuaikan nangseuphim phim thai" [The case of the murder of Ari Liwira, the director of *Phim Thai* newspaper], in *Neung satawas nangseuphim thai* [A century of Thai newspapers] (Bangkok: Ruamsan Ltd. Partnership, 1967), 473–510.

197 Reynolds, *Thai Radical Discourse*, 32–33; Mongkol, "Wikhrao reuangsan," 41–42.

198 Supha, interview, October 28, 1979; Thaweep Voradilok, panel discussion on "Prison and Writers," Thammasat University, February 2, 1989.

199 Mongkol, "Wikhrao reuangsan," 43–46; Thongbai, *Khommunit ladyao*, 90–191, 278–99, passim. My idea in this passage is inspired by the penetrating critique of bourgeois civil society in Ellen Meiksins Wood, "The Uses and Abuses of 'Civil Society,'" *The Socialist Register 1990*, ed. Ralph Miliband, Leo Panitch, and John Saville (London: The Merlin Press, 1990), especially 73–74.

Chapter 9

1 Asvabahu (King Vajiravudh), *Phuak jew haeng buraphathis lae meuang thai jong teun thoed khong asvabahu phrom duai laiphrarajhat khamplae phasa anglis* [The Jews of the Orient and Awake, Siam by Asvabahu with His Majesty's manuscript of the English translation] (Bangkok: Moonnithi Phrabaromrajanusorn Phrabatsomdej Phramongkutklaojaoyoohua, 1985).

2 For further details, see my "Imagined Uncommunity: The *Lookjin* Middle Class and Thai Official Nationalism," in *Essential Outsiders: Chinese and Jews in the Modern Transformation of Southeast Asia and Central Europe*, ed. Daniel Chirot and Anthony Reid (Seattle and London: University of Washington Press, 1997), 75–98.

3 Vajiravudh, *Pakinnakakhadi*, 241–47.

4 Prince Damrong, "Laksana kanpokkhrong," 5–8.
5 Thaemsook Numnond, "Meuangthai yuk cheua phoonam" [Thailand in the obey-the-leader age], *Thammasat University Journal* 6, no. 1 (June–September 1976): 144–45.
6 This suggestive idea of "fishing for meaning" is fished out from Vicente L. Rafael's introduction to *Contracting Colonialism: Translation and Christian Conversion in Tagalog Society under Early Spanish Rule* (Ithaca: Cornell University Press, 1988), entitled "Fishing Out the Past":

> [to] "fish out" discrete words from the stream of the sermon, arbitrarily attaching them to their imaginings...a distinctive Tagalog strategy of decontextualizing the means by which colonial authority represents itself. Such a strategy short-circuits the linkages among the priest's message, the language in which it is put, and the intended effect of both on the congregation. (2–3)

As it turned out, Marxism suffered the same fate in the eyes of the Thai reading public as Christianity did in the ears of the listening Tagalog congregation, that is, being fished out of its context.
7 Reynolds, *Thai Radical Discourse*, 26.
8 I derive this apt concept of Prasenjit Duara from Craig J. Reynolds, "Identity, Authenticity and Reputation in the Postcolonial History of Mainland Southeast Asia" (keynote speech at the International Conference on Post Colonial Society and Culture in Southeast Asia, Yangon, Myanmar, December 16–18, 1998). Otherwise, the idea in this part is generally inspired by Thongchai Winichakul, *Siam Mapped: A History of the Geo-Body of a Nation* (Honolulu: University of Hawaii Press, 1994), especially a section entitled "The Border of Thainess," 169–70.
9 Prince Narathipphongpraphan (M.C. Wan Waithayakon Worawan), "Pathakatha reuang siamphak" [A lecture on Siamese language], in *Chumnum phraniphon khong sassatrajan pholtri phrajaoworawongthoe krommeun narathipphongpraphan* [Selected writings of Professor, Major General, Prince Narathipphongpraphan], ed. Songwit Kaeosri (Bangkok: Bangkok Bank, 1979), 416.
10 Murashima, *Kanmeuang jinsiam*, 100.
11 Some earlier attempts at translating Chinese communist propaganda materials into Thai by the CPS propagandists in the 1930s, as related in Chapter 3, seemed sporadic and left no traceable legacy for the post-war CPT.
12 See Krom Tamra, Krasuang Thammakan [Department of Textbooks, Ministry of Public Instruction], *Pathanukrom krom tamra krasuang thammakan* [Dictionary of the Department of Textbooks, Ministry of Public Instruction] (Bangkok: Department of Textbooks, Ministry of

Public Instruction, 1927), 13; and Rajbandittayasathan [Royal Institute], *Photjananukrom chabab rajbandittayasathan* [The Royal Institute's Dictionary](Bangkok: Rajbandittayasathan, 1950), 18.

13 Damri and Jaroon, 146–48.

14 No.Mo.So. (Prince Phitthayalongkorn), *Klon lae nakklon* [Rhymes and rhymers] (Bangkok: Sophonphiphatthanakorn Printing House, 1930), 1–2.

15 Intharayut (Atsani Phonlajan), "Wannakhadi kao kao" [Old literature], *Aksornsarn* 1, no. 11 (February 1950): 85.

16 Laong Misetthi, *Photjananukrom lamdub sara* [Rhyming dictionary] (Bangkok: Rungreuangsan Publisher, 1961), 1218–19, 1236–50.

17 Suffice it to point out that 30 years ago, I, as a shy early teenager in secondary school, composed a lengthy Thai poem to express my bliss and lament my anguish upon my first puppy love. Consisting of a total of 200 different stanzas, it basically says: "Oh, Lady, how beautiful you are! How much I love and long for you! Well, do you love me?" Alas, as a matter of fact, she didn't even notice me, let alone read my poem, but all the same...

18 Thaweepvorn (Thaweep Voradilok), "Namthuam kab satpa" [Flood and beasts], *Aksornsarn* 2, no. 11 (February 1951): 17.

19 Mani Chotiros (Jaroenphron Phutthiwiwat), "Mon bot neung seung mai khuan leum" [A mantra that should not be forgotten], *Aksornsarn* 2, no. 7 (October 1950): 19–20. The word in question was *samneuk nak sangkhomniyom* (the socialist consciousness).

Bibliography

I. Interviews and Discussions

Chan Kaeochoosai. Interview by author on post-war Thai politics and the radical press. Bangkok, February 5, 1989.

Chinda Sirimanond. Interview by author and Wiwat Catithammanit on Supha Sirimanond and *Aksornsarn* monthly magazine. Bangkok, September 27, 1988.

Kanlaya Phichaikul. Interview by author on her life and lookjin communists. Rayong, March 26, 1989.

Kanya Lilalai. Interview by author on her life and the Voice of the People of Thailand radio station. Bangkok, January 27, 1989.

Khamsing Srinawk. Interview by author on his life, writings, and radical literature. Nonthaburi, April 12, 1989.

Phichit Dijai. Interview by author on his life and political activities. Bangkok, April 23, 1989.

———— Interview by author on his life and political activities. Bangkok, May 15, 1989.

Phin Bua-on. Interview by Craig J. Reynolds on his life and the Thai communist movement. Bangkok, August 31, 1984.

———— Interview by Somsak Jeamteerasakul on his life and the Thai communist movement. Bangkok, July 31, 1985.

Prawut Srimantra. Interview by Craig J. Reynolds on Jit Poumisak and the Thai left. Bangkok, December 18, 1983.

Somkhuan Phichaikul. Interview by author on the post-war movement of radical students and intellectuals. Rayong, March 26, 1989.

Supha Sirimanond. Interview by Craig J. Reynolds on his life, the Thai left, and Jit Poumisak. Bangkok, September 16, 1979.

———— Interview by Craig J. Reynolds on his life, the Thai left, and Jit Poumisak. Bangkok, October 17, 1979.

———— Interview by Craig J. Reynolds on his life, the Thai left, and Jit Poumisak. Bangkok, October 28, 1979.

———— Interview by Napaporn Ativanichayapong on the development of Marxist political economy in Thailand. Bangkok, September 4, 1985.

Suphat Sukhonthaphirom. Interview by Napaporn Ativanichayapong on the development of Marxist political economy in Thailand. Bangkok, September 7, 1985.

Sawai Malayavej. Interview by author on his life and the Thai communist movement. Bangkok, April 22, 1989.

Thaweep Voradilok. Interview by Craig J. Reynolds on Jit Poumisak and radical literature and politics. Bangkok, September 27, 1979.

———— Interview by Craig J. Reynolds on Jit Poumisak and radical literature and politics. Bangkok, January 13, 1984.

———— Interview by author on post-war radical literature and Thammasat University student movement. Bangkok, December 27, 1988.

———— Panel discussion on "Soviet Russian Literature." Thammasat University, Bangkok, December 16, 1988.

———— Panel discussion on "Prison and Writers." Thammasat University, Bangkok, February 2, 1989.

Udom Sisuwan. Interview by Craig J. Reynolds on communism and literature in Thailand. Bangkok, December 27, 1983.

———— Interview by Craig J. Reynolds on communism and literature in Thailand. Bangkok, January 19, 1984.

Uphai Phinthuyothin. Interview by Suphaphorn Jaralphat, Nakharin Mektrairat, Sunthari Asawai, and Suvimol Roongcharoen on the history of Thammasat University. Bangkok, March 7, 1983.

II. Unpublished Documents

A. In Thai

Communist Party of Thailand. "Kham hai samphas khong khoesok phak khommunit haeng prathet thai kiaokab phreuttikan khong nai prasert sapsunthorn thi thorayos to kanpatiwat lae thorayos to prachachon" [Interview of the spokesman of the Communist Party of Thailand about Mr. Prasert Sapsunthorn's traitorous behaviour against the Revolution and the people]. Radio Broadcast. VOPT, Kunming, July 27, 1968.

———— Untitled Internal Study Document: Glossary of Political Economic Terms. N.p., n.d.

Royal Thai Government. Criminal Court, Ministry of Justice. "The Testimony of Phramaha Dilok Suwannarat (Thammathatto Bhikkhu)." Criminal Court Proceedings of the Cases No. Black 158, 168, 202/2496. 1953.

————— Department of Commercial Registration, Ministry of Commerce. "Aksornsarn Limited Partnership." Registration Profile File No.738. N.d.

————— Department of Commercial Registration, Ministry of Commerce. "Dazhong Wenhua Company Limited." Registration Profile File No.1024. N.d.

————— Department of Commercial Registration, Ministry of Commerce. "Rungnakhorn Company Limited." Registration Profile File No. 2349. N.d.

B. In English

United States. American Embassy, Bangkok. "Fortnightly Summary of Political Events in Siam for the Period March 16–March 31, 1947." NADD, Washington, D.C., April 7, 1947.

————— "Fortnightly Summary of Political Events in Siam for the Period April 16–April 30, 1947." NADD, Washington, D.C., May 23, 1947.

————— "The Sahacheep Party: A Chronology." Enclosure No. 2 to "Fortnightly Summary of Political Events in Siam for the Period July 16–July 31, 1947." NADD, Washington, D.C., July 16–31, 1947.

————— "Fortnightly Summary of Political Events in Siam for the Period August 1–August 15, 1947." NADD, Washington, D.C., August 27, 1947.

————— "The Free Thais: A Chronology." NADD, Washington, D.C., August 27, 1947.

————— "Phya Wichit Case: A Special Chronology." NADD, Washington, D.C., October 15–27, 1947.

————— "Fortnightly Summary of Political Events in Siam for the Period November 1–November 15, 1947." NADD, Washington, D.C., November, 1947.

————— "Outline of Events: Coup D' Etat November 9, 1947." NADD, Washington, D.C., n.d.

————— "Airgram A-357, August 18, 1949." NADD, Washington, D.C., August 31, 1949.

United States. American Legation, Bangkok. "Appendix: Brief Guide to Political Parties in Siam." NADD, Washington, D.C., n.d.

————— "The Political Situation in Siam." NADD, Washington, D.C., November 21, 1945.

————— Letter dated 16 September 1945 from Major Arkadej Bijayendrayothin. Enclosure to "The Political Situation in Siam." NADD, Washington, D.C., November 21, 1945.

————— "Fortnightly Summary of Political Events in Siam for the Period July 15–July 30, 1946." NADD, Washington, D.C., July 30, 1946.

————— "Fortnightly Summary of Political Events in Siam for the Period July 31–August 15, 1946." NADD, Washington, D.C., August 19, 1946.

United States. Department of State, Office of Far Eastern Affairs, Division of Southeast Asian Affairs. Office Memorandum to FE-Mr. Butterworth from SEA-Mr. Reed, "Siamese Politics." NADD, Washington, D.C., June 2, 1948.

————— Memorandum of Conversation, "Siam." NADD, Washington, D.C., November 12, 1948.

United States. Department of State, Division of Southwest Pacific Affairs. "Annex D: Thailand, Controls during and after Liberation." NADD, Washington, D.C., June 7, 1945.

————— "Annex E: Thai Resistance." NADD, Washington, D.C., June 7, 1945.

————— "Annex F: Thai Declaration of War against Japan." NADD, Washington, D.C., June 7, 1945.

United States. Department of State, Research and Intelligence Service, Bangkok, Siam. "Royal Crown Property in Siamese Politics." NADD, Washington, D.C., November 24, 1945.

United States. Office of Strategic Services. "Appendix C: Political Warfare Executive, Plan of Political Warfare against Japan, Appreciation of Siam, Siamese Personalities." NADD, Washington, D.C., June, 1945.

III. Serials

Aksornsarn. 1949–1952.

Aksornsatphijan. Special Double Issue on Jit Poumisak. 1976.

Karnmuang. 1946–1951.

Mahachon. 1947–1948.

Nitisat Rab Satawas Mai [Journal of law: The new century issue]. 1957.

Pituphoom (La Patrie). 1955–1957.

Rajkijjanubeksa [Royal Thai government gazette]. 1933–1957.

Saithan. 1958.

Samakkhi Soorob. 1977–1979.

Sethasarn. 1953–1958.

Siam Nikorn. 1951–1952.

IV. Published Works, Dissertations, Papers, and Cassette Tape

A. In Thai

Anonymous. *Aksornsarn samrab hok rob ayu supha sirimanond* [*Aksornsarn* published in memory of the 72nd anniversary of Supha Sirimanond's birthday]. Bangkok: Journalistic Science Foundation, 1986.

————— "Beuanglang khon kheu khwamkhid beuanglang jit kheu khwamjing" [Behind the man is the thought, Behind Jit is reality]. *Thanon Nangseu* 3, no. 11 (1986): 18–22.

————— *Dae thanong satthathip* [For Thanong Satthathip]. Published on the Occasion of the One Hundredth Day after Thanong Satthathip's Death. Amphoe Pakthongchai, Nakhon Ratchasima, 1973.

————— "Lakhorn haeng chiwit khong supha sirimanond" [Supha Sirimanond's circus of life]. *Thanon Nangseu* 1, no. 4 (1983): 9–27.

————— *Phichananusorn* [In memory of Phichan]. Cremation Volume of Phichan Bulyong. Thepsirintharawas Temple, Bangkok, 1963.

————— "Phrarajbanyat waduai khommunit phutthasakkaraj 2476" [The Royal Act on Communism, B.E. 2476]. *Rajkijjanubeksa* [Royal Thai government gazette] 50 (1933): 10–12.

————— "Phrarajbanyat pongkan kankratham an pen khommunit phutthasakkaraj 2495" [The Anti-Communist Activities Act, B.E. 2495]. *Rajkijjanubeksa* [Royal Thai government gazette] 69, no. 18 (1952).

————— "Pleuang wannasri 'kheunmeuang': Pho.kho.tho. nai sathanakan thodthoi jak sam sib ha leua kao khon" [Pleuang Wannasri "Back to the city": The CPT at a low ebb from thirty-five to nine men]. *Matichon Sudsapda* 10, no. 492 (1990): 26–28.

————— "Prasit kanjanawat phoosang tamnan kanmeuang-thurakij" [Prasit Kanjanawat, Creator of a political-business legend]. *Phoonam Thurakij* 3, no. 26 (1989): 15–64.

————— "Prawat nai thianthai aphichatbut" [Profile of Mr.Thianthai Aphichatbut]. Cremation Volume of Mr. Thianthai Aphichatbut. Makudkasattriyaram Temple, Bangkok, 1976.

————— "Yiam ban nakkhian: Suwat voradilok" [Visiting a writer's house: Suwat Voradilok]. *Parithassan* 2, no. 14 (1983): 42–46.

Akatdamkoeng Raphiphat, M.C. *Lakhorn haeng chiwit* [The circus of life]. Bangkok: Prae Pittaya Press, 1960.

Amnaj Yutthawiwat (Phin Bua-on). *Wiphak naiphi* [A critique of Naiphi]. Bangkok: Sanseuksa Kanphim, 1975.

Amnuaichai Patiphatphaophong. "Botbat khong nakseuksa to rabob prachathipatai" [The role of university students towards democracy]. In

Ha sib pi bon senthang prachathipatai Pho.So. 2475–2525 [Fifty years on the path of democracy, B.E. 2475–2525], Editorial Board of the *Journal of Political Economy*, 56–90, 347–91. Bangkok: Social Research Institute, Chulalongkorn University, 1983.

Anand Senakhan, Police Major. *Beuanglang kamphaeng* [Behind the walls]. Bangkok: Chanuan, 1988.

Asvabahu (King Vajiravudh). *Phuak jew haeng buraphathis lae meuang thai jong teun thoed khong asvaphahu phrom duai laiphrarajhat khamplae phasa anglis* [The Jews of the Orient and Awake, Siam by Asvabahu with His Majesty's manuscript of the English translation]. Bangkok: Moonnithi Phrabaromrajanusorn Phrabatsomdej Phramongkutklaojaoyoohua, 1985.

Athikhom Krongkredphej. *Latthi watthuniyom thang prawattisat lae wiwatthanakan thang sangkhom* [Historical materialism and social evolution]. Bangkok: Daoneua Book Club, 1975.

Atsani Phonlajan. *Rao chana laew mae ja* [We won, Mom]. Bangkok: Yaowachon Press, 1979.

Aurasom Sutthisakhorn. *Nakfan khonkla or. udakorn* [Bold dreamer: Or. Udakorn]. Chomrom nakkhian [Writers' Circle] Series, no. 5, edited by Chuai Phulphoem. Bangkok: Dokya Press, 1989.

Bamrung Phairachwathi (Lom Loetpricha), trans. *Lak latthi lenin* [The foundations of Leninism], by Joseph Stalin. Bangkok: Chomrom Nangseu Saengtawan, 1976.

Banjob Banruji. *Phra sri arya ma laew?* [Has Phra Sri Arya come?] Bangkok: Sukhaphapjai Press, 1986.

Banjong Banjoedsil (Udom Sisuwan). "Phak phanuak: Bantheuk khong 'banjong banjoedsil' kiaokab khwamkhid kaona kon khleuanwai wannakam kaona" [Appendix: "Banjong Banjoedsil"'s memoir on progressive ideas before the Progressive Literary Movement]. In *Saithan wannakam pheua chiwit khong thai* [The current of Thai Literature for Life's Sake], edited by Sathian Janthimathorn, 237–245. Bangkok: Chaophraya Press, 1982.

Banleu Reuangtrakul, Police Major General. *Khoomeu kansobsuan khadi aya ton thi neung* [A handbook of criminal investigation, part one]. Bangkok: Police Department, 1962.

Buncha Suma. "Kankhleuanwai khong phuak khommunit kab nayobai pongkan lae prabpram khong ratthabal (Pho.So. 2500–2523)" [The communist movement and the preventive and suppressive policies of the Thai government, 1957–1980]. Master's thesis, Chulalongkorn University, 1985.

Bunchai Jaiyen. *Ruai baeb jaosua neung* [Rich-tycoon style, volume one]. Bangkok: Bunchai Press, 1990.

Bunloet Changyai. "Kathao chiwit phichit dijai manus si khuk bangkhwang
    theung khuktai vietnam" [Cracking the life of Phichit Dijai, a man of four
    prisons from Bangkhwang to the Vietnamese Death Prison]. *Matichon
    Weekend Magazine* 9, no. 445 (1989): 46–47.

Carabao. *Made in Thailand*. Ligo, C-27106, 1984.

Chai-anan Samudavanija. *Kanmeuang-kanplianplaeng thang kanmeuang thai
    (Pho.So. 1893–2475)* [Politics and political change in Thailand, B.E.
    1893–2475]. Bangkok: Social Science Association of Thailand, 1975.

————— and Phirasak Janthawarin, comp. *Khomoon pheunthan keung satawas
    haeng kanplianplaeng kanpokkhrong thai* [Basic data of half a century
    of Thailand's change of regime]. Bangkok: Social Science Association
    of Thailand, 1982.

————— and Suwadee Charoenphong, eds. *Kanmeuang-kanpokkhrong thai
    samai mai: Ruam nganwijai thang prawattisat lae ratthasat* [Modern
    Thai politics and government: A collection of researches in history and
    political science]. Bangkok: Chulalongkorn University, 1979.

Chaiwat Bunnag. "Kanpatiwat meua wanthi 24 mithunayon 2475" [The
    revolution of 24 June B.E. 2475]. Paper presented in the seminar, "The
    People's Party in Thai History," Krirk College, May 9–10, 1985.
    Mimeographed.

————— et al. "Khana ratsadorn nai prawattisat thai" [The People's Party in
    Thai history]. Papers presented in the seminar, "The People's Party in
    Thai History," Krirk College, May 9–10, 1985. Mimeographed.

Chaiwat Satha-anand. "Thewawitthaya haeng wathakam: Tham khwamkhaojai
    amnaj haeng wathakam duai 'Narai Sib Pang'" [Theology of discourse:
    Understanding the power of discourse through "The ten incarnations of
    Vishnu"]. Paper presented at the annual meeting of the Historical
    Association of Thailand, Chulalongkorn University, February 1990.
    Mimeographed.

Chaiwat Yonpiam. *Fan rai khong meuang thai* [Thailand's nightmare].
    Bangkok: Chaophraya Press, 1985.

Chaloemkiat Phiunual. "Khwamkhid thang kanmeuang khong pridi banomyong"
    [The political thought of Pridi Banomyong]. Academic paper no. 48
    presented in the seminar, "Keung satawas thammasat: 2477–2527" [Half a
    century of Thammasat: B.E. 2477–2527], Thai Khadi Research Institute,
    Thammasat University, 1984. Mimeographed.

Chan Kratsanaipura (Chao Phongphichit). *Watthanakan khwamkhid
    sangkhomniyom* [The evolution of socialist thoughts]. Bangkok:
    Naewruamnakseuksa, Chiang Mai University, 1974.

Charnvit Kasetsiri et al. *Raingan kanwijai reuang prawat mahawitthayalai thammasat* [Research report on the history of Thammasat University]. Bangkok: Thai Khadi Research Institute, Thammasat University, 1989.

Charnvit Kasetsiri, ed. *Thammasat ha sib pi* [Fifty years of Thammasat]. Published on the Occasion of the 50th Anniversary of the Establishment of Thammasat University on June 27, B.E. 2477. Bangkok: Thammasat University, 1984.

Chat Chawangkun, Police Colonel. "Kantosoo rawang latthi" [Struggle between doctrines]. Unpublished personal research in political science, Class 5, academic year 1962–1963, Witthayalai Pongkan Rajanajak.

Chatthip Nartsupha and Santisuk Sophonsiri. *Khwamkid sahakorn khong pridi banomyong lae Pridi banomyong kab kansangsan satipanya yang thai* [Pridi Banomyong's ideas on co-operative and Pridi Banomyong and the Thai way of intellectual creativity]. Bangkok: Aksornsarn Press, 1987.

Chiab Amphunan (Chiab Chaisong). "Bantheuk reuang khaphajao mai dai khai chat" [I did not sell the nation: A memoir]. *Thai Nikorn* [98] (1979): 10–16.

———— *Mahawitthayalai khong khaphajao* [My university]. Bangkok: Ruamsan Press, 1958.

Chinda Sirimanond. *Anusorn nai supha sirimanond* [In memory of Mr. Supha Sirimanond]. Cremation Volume of Supha Sirimanond. Somnaswarawihan Temple, Bangkok, 1986.

Chit Wiphasthawat. *Phao saraphap (Burus lek haeng asia)* [Phao confesses (The Iron Man of Asia)]. Bangkok: "Thainoi" and Prae Pittaya Press, 1960.

Cholthira Sattayawatthana. "Wanakhadi chud 'Phlik adit: Kankhleuanwai khong sattri thai nakpatiwat run bukboek'" ['Digging up the past: The activities of Thai female revolutionary pioneers' Junglelogue series]. *Samakkhi Soorob* 1, no. 5 (1977): 59–68.

————, ed. *Khroo thep* [Teacher Thep]. Bangkok: Khrongkan Tamra Sangkhomsat Lae Manussat, Social Science Association of Thailand, 1983.

Chuai Phulphoem. *Chiwit lae ngan khong nakpraphan nai khrongkan anurak wannakam kao lae hayak* [The lives and works of authors in the Old and Rare Literature Conservation Project]. Bangkok: Dokya Press, 1988.

Damri Reuangsutham and Jaroon Lasa. *Khabuankan kammakorn nai prathet thai kab kantosoo khleuanwai lae phatthanakan khong raengngan* [Workers' movement in Thailand and the struggle, activities and development of labor]. Bangkok: Santitham Press, 1986.

Damrongrachanuphap, Prince. "Laksana kanpokkhrong prathet siam tae boran" [The character of the administration of ancient Siam]. Cremation Volume of Mr. Dao Buphawes, 1–38. Rasbamrung Temple, Chon Buri, 1968.

Decha Rattayothin (Damri Reuangsutham). *Wiwatthanakan khong sangkhom* [The evolution of society]. Bangkok: Prawattisat Press, 1979.

Duangmon Jitjamnong et al. *Tho mai nai sainam: Song roi pi wannakhadi wijan thai* [Weaving silk in the stream: Two hundred years of Thai literary criticism]. Edited by Suvanna Kriangkraiphej and Sujittra Jongsathitwatthana. Bangkok: Pajarayasan, 1989.

Fongjan Thaleya (Wimol Phonlajan). "Phak tam: Khwamngam khong chiwit" [Appendix: The beauty of life]. In *Ramleuk theung naiphi jak pa lom: Chuang chiwit lae phonngan thi pheung poed phoey pen khrang raek* [Auntie Lom's remembrance of Naiphi: Episodes in his life and some of his writings revealed for the first time], compiled by Wimol Phonlajan and edited by Chuai Phulphoem, 77–144. Bangkok: Dokya Press, 1990.

Homhual Cheunjit. *Kanplae: Achip soo puangchon* [Translation: Career for the people]. Bangkok: United Productions Publisher, 1984.

Hutcheson, J.F. and Dr. Thawi Tawethikul. *Latthi setthakij* [Economic doctrines]. Bangkok: Thammasat University Press, 1980.

Intharayut (Atsani Phonlajan). "Phak phanuak: Bantheuk khong 'intharayut' kiaokab jamkad phlangkoon lae nangseu ekkachon" [Appendix: "Intharayut"'s memoir on Jamkad Phlangkoon and *Ekkachon* newspaper]. In *Saithan wannakam pheua chiwit khong thai* [The current of Thai Literature for Life's Sake], edited by Sathian Janthimathorn, 227–35. Bangkok: Chaophraya Press, 1982.

————— "Phak phanuak: Bantheuk khong 'intharayut' kiaokab run khong issara amantakul" [Appendix: "Intharayut"'s memoir on Issara Amantakul's generation]. In *Saithan wannakam pheua chiwit khong thai* [The current of Thai Literature for Life's Sake], edited by Sathian Janthimathorn, 221–25. Bangkok: Chaophraya Press, 1982.

Issara Amantakul (Abrahim Aman). *Huarao lae namta: Chud ruam reuangsan lem neung* [Laughter and tears: A collection of short stories, volume one]. Khrongkan anurak wannakam kao lae hayak [Old and Rare Literature Conservation Project] Series, ed. Chuai Phulphoem, no. 28. Bangkok: Dokya Press, 1988.

Jamroen Saengduangkhae. "Wikhrao wannakam khong jit poumisak" [An analysis of Jit Poumisak's literary works]. Master's thesis, Srinakharinwirot University, 1977.

Jareuk Chomphoophol (Chat Bunyasirichai). "Bantheuk jak bangkhwang" [Bangkhwang memoir]. In *Beuangraek prachathipatai: Bantheuk khwamsongjam khong phoo yoo nai hetkan samai Pho.So. 2475–2500* [The early days of democracy: Memoirs of participants in the events during B.E. 2475–2500]. Bangkok: The News Reporters Association of Thailand, 1973.

Jaroen Wanngam. *Khrai sang khrai tham?* [Who makes, Who builds?] Bangkok: Chomrom Daorung, n.d.

Jintana Kotrakul. "Chuang neung khong prasobkan thi dai phanphob jit poumisak" [My acquaintance of Jit Poumisak]. *Thanon Nangseu* 3, no. 11 (1986): 23–29.

Jit Poumisak. *Khwamfaifan saen ngam: Ruam ngankawiniphon chudsomboon 2489–2509* [Beautiful dream: A complete anthology of Jit Poumisak's poetry, B.E. 2489–2509]. Edited by Meuang Boyang. Bangkok: Dokya Press, 1981.

Kan Chong. "Naiphi: Atsani phonlajan phookhrawi wiriya awut nai wangwon khong khwamkhadyaeng" [Naiphi: Atsani Phonlajan, who brandishes the weapon of diligence in the whirlwind of conflict]. *Parithassan* 2, no. 15 (1983): 58–65.

Kanya Lilalai. "Prawat kantosoo khong kammakorn thai" [A history of Thai workers' struggle]. Unpublished manuscript. 1980.

Kawikanmeuang (Jit Poumisak). *Ruam botkawi lae ngan wijan sinlapawannakhadi khong kawikanmeuang* [Collected poems, art, and literary criticisms of Kawikanmeuang]. Bangkok: Naewruam Nakseuksa Chiangmai, 1974.

Khajorn Sukphanich. *Kao raek khong nangseuphim nai prathet thai* [The first step of newspapers in Thailand]. Bangkok: Ongkankha Khong Khurusapha, 1983.

Khomsan Matukham. *Khrong jandawong khao kheu khrai?* [Khrong Jandawong, Who was he?] Bangkok: Phitakpracha, 1978.

Kittisak Sriamphai. *Prachathipatai samai Phol.T.O. Phao Sriyanond: Yuk assawin phayong thamil khrong meuang* [Democracy under Police General Phao Sriyanond: The age of overbearing knights and evil rulers]. Bangkok: Prakasit Law Office, n.d.

Kong Kanwijai, Krom Wichakan, Krasuang Seuksathikan (Research Division, Academic Department, Ministry of Education). *Sathiti kanseuksa bang prakan pi 2485–2496* [Some educational statistics, B.E. 2485–2496]. Bangkok: Research Division, Academic Department, Ministry of Education, n.d.

Kongbannathikan "Lok Nangseu" et al. *Dang thian phoo thongthae kae khon: Ruam botkhwam kiaokab jit poumisak* [Like a clear candle for men: Collected articles on Jit Poumisak]. Bangkok: Puifai Press, 1980.

Krasuang Mahadthai [Ministry of Interior]. "Prakas krasuang mahadthai reuang kanjodthabian phak kanmeuang kammakorn" [The proclamation of the Ministry of Interior on the registration of the Worker Party]. *Rajkijjanubeksa* [Royal Thai government gazette] 72, no. 86 (1955): 2685–2688.

———— "Prakas krasuang mahadthai reuang kanjodthabian phak kanmeuang khabuankan hyde park" [The proclamation of the Ministry of Interior on the registration of the Hyde Park Movement Party]. *Rajkijjanubeksa* [Royal Thai government gazette] 73, no. 30 (1956): 1101–1106.

———— "Prakas krasuang mahadthai reuang kanjodthabian phak kanmeuang sangkhomniyom" [The proclamation of the Ministry of Interior on the registration of the Socialist Party]. *Rajkijjanubeksa* [Royal Thai government gazette] 73, no. 25 (1956): 1036–1045.

———— "Prakas krasuang mahadthai reuang kanjodthabian phak kanmeuang setthakorn" [The proclamation of the Ministry of Interior on the registration of the Economist Party]. *Rajkijjanubeksa* [Royal Thai government gazette] 72, no. 86 (1955): 2689–2696.

———— "Prakas krasuang mahadthai reuang kanjodthabian phak kanmeuang sri arya mettraya" [The proclamation of the Ministry of Interior on the registration of the Sri Arya Mettraya Party]. *Rajkijjanubeksa* [Royal Thai government gazette] 74, no. 8 (1957): 217–223.

———— "Prakas krasuang mahadthai reuang kanplianplaeng huana phak khabuankan hyde park" [The proclamation of the Ministry of Interior on the change of the head of the Hyde Park Movement Party]. *Rajkijjanubeksa* [Royal Thai government gazette] 73, no. 74 (1956): 2658.

Krasnai Porachat (Sakchai Bamrungphong), trans. *Wara sudthai khong sevastopol* [The last days of Sevastopol], by Boris Voyetekhov. Bangkok: Noppharat Press, 1980.

Krit Sombatsiri. *Jek sakdina* [Feudalized Chinese]. Bangkok: Kaeoprakai Press, 1986.

Krom Mahadthai, Krasuang Mahadthai [Department of Interior, Ministry of Interior]. *Kansamruaj sammanokhrua thua rajanajak-kanseuksa* [Whole-Kingdom census survey-education]. Bangkok: Department of Interior, Ministry of Interior, n.d.

Krom Sinlapakorn, Krasuang Seuksathikan [Department of Fine Arts, Ministry of Education]. *Nampraphan nakkhian thai thi chai nai batraikan khong hosamud haeng chat* [Thai authors and their pen-names compiled from the catalogue cards of the National Library]. Bangkok: National Library, Department of Fine Arts, 1986.

———— *Prawat nakkhian thai lem neung* [Profiles of Thai writers, vol. one]. Bangkok: Department of Fine Arts, Ministry of Education, 1981.

——— *Prawat nakkhian thai lem song* [Profiles of Thai writers, vol. two]. Bangkok: Department of Fine Arts, Ministry of Education, 1980.

Krom Tamra, Krasuang Thammakan [Department of Textbooks, Ministry of Public Instruction]. *Pathanukrom krom tamra krasuang thammakan* [Dictionary of the Department of Textbooks, Ministry of Public Instruction]. Bangkok: Department of Textbooks, Ministry of Public Instruction, 1927.

Krom Wisamanseuksa, Krasuang Seuksathikan [Department of Secondary Education, Ministry of Education]. *Sathiti kanseuksa rob yi sib paed pi* [Statistics of education in twenty-eight years]. Bangkok: Department of Secondary Education, Ministry of Education, 1960.

Kukrit Pramoj, M.R. *Farang sakdina* [Feudal Europe]. Bangkok: Siam Rat Press, 1986.

——— *Pathakatha khong kukrit* [Kukrit's lectures]. Bangkok: Klang Vidhaya Publishing House, 1960.

——— *Tob panha prajamwan chudmaimai* [Answers to daily questions: New installments]. Bangkok: Kaona Press, 1964.

Kulap Saipradit. *Adit thi pen botrian* [Lessons from the past]. Bangkok: Saengthian Group, 1979.

——— *Khaphajao dai hen ma* [I have seen]. Bangkok: Kwianthong Press, 1957.

——— *Pai sahaphap soviet* [To the Soviet Union]. Bangkok: Suphapburus Press, 1958.

——— *Rabiab sangkhom khong manus* [Human social order]. Khwamroo [Knowledge] Series, no. 3. Bangkok: P.P. Press, 1978.

Lao Khamhom (Khamsing Srinawk). *Fa bo kan* [The sky is no barrier]. Bangkok: Ko Phai Press, 1987.

Laong Misetthi. *Photjananukrom lamdub sara* [Rhyming dictionary]. Bangkok: Rungreuangsan Publisher, 1961.

Laortong Amarinratana. "Kansong nakrian pai seuksato tangprathet tangtae Pho.So. 2411–2475" [The sending of students abroad from 1868–1932]. Master's thesis, Chulalongkorn University, 1979.

Leuan Saraphaiwanich (Captain Phraya Saraphaiphiphat). *Fan rai khong khaphajao* [My nightmare]. Bangkok: Bannakhan Press, 1959.

Mao Zedung. *Khatiphoj prathan maozedung* [Quotations from Chairman Mao Zedung]. Bangkok: Klum Seuksa Panha Kanmeuang, n.d.

Maung Htin Aung. *Prawattisat Phama* [A history of Burma]. Translated by Petchari Sumit. Bangkok: Social Association of Thailand, 1976.

Meuang Boyang. *Botphleng haeng rungarun: Waduai chiwaprawat nai waiyao*

khong jit poumisak [The song of dawn: On Jit Poumisak's early life].
Bangkok: Tonkla Book Club, 1980.

Mit Ruamrob (Prawut Srimantra). "Chiwaprawat bangton khong jit poumisak"
[Some episodes from Jit Poumisak's biography]. *Aksornsatphijan*
(Special Double Issue on Jit Poumisak) 3, no. 11–12 (1976): 23–44.

Mongkol Poonpermsuksombat. "Wikhrao reuangsan khong Issara amantakul"
[An analytical study of Isara Amantakool's short stories]. Master's
thesis, Srinakharinwirot University, 1981.

Murashima, Eiji. *Kanmeuang jinsiam: kan khleuanwai thang kanmeuang
khong chao jin phonethale nai prathet thai kho.so. 1924–1941* [Sino-
Siamese politics: The overseas Chinese political movement in Thailand,
A.D. 1924–1941]. Translated by Eiji Murashima and Worasak
Mahatthanobol. Bangkok: Chinese Studies Center, Institute of Asian
Studies, Chulalongkorn University, 1996.

——— "Samphanthamit thai-yipun kab chaojin nai prathet thai samai
songkhram lok khrang thi song" [The Thai-Japanese alliance and
overseas Chinese in Thailand]. Translated by Eiji Murashima and
Nakharin Mektrairat. In *Yipun-thai-usakhane* [Japan-Thailand-Southeast
Asia], edited by Charnvit Kasetsiri and Hayao Fukui. Bangkok:
Thammasat-Kyoto Core University Program and the Foundation for the
Promotion of Social Sciences and Humanities Textbooks Project, 1998.

Naiphi (Atsani Phonlajan). *Kaapklon naiphi* [Naiphi's poems]. Thonburi:
Aksornwatthana Publishing House, 1958.

——— "Khloong-chand khong 'naiphi'" ["Naiphi"'s *khloong* and *chand*]. In
*Ramleuk theung naiphi jak pa lom: Chuang chiwit lae phonngan thi
pheung poed phey pen khrang raek* [Auntie Lom's remembrance of
Naiphi: Episodes in his life and some of his writings revealed for the first
time], edited by Chuai Phulphoem, 17–76. Bangkok: Dokya Press, 1990.

——— *Khwamplianplaeng* [Change]. Bangkok: Kiao-Klao (K.K.)
Phimphakan Press, 1990.

Nakharin Mektrairat. "Prawattisat phoompanya khong kanplian rabob
kanpokkhrong siam rawang Pho.So. 2470–2480" [An intellectual history
of Siam's political transformation during 2470–2480 B.E.]. Master's
thesis, Chulalongkorn University, 1985.

——— "Wathakam kanmeuang waduai prachathipatai khong thai" [Political
discourse of Thai democracy]. Paper presented in a trial lecture on the
same topic at the Faculty of Political Science, Thammasat University,
1988. Mimeographed.

Napaporn Ativanichayapong. *Phatthanakan khwamkhid setthasat
kanmeuang thai tangtae Pho.So. 2475-pajjuban* [The development of

Thai political economy thought from B.E. 2475 to the present].
Bangkok: The Political Economy Group, Social Research Institute,
Chulalongkorn University, 1988.

Narathipphongpraphan, Prince (M.C. Wan Waithayakon Worawan). *Chumnum
phraniphon khong sassatrajan pholtri phrajaoworawongthoe krommeun
narathipphongpraphan* [Selected writings of Professor, Major General,
Prince Narathipphongpraphan]. Edited by Songwit Kaeosri. Bangkok:
Bangkok Bank, 1979.

————— et al. *Narathipphongpraphan*. Cremation Volume of Princee
Narathipphongpraphan. Thepsirintharawas Temple, 1976.

Narong Phuangphis. "Khwamkhleuanwai thang kanmeuang khong khon jin nai
prathet thai nai rajsamai phrabatsomdej phrapokklao jaoyoohua"
[Political movements of the Chinese in Thailand in the reign of King
Prajadhipok]. *Warasan Thammasat* 1, no. 3 (1972): 1–12.

Nidhi Aeusrivongse. "Phasa thai mattrathan kab kanmeuang" [Standard Thai
language and politics]. *Phasa lae nangseu* 17, no. 2 (1984–1985): 11–37.

Nimitmongkhol Nawarat, M.R. *Meuangnimit lae chiwit haeng kankabot song
khrang* [The sight of future Siam and The victim of the two political
purges]. Bangkok: Aksornsamphan Press, 1970.

Nittaya Mapheungphong. "Khwamkhidhen thang setthakij khong khroothep"
[Khroothep's economic ideas]. In *Khroothep* [Teacher Thep], edited by
Cholthira Sattayawatthana. Bangkok: Khrongkan Tamra Sangkhomsat
Lae Manussat, Social Science Association of Thailand, 1983.

Niyom Sukrongphaeng. *Thahanreua kabot manhattan* [The Navy's Manhattan
Rebellion]. Bangkok: Sinlapawatthanatham Press, 1986.

No.Mo.So. (Prince Phitthayalongkorn). *Klon lae nakklon* [Rhymes and
rhymers]. Bangkok: Sophonphiphatthanakorn Printing House, 1930.

No. Praphasathit (Nongphot Praphasathit). *Kao pi nai pakking* [Nine years in
Peking]. Bangkok: Prae Pittaya Press, 1966.

Nopadol Riewcharoen. "Kodmai kab seriphap nangseuphim" [Law and
freedom of the press]. LL.M. thesis, Chulalongkorn University, 1981.

Nopphorn Suwanphanich and Kraisak Chunhawan. "Phak khommunit haeng
prathet thai kab khwamkhadyaeng nai indojin" [The Communist Party of
Thailand and conflict in Indochina]. *Mitthai* 24 (1981): 6–19.

Ongkankha Khong Khurusapha (Trading Agency of the Teachers Council).
Photjananukrom samrab nakrian [Dictionary for students]. Bangkok:
Ongkankha Khong Khurusapha, 1982.

Or. Udakorn (Udom Udakorn). *Teuk gross: Ruam reuangek* [Gross building:
Collected best stories]. Edited by Suwit Wongwira. Bangkok: Anthai
Press, 1988.

Pan Kaeomat. "Phak khommunit haeng prathet thai nai sam sib pi thi phom roojak" [Thirty years of my acquaintance with the Communist Party of Thailand]. *Samakkhi Soorob* 2, no. 1 (1978).

Phaisal Malaphan (Sawai Malayavej). *Bantheuk nakthos kanmeuang* [Memoir of a political prisoner]. Bangkok: Santitham Press, 1985.

————— "Sriburapha: Atyakorn phooploi nokphirab" [Sriburapha: A criminal who set the pigeons free]. *Thanon Nangseu* 1, no. 12 (1984): 50–56.

Phaithoon Sinlarat. *Rabob kanseuksa thai nai rob sam thossawas (Pho.So. 2490– 2520): Kanseuksa pheua sanongtob lae pentua khong tuaeng* [The Thai educational system in three decades (B.E. 2490–2520): Education for responsiveness and autonomy]. Bangkok: Chulalongkorn University, 1983.

Phanni Bualek. *Wikhrao naithun thanakan phanich khong thai Pho.So. 2475– 2516* [An analysis of Thai commercial banking capitalists, B.E. 2475–2516]. Khrongkan nangseulem sathaban wijaisangkhom chulalongkorn mahawitthayalai [Chulalongkorn University's Social Research Institute Book Publications] Project Series, ed. Kanoksak Kaewthep. Bangkok: Sangsan Publishing House, 1986.

Phayap Rojjanawiphat. *Yuk thamil* [Evil age]. Bangkok: Anthai Press, 1989.

Pheuan ruam khuk 2495–2500 lae Sahathammik. *Ramleuk theung kulap saipradit* [Remembering Kulap Saipradit]. Bangkok: Santitham Press, 1985.

Phimphawal Sethaputra. *Chiwaprawat kanthamphotjananukrom angklis-thai thai-angklis khong so sethaputra* [So Sethaputra and the making of his English-Thai, Thai-English dictionary: A biography]. Bangkok: Phimphawal Sethaputra, 1971.

Phinyo Rojjana. "Kanphoeyphrae sajjatham latthi marx nai prathet thai" [The dissemination of Marxist truth in Thailand]. *Mahachon-Thaiphijan* 1, no. 1 (1983): 42–47.

Pho. Meuangchomphoo (Udom Sisuwan). *Soo samoraphoom phoophan [phrom phak phanuak] pai meuang hang* [To the Phoophan battlefront with an appendix: To the Hang Town]. Bangkok: Matichon Press, 1987.

Phoonsuk Banomyong et al. *Photjanalai supha sirimanond* [Eulogies to Supha Sirimanond]. Bangkok: Songphorn Woraphithaksanond, 1986.

Phornphirom Iamtham. *Botbat thang kanmeuang khong nangseuphim thai tangtae plianplaeng kanpokkhrong Pho.So. 2475 theung sinsud songkhramlok khrang thi song* [The political roles of Thai newspapers from the change of regime in B.E. 2475 until the end of World War II]. Bangkok: Khrongkan Tamra Sangkhomsat Lae Manussat, Social Science Association of Thailand, 1977.

————— "Phatthanakan khong 'khabuankan sangkhomniyom' nai prathet thai lang songkhram lok khrang thi song theung Pho.So. 2526" [The development of the "socialist movement" in Thailand from after the Second World War until B.E. 2526]. *Journal of Political Economy* 5, no. 1–2 (1985–1986): 109–121.

Po. Pawarohit (Sanao Phanichjaroen), trans. *Anathipatai reu sangkhomniyom* [Anarchism or socialism], by Joseph Stalin. Bangkok: Saengtawan Book Club, 1976.

Po. Watcharaphorn (Prakas Watcharaphorn). *Chomrom nakkhian* [Writers' circles]. Bangkok: Ruamsan, 1966.

————— *Khon nangseuphim* [Journalists]. Bangkok: Odion Store, 1963.

————— *Prawat nakpraphan* [Author profiles]. Bangkok: Prae Pittaya Press, 1973.

————— *Thamniab nakpraphan* [Author directory]. Bangkok: Phadungseuksa Press, 1963.

Prajadhipok, King. "Phrabaromrajwinijchai khong phrabatsomdej phrapokklao jaoyoohua rabsanong phrabaromrajongkan doi phraya manopakornnitithada nayokratthamontri" [King Prajadhipok's consideration with Prime Minister Manopakorn at His Majesty's command]. In *Pridi banomyong kab sangkhom thai: Ruam khokhian khong pridi banomyong* [Pridi Banomyong and Thai society: Collected writings of Pridi Banomyong], by Pridi Banomyong, 173–259. Bangkok: Thammasat University Press and the Pridi Banomyong Kab Sangkhom Thai Project, 1983.

Prakas Watcharaphorn. *'Suphapburus' nakpraphan* [The "gentlemen" authors]. Chomrom nakkhian (Writers' Circle) Series, ed. Chuai Phulphoem, no. 4. Bangkok: Dokya Press, 1988.

Praphai Wisesthani (Atsani Phonlajan), trans. *Kaapklon maozedong* [The poems of Mao Zedong]. Bangkok: Thapnaram, 1975.

Prasan (Udom Sisuwan). *San dae nid* [Letters to Nid]. Bangkok: Maengsab Press, n.d.

Prasert Jandam, ed. *Tamnan naiphi atsani phonlajan* [The legends of Naiphi, Atsani Phonlajan]. Bangkok: Dokya Press, 1989.

Prasert Pathamasukhon. *Ratthasapha thai nai rob si sib song pi (2475–2517)* [Thai parliament in forty-two years, B.E. 2475–2517]. Bangkok: Ratthakijseri Group, 1974.

Prasert Sapsunthorn. *Chiwathas yaowachon* [The life conception of the youth]. Bangkok: n.p., n.d.

Prathip Saisen. *Kabot wangluang kab sathana khong pridi banomyong* [The

Royal Palace Rebellion and Pridi Banomyong's status]. Bangkok: Aksornsarn Press and Santiprachatham Institute, 1989.

Pridi Banomyong. *Chiwaprawat yo khong nai pridi banomyong [Jon theung 24 karakadakhom 2525]* [A short biography of Mr. Pridi Banomyong up to July 24, 1982]. Bangkok: Khrongkan Pridi Banomyong Kab Sangkhom Thai, 1983.

————— *Khokhian thang pratya* [Philosophical writings]. Bangkok: Sathaban Siam Pheua Kanseuksa Witthayasat Lae Watthanatham, 1975.

————— *Khwampenanijjang khong sangkhom* [The impermanence of society]. Bangkok: Pal Banomyong, 1970.

————— "Prawat pramot lae botkhwam bangreuang khong nai pridi banomyong" [Pramot's profile and selected articles of Pridi Banomyong]. In *Anusorn nai pramot pheungsunthorn, nakaphiwat, serithai, naisanammuai wethirajdamnoen khonraek* [In memory of Mr. Pramot Pheungsunthorn, a revolutionary, a Free Thai, and the first director of the Rajdamnoen Boxing Stadium]. Bangkok: Bunphring T. Suwan, 1982.

————— *Pridi banomyong kab sangkhom thai: Ruam khokhian khong pridi banomyong* [Pridi Banomyong and Thai society: Collected writings of Pridi Banomyong]. Bangkok: Thammasat University Press and the Pridi Banomyong Kab Sangkhom Thai Project, 1983.

————— "Sakul banomyong" [The Banomyong family]. In *Banomyong pradistham: Jad phim nai okas satamahawan haeng asanyakam khong phanathan pridi banomyong, 9 singhakhom 2526* [Banomyong Pradistham: A publication on the occasion of the one hundredth day of the passing away of His Excellency Pridi Banomyong, 9 August B.E. 2526], 1–19. Bangkok: Khana Kammakan Sassana Pheua Kanphatthana, 1983.

Rajbandittayasathan [Royal Institute]. *Photjananukrom chabab rajbandittayasathan* [The Royal Institute's dictionary]. Bangkok: Rajbandittayasathan, 1950.

————— *Sapbanyat angklis-thai thai-angklis* [Decreed coinages: English-Thai, Thai-English]. Bangkok: Rajbandittaya sathan, 1987.

Rangsan Thanapornpun. *Krabuankan kamnod nayobai setthakij nai prathet thai: Botwikhrao choeng prawattisat setthakij kanmeuang Pho.So. 2475–2530* [The process of economic policy formation in Thailand: A historical analysis of political economy, B.E. 2475–2530]. Bangkok: The Social Science Association of Thailand, 1989.

Rawewan Prakobpol. *Nittayasan thai* [Thai magazine]. Research Report Series, no. 19. Bangkok: Research Dissemination Project, Research Division, Chulalongkorn University, 1987.

Rungwit Suwanaphichon. *Sriburapha sri haeng wannakam thai* [Sriburapha, the glory of Thai literature]. Bangkok: Pasiko Press, 1979.

Sairung (Sak Suphakasem), trans. *Kawiniphon maozedung* [The poems of Mao Zedong]. Bangkok: Jatujak Press, 1981.

Sajjaphirom, Phraya (Sruang Sriphen). *Thewakamnoed: Khao khwampenma khong puang thep thewada thanglai phromduai aphinihan khwamsaksit* [Theogenesis: The story of all gods and angels with their might and miracles]. Bangkok: Sermwitbannakhan, 1968.

Sak Suriya (Bunmi Latthiprasat). *Pratya chaoban* [Popular philosophy]. Bangkok: Wangna Press, 1978.

Sakdina Chatkul na Ayudhya. "Narin phasit: Khonkhwanglok" [Narin Phasit: A heretic]. *Jodmaikhao Sangkhomsat* 10, no. 4 (1988): 4–42.

Sakol Wannakon Worawan, M.C. et al. *Khamprakas momchao sakol wannakon worawan nak sangkhomniyom khong meuang thai* [Manifesto of M.C. Sakol Wannakon Worawan, a socialist of Thailand]. Bangkok: Chesthaburus Press, n.d.

Salao Lekharuji. *Neung satawas nangseuphim thai* [A century of Thai newspapers]. Bangkok: Ruamsan, 1967.

Samak Burawas. *Panyawiwat: Kamnoed lae wiwatthanakan haeng panya khong manussayachat nai adit, song lem* [Intellectual evolution: The origins and evolution of human intellect in the past, two volumes]. Bangkok: Prae Pittaya Press, 1982.

——— *Phutthapratya yi sib ha satawas* [Twenty-five centuries of Buddhist philosophy]. Bangkok: Klang Vidhaya Publishing House, 1957.

——— *Witthayasat mai lae phrasriarya* [New sciences and Phra Sri Arya]. Bangkok: Prae Pittaya Press, 1970.

——— et al. *Anusorn nai ngan phrarajthan phloeng sop phanek samak burawas* [Cremation volume of Colonel Samak Burawas]. The Army Crematorium, Wat Sommanaswihan, Bangkok, 1975.

——— et al. *Ruam pathakatha phises phak reudooron 2495* [Collection of summer special lectures, B.E. 2495]. Bangkok: n.p., 1952.

Samakhom Wannakhadi [The Literary Society]. *Bantheuk samakhom wannakhadi* [Minutes of the Literary Society]. Cremation Volume of Dej Khongsaisin. Thepsirintharawas Temple, Bangkok, 1973.

Samnakngan Khana Kammakan Kanseuksa Haeng Chat, Samnak Nayokratthamontri [Office of the National Education Commission, Office of the Prime Minister]. *Sathiti prachakorn phoomairoo nangseu khong prathet thai Pho.So. 2490–2513* [Statistics of the illiterate population of Thailand, B.E. 2490–2513]. Bangkok: Office of the National Education Commission, Office of the Prime Minister, 1977.

Samnakngan Sathiti Haeng Chat, Samnak Nayokratthamontri [National Statistical Office, Office of the Prime Minister]. *Samud sathiti raipi prathet thai* [Thailand's yearbook of statistics]. Bangkok: National Bureau of Statistics, Prime Minister's Office, n.d.

Sanchawi Saibua. *Lak kanplae* [Principles of translation]. Bangkok: Thammasat University Press, 1982.

Saneh Jamarik. *Kanmeuang kab kanseuksa khong thai* [Thai politics and education]. Bangkok: Development of Education-Related Social Sciences Project, Office of the National Education Committee, Office of the Prime Minister, 1983.

————— *Kanmeuang thai kab phatthanakan ratthathammanoon* [Thai politics and constitutional development]. Phatthanakan sitthi manussayachon nai prathet thai [Development of Human Rights in Thailand] Research Series. Bangkok: Thai Khadi Research Institute, Thammasat University, and the Social Sciences and Humanities Textbooks Project Foundation, 1986.

————— *Saneh Chamarik: Ratthasat kab kanmeuang thai* [Saneh Jamarik: Political science and Thai politics]. Edited by Rangsan Thanapornpun and Ukris Patthamanan. Bangkok: Social Sciences and Humanities Textbooks Project Foundation, 1987.

————— et al. *Pridiparithas: Pathakatha chud pridi banomyong anusorn* [Pridi Commentary: Lectures in memory of Pridi Banomyong]. Khon kab khwamkhid [Men and Ideas] Series. Bangkok: Tianwan Press, 1983.

Sang Phatnothai. *Pathanukrom sapkanmeuang angklis-thai* [English-Thai political dictionary]. Bangkok: Prae Pittaya Press, 1968.

Sangwian Miphaophong. "Phrasong thai pi meuang jin laew thook jab tidkhuk" [Thai monks visited China and were put in jail]. *Sinlapa Watthanatham* 7, no. 9 (1986): 62–80.

Saraphaiphiphat, Captain, Phraya (Leuan Saraphaiwanich). "Udomkhati khong sangkhomniyom" [The ideal of socialism]. In *Khamprakas momchao sakol wannakon worawan nak sangkhomniyom khong meuang thai* [Manifesto of M.C. Sakol Wannakon Worawan, a socialist of Thailand], by M.C. Sakol Wannakon Worawan et al., 30–50. Bangkok: Chesthaburus Press, n.d.

Sathian Janthimathorn. *Saithan wannakam pheua chiwit khong thai* [The current of Thai Literature for Life's Sake]. Bangkok: Chaophraya Press, 1982.

—————, ed. *Jed sib song pi sakchai bamrungphong nakkhian samanchon* [Seventy-two years of Sakchai Bamrungphong, a commoner writer]. Bangkok: Matichon Press, 1990.

Sathiankoses (Phraya Anumanrajthon). *Lao reuang nai traiphoom* [Telling the story in *Traiphoom*]. Bangkok: Klang Vidhaya Publishing House, 1959.

Sawai Sutthiphithak. *Dr. pridi banomyong* [Dr. Pridi Banomyong]. Bangkok: n.p., 1983.

Seni Pramoj, M.R. *Faem kanmeuang* [Political dossier]. Bangkok: Bunsawas Duangjaiekraj, M.P. Chiang Rai, 1970.

————— *Pathakatha reuang kanplae khampraphan thai lae sila jareuk pho khunramkhamhaeng* [Lectures on the translation of Thai verses and the stone inscriptions of King Ramkhamhaeng]. Bangkok: Ongkankha Khong Khurusapha, 1976.

Seni Saowaphong (Sakchai Bamrungphong). *Pisaj* [The specter]. Bangkok: Anthai Press, 1988.

————— *Sinlapa lae wannakhadi* [Art and literature]. Bangkok: Sahabannakorn Press, 1952.

————— "Yiap yurop kab supha sirimanond" [Roaming Europe with Supha Sirimanond]. In *Photjanalai supha sirimanond* [Eulogies to Supha Sirimanond], 48–54. Bangkok: Songphorn Woraphithaksanond, 1986.

Siriusa Phonlajan (Cholthira Sattayawatthana). "Ajan jit poumisak kab chaosinlapakorn" [Lecturer Jit Poumisak and Fine Arts University's people]. *Aksornsatphijan* (Special Double Issue on Jit Poumisak) 3, no. 11–12 (1976): 5–22.

Siva Ronnachit (Suwat Voradilok). *Jodmai jak ladyao* [Letters from Ladyao]. Bangkok: Prakai Press, 1978.

Somboon Woraphong. *Bon senthang nangseuphim* [On the journalistic road]. Bangkok: Pheuanchiwit Press, 1984.

Somkhuan Kawiya et al. "Sammananusorn ajan supha sirimanond" [Seminar in memory of Supha Sirimanond]. Papers presented in the seminar on Supha Sirimanond's journalistic works, Department of Journalism and Mass Media, Thammasat University and the Institute of Professional Journalism of Thailand, 1986. Mimeographed.

Somkiat Wanthana. "Song satawas khong rat lae prawattisat niphon thai samai mai" [Two centuries of the Thai state and modern Thai historiography]. *Thammsat University Journal* 13, no. 3 (1984): 152–71.

————— "Wiwatthanakan chonchan raengngan thai: Khaokhrong prawattisat raengngan khrob rob songroi pi" [The evolution of the Thai laboring class: An outline of labor history in two hundred years]. Academic Paper no. 23 presented in the seminar, "Song satawas rattanakosin: Khwamplianplaeng khong sangkhom thai" [Rattanakosin bicentennial: The changes in Thai society], organized by Thai Khadi Research Institute of Thammasat University, Institute of Social Research of Chulalongkorn University, Social Science Association of Thailand, Social Sciences and Humanities Textbooks Project Foundation, and

Thammasat University Journal, at Thammasat University, 1982. Mimeographed.

Somphop Jantharaprapha et al. *Prawat kanrajthan song roi pi* [Two hundred years' history of the penitentiary]. Bangkok: Department of Penitentiary, Ministry of Interior, 1982.

Somsak Jeamteerasakul. "Mahawittayalai thammasat lae kanmeuang kab kanmeuang thai: Khaokhrong prawattisat ha sib pi" [University of Moral and Political Sciences and Thai politics: An outline of its fifty-year history]. *Warasan Thammasat* 14, no 4 (1984): 8–33.

Sornsak Ngamkhajornkulkij. *Khabuankan serithai kab khwamkhadyaeng thang kanmeuang phainai prathet thai rawang Pho.So. 2481–2492* [The Free Thai Movement and political conflict in Thailand during B.E. 2481– 2492]. Bangkok: Sathaban Asia Seuksa, Chulalongkorn University, 1989.

Sriburapha (Kulap Saipradit). *Kho raeng noi thoe: Ruam reuangsan pheua chiwit* [Lend a helping hand: An anthology of short stories for life]. Khrongkan anurak wannakam kao lae hayak [Old and Rare Literature Conservation Project] Series, no. 14. Bangkok: Dokya Press, 1987.

———— *La kon ratthathammanoon* [Farewell constitution]. Bangkok: Witthawas Press, 1979.

———— *Lae pai khangna: Phak majchimwai* [Looking forward: The middle age]. Khrongkan anurak wannakam kao lae hayak [Old and Rare Literature Conservation Project] Series, ed. Chuai Phulphoem, no. 36. Bangkok: Dokya Press, 1988.

———— *Lae pai khangna: Phak pathomwai* [Looking forward: The tender age]. Khrongkan anurak wannakam kao lae hayak [Old and Rare Literature Conservation Project] Series, ed. Chuai Phulphoem, no. 36. Bangkok: Dokya Press, 1988.

———— *Udomtham kab pholngan chud phutthasassana* [Udomtham and works on Buddhism], Khrongkan anurak wannakam kao lae hayak [Old and Rare Literature Conservation Project] Series, ed. Chuai Phulphoem, no. 27. Bangkok: Dokya Press, 1988.

————, trans. *Mae* [Mother], by Maxim Gorky. Bangkok: Busbaban Press, 1958.

Suchat Phoomborirak. "Chiwit sriburapha nai satharanarat prachachon jin" [Sriburapha's life in the People's Republic of China]. *Ongkorn Wannakam* 12 (1982): 4–7.

Suchira Guptarak. "Wikhrao bot roikrong khong nai phi" [An analysis of Nai Phee's poetical works]. Master's thesis, Srinakharinwirot University, 1983.

Sukanya Tirawanich. *Nangseuphim thai jak patiwat 2475 su patiwat 2516*

[Thai newspapers from the revolution of B.E. 2475 to the revolution of B.E. 2516]. Bangkok: Thai Watana Panich, 1983.

———— *Prawat kannangseuphim nai prathet thai phaitai rabob somboonnayasitthiraj (Pho.So. 2325–2475)* [A history of journalism in Thailand under absolute monarchy (B.E. 2325–2475)]. Bangkok: Thai Watana Panich, 1977.

Sungsidh Piriyarangsan. *Prawat kantosoo khong kammakorn thai* [A history of Thai workers' struggle]. Bangkok: Social Research Institute, Chulalongkorn University, 1986.

———— *Thunniyom khunnang thai (Pho.So.2 475–2503)* [Thai bureaucratic capitalism (B.E. 2475–2503)]. Bangkok: Chulalongkorn University Social Research Institute, 1983.

Supha Sirimanond. *Jengghizkhan: Nawaniyai ing prawattisat* [Genghis Khan: A historical novel]. Bangkok: Supha Sirimanond Foundation, 1988.

———— *Jodmai jak bannathikan* [Letters from the editor]. Bangkok: Supha Sirimanond Foundation, 1988.

———— *Khaepitalist: khambanyai waduai kamnoed, khrongsang, khwamsongyoo lae kod haeng khwamkhleuanwai khong yuk khaepitalist* [Capitalism: Lectures on the origins, structure, existence and laws of motion of the age of capitalism]. Bangkok: Chulalongkorn University Social Research Institute Publications, 1986.

———— *Khambanyai marx jongjai ja phisuj arai yangrai?: Khokhid bangprakan khong rabob marxist* [Lecture on what Marx intends to prove, and how: Some Marxist ideas]. Bangkok: Chaoaksorn Press, 1987.

———— *Wannasan samneuk: Khwamsamneuk nai itthiphol seusan khong nangseu, song lem* [Literary consciousness: The consciousness of the communicative influence of books, two volumes]. Bangkok: Supha Sirimanond Foundation, 1986.

Suphat Sukhonthaphirom na Phatthalung. *Phutthapratya kab pratya marxist* [Buddhist and Marxist philosophies]. Bangkok: The Star Library, 1981.

———— *Phutthapratya prayuk* [Applied Buddhist philosophy]. Bangkok: Santitham Press, 1985.

Suphot Dantrakul. *Pathanukrom kanmeuang chabab chaoban* [Popular dictionary of politics]. Bangkok: Santitham Press, 1985.

———— *Prasert sapsunthorn, adit kammakanklang phak khommunit haeng prathet thai; Khrai? Ma jak nai? Lae khid yangrai?* [Prasert Sapsunthorn, Former Central Committee member of the Communist Party of Thailand; Who? whence? and how does he think?]. Bangkok: n.p., 1981.

Suthachai Yimprasert. "Kankhleuanwai thang kanmeuang thi totan ratthabal samai jomphol plaek phibunsongkhram (Pho.So. 2491–2500)" [Political

movement against Field Marshal Pibulsonggram's regime, 1948–1957].
Master's thesis, Chulalongkorn University, 1989.

Sutin Gulayapruk. "Sriburapha nai thana nakmanussayatham" [Sriburapa as a
humanist]. Master's thesis, Srinakharinwirot University, 1981.

Suvimol Roongcharoen. "Botbat khong naknangseuphim nai kanmeuang thai
rawang Pho.So. 2490–2501" [Roles of journalists in Thai politics during
1947–1958 A.D.]. Master's thesis, Chulalongkorn University, 1983.

————— et al. "Prawat phoompanya khong sangkhom thai: Chiwit lae ngan
khong supha sirimanond" [An intellectual history of Thai society: The
life and works of Supha Sirimanond]. Papers presented in the seminar,
"Prawat phumpanya khong sangkhom thai: Chiwit lae ngan khong supha
sirimanond" [An intellectual history of Thai society: The life and works
of Supha Sirimanond] on the occasion of the seventy-second anniversary
of Supha Sirimanond's birth, organized by the Political Economy Group
of the Social Research Institute, the Economic History Group, the Komol
Khimthong Foundation, the Pridi Banomyong Foundation, the Social
Science Association of Thailand, and the *Matichon* newspaper, at
Chulalongkorn University, 1986. Mimeographed.

Suwadee Charoenphong. "Bot thi ha: Patikiriya khong ratthabal phrabatsomdej
phrapokklaojaoyoohua to kankhleuanwai thang khwamkhid
sangkhomniyom khommunit (Pho.So. 2468–2475)" [Chapter 5: The
reaction of King Prajadhipok's government to the communist-socialist
ideological movement, B.E. 2468–2475]. In *Kanmeuang-kanpokkhrong
thai samai mai: Ruam nganwijai thang prawattisat lae ratthasat* [Modern
Thai politics and government: A collection of researches in history and
political science], edited by Chai-anan Samudavanija and Suwadee
Charoenphong. Bangkok: Chulalongkorn University, 1979.

Suwanna Kriangkraiphej, ed. *No.Mo.So.* Bangkok: Moonnithi Khrongkan
Tamra Sangkhomsat Lae Manussayasat Haeng Prathet Thai, 1984.

Thaemsook Numnond. "Meuangthai yuk cheua phoonam" [Thailand in the
obey-the-leader age]. *Thammasat University Journal* 6, no. 1 (June–
September 1976): 144–145.

————— *Yangtoek run raek: Kabot R.S.130* [The first Young Turks: The 1912
conspiracy]. Bangkok: Reuangsin Press, 1979.

Thammakiat Kanari. "Supha sirimanond nakwichanangseuphim namkhang
haeng thalesai nai wan thi kheun soo mahannop" [Supha Sirimanond, a
journalistic scholar, a dew of the desert on the day it returns to the sea].
In *Photjanalai supha sirimanond* [Eulogies to Supha Sirimanond], 85–
92. Bangkok: Songphorn Woraphithaksanond, 1986.

Thammasakmontri, Chaophraya. *Khlong klon khong khroo thep* [Teacher

Thep's poetry]. Cremation Volume of Rong Ammat Ek Luang Suphakornphanomkij. Makutkasattriyaram Temple, Bangkok, 1960.
————— *Khlong klon khong khroo thep lem song* [Khruthep's poetry, vol. two]. Bangkok: Ongkankha Khong Khurusapha, 1983.
Thamrongsak Phechleotanan. "Botnam" [Introduction]. In *Yuk thamil* [Dark age], by Phayap Rojjanawiphat, [14]–[27]. Bangkok: Anthai Press, 1989.
Thanin Kraivichien. *Kanchai kodmai pongkan khommunit* [The application of anti-communist laws]. Bangkok: Security Center, Ministry of Defense, 1974.
————— *Latthi lae withikan khong khommunit* [The doctrine and methods of communism]. Bangkok: Security Center, Ministry of Defense, 1974.
Thatri Niwatthanathamrong (Phornchai Saengchaj), trans. *Pratya prayuk* [Handbook of philosophy], by Howard Selsam. Bagnkok: n.p., 1954.
Thaweep Voradilok. "Naknangseuphim kab thoraraj" [Journalists and tyrants]. *Matichon* 9 (1986): 18–21.
————— "Supha sirimanond pheua khwampenloet khong nangseuphim thai" [Supha Sirimanond for the excellence of Thai newspapers]. In *Photjanalai supha sirimanond* [Eulogies to Supha Sirimanond], 30–47. Bangkok: Songphorn Woraphithaksanond, 1986.
————— *Wijan ngankawi khong jit poumisak lae khokhian eun eun* [Criticism of Jit Poumisak's poetry and other writings]. Bangkok: Dokkaeo Press, 1980.
Thaweepvorn (Thaweep Voradilok). *Jong pen athit meua uthai: Ruam kawiniphon nai rob si thossawas* [Be the sun at dawn: Collected poems in four decades]. Bangkok: Anthai Press, 1989.
————— trans. *Kawiniphon maozedong* [The poems of Mao Zedong]. Bangkok: Walee Publishing House, 1981.
Thianchai Iamworamet. *Photjananukrom jin-thai* [Chinese-Thai dictionary]. Bangkok: Bamrungsan Press, 1986.
Thipphawan Jeamteerasakul. *Pathomthas thang kanmeuang khong pridi Banomyong* [Pridi Banomyong's early political thought]. Bangkok: Aksornsarn Press, 1988.
Thongbai Thongpao. *Khommunit ladyao* [Communists of Ladyao Prison]. Bangkok: Khonnum Press, 1974.
Thongchai Phuengkanthai. "Latthi khommunit lae nayobai totan khong ratthabal thai Pho.So. 2468–2500" [Communism in Thailand and government policy against communism, B.E. 2468–2500]. Master's thesis, Chulalongkorn University, 1978.
Thongthae Rojjanasan. *Pathanukrom thai-jin* [Thai-Chinese dictionary]. Bangkok: n.p., 1956.

Trisilp Bunkhajorn. *Nawaniyai kab sangkhom thai (2475–2500)* [Novels and Thai society (B.E. 2475–2500)]. Bangkok: Sangsan Press, 1980.

——— *Phatthanakan seuksa khonkhwa lae wijai wannakhadi thai* [The development of Thai literary studies and research]. Bangkok: the Faculty of Arts, Chulalongkorn University, 1987.

Uayporn Milindankura. "Laksana khampraphan roikrong khong thai tangtae Pho.So. 2475–2501" [The characteristics of Thai poetical works, 1932–1958 A.D.]. Master's thesis, Chulalongkorn University, 1976.

Ujcheni (Prakhin Chumsai na Ayudhya). *Khobfa khlibthong* [The golden horizon]. Edited by Suchart Sawatsri. Bangkok: Duang Kamol Press, 1980.

——— and Nid Nararak (Prakhin Chumsai na Ayudhya). *Daophong naphadin* [Starry sky and earth]. Bangkok: Phikkhanes Press, 1974.

Ukris Patthamanan. "Khana ratsadorn kab kanplianplaeng sangkhom thai dan kanthahan" [The People's Party and the transformation of the military in Thai society]. In "Khana ratsadorn nai prawattisat thai" [The People's Party in Thai history], Papers presented in the seminar, "The People's Party in Thai History," Krirk College, May 9–10, 1985. Mimeographed.

Uthis Prasansapha (Atsani Phonlajan). *Toe latthikae thai lae wijan haeng wijan* [Against Thai revisionism and critique of criticism]. Bangkok: Prakaifaimailamthung Press, 1975.

Vajiravudh, King. *Jodmaihet raiwan khong phrabatsomdej phramongkutklao jaoyoohua R.S. 131* [Diary of King Vajiravudh, 1912 A.D.]. Bangkok: Duang Kamol Press, 1981.

——— *Pakinnakakhadi* [Miscellanies]. Bangkok: Klang Vidhaya Publishing House, 1975.

——— *Phuak yew haeng buraphathis lae Meuang thai jong teun thoed* [The Jews of the Orient and Wake up, Siam! with His Majesty's manuscripts of the English translations]. Bangkok: Moonnithi Phrabaromrajanusorn Phrabatsomdej Phramongkutklaojaoyoohua, 1985.

——— *Uttarakuru: Dindaen assajan khong asia* [Uttarakuru: An Asiatic wonderland]. Translated by Prince Dhani. Bangkok: Mahamakud Rajwitthayalai, 1965.

Wat Wanlayangkoon. *Duai rak haeng udomkan* [With ideological love]. Bangkok: Nokhook Press, 1981.

Wimol Phonlajan, comp. *Ramleuk theung naiphi jak pa lom: Chuang chiwit lae phonngan thi pheung poed phey pen khrang raek* [Auntie Lom's remembrance of Naiphi: Episodes in his life and some of his writings revealed for the first time]. Edited by Chuai Phulphoem. Bangkok: Dokya Press, 1990.

Witthayakorn Chiangkul. *Panyachon thai kab kanplianplaeng sangkhom* [Thai intellectuals and social change]. Bangkok: Community for Development Research Project and Phleuk Press, 1987.

————— *Seuksa botbat lae khwamkhid sriburapha* [A study of the role and thought of Sriburapha]. Bangkok: Community for Development Research Project and Phleuk Press, 1989.

Wiwat Catithammanit. "Kabot santiphap" [Peace Rebellion]. Master's thesis, Chulalongkorn University, 1989.

Yanyong Jariyaphas. "Prawat nangseuphim jin nai prathet thai" [A history of Chinese newspapers in Thailand]. Translated by Suthi Techawiriyathawisin. In *Bannanukrom nangseuphim lae warasan phasa jin nai prathet thai* [Bibliography of Chinese newspapers and magazines in Thailand], 1–116. Bangkok: National Library, Department of Fine Arts, 1976.

Yos Watcharasathian. *Kulap saipradit: Sriburapha thi khaphajao roojak* [Kulap Saipradit: The Sriburapha I knew]. Bangkok: Arts and Sciences Press, 1982.

B. In Western Languages

Adorno, Theodor. *Minima Moralia: Reflections from Damaged Life.* Translated by E.F.N. Jephcott. New York: Verso Press, 1991.

Anderson, Benedict R. O'G. *Imagined Communities: Reflections on the Origin and Spread of Nationalism.* London: Verso, 1983.

————— "Murder and Progress in Modern Siam." *New Left Review* 181 (1990): 33–48.

————— *The Spectre of Comparisons: Nationalism, Southeast Asia, and the World* London: Verso, 1998.

————— "Studies of the Thai State: The State of Thai Studies." In *The Study of Thailand: Analysis of Knowledge, Approaches, and Prospects in Anthropology, Art History, Economics, History and Political Science*, edited by Eliezer B. Ayal, 193–247. Athens, Ohio: Center for International Studies, Ohio University, 1979.

————— and Ruchira Mendiones, eds. and trans. *In the Mirror: Literature and Politics in Siam in the American Era.* Bangkok: Editions Duang Kamol, 1985.

Anderson, Perry. "Components of the National Culture." *New Left Review* 50 (1968): 3–57.

Barmé, Scot. *Kulap in Oz: A Thai View of Australian Life and Society in the Late 1940s.* Clayton, Victoria: Monash Asia Institute, Monash University, 1995.

Batson, Benjamin A. *The End of the Absolute Monarchy in Siam*. Asian Studies
    Association of Australia Southeast Asia Publications Series, no. 10. New
    York: Oxford University Press, 1986.
Benjamin, Walter. "Eduard Fuchs, Collector and Historian." In *One-Way Street
    and Other Writings*, 349–386. Translated by Edmund Jephcott and
    Kingsley Shorter. London: Verso, 1985.
————— "N" [Theoretics of knowledge, Theory of progress]. *The
    Philosophical Forum* 15, no. 1–2 (1983–1984): 1–40.
————— "Theses on the Philosophy of History." In *Illuminations*, 253–264.
    Translated by Harry Zohn and edited by Hannah Arendt. New York:
    Schocken Books, 1969.
Berman, Marshall. *All That Is Solid Melts into Air: The Experience of
    Modernity*. New York: Simon and Schuster, 1982.
Bernath, Frances A., comp. *Catalogue of Thai Language Holdings in the
    Cornell University Libraries through 1964*. Cornell University Southeast
    Asia Program Data Paper, no. 54. Ithaca: Cornell University Southeast
    Asia Program, 1964.
Bottomore, Tom et al., eds. *A Dictionary of Marxist Thought*. Cambridge,
    Massachusetts: Harvard University Press, 1983.
Brailey, Nigel J. *Thailand and the Fall of Singapore: A Frustrated Asian
    Revolution*. Boulder: Westview Press, 1986.
Brimmell, J.H. *Communism in South East Asia: A Political Analysis*. New
    York: Oxford University Press, 1959.
Buck-Morss, Susan. *The Dialectics of Seeing: Walter Benjamin and the
    Arcades Project*. Studies in Contemporary German Social Thought
    Series, edited by Thomas McCarthy. Cambridge, Massachusetts: The
    MIT Press, 1989.
Campbell, Joseph. *The Masks of God: Oriental Mythology*. New York: Penguin
    Books, 1987.
————— and Bill Moyers. *The Power of Myth*. Edited by Betty Sue Flowers.
    New York: Double Day, 1988.
Charivat Santaputra. *Thai Foreign Policy, 1932–1946*. Bangkok: Thai Khadi
    Research Institute, Thammasat University, 1985.
Charnvit Kasetsiri. "From Siam To Thailand: What Is in a Name?" Paper
    presented at the International Conference on Post Colonial Society and
    Culture in Southeast Asia, Yangon, Myanmar, 1998.
Cheah Boon Kheng. *Red Star over Malaya: Resistance and Social Conflict
    during and after the Japanese Occupation of Malaya, 1941–1946*.
    Singapore: Singapore University Press, National University of
    Singapore, 1983.

Colbert, Evelyn. *Southeast Asia in International Politics, 1941-1965*. Ithaca: Cornell University Press, 1977.

Communist Party of Thailand. "VOPT Marks Anniversary of End of Absolute Monarchy." *Foreign Broadcast Information Service, Daily Report: Asia & Pacific* 4, no. 128 (July 2, 1975): J9–J11.

————— "VOPT Recounts CPT History Covering 1942-1977." *Foreign Broadcast Information Service, Daily Report: Asia & Pacific* 4, no. 241 (December, 15, 1977): J6–J15.

Cowie, A.P., and A. Evison, comps. *Concise English-Chinese, Chinese-English Dictionary*. Hong Kong and Beijing: Oxford University Press and The Commercial Press, 1988.

Daniels, Robert V., ed. *A Documentary History of Communism*, Vol. 2: *Communism and the World*. Hanover: University Press of New England, 1984.

Deutscher, Isaac. "Marxism and the New Left." In *Marxism in Our Time*, edited by Tamara Deutscher, 63–77. Berkeley, California: The Ramparts Press, 1971.

Dirlik, Arif. *The Origins of Chinese Communism*. New York: Oxford University Press, 1989.

————— "Socialism and Capitalism in Chinese Socialist Thinking: The Origins." *Studies in Comparative Communism* 21, no. 2 (1988): 131–152.

Droz, Jacques, ed. *Histoire générale du socialisme, Tome III: De 1919 à 1945*. Paris: Presses Universitaires de France, 1977.

Fistié, Pierre. *Sous-développement et utopie au Siam: Le programme de réformes présenté en 1933 par Pridi Phanomyong*. Matériaux pour l'étude de l'extrême-orient moderne et contemporain, Travaux 5. Paris: Mouton and Maison des Sciences de l'Homme, 1969.

Flood, Thadeus. "The Thai Left Wing in Historical Context." *Bulletin of Concerned Asian Scholars* 7, no. 2 (1975): 55–67.

Gamson, William A. *Political Discourse and Collective Action*. Working Paper no. 4. Boston: Social Economy and Social Justice Program, Boston College, 1986.

Garraty, John A., and Peter Gay, eds. *The Columbia History of the World*. New York: Harper & Row, 1981.

Girling, John. "Thailand in Gramscian Perspective." *Pacific Affairs* 57, no. 3 (1984): 385–403.

————— *Thailand: Society and Politics*. Ithaca: Cornell University Press, 1985.

Goscha, Christopher E. *Thailand and the Southeast Asian Networks of the Vietnamese Revolution, 1885-1954*. Nordic Institute of Asian Studies Monograph Series, no. 79. Surrey: Curzon Press, 1999.

Gramsci, Antonio. *Selections from the Prison Notebooks of Antonio Gramsci.* Edited and translated by Quintin Hoare and Geoffrey Nowell Smith. New York: International Publishers, 1983.

Huynh Kim Khanh. *Vietnamese Communism, 1925–1945.* Published under the auspices of the Institute of Southeast Asian Studies, Singapore. Ithaca: Cornell University Press, 1986.

Jarvis, Helen. "Tan Malaka: Revolutionary or Renegade?" *Bulletin of Concerned Asian Scholars* 19, no. 1 (1987): 41–54.

Kasian Tejapira. "Independent Siam and Colonial Burma: A Comparative Historical Perspective." In *Asian Review 1993*, edited by Suwanna Satha-Anand, 1–62. Bangkok: Institute of Asian Studies, Chulalongkorn University, 1994.

Keyes, Charles F. *Thailand: Buddhist Kingdom as Modern Nation-State.* Bangkok: Editions Duang Kamol, 1989.

Khin Maung Kyi. "Western Enterprise and Economic Development." *Journal of the Burma Research Society* 53, no. 1 (1970): 25–51.

Kiernan, Ben. *How Pol Pot Came to Power: A History of Communism in Kampuchea, 1930–1975.* London: Verso, 1985.

Kloppenberg, James T. *Uncertain Victory: Social Democracy and Progressivism in European and American Thought, 1870–1920.* New York: Oxford University Press, 1986.

Labica, Georges, and Gérard Bensussan, eds. *Dictionnaire critique du marxisme.* Paris: Presses Universitaires de France, 1985.

Lacouture, Jean. *Ho Chi Minh: A Political Biography.* Translated by Peter Wiles. New York: Vintage Books, 1968.

Le Manh Trinh. "In Canton and Thailand." In *Days with Ho Chi Minh*, 104–131. Hanoi: Foreign Languages Publishing House, 1962.

Lew, Roland. "Maoism, Stalinism and the Chinese Revolution." In *The Stalinist Legacy: Its Impact on Twentieth-Century World Politics*, edited by Tariq Ali, 273–320. Middlesex: Penguin Books, 1984.

Mabry, Bevars D. *The Development of Labor Institutions in Thailand.* Data paper no. 112. Ithaca, New York: Department of Asian Studies, Cornell University, 1979.

Mao Tse-tung. *Mao Tse-tung on Literature and Art.* Peking: Foreign Languages Press, 1967.

——— *Poems of Mao Tse-tung.* Translated by Hua-ling Nieh Engle and Paul Engle. New York: Simon and Schuster, 1972.

——— *Quotations from Chairman Mao Tsetung.* Peking: Foreign Languages Press, 1972.

————— *Selected Readings from the Works of Mao Tsetung*. Peking: Foreign
    Languages Press, 1971.
Marr, David G. *Vietnamese Tradition on Trial, 1920–1945*. Berkeley:
    University of California Press, 1984.
Marx, Karl, and Frederick Engels. *Selected Works*. Moscow: Progress
    Publishers, 1986.
McDougall, Bonnie. *Mao Zedong's "Talks at the Yan'an Conference on
    Literature and Art": A Translation of the 1943 Text with Commentary*.
    Michigan Papers in Chinese Studies Series, no. 39. Ann Arbor: Center
    for Chinese Studies, University of Michigan, 1980.
McVey, Ruth T. *The Rise of Indonesian Communism*. Modern Indonesia
    Project, Southeast Asia Program, Cornell University. Ithaca, New York:
    Cornell University Press, 1965.
Mit Samanan (Jaroen Wanngam). "VOPT Carries Article Commemorating 35th
    CPT Anniversary." *Foreign Broadcast Information Service, Daily
    Report: Asia & Pacific* 4, no. 232 (December 2, 1977): J7–J11.
Morell, David, and Chai-anan Samudavanija. *Political Conflict in Thailand:
    Reform, Reaction, Revolution*. Cambridge, Massachusetts: Oelgeschlager,
    Gunn & Hain, 1982.
Murashima, Eiji. "The Origin of Modern Official State Ideology in Thailand."
    Journal of Southeast Asian Studies 19, no. 1 (1988): 80–96.
Nakhorn That (Jit Poumisak). "Phi tong luang" [The spirits of the yellow
    leaves]. Translated by Craig J. Reynolds, Echols Collection, Kroch
    Library, Cornell University. Mimeographed.
Napaporn Ativanichayapong. "The Development of Political Economy
    Thought in Thailand, 1932–1982." Master's thesis, Thammasat Uni-
    versity, 1986.
Nisbet, Robert. *Sociology as an Art Form*. New York: Oxford University Press,
    1976.
Onions, C.T. *The Oxford Universal Dictionary on Historical Principles*.
    Oxford: Clarendon Press, 1955.
Prachoom Chomchai. "Thailand." Chapter 4 of *The Economic Development of
    East and Southeast Asia*, edited by Shinichi Ichimura. Honolulu: The
    University Press of Hawaii, 1955.
Pridi Banomyong. *Ma vie mouvementée et mes 21 ans d'exil en Chine
    Populaire*. Paris: Varap, 1974.
Putrin, Boris, comp. *Political Terms: A Short Guide*. Translated by Valentin
    Kochetkov. Moscow: Novosti Press Agency Publishing House, 1982.
Rafael, Vicente L. *Contracting Colonialism: Translation and Christian*

Conversion in Tagalog Society under Early Spanish Rule. Ithaca: Cornell University Press, 1988.

Reynolds, Craig J. "Identity, Authenticity and Reputation in the Postcolonial History of Mainland Southeast Asia." Keynote speech at the International Conference on Post Colonial Society and Culture in Southeast Asia, Yangon, Myanmar, 1998.

———— *Thai Radical Discourse: The Real Face of Thai Feudalism Today*. Ithaca: Southeast Asia Program, Cornell University, 1987.

———— and Hong Lysa. "Marxism in Thai Historical Studies." *Journal of Asian Studies* 43, no. 1 (1983): 77–104.

Seksan Prasertkul. "The Transformation of the Thai State and Economic Change (1855–1945)." Ph.D. diss., Cornell University, 1989.

Shiraishi, Takashi. "The Military in Thailand, Burma and Indonesia." In *Asian Political Institutionalization*, edited by Robert A. Scalapino et al. Research Papers and Policy Studies Series, no. 15. Berkeley, California: Institute of East Asian Studies, University of California at Berkeley, 1986.

Siburapha (Kulap Saipradit). *Behind the Painting and Other Stories*. Translated by David Smyth. New York: Oxford University Press, 1990.

Skinner, G. William. *Chinese Society in Thailand: An Analytical History*. Ithaca, New York: Cornell University Press, 1957.

Smyth, David. "Kulap Saipradit (Siburapha): His Life and Times." Introduction to *Behind the Painting and Other Stories*, by Siburapha (Kulap Saipradit), translated by David Smyth, 1–44. New York: Oxford University Press, 1993.

Somsak Jeamteerasakul. "The Communist Movement in Thailand." Ph.D. diss., Monash University, 1993.

Spence, Jonathan D. *The Gate of Heavenly Peace: The Chinese and Their Revolution, 1895–1980*. New York: Penguin Books, 1983.

———— *The Search for Modern China*. New York: W.W. Norton, 1990.

Stalin, J.V. *Selected Works*. Albania: The "8 Nentori" Publishing House, 1979.

Steinberg, David Joel, ed. *In Search of Southeast Asia: A Modern History*. Honolulu: University of Hawaii Press, 1987.

Suehiro Akira. *Capital Accumulation in Thailand, 1855–1985*. Tokyo: The Centre for East Asian Cultural Studies, 1989.

Sworakowski, Witold S., ed. *World Communism: A Handbook 1918–1965*. Stanford, California: Hoover Institution Press, 1973.

Tarrow, Sidney. *Struggling to Reform: Social Movements and Policy Change During Cycles of Protest*. Western Societies Program's Occasional Paper, no. 15. Ithaca: Center for International Studies, Cornell University, 1983.

Terwiel, B.J. "Thai Nationalism and Identity: Popular Themes of the 1930s." In *National Identity and Its Defenders, Thailand, 1939–1989*, edited by Craig J. Reynolds, 133–154. Clayton, Victoria: Centre of Southeast Asian Studies, Monash University, 1991.

Thak Chaloemtiarana. *Thailand: The Politics of Despotic Paternalism*. Bangkok: Social Science Association of Thailand and the Thai Khadi Research Institute, Thammasat University, 1979.

————, ed. *Thai Politics: Extracts and Documents, 1932–1957*. Bangkok: The Social Science Association of Thailand, 1979.

Thanet Aphornsuvan. "The United States and the Coming of the Coup of 1947 in Siam." *Journal of the Siam Society* 75 (1987): 187–214.

Tharatatukaro. "Kali Yuga Is the Cause of Freedom, Migasanyi Is the Cause of Equality." In *The Political Economy of Siam, 1910–1932*, edited and translated by Chatthip Nartsupha et al., 246–49. Bangkok: Social Science Association of Thailand, 1981.

———— "Phra Sri Araya's Envoy." In *The Political Economy of Siam, 1910–1932*, edited and translated by Chatthip Nartsupha et al., 250–53. Bangkok: Social Science Association of Thailand, 1981.

Therborn, Göran. *What Does the Ruling Class Do When It Rules?* London: New Left Books, 1978.

Third World Studies, ed. *Marxism in the Philippines: Marx Centennial Lectures*. Quezon City: Third World Studies Center, University of the Philippines, 1984.

Thompson, Virginia, and Richard Adloff. *The Left Wing in Southeast Asia*. Published under the auspices of the International Secretariat, Institute of Pacific Relations. New York: William Sloane, 1950.

Thongchai Winichakul. *Siam Mapped: A History of the Geo-Body of a Nation*. Honolulu: University of Hawaii Press, 1994.

Too, Tan Sri C.C. "Malaysia's Communist Threat." *Far Eastern Economic Review*, 146, no. 49 (1989): 29–33.

Trotsky, Leon. *Leon Trotsky on Literature and Art*. Edited by Paul N. Siegel. New York: Pathfinder Press, 1981.

Uhalley, Jr., Stephen. *A History of the Chinese Communist Party*. Histories of Ruling Communist Parties Series, edited by Richard F. Starr. Stanford, California: Hoover Institution Press, 1988.

Vadney, T.E. *The World since 1945*. New York: Penguin Books, 1987.

Vajiravudh, King. *Uttarakuru: An Asiatic Wonderland*. Bangkok: Mahamakud Rajwitthayalai, 1965.

Van Slyke, Lyman P. *Enemies and Friends: The United Front in Chinese Communist History*. Stanford, California: Stanford University Press, 1967.

Vargas Llosa, Mario. *The Real Life of Alejandro Mayta*. Translated by Alfred MacAdam. New York: Vintage International, 1989.

Vella, Walter F. *Chaiyo! King Vajiravudh and the Development of Thai Nationalism*. Honolulu: The University Press of Hawaii, 1978.

Vichitvong na Pombhejara. *Pridi Banomyong and the Making of Thailand's Modern History*. Bangkok: n.p., n.d.

Wibha Senanan. *The Genesis of the Novel in Thailand*. Bangkok: Thai Watana Panich, 1975.

Williams, Raymond. *Keywords: A Vocabulary of Culture and Society*. London: Flamingo Edition, 1983.

————— *Marxism and Literature*. New York: Oxford University Press, 1977.

————— *Problems in Materialism and Culture*. London: New Left Books, 1980.

————— *Resources of Hope: Culture, Democracy, Socialism*. Edited by Robin Gable. London: Verso, 1989.

Wilson, Constance M. *Thailand: A Handbook of Historical Statistics*. International Historical Statistics Series, edited by Oliver Pollak. Boston: G.K. Hall, 1983.

Wilson, David A. "Thailand and Marxism." In *Marxism in Southeast Asia: A Study of Four Countries*, edited by Frank N. Trager, 58–101. Stanford, California: Stanford University Press, 1965.

Wood, Ellen Meiksins. "The Uses and Abuses of 'Civil Society.'" In *The Socialist Register 1990*, edited by Ralph Miliband, Leo Panitch, and John Saville, 60–84. London: The Merlin Press, 1990.

Wyatt, David K. *Thailand: A Short History*. New Haven: Yale University Press, 1984.

Yuangrat Wedel. *Modern Thai Radical Thought: The Siamization of Marxism and Its Theoretical Problems*. Bangkok: Thai Khadi Research Institute, Thammasat University, 1982.

————— and Paul Wedel. *Radical Thought, Thai Mind: The Development of Revolutionary Ideas in Thailand*. Bangkok: Assumption Business Administration College, 1987.

Zizek, Slavoj. *Enjoy Your Symptom! Jacques Lacan in Hollywood and Out*. London: Routledge, 1992.

Index

This book contains both a name index and a subject index. In general, entries and subentries are arranged alphabetically. However, as far as long and complicated subject entries such as 'Anti-communism' or 'Communist movements in Thailand' are concerned, the subentries therein follow an organization-based, chronological order: sub-subentries are alphabetically arranged and grouped under an organizational heading, and then these headings are further arranged chronologically.

Name Index

Subject Index